Binary Neural Networks

Deep learning has achieved impressive results in image classification, computer vision, and natural language processing. To achieve better performance, deeper and wider networks have been designed, which increase the demand for computational resources. The number of floating-point operations (FLOPs) has increased dramatically with larger networks, and this has become an obstacle for convolutional neural networks (CNNs) being developed for mobile and embedded devices. In this context, *Binary Neural Networks: Algorithms, Architectures, and Applications* will focus on CNN compression and acceleration, which are important for the research community. We will describe numerous methods, including parameter quantization, network pruning, low-rank decomposition, and knowledge distillation. More recently, to reduce (from binary to low-bit) the burden of handcrafted architecture design, neural architecture search (NAS) has been used to automatically build neural networks by searching over a vast architecture space. Our book will also introduce NAS and binary NAS and its superiority and state-of-the-art performance in various applications, such as image classification and object detection. We also describe extensive applications of compressed deep models on image classification, speech recognition, object detection, and tracking. These topics can help researchers better understand the usefulness and the potential of network compression on practical applications. Moreover, interested readers should have basic knowledge of machine learning and deep learning to better understand the methods described in this book.

Key Features
- Reviews recent advances in CNN compression and acceleration
- Elaborates recent advances on binary neural network (BNN) technologies
- Introduces applications of BNN in image classification, speech recognition, object detection, and more

Multimedia Computing, Communication and Intelligence
Series Editor
Chang Wen Chen & Shiguo Lian

PUBLISHED

Effective Surveillance for Homeland Security:

Balancing Technology and Social Issues

By Francesco Flammini, Roberto Setola, and Giorgio Franceschetti

ISBN: 9781138199705

Advances in Visual Data Compression and Communication:

Meeting the Requirements of New Applications

By Feng Wu

ISBN: 9781482234138

TV Content Analysis:

Techniques and Applications

By Yiannis Kompatsiaris, Bernard Merialdo, and Shiguo Lian

ISBN: 9780367900946

Music Emotion Recognition

By Yi-Hsuan and Homer H. Chen

ISBN: 9781439850466

Binary Neural Networks:

Algorithms, Architectures, and Applications

By Baochang Zhang, Sheng Xu, Mingbao Lin, Tiancheng Wang, and David Doermann

ISBN: 9781032452487

Binary Neural Networks
Algorithms, Architectures, and Applications

Baochang Zhang, Sheng Xu, Mingbao Lin,
Tiancheng Wang, and David Doermann

CRC Press
Taylor & Francis Group
Boca Raton London New York

CRC Press is an imprint of the
Taylor & Francis Group, an **informa** business

Cover Image Credit: Shutterstock_2045393252

First edition published 2024
by CRC Press
2385 NW Executive Center Drive, Suite 320, Boca Raton FL 33431

and by CRC Press
4 Park Square, Milton Park, Abingdon, Oxon, OX14 4RN

CRC Press is an imprint of Taylor & Francis Group, LLC

© 2024 Baochang Zhang, Sheng Xu, Mingbao Lin, Tiancheng Wang, David Doermann

ISBN: 978-1-032-45248-7 (hbk)
ISBN: 978-1-032-45250-0 (pbk)
ISBN: 978-1-003-37613-2 (ebk)

DOI: 10.1201/9781003376132

Typeset in CMR10
by KnowledgeWorks Global Ltd.

Publisher's note: This book has been prepared from camera-ready copy provided by the authors.

Dedication
To all our collaborators working
on binary neural networks

Contents

About the Authors   xi

1 Introduction   1
    1.1 Principal Methods 2
       1.1.1 Early Binary Neural Networks 2
       1.1.2 Gradient Approximation 3
       1.1.3 Quantization 3
       1.1.4 Structural Design 6
       1.1.5 Loss Design 9
       1.1.6 Neural Architecture Search 10
       1.1.7 Optimization 10
    1.2 Applications 12
       1.2.1 Image Classification 13
       1.2.2 Speech Recognition 13
       1.2.3 Object Detection and Tracking 13
       1.2.4 Applications 14
    1.3 Our Works on BNNs 14

2 Quantization of Neural Networks   16
    2.1 Overview of Quantization 16
       2.1.1 Uniform and Non-Uniform Quantization 16
       2.1.2 Symmetric and Asymmetric Quantization 17
    2.2 LSQ: Learned Step Size Quantization 18
       2.2.1 Notations 18
       2.2.2 Step Size Gradient 19
       2.2.3 Step Size Gradient Scale 20
       2.2.4 Training 20
    2.3 Q-ViT: Accurate and Fully Quantized Low-Bit Vision Transformer 21
       2.3.1 Baseline of Fully Quantized ViT 22
       2.3.2 Performance Degeneration of Fully Quantized ViT Baseline 23
       2.3.3 Information Rectification in Q-Attention 24
       2.3.4 Distribution Guided Distillation Through Attention 26
       2.3.5 Ablation Study 27
    2.4 Q-DETR: An Efficient Low-Bit Quantized Detection Transformer 28
       2.4.1 Quantized DETR Baseline 30
       2.4.2 Challenge Analysis 31
       2.4.3 Information Bottleneck of Q-DETR 32
       2.4.4 Distribution Rectification Distillation 33
       2.4.5 Ablation Study 34

3   Algorithms for Binary Neural Networks   **37**
    3.1   Overview   37
    3.2   BNN: Binary Neural Network   38
    3.3   XNOR-Net: Imagenet Classification Using Binary Convolutional Neural Net-
          works   38
    3.4   MCN: Modulated Convolutional Network   40
          3.4.1   Forward Propagation with Modulation   41
          3.4.2   Loss Function of MCNs   43
          3.4.3   Back-Propagation Updating   44
          3.4.4   Parameters Evaluation   45
          3.4.5   Model Effect   47
    3.5   PCNN: Projection Convolutional Neural Networks   49
          3.5.1   Projection   51
          3.5.2   Optimization   51
          3.5.3   Theoretical Analysis   52
          3.5.4   Projection Convolutional Neural Networks   53
          3.5.5   Forward Propagation Based on Projection Convolution Layer   54
          3.5.6   Backward Propagation   54
          3.5.7   Progressive Optimization   55
          3.5.8   Ablation Study   58
    3.6   RBCN: Rectified Binary Convolutional Networks with Generative Adversar-
          ial Learning   60
          3.6.1   Loss Function   62
          3.6.2   Learning RBCNs   62
          3.6.3   Network Pruning   64
          3.6.4   Ablation Study   66
    3.7   BONN: Bayesian Optimized Binary Neural Network   67
          3.7.1   Bayesian Formulation for Compact 1-Bit CNNs   69
          3.7.2   Bayesian Learning Losses   69
          3.7.3   Bayesian Pruning   71
          3.7.4   BONNs   71
          3.7.5   Forward Propagation   72
          3.7.6   Asynchronous Backward Propagation   73
          3.7.7   Ablation Study   76
    3.8   RBONN: Recurrent Bilinear Optimization for a Binary Neural Network . .   79
          3.8.1   Bilinear Model of BNNs   81
          3.8.2   Recurrent Bilinear Optimization   81
          3.8.3   Discussion   83
          3.8.4   Ablation Study   84
    3.9   ReBNN: Resilient Binary Neural Network   85
          3.9.1   Problem Formulation   86
          3.9.2   Method   86
          3.9.3   Ablation Study   88

4   Binary Neural Architecture Search   **91**
    4.1   Background   91
    4.2   ABanditNAS: Anti-Bandit for Neural Architecture Search   92
          4.2.1   Anti-Bandit Algorithm   93
          4.2.2   Search Space   95
          4.2.3   Anti-Bandit Strategy for NAS   95
          4.2.4   Adversarial Optimization   97

| | 4.2.5 | Analysis | 97 |

4.3 CP-NAS: Child-Parent Neural Architecture Search for 1-bit CNNs 98
    4.3.1 Child-Parent Model for Network Binarization 100
    4.3.2 Search Space 102
    4.3.3 Search Strategy for CP-NAS 103
    4.3.4 Optimization of the 1-Bit CNNs 103
    4.3.5 Ablation Study 104
4.4 DCP-NAS: Discrepant Child-Parent Neural Architecture Search for 1-Bit CNNs 105
    4.4.1 Preliminary 105
    4.4.2 Redefine Child-Parent Framework for Network Binarization 107
    4.4.3 Search Space 108
    4.4.4 Tangent Propagation for DCP-NAS 109
    4.4.5 Generalized Gauss-Newton Matrix (GGN) for Hessian Matrix 110
    4.4.6 Decoupled Optimization for Training the DCP-NAS 111
    4.4.7 Ablation Study 115

5 Applications in Natural Language Processing   **118**
5.1 Background 118
    5.1.1 Quantization-Aware Training (QAT) for Low-Bit Large Language Models 118
    5.1.2 Post-Training Quantization (PTQ) for Low-Bit Large Language Models 118
    5.1.3 Binary BERT Pre-Trained Models 119
5.2 Fully Quantized Transformer for Machine Translation 121
    5.2.1 Quantization Scheme 121
    5.2.2 What to Quantize 122
    5.2.3 Tensor Bucketing 123
    5.2.4 Dealing with Zeros 124
5.3 Q-BERT: Hessian-Based Ultra Low-Precision Quantization of BERT 125
    5.3.1 Hessian-Based Mix-Precision 125
    5.3.2 Group-Wise Quantization 125
5.4 I-BERT: Integer-Only BERT Quantization 127
    5.4.1 Integer-Only Computation of GELU and Softmax 128
    5.4.2 Integer-Only Computation of LayerNorm 128
5.5 Toward Efficient Post-Training Quantization of Pre-Trained Language Models 129
    5.5.1 Module-Wise Reconstruction Error Minimization 129
    5.5.2 Model Parallel Strategy 130
    5.5.3 Annealed Teacher Forcing 130
5.6 Outlier Suppression: Pushing the Limit of Low-Bit Transformer Language Models 132
    5.6.1 Analysis 132
    5.6.2 Gamma Migration 133
    5.6.3 Token-Wise Clipping 134
5.7 BinaryBERT: Pushing the Limit of BERT Quantization 134
    5.7.1 Ternary Weight Splitting 136
    5.7.2 Knowledge Distillation 136
5.8 BEBERT: Efficient and Robust Binary Ensemble BERT 138
5.9 BiBERT: Accurate Fully Binarized BERT 139
    5.9.1 Bi-Attention 139

| | 5.9.2 | Direction-Matching Distillation | 141 |

5.10   BiT: Robustly Binarized Multi-Distilled Transformer 142
        5.10.1 Two-Set Binarization Scheme 143
        5.10.2 Elastic Binarization Function 144
        5.10.3 Multi-Distilled Binary BERT 145
5.11   Post-Training Embedding Binarization for Fast Online Top-K Passage
        Matching 146
        5.11.1 Semantic Diffusion 146
        5.11.2 Gradient Estimation 147

6 Applications in Computer Vision   149
6.1   Introduction 149
        6.1.1 Person Re-Identification 149
        6.1.2 3D Point Cloud Processing 149
        6.1.3 Object Detection 150
        6.1.4 Speech Recognition 150
6.2   BiRe-ID: Binary Neural Network for Efficient Person Re-ID 151
        6.2.1 Problem Formulation 151
        6.2.2 Kernel Refining Generative Adversarial Learning (KR-GAL) 152
        6.2.3 Feature Refining Generative Adversarial Learning (FR-GAL) 153
        6.2.4 Optimization 154
        6.2.5 Ablation Study 156
6.3   POEM: 1-Bit Point-Wise Operations Based on E-M for Point Cloud
        Processing 157
        6.3.1 Problem Formulation 158
        6.3.2 Binarization Framework of POEM 159
        6.3.3 Supervision for POEM 160
        6.3.4 Optimization for POEM 161
        6.3.5 Ablation Study 164
6.4   LWS-Det: Layer-Wise Search for 1-bit Detectors 166
        6.4.1 Preliminaries 167
        6.4.2 Formulation of LWS-Det 168
        6.4.3 Differentiable Binarization Search for the 1-Bit Weight 169
        6.4.4 Learning the Scale Factor 170
        6.4.5 Ablation Study 171
6.5   IDa-Det: An Information Discrepancy-Aware Distillation for 1-bit Detectors 171
        6.5.1 Preliminaries 174
        6.5.2 Select Proposals with Information Discrepancy 174
        6.5.3 Entropy Distillation Loss 176
        6.5.4 Ablation Study 176

Bibliography   179

Index   203

About the Authors

Baochang Zhang is a full professor with the Institute of Artificial Intelligence, Beihang University, Beijing, China; and also with Zhongguancun Laboratory, Beijing, China. He was selected by the Program for New Century Excellent Talents in the University of Ministry of Education of China, chosen as the Academic Advisor of the Deep Learning Lab of Baidu Inc., and was honored as a Distinguished Researcher of Beihang Hangzhou Institute in Zhejiang Province. His research interests include explainable deep learning, computer vision, and pattern recognition. His HGPP and LDP methods were state-of-the-art feature descriptors, with 1234 and 768 Google Scholar citations, respectively, and both "Test-of-Time" works. His team's 1-bit methods achieved the best performance on ImageNet. His group also won the ECCV 2020 Tiny Object Detection, COCO Object Detection, and ICPR 2020 Pollen recognition challenges.

Sheng Xu received a BE in automotive engineering from Beihang University, Beijing, China. He has a PhD and is currently at the School of Automation Science and Electrical Engineering, Beihang University, specializing in computer vision, model quantization, and compression. He has made significant contributions to the field and has published about a dozen papers as the first author in top-tier conferences and journals such as *CVPR, ECCV, NeurIPS, AAAI, BMVC, IJCV,* and *ACM TOMM.* Notably, he has 4 papers selected as oral or highlighted presentations by these prestigious conferences. Furthermore, Dr. Xu actively participates in the academic community as a reviewer for various international journals and conferences, including *CVPR, ICCV, ECCV, NeurIPS, ICML,* and *IEEE TCSVT.* His expertise has also led to his group's victory in the ECCV 2020 Tiny Object Detection Challenge.

Mingbao Lin finished his MS-PhD study and obtained a PhD in intelligence science and technology from Xiamen University, Xiamen, China in 2022. In 2016, he received a BS from Fuzhou University, Fuzhou, China. He is currently a senior researcher with the Tencent Youtu Lab, Shanghai, China. His publications on top-tier conferences/journals include: *IEEE TPAMI, IJCV, IEEE TIP, IEEE TNNLS, CVPR, NeurIPS, AAAI, IJCAI, ACM MM,* and more. His current research interests include developing an efficient vision model, as well as information retrieval.

Tiancheng Wang received a BE in automation from Beihang University, Beijing, China. He is currently pursuing a PhD with the Institute of Artificial Intelligence, Beihang University. During his undergraduate studies, he was given the Merit Student Award for several consecutive years, and has received various scholarships including academic excellence and academic competitions scholarships. He was involved in several AI projects including behavior detection and intention understanding research and unmanned air-based vision platform, and more. Now his current research interests include deep learning and network compression; his goal is to explore a high energy-saving model and drive the deployment of neural networks in embedded devices.

Dr. David Doermann is a professor of empire innovation at the University at Buffalo (UB), New York, US, and the director of the University at Buffalo Artificial Intelligence Institute. Prior to coming to UB, he was a program manager at the Defense Advanced Research Projects Agency (DARPA) where he developed, selected, and oversaw approximately $150 million in research and transition funding in the areas of computer vision, human language technologies, and voice analytics. He coordinated performers on all projects, orchestrating consensus, evaluating cross team management, and overseeing fluid program objectives.

1

Introduction

Recently, we have witnessed a trend in deep learning in which models are rapidly increasing in complexity [84, 211, 220, 90, 205, 286]. However, the host hardware where the models are deployed has yet to keep up performance-wise due to practical limitations such as latency, battery life, and temperature. It results in a large, ever-increasing gap between computational demands and resources. To address this issue, network quantization [48, 199, 115, 149], which maps single-precision floating point weights or activations to lower bits integers for compression and acceleration, has attracted considerable research attention. The binary neural network (BNN) is the simplest version of low-bit networks and has gained much attention due to its highly compressed parameters and activation features [48]. The artificial intelligence company Xnor.ai is the most famous one focusing on BNNs. The company, founded in 2016, raised a lot of money to build tools that help AI algorithms run on devices rather than remote data centers. Apple Inc. bought the company and planned to apply BNN technology on its devices to keep user information more private and speed-up processing.

This chapter reviews recent advances in BNNs technologies well suited for front-end, edge-based computing. We introduce and summarize existing works by classifying them based on gradient approximation, quantization, architecture, loss functions, optimization method, and binary neural architecture search. We also introduce computer vision and speech recognition applications and discuss future applications of BNNs.

Deep learning has become increasingly important because of its superior performance. Still, it suffers from a large memory footprint and high computational cost, making it difficult to deploy on front-end devices. For example, in unmanned systems, UAVs serve as computing terminals with limited memory and computing resources, making it difficult to perform real-time data processing based on convolutional neural networks (CNNs). To improve storage and computation efficiency, BNNs have shown promise for practical applications. BNNs are neural networks where the weights are binarized. 1-bit CNNs are a highly compressed version of BNNs that binarize both the weights and the activations to decrease the model size and computational cost. These highly compressed models make them suitable for front-end computing. In addition to these two, other quantizing neural networks, such as pruning and sparse neural networks, are widely used in edge computing.

This chapter reviews the main advances of BNNs and 1-bit CNNs. Although binarization operations can make neural networks more efficient, they almost always cause a significant performance drop. In the last five years, many methods have been introduced to improve the performance of BNNs. To better review these methods, we describe six aspects: gradient approximation, quantization, structural design, loss design, optimization, and binary neural architecture search. Finally, we will also review the object detection, object tracking, and audio analysis applications of BNNs.

DOI: 10.1201/9781003376132-1

TABLE 1.1
Results reported in BinaryConnect [48] and BinaryNet [99].

Method	MNIST	CIFAR-10
BinaryConnect (only binary weights)	1.29±0.08%	9.90%
BinaryNet (binary both weights and activations)	1.40%	10.15%

1.1 Principal Methods

This section will review binary and 1-bit neural networks and highlight their similarities and differences.

1.1.1 Early Binary Neural Networks

BinaryConnect [48] was the first work presented that tried to restrict weights to +1 or −1 during propagation but did not binarize the inputs. Binary operations are simple and readily understandable. One way to binarize CNNs is by using a sign function:

$$\omega_b = \begin{cases} +1, & if \quad \omega \geq 0 \\ -1, & otherwise \end{cases},$$ (1.1)

where ω_b is the binarized weight and ω the real-valued weight. A second way is to binarize scholastically:

$$\omega_b = \begin{cases} +1, & with \quad probability \quad p = \sigma(\omega) \\ -1, & with \quad probability \quad 1-p \end{cases},$$ (1.2)

where σ is the "hard sigmoid" function. The training process for these networks is slightly different from full-precision neural networks. The forward propagation utilizes the binarized weights instead of the full-precision weights, but the backward propagation is the same as conventional methods. The gradient $\frac{\partial C}{\partial \omega_b}$ needs to be calculated (C is the cost function) and then combined with the learning rate to update the full-precision weights directly.

BinaryConnect only binarizes the weights, while BinaryNet [99] quantizes both the weights and activations. BinaryNet also introduces two ways to constrain weights and activations to be either +1 or −1, like BinaryConnect. BinaryNet also makes several changes to adapt to binary activations. The first is shift-based Batch Normalization (SBN), which avoids additional multiplications. The second is shift-based AdaMax instead of the ADAM learning rule, which also decreases the number of multiplications. The one-third change is to the operation to the input of the first layer. BinaryNet handles continuous-valued inputs of the first layer as fixed-point numbers, with m bits of precision. Training neural networks with extremely low-bit weights and activations were proposed as QNN [100]. As we are primarily reviewing work on binary networks, the details of QNN are omitted here. The error rates of these networks on representative datasets are shown in Table 1.1. However, these two networks perform unsatisfactorily on larger datasets since weights constrained to +1 and −1 cannot be learned effectively. New methods for training [BNNs] and 1-bit networks need to be raised.

Wang et al. [234] proposed Binarized Deep Neural Networks (BDNNs) for image classification tasks, where all the values and operations in the network are binarized. While BinaryNet deals with CNNs, BDNNs target basic artificial neural networks consisting of full-connection layers. Bitwise neural networks [117] also present a completely bitwise network where all participating variables are bipolar binaries.

1.1.2 Gradient Approximation

As described in Section 1.1.1, while updating the parameters in BNNs and 1-bit networks, the full-precision weights are updated with the gradient $\frac{\partial C}{\partial \omega_b}$. But forward propagation has a sign function between full-precision weights and binarized weights. In other words, the gradient of the sign function should be considered when updating full-precision weights. Note that the derivative of the sign function keeps zero and only becomes infinity at zero points, and a derivable function is widely utilized to approximate the sign function.

The first one to solve this problem in a 1-bit network is BinaryNet [99]. Assuming that an estimator of g_q of the gradient $\frac{\partial C}{\partial q}$, where q is $Sign(r)$, has been obtained. Then, the straight-through estimator of $\frac{\partial C}{\partial r}$ is simply

$$g_r = g_q 1_{|r| \leq 1}, \tag{1.3}$$

where $1_{|r| \leq 1}$ equals 1 when $|r| \leq 1$. And it equals 0 in other cases. It can also be seen as propagating the gradient through the hard *tanh*, which is a piecewise-linear activation function.

The Bi-real Net [159] approximates the derivative of the sign function for activations. Unlike using *Htanh* [99] to approximate the sign function, the Bi-real Net uses a piecewise polynomial function for a better approximation.

Bi-real Net also proposes a magnitude-aware gradient for weights. When training BNNs, the gradient $\frac{\partial C}{\partial W}$ is only related to the sign of weights and is independent of its magnitude. So, the Bi-real Net replaces the sign function with a magnitude-aware function.

Xu et al. [266] use a higher-order approximation for weight binarization. They propose a long-tailed approximation for activation binarization as a trade-off between tight approximation and smooth backpropagation.

Differentiable Soft Quantization (DSQ) [74] also introduces a function to approximate the standard binary and uniform quantization process called differentiable soft quantization. DSQ employs hyperbolic tangent functions to gradually approach the staircase function for low-bit quantization (sign function in 1-bit CNN). The binary DSQ function is as follows:

$$Q_s(x) = \begin{cases} -1, & x < -1 \\ 1, & x > 1 \\ stanh(kx), & otherwise \end{cases}, \tag{1.4}$$

with

$$k = \frac{1}{2}log(\frac{2}{\alpha} - 1), s = \frac{1}{1 - \alpha}. \tag{1.5}$$

Especially when α is small, DSQ can closely approximate the uniform quantization performance. This means that a suitable α will allow DSQ to help train a quantized model with higher accuracy. Note that DSQ is differentiable, and thus the derivative of this function can be used while updating the parameters directly.

According to the above methods, we can summarize that they all introduce a different function to approximate the sign function in BinaryConnect so that the gradient to full-precision weights or activations can be obtained more accurately. Therefore, the BNN or 1-bit network converges easier in the training process, and the network performance improves.

1.1.3 Quantization

BinaryConnect and BinaryNet use simple quantization methods. After the full-precision weights are updated, the new binary weights are generated by taking the sign of real-value weights. But when the binary weights are decided only by the sign of full-precision weights, this may cause significant errors in quantization. Before introducing new methods to improve the quantization process, we highlight the notations used in XNOR-Net [199] that will be used in our discussions. For each layer in a CNN, I is the input, W is the weight filter, B is the binarized weight $(+-1)$, and H is the binarized input.

Rastegari et al. [199] propose Binary-Weight-Networks (BWN) and XNOR-Networks. BWN approximates the weights with binary values, a variation of a BNN. XNOR-Networks binarize both the weights and activation bits and is considered a 1-bit network. Both networks use the idea of a scaling factor. In BWN, the real-valued weight filter W is estimated using a binary filter B and a scaling factor α. The convolutional operation is then approximated by:

$$I * W \approx (I \oplus B)\alpha, \tag{1.6}$$

where $\oplus$ indicates a convolution without multiplication. By introducing the scaling factor, binary weight filters reduce memory usage by a factor of $32\times$ compared to single precision filters. To ensure W is approximately equal to αB, BWN defines an optimization problem, and the optimal solution is:

$$B^* = sign(W), \tag{1.7}$$

$$\alpha^* = \frac{W^T sign(W)}{n} = \frac{\sum |W_i|}{n} = \frac{1}{n}\|W_r\|_{l_1}. \tag{1.8}$$

Therefore, the optimal estimation of a binary weight filter can be achieved by taking the sign of weight values. The optimal scaling factor is the absolute average of the absolute weight values. The scaling factor is also used to calculate the gradient in backpropagation. The core idea of XNOR-Net is the same as BWN, but another scaling factor, β, is used when binarizing the input I into H. As the experiments show, this approach outperforms BinaryConnect and BNN by a large margin on ImageNet. Unlike the XNOR-Net, which sets the mean weights to the scaling factor, Xu et al. [266] define a trainable scaring factor for both weights and activations. LQ-Nets [284] quantize both weights and activations with arbitrary bit-widths, including 1-bit. The learnability of the quantizers makes them compatible with bitwise operations to keep the fast inference merit of properly quantized neural networks (QNNs).

Based on XNOR-Net [199], the High-Order Residual Quantization (HORQ) [138] provides a high-order binarization scheme, which achieves a more accurate approximation while still having the advantage of binary operations. HORQ calculates the residual error and then performs a new round of thresholding operations to approximate the residual further. This binary approximation of the residual can be considered a higher-order binary input. Following XNOR, HORQ defines the first-order residual tensor $R_1(x)$ by computing the difference between the real input and the first-order binary quantization:

$$R_1(x) = X - \beta_1 H_1 \approx \beta_2 H_2, \tag{1.9}$$

where $R_1(x)$ is a real value tensor. By this analogy, $R_2(x)$ can be seen as the second-order residual tensor, and $\beta_3 H_3$ also approximates it. After recursively performing the above operations, they obtain order-K residual quantization:

$$X = \sum_{i=1}^{K} \beta_i H_i. \tag{1.10}$$

During the training of the HORQ network, the input tensor can be reshaped into a matrix and expressed as any order residual quantization. Experiments show that HORQ-Net outperforms XNOR-Net in accuracy in the CIFAR dataset.

ABC-Net [147] is another network designed to improve the performance of binary networks. ABC-Net approximates the full precision weight filter W with a linear combination of M binary filters $B_1, B_2, ..., B_M \in \{+1, -1\}$ such that $W \approx \alpha_1 \beta_1 + ... + \alpha_M \beta_M$. These binary filters are fixed as follows:

$$B_i = F_{u_i}(W) := sign(\bar{W} + u_i std(W)), i = 1, 2, ..., M, \tag{1.11}$$

where $\bar{W}$ and $std(W)$ are the mean and standard derivation of W, respectively. For activations, ABC-Net employs multiple binary activations to alleviate information loss. Like the binarization weights, the real activation I is estimated using a linear combination of N activations $A_1, A_2, ..., A_N$ such that $I = \beta_1 A_1 + ... + \beta_N A_N$, where

$$A_1, A_2, ..., A_N = H_{v_1}(R), H_{v_2}(R), ..., H_{v_N}(R). \tag{1.12}$$

$H(R)$ in Eq. 4.35 is a binary function, h is a bounded activation function, I is the indicator function, and v is a shift parameter. Unlike the input weights, the parameters β and v are trainable. Without explicit linear regression, the network tunes $\beta'_n s$ and $v'_n s$ during training and is fixed for testing. They are expected to learn and utilize the statistical features of full-precision activations.

Ternary-Binary Network (TBN) [228] is a CNN with ternary inputs and binary weights. Based on accelerated ternary-binary matrix multiplication, TBN uses efficient operations such as XOR, AND, and bit count in standard CNNs, and thus provides an optimal trade-off between memory, efficiency, and performance. Wang et al. [233] propose a simple yet effective two-step quantization framework (TSQ) by decomposing network quantization into two steps: code learning and transformation function learning based on codes learned. TSQ fits primarily into the class of 2-bit neural networks.

Local Binary Convolutional Network (LBCNN) [109] proposes a local binary convolution (LBC), which is motivated by local binary patterns (LBP), a descriptor of images rooted in the face recognition community. The LBC layer has a set of fixed, sparse predefined binary convolutional filters that are not updated during the training process, a non-linear activation function, and a set of learnable linear weights. The linear weights combine the activated filter responses to approximate a standard convolutional layer's corresponding activated filter responses. The LBC layer often affords significant parameter savings of $9x$ to $169x$ fewer learnable parameters than a standard convolutional layer. Furthermore, the sparse and binary nature of the weights also results in up to $169x$ savings in model size compared to a conventional convolution.

Modulated Convolutional Networks (MCN) [236] first introduce modulation filters (M-Filters) to recover the binarized filters. M-Filters are designed to approximate unbinarized convolutional filters in an end-to-end framework. Each layer shares only one M-Filter, leading to a significant reduction in model size. To reconstruct the unbinarized filters, they introduce a modulated process based on the M-Filters and binarized filters. Figure 1.1 is an example of the modulation process. In this example, the M-Filter has four planes, each of which can be expanded to a 3D matrix according to the channels of the binarized filter. After the ∘ operation between the binarized filter and each expanded M-Filter, the reconstructed filter Q is obtained.

As shown in Fig. 1.2, the reconstructed filters Q are used to calculate the output feature maps F. There are four planes in Fig. 1.2, so the number of channels in the feature maps is also 4. Using MCNs convolution, every feature map's input and output channels are the same, allowing the module to be replicated and the MCNs to be easily implemented.

Unlike previous work in which the model binarizes each filter independently, Bulat et al. [23] propose parameterizing each layer's weight tensor using a matrix or tensor decomposition. The binarization process uses latent parametrization through a quantization function

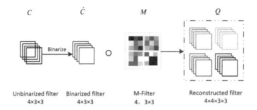

FIGURE 1.1
Modulation process based on an M-Filter.

(e.g., sign function) for the reconstructed weights. While the reconstruction is binarized, the computation in the latent factorized space is done in the real domain. This has several advantages. First, the latent factorization enforces a coupling of filters before binarization, which significantly improves the accuracy of trained models. Second, during training, the binary weights of each convolutional layer are parametrized using a real-valued matrix or tensor decomposition, while during inference, reconstructed (binary) weights are used.

Instead of using the same binary method for weights and activations, Huang et al. [93] believe that the best performance for binarized neural networks can be obtained by applying different quantization methods to weights and activations. They simultaneously binarize the weights and quantize the activations to reduce bandwidth.

ReActNet [158] proposes a simple channel-wise reshaping and shifting operation for the activation distribution, which replaces the sign function with ReAct-Sign, and replaces the PReLU function with ReAct-PReLU. The parameters in ReAct-Sign and ReAct-PReLU can be updated.

Compared to XNOR-Net [199], both HORQ-Net [138] and ABC-Net [147] use multiple binary weights and activations. As a result, HORQ-Net and ABC-Net outperform XNOR-Net on binary tasks, but they also increase complexity, which goes against the initial intention of BNNs. New neural networks that perform better and retain the advantage of speediness are waiting to be explored. MCN [236] and LBCNN [109] proposed new filters while quantizing parameters and introducing a new loss function to learn these auxiliary filters.

1.1.4   Structural Design

The basic structure of networks such as BinaryConnect [48] and BinaryNet [99] is essentially the same as traditional CNNs, which may not fit the binary process. Some attempts have been made to modify the structure of BNNs for better accuracy.

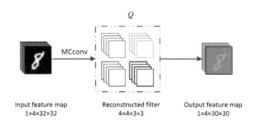

FIGURE 1.2
MCNs convolution.

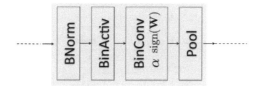

FIGURE 1.3
A block in XNOR-Net.

XNOR-Net [199] changes the block structure in a typical CNN. A typical block in a CNN contains different layers: 1-Convolutional, 2-BatchNorm, 3-Activation, and 4-Pooling. To further decrease information loss due to binarization, XNOR-Net normalizes the input before binarization. This ensures the data have zero mean, so thresholding at zero minimizes quantization error. The order of the layers in XNOR-Net is shown in Fig. 1.3.

The Bi-real Net [159] attributes the poor performance of 1-bit CNNs to their low representation capacity. The representation capacity is defined as the number of all possible configurations of x, where x could be a scalar, vector, matrix, or tensor. Bi-real Net proposes a simple shortcut to preserve real activations before the sign function to increase the representation capability of the 1-bit CNN. As shown in Fig. 1.4, the block indicates the structure "Sign $\rightarrow$ 1-bit convolution $\rightarrow$ batch normalization $\rightarrow$ addition operator." The shortcut connects the input activations to the sign function in the current block to the output activations after the batch normalization in the same block. These two activations are added through an addition operator, and then the combined activations are passed to the sign function in the next block.

The simple identity shortcut significantly enhances the representation capability of each block in the 1-bit CNN. The only additional cost of computation is the addition operation of two real activations without additional memory cost.

BinaryDenseNet [12] designs a new BNN architecture that addresses the main drawbacks of BNNs. DenseNets [92] apply shortcut connections so that new information gained in one layer can be reused throughout the depth of the network. This is a significant characteristic that helps to maintain the information flow. The bottleneck design in DenseNets significantly reduces the filters and values between layers, resulting in less information flow in the BNNs. These bottlenecks must be eliminated. Due to the limited representation capacity of binary layers, the DenseNet architecture does not perform satisfactorily. This problem is solved by increasing the growth rate or using a larger number of blocks. To keep the number

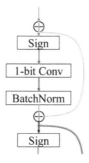

FIGURE 1.4
1-bit CNN with shortcut.

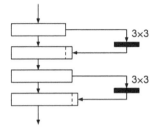

FIGURE 1.5
BinaryDenseNet.

of parameters equal for a given BinaryDenseNet, they halve the growth rate and double the number of blocks simultaneously. The architecture of BinaryDenseNet is shown in Fig. 1.5

MeliusNet [10] presents a new architecture alternating with a DenseBlock, which increases the feature capacity. They also propose an ImprovementBlock, which increases the quality of the features. With this method, 1-bit CNNs can match the accuracy of the popular compact network MobileNet-v1 in terms of model size, number of operations, and accuracy. The building blocks of MeliusNet are shown in Fig. 1.6.

Group-Net [303] also improves the performance of 1-bit CNNs through structural design. Inspired by a fixed number of binary digits representing a floating point number in a computer, Group-Net proposes decomposing a network into binary structures while preserving its representability rather than directly doing the quantization via "value decomposition."

Bulat et al. [25] are the first to study the effect of neural network binarization on localization tasks, such as human pose estimation and face alignment. They propose a novel hierarchical, parallel, and multiscale residual architecture that significantly improves performance over the standard bottleneck block while maintaining the number of parameters, thus bridging the gap between the original network and its binarized counterpart. The new architecture increases the size of the receptive field, as well as the gradient flow.

LightNN [57] replaces multiplications with one shift or a constrained number of shifts and adds, which forms a new kind of model. The experiments show that LightNN has better accuracy than BNNs, with only a slight increase in energy.

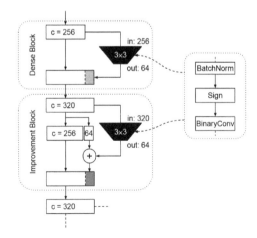

FIGURE 1.6
Building blocks of MeliusNet (c denotes the number of channels in the feature map).

In this section, we list several works that modify the structure of [BNNs], contributing to better performance or convergence of the network. XNOR-Net and Bi-real Net make minor adjustments to the original networks, while MCN proposes new filters and convolutional operations. The loss function is also adjusted according to the new filters, which will be introduced in Section 1.1.5.

1.1.5   Loss Design

During neural network optimization, the loss function is used to estimate the difference between the real and predicted values of a model. Some classical loss functions, such as least squares loss and cross-entropy loss, are widely used in classification and regression problems. This section will review the specific loss function used in [BNNs].

MCNs [236] propose a novel loss function that considers filter loss, center loss, and softmax loss in an end-to-end framework. The loss function in MCNs consists of two parts:

$$L = L_M + L_S. \tag{1.13}$$

The first part L_M is:

$$L_M = \frac{\theta}{2} \sum_{i,l} \left\| C_i^l - \hat{C}_i^l \circ M^l \right\|^2 + \frac{\lambda}{2} \sum_m \left\| f_m(\hat{C}, \vec{M}) - \bar{f}(\hat{C}, \vec{M}) \right\|^2, \tag{1.14}$$

where C is the full precision weights, $\hat{C}$ is the binarized weights, M is the M-Filters defined in Section 1.1.4, f_m denotes the feature map of the last convolutional layer for the mth sample, and $\bar{f}$ denotes the class-specific mean feature map of previous samples. The first entry of L_M represents the filter loss, while the second entry calculates the center loss using a conventional loss function, such as the softmax loss.

PCNNs [77] propose a projection loss for discrete backpropagation. It is the first to define the quantization of the input variable as a projection onto a set to obtain a projection loss. Our BONNs [287] propose a Bayesian-optimized 1-bit CNN model to improve the performance of 1-bit CNNs significantly. BONNs incorporate the prior distributions of full-precision kernels, features, and filters into a Bayesian framework to construct 1-bit CNNs comprehensively, end-to-end. They denote the quantization error as y and the full-precision weights as x. They maximize $p(x|y)$ to optimize x for quantization to minimize the reconstructed error. This optimization problem can be converted to a maximum a posteriori since the distribution of x is known. For feature quantization, the method is the same. Therefore, the Bayesian loss is as follows:

$$
\begin{aligned}
L_B = \frac{\lambda}{2} \sum_{l=1}^{l} \sum_{i=1}^{C_o^l} \sum_{n=1}^{C_i^l} \{ & \left\| \hat{k}_n^{l,i} - w^l \circ k_n^{l,i} \right\|_2^2 \\
& + v(k_{n+}^{l,i} - \mu_{i+}^l)^T (\Psi_{i+}^l)^{-1} (k_{n+}^{l,i} - \mu_{i+}^l) \\
& + v(k_{n-}^{l,i} - \mu_{i-}^l)^T (\Psi_{i-}^l)^{-1} (k_{n-}^{l,i} - \mu_{i-}^l) \\
& vlog(det(\Psi^l)) \} + \frac{\theta}{2} \sum_{m=1}^{M} \{ \left\| f_m - c_m \right\|^2 \\
& + \sum_{n=1}^{N_f} \left[\sigma_{m,n}^{-2} (f_{m,n} - c_{m,n})^2 + log(\sigma_{m,n}^2) \right] \},
\end{aligned} \tag{1.15}
$$

where k is the full precision kernels, w is the reconstructed matrix, v is the variance of y, μ is the mean of the kernels, Ψ is the covariance of the kernels, f_m are the features of class m, and c is the mean of f_m.

Zheng et al. [288] define a new quantization loss between binary weights and learned real values, where they theoretically prove the necessity of minimizing the weight quantization loss. Ding et al. [56] propose using distribution loss to explicitly regularize the activation flow and develop a framework to formulate the loss systematically. Empirical results show that the proposed distribution loss is robust to selecting the training hyper-parameters.

Reviewing these methods, they all aim to minimize the error and information loss of quantization, which improves the compactness and capacity of 1-bit CNNs.

1.1.6   Neural Architecture Search

Neural architecture search (NAS) has attracted significant attention with remarkable performance in various deep learning tasks. Impressive results have been shown for reinforcement learning (RL), for example,[306]. Recent methods such as differentiable architecture search (DARTs) [151] reduce search time by formulating the task in a differentiable manner. To reduce redundancy in the network space, partially connected DARTs (PC-DARTs) were recently introduced to perform a more efficient search without compromising DARTS performance [265].

In Binarized Neural Architecture Search (BNAS) [35], the neural architecture search is used to search BNNs, and the BNNs obtained by BNAS can outperform conventional models by a large margin. Another natural approach is to use 1-bit CNNs to reduce the computation and memory cost of NAS by taking advantage of the strengths of each in a unified framework [304]. To accomplish this, a Child-Parent (CP) model is introduced to a differentiable NAS to search the binarized architecture (Child) under the supervision of a full precision model (Parent). In the search stage, the Child-Parent model uses an indicator generated by the accuracy of the Child-Parent (cp) model to evaluate the performance and abandon operations with less potential. In the training stage, a kernel-level CP loss is introduced to optimize the binarized network. Extensive experiments demonstrate that the proposed CP-NAS achieves a comparable accuracy with traditional NAS on both the CIFAR and ImageNet databases.

Unlike conventional convolutions, BNAS is achieved by transforming all convolutions in the search space O into binarized convolutions. They denote the full-precision and binarized kernels as X and $\hat{X}$, respectively. A convolution operation in O is represented as $B_j = B_i \otimes \hat{X}$, where $\otimes$ denotes convolution. To build BNAS, a key step is to binarize the kernels from X to $\hat{X}$, which can be implemented based on state-of-the-art BNNs, such as XNOR or PCNN. To solve this, they introduce channel sampling and reduction in operating space into differentiable NAS to significantly reduce the cost of GPU hours, leading to an efficient BNAS.

1.1.7   Optimization

Researchers also explore new training methods to improve BNN performance. These methods are designed to handle the drawbacks of BNNs. Some borrow popular techniques from other fields and integrate them into BNNs, while others make changes based on classical BNNs training, such as improving the optimizer.

Sari et al. [234] find that the BatchNorm layer plays a significant role in avoiding exploding gradients, so the standard initialization methods developed for full-precision networks are irrelevant for BNNs. They also break down BatchNorm components into centering and scaling, showing only minibatch centering is required. Their work provides valuable information for research on the BNN training process. The experiments of Alizadeh et al. [2] show that most of the tricks commonly used in training binary models, such as gradient and weight clipping, are only required during the final stages of training to achieve the best performance.

XNOR-Net++ [26] provides a new training algorithm for 1-bit CNNs based on XNOR-Net. Compared to XNOR-Net, this new method combines activation and weight scaling factors into a single scalar learned discriminatively through backpropagation. They also try different ways to construct the shape of the scale factors on the premise that the computational budget remains fixed.

Borrowing an idea from the Alternating Direction Method of Multipliers (ADMM), Leng et al. [128] decouple the continuous parameters from the discrete constraints of the network and divide the original hard problem into several subproblems. These subproblems are solved by extra gradient and iterative quantization algorithms, leading to considerably faster convergence than conventional optimization methods.

Deterministic Binary Filters (DBFs) [225] learn weighted coefficients of predefined orthogonal binary bases instead of the conventional approach, which directly learns the convolutional filters. The filters are generated as a linear combination of orthogonal binary codes and thus can be generated very efficiently in real time.

BWNH [91] trains binary weight networks by hashing. They first reveal the strong connection between inner-product preserving hashing and binary weight networks, showing that training binary weight networks can be intrinsically regarded as a hashing problem. They propose an alternating optimization method to learn the hash codes instead of directly learning binary weights.

CI-BCNN [239] learns BNNs with channel-wise interactions for efficient inference. Unlike existing methods that directly apply XNOR and BITCOUNT operations, this method learns interacted bitcount according to the mined channel-wise interactions. The inconsistent signs in binary feature maps are corrected based on prior knowledge provided by channel-wise interactions so that the information of the input images is preserved in the forward propagation of BNNs. Specifically, they employ a reinforcement learning model to learn a directed acyclic graph for each convolutional layer, representing implicit channel-wise interactions. They obtain the interacted bitcount by adjusting the output of the original bitcount in line with the effects exerted by the graph. They train the BCNN and the graph structure simultaneously.

BinaryRelax [272] is a two-phase algorithm to train CNNs with quantized weights, including binary weights. They relax the hard constraint into a continuous regularizer via Moreau envelope [176], the squared Euclidean distance to the set of quantized weights. They gradually increase the regularization parameter to close the gap between the weights and the quantized state. In the second phase, they introduce the exact quantization scheme with a small learning rate to guarantee fully quantized weights.

CBCNs [149] propose new circulant filters (CiFs) and a circulant binary convolution (CBConv) to enhance the capacity of binarized convolutional features through circulant backpropagation. A CiF is a 4D tensor of size $K \times K \times H \times H$, generated based on a learned filter and a circulant transfer matrix M. The matrix M here rotates the learned filter at different angles. The original 2D $H \times H$ learned filter is modified to 3D by replicating it three times and concatenating them to obtain 4D CiF, as shown in Fig. 1.7. The method can improve the representation capacity of BNNs without changing the model size.

Rectified binary convolutional networks (RBCNs) [148] use a generative adversarial network (GAN) to train the 1-bit binary network with the guidance of its corresponding full-precision model, which significantly improves the performance of 1-bit CNNs. The rectified convolutional layers are generic and flexible and can be easily incorporated into existing DCNNs such as WideResNets and ResNets.

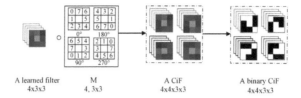

FIGURE 1.7
The generation of CiF.

Martinez et al. [168] attempt to minimize the discrepancy between the binary output and the corresponding real-valued convolution. They proposed real-to-binary attention matching suited for training 1-bit CNNs. They also devised an approach in which the architectural gap between real and binary networks is progressively bridged through a sequence of teacher-student pairs.

Instead of using a pre-trained full-precision model, Bethge et al. [11] directly train a binary network from scratch, which does not benefit from other standard methods. Their implementation is based on the BMXNet framework [268].

Helwegen et al. [85] believe that latent weights with real values cannot be treated analogously to weights in real-valued networks, while their primary role is to provide inertia during training. They introduced the Binary Optimizer (Bop), the first optimizer designed for BNNs.

BinaryDuo [115] proposes a new training scheme for binary activation networks in which two binary activations are coupled into a ternary activation during training. They first decouple a ternary activation into two binary activations. Then the number of weights is doubled after decoupling. They reduce the coupled ternary model to match the parameter size of the decoupled model and the baseline model. They update each weight independently to find a better value since the two weights no longer need to share the same value.

BENN [301] uses classical ensemble methods to improve the performance of 1-bit CNNs. While ensemble techniques have been broadly believed to be only marginally helpful for strong classifiers, such as deep neural networks, their analysis, and experiments show that they are naturally a perfect fit to boost BNNs. The main uses of the ensemble strategies are shown in [19, 32, 184].

TentacleNet [173] is also inspired by the theory of ensemble learning. Compared to BENN [301], TentacleNet takes a step forward, showing that binary ensembles can reach high accuracy with fewer resources.

BayesBiNN [170] uses a distribution over the binary variable, resulting in a principled approach to discrete optimization. They used a Bernoulli approximation to the posterior and estimated it using the Bayesian learning rule proposed in [112].

1.2 Applications

The success of BNNs makes it possible to apply deep learning models to edge computing. Neural network models have been used in various real tasks with the help of these binary methods, including image classification, image classification, speech recognition, and object detection and tracking.

TABLE 1.2

Experimental results of some famous binary methods on ImageNet.

Methods	Weights	Activations	Model	Binarized Acc.		Full-precision Acc.	
				Top-1	Top-5	Top-1	Top-5
XNOR-Net [199]	Binary	Binary	ResNet-18	51.2	73.2	69.3	89.2
ABC-Net [147]	Binary	Binary	ResNet-50	70.1	89.7	76.1	92.8
LBCNN [109]	Binary	–	–	62.43[1]	–	64.94	–
Bi-Real Net [159]	Binary	Binary	ResNet-34	62.2	83.9	73.3	91.3
PCNN [77]	Binary	Binary	ResNet-18	57.3	80.0	69.3	89.2
RBCN [148]	Binary	Binary	ResNet-18	59.5	81.6	69.3	89.2
BinaryDenseNet [12]	–	–	–	62.5	83.9	–	–
BNAS [36]	–	–	–	71.3	90.3	–	–

1.2.1   Image Classification

Image classification aims to group images into different semantic classes together. Many works regard the completion of image classification as the criterion for the success of BNNs. Five datasets are commonly used for image classification tasks: MNIST [181], SVHN, CIFAR-10 [122], CIFAR-100 and ImageNet [204]. Among them, ImageNet is the most difficult to train and consists of 100 classes of images. Table 1.2 shows the experimental results of some of the most popular binary methods on ImageNet.

1.2.2   Speech Recognition

Speech recognition is a technique or capability that enables a program or system to process human speech. We can use binary methods to complete speech recognition tasks in edge computing devices.

Xiang et al. [252] applied binary DNNs to speech recognition tasks. Experiments on TIMIT phone recognition and 50-hour Switchboard speech recognition show that binary DNNs can run about four times faster than standard DNNs during inference, with roughly 10.0%.

Zheng et al. [290] and Yin et al. [273] also implement binarized CNN-based speech recognition tasks.

1.2.3   Object Detection and Tracking

Object detection is the process of finding a target from a scene, while object tracking is the follow-up of a target in consecutive frames in a video.

Sun et al. [218] propose a fast object detection algorithm based on BNNs. Compared to full-precision convolution, this new method results in 62 times faster convolutional operations and 32 times memory saving in theory.

---

[1]13×13 Filter

TABLE 1.3

Results reported in Liu et al. [148].

Dataset	Index	SiamFC	XNOR	RB-SF
GOT-10K	AO	0.348	0.251	0.327
	SR	0.383	0.230	0.343
OTB50	Precision	0.761	0.457	0.706
	SR	0.556	0.323	0.496
OTB100	Precision	0.808	0.541	0.786
	SR	0.602	0.394	0.572
UAV123	Precision	0.745	0.547	0.688
	SR	0.528	0.374	0.497

Liu et al. [148] experiment on object tracking after proposing RBCNs. They used the SiamFC network as the backbone for object tracking and binarized the SiamFC as the Rectified Binary Convolutional SiamFC Network (RB-SF). They evaluated RBSF in four datasets, GOT-10K [94], OTB50 [250], OTB100 [251], and UAV123 [177], using accuracy occupy (AO) and success rate (SR). The results are shown in Table 1.3.

Yang et al. [269] propose a new method to optimize a deep neural network based on YOLO-based object tracking simultaneously using approximate weight binarization, trainable threshold group binarization activation function, and separable convolution methods according to depth, significantly reducing the complexity of computation and model size.

1.2.4 Applications

Other applications include face recognition and face alignment. Face recognition: Liu et al. [160] apply Weight Binarization Cascade Convolution Neural Network to eye localization, a face recognition field. BNNs here help reduce the storage size of the model, as well as speed up calculation.

Face Alignment: Bulat et al. [25] test their method on three challenging datasets for significant pose face alignment: AFLW [121], AFLW-PIFA [108], and AFLW2000-3D [302], reporting in many cases state-of-the-art performance.

1.3   Our Works on BNNs

We have designed several BNNs and 1-bit CNNs. MCN [236] was our first work, in which we introduced modulation filters to approximate unbinarized filters in the end-to-end framework. Based on MCN, we introduce projection convolutional neural networks (PCNNs) [77] with discrete backpropagation via projection. Similarly to PCNN, our CBCNs [149] aims to improve backpropagation by improving the representation ability based on a circular backpropagation method. On the other hand, our RBCN [148] and BONN [287] improve the training of new models by changing the loss function and the optimization process. RBCNs introduce GAN, while BONNs are based on Bayesian learning. Recurrent bilinear optimization for binary neural networks (RBONNs) is introduced to investigate the relationship between full-precision parameters and their binary counterparts. This is implemented by controlling the backpropagation process, where the sparse real-valued parameters are backtracked to wait for other parameters well trained to their full performance. Resilient Binary Neural Networks (ReBNNs) are introduced to mitigate the gradient oscillation prob-

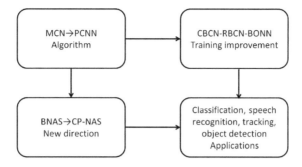

FIGURE 1.8
Our research agenda on BNNs.

lem in a theoretical framework. In ReBNNs, the reconstruction loss introduced in MCN can theoretically decrease the gradient oscillation by changing its balanced factor.

Although the performance of BNNs has improved dramatically in the last three years, the gap remains large compared to that of their full-precision counterparts. One possible solution could come from the neural architecture search (NAS), which has led to state-of-the-art performance in many learning tasks. Neural architecture search (NAS) has led to state-of-the-art performance on many learning tasks. A natural idea is introducing NAS into BNNs, leading to our binarized neural architecture search (BNAS) [35]. In our BNAS framework, we show that the BNNs obtained by BNAS can outperform conventional models by a large margin. While BNAS only focuses on kernel binarization to achieve 1-bit CNNs, our CP-NAS [304] advances this work to binarize both weights and activations. In CP-NAS, a Child-Parent (CP) model is introduced to a differentiable NAS to search the binarized architecture (child) under the supervision of a full precision model (Parent). Based on CP-NAS, we achieve much better performance than conventional binarized neural networks. Our research agenda on BNNs is shown in Fig. 1.8.

2

Quantization of Neural Networks

Quantization is a strategy that has demonstrated outstanding and consistent success in both the training and inference of neural networks (NN). NN present unique opportunities for advancement even though the issues of numerical representation and quantization are as old as digital computing. Although most of this quantization survey is concerned with inference, it is essential to note that quantization has also been successful in NN training [8, 42, 63, 105]. Innovations in half-precision and mixed-precision training in particular [47, 80] have enabled greater throughput in AI accelerators. However, going below half-precision without significant tuning has proven to be challenging, and most recent quantization research has concentrated on inference.

2.1 Overview of Quantization

Given an NN model of N layers, we denote its weight set as $\mathbf{W} = \{\mathbf{w}^n\}_{n=1}^N$ and the input feature set as $\mathbf{A} = \{\mathbf{a}_{in}^n\}_{n=1}^N$. The $\mathbf{w}^n \in \mathbb{R}^{C_{out}^n \times C_{in}^n}$ and $\mathbf{a}_{in}^n \in \mathbb{R}^{C_{in}^n}$ are the convolutional weight and the input feature map in the n-th layer, respectively, where C_{in}^n and C_{out}^n respectively stand for the input channel number and the output channel number. Then, the outputs $\mathbf{a}_{out}^n$ can be technically formulated as:

$$\mathbf{a}_{out}^n = \mathbf{w}^n \cdot \mathbf{a}_{in}^n, \tag{2.1}$$

where $\cdot$ represents matrix multiplication. In this paper, we omit the non-linear function for simplicity. Following the prior works [100], quantized neural network (QNN) intends to represent $\mathbf{w}^n$ and $\mathbf{a}^n$ in a low-bit format as

$$\mathbb{Q} := \{q_1, \cdots, q_U\},$$

where $q_i,\ i = 1, \cdots, U$ satisfying $q_1 < \cdots < q_U$, are defined as quantized values of the original variable. Note that x can be the input feature $\mathbf{a}^n$ or the weights $\mathbf{w}^n$. In this way, $\mathbf{q}^{\mathbf{w}^n} \in \mathbb{Q}^{C_{out}^n \times C_{in}^n}$ and $\mathbf{q}^{\mathbf{a}_{in}^n} \in \mathbb{Q}^{C_{in}^n}$ such that the float-point convolutional outputs can be approximated by the efficient XNOR and bit-count instructions as:

$$\mathbf{a}_{out}^n \approx \mathbf{q}^{\mathbf{w}^n} \odot \mathbf{q}^{\mathbf{a}_{in}^n}. \tag{2.2}$$

The core item of QNNs is how to define a quantization set $\mathbb{Q}$, which is described next.

2.1.1 Uniform and Non-Uniform Quantization

First, we must define a function capable of quantizing the weights and activations of the NN to a finite set of values. The following is a popular choice for a quantization function:

$$\mathbf{q}^x = \text{INT}(\frac{x}{S}) - Z, \tag{2.3}$$

DOI: 10.1201/9781003376132-2

where, x is a real-valued input (activation or weight), S is a real-valued scaling factor, and Z is an integer zero point. In addition, the INT function converts a real number to an integer value via a rounding technique (e.g., round to nearest and truncation). This function is just a mapping from real values x to some integer value. This method of quantization is also known as uniform quantization.

Besides, non-uniform quantization methods produce quantized values that are not necessarily uniformly spaced. The formal definition of non-uniform quantization is shown as

$$\mathbf{q}^x = \begin{cases} q_1, & \text{if } x \leq \Delta_1, \\ \dots \\ q_i, & \text{if } \Delta_{i-1} < x \leq \Delta_i, \\ \dots \\ q_U, & \text{if } x > \Delta_U. \end{cases} \tag{2.4}$$

where q_i represents the discrete quantization levels and Δ_i denotes the quantization steps. When the value of a real number x falls between the quantization steps $\Delta_i - 1$ and $i + 1$, the quantizer Q projects it to the associated quantization level q_i. It should be noted that neither q_i nor Δ_i are evenly spaced.

Nonuniform quantization can achieve higher accuracy for a fixed bit width because it allows for better capturing of distributions by focusing on important value regions or determining appropriate dynamic ranges. For example, various nonuniform quantization techniques have been developed for bell-shaped distributions of weights and activations, which often exhibit long tails. A commonly employed rule-based nonuniform quantization method uses a logarithmic distribution, where the quantization steps and levels increase exponentially rather than linearly.

Recent advances have approached it as an optimization problem to enhance quantization performance. The goal is to minimize the difference between the original tensor and its quantized counterpart by adjusting the quantization steps/levels in the quantizer $\mathbf{q}^x$.

$$min_{\mathbf{q}}\|\mathbf{q}^x - x\|_2^2 \tag{2.5}$$

Nonuniform quantization can also be improved by making the quantizer itself trainable. These methods are called learnable quantizers, and the quantization steps/levels are optimized through an iterative process or gradient descent along with the model parameters.

Overall, nonuniform quantization can better represent data by distributing bits and unevenly discretizing the range of parameters. However, this quantization type can be challenging to implement effectively on standard computation hardware such as a GPU and a CPU. As a result, uniform quantization remains the prevalent method because of its straightforward implementation and efficient mapping to hardware.

2.1.2 Symmetric and Asymmetric Quantization

The choice of the scaling factor, S, in Eq. 2 is crucial in uniform quantization. S determines the size of each partition by dividing the range of real values, x, into a specified number of segments. The value of S affects the granularity of the quantization and ultimately impacts the accuracy of the quantized representation:

$$S = \frac{\beta - \alpha}{2^b - 1}, \tag{2.6}$$

where $[\alpha, \beta]$ is the clip range and b is the bit-width. The clipping range, $[\alpha, \beta]$, determines the range of real values that should be quantized. The choice of this range is crucial, as it determines the quantization's precision and the quantized model's overall quality. This process is known as calibration, an important step in uniform quantization. where $[\alpha, \beta]$ is the clip range and b is the bit-width. The clipping range, $[\alpha, \beta]$, determines the range of real values that should be quantized. The choice of this range is crucial, as it determines the quantization's precision and the quantized model's overall quality. This process is known as calibration, an important step in uniform quantization. The clipping range can be tighter in asymmetric quantization than in symmetric quantization. This is especially important for signals with imbalanced values, like activations after ReLU, which always have non-negative values. Furthermore, symmetric quantization simplifies the quantization function by centering the zero point at $Z = 0$, making the quantization process more straightforward as follows:

$$\mathbf{q}^x = \text{INT}(\frac{x}{S}). \tag{2.7}$$

In general, the full-range approach provides greater accuracy. Symmetric quantization is commonly used for quantizing weights due to its simplicity and reduced computational cost during inference. However, asymmetric quantization may be more effective for activations because the offset in asymmetric activations can be absorbed into the bias or used to initialize the accumulator.

2.2   LSQ: Learned Step Size Quantization

Fixed quantization methods that rely on user-defined settings do not guarantee optimal network performance and may still produce suboptimal results even if they minimize quantization error. An alternative approach is learning the quantization mapping by minimizing task loss, directly improving the desired metric. However, this method is challenging because the quantizer is discontinuous and requires an accurate approximation of its gradient, which existing methods [43] have done roughly that overlooks the effects of transitions between quantized states.

This section introduces a new method for learning the quantization mapping for each layer in a deep network called Learned Step Size Quantization (LSQ) [61]. LSQ improves on previous methods with two key innovations. First, we offer a simple way to estimate the gradient of the quantizer step size, considering the impact of transitions between quantized states. This results in more refined optimization when learning the step size as a model parameter. Second, we introduce a heuristic to balance the magnitude of step size updates with weight updates, leading to improved convergence. Our approach can be used to quantize both activations and weights and is compatible with existing techniques for backpropagation and stochastic gradient descent.

2.2.1   Notations

The goal of quantization in deep networks is to reduce the precision of the weights and the activations during the inference time to increase the computational efficiency. Given the data to quantize v, the quantizer step size s, and the number of positive and negative quantization levels (Q_P and Q_N), a quantizer is used to compute $\hat{v}$, a quantized representation on the whole scale of the data, and $\hat{v}$, a quantized representation of the data at the same scale as v:

$$\bar{v} = \lfloor clip(v/s, -Q_N, Q_P) \rceil \tag{2.8}$$

$$\hat{v} = \bar{v} \times s \tag{2.9}$$

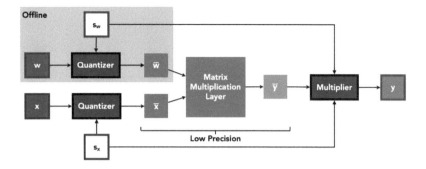

FIGURE 2.1
Computation of a low-precision convolution or fully connected layer, as envisioned here.

This technique uses low-precision inputs, represented by $\bar{w}$ and $\bar{x}$, in matrix multiplication units for convolutional or fully connected layers in deep learning networks. The low-precision integer matrix multiplication units can be computed efficiently, and a step size then scale the output with a relatively low-cost high-precision scalar-tensor multiplication. This scaling step has the potential to be combined with other operations, such as batch normalization, through algebraic merging, as shown in Fig. 2.1. This approach minimizes the memory and computational costs associated with matrix multiplication.

2.2.2 Step Size Gradient

LSQ offers a way of determining s based on the training loss through the incorporation of a gradient into the step size parameter of the quantizer as:

$$\frac{\partial \hat{v}}{\partial s} = \begin{cases} -v/s + \lfloor v/s \rceil, & \text{if } -Q_N < v/s < Q_p, \\ -Q_N, & \text{if } v/s \leq x, \\ Q_P, & \text{if } v/s \geq Q_p. \end{cases} \tag{2.10}$$

The gradient is calculated using the straight-through estimator, as proposed by [9], to approximate the gradient through the round function as a direct pass. The round function remains unchanged to differentiate downstream operations, while all other operations are differentiated conventionally.

The gradient calculated by LSQ is different from other similar approximations (Fig. 2.2) in that it does not transform the data before quantization or estimate the gradient by algebraically canceling terms after removing the round operation from the forward equation resulting in $\partial \hat{v}/\partial s = 0$ when $-Q_N < v/s < Q_P$ [43]. In these previous methods, the proximity of v to the transition point between quantized states does not impact the gradient of the quantization parameters. However, it is intuitive that the closer a value of v is to a quantization transition point, the more likely it is to change its quantization bin $\hat{v}$ with a small change in s, resulting in a large jump in $\hat{v}$. This means that $\partial \hat{v}/\partial s$ should increase as the distance from v to a transition point decreases, as observed in the LSQ gradient. Notably, this gradient emerges naturally from the simple quantizer formulation and the use of the straight-through estimator for the round function.

In LSQ, each layer of weights and each layer of activations have their unique step size represented as a 32-bit floating point value. These step sizes are initialized to $2|v|/\sqrt{Q_P}$ and are calculated from the initial weight values or the first batch of activations, respectively.

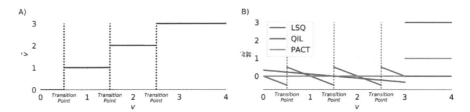

FIGURE 2.2
Given $s = 1, Q_N = 0, Q_P = 3$, A) quantizer output and B) gradients of the quantizer output concerning step size, s, for LSQ, or a related parameter controlling the width of the quantized domain (equal to $s(Q_P + Q_N)$) for QIL [110] and PACT [43]. The gradient employed by LSQ is sensitive to the distance between v and each transition point, whereas the gradient employed by QIL [110] is sensitive only to the distance from quantizer clip points and the gradient employed by PACT [43] is zero everywhere below the clip point. Here, we demonstrate that networks trained with the LSQ gradient reach a higher accuracy than those trained with the QIL or PACT gradients in prior work.

2.2.3 Step Size Gradient Scale

It has been demonstrated that good convergence during training can be achieved when the ratio of average update magnitude to average parameter magnitude is consistent across all weight layers in a network. Setting the learning rate correctly helps prevent updates from being too large and causing repeated overshooting of local minima or too small, leading to a slow convergence time. Based on this reasoning, it is reasonable to assume that each step size should also have its update magnitude proportional to its parameter magnitude, similarly to the weights. Therefore, for a network trained on a loss function L, the ratio

$$R = \frac{\nabla_s L}{s} / \frac{\|\nabla_w L\|}{\|w\|}, \tag{2.11}$$

should be close to 1, where $\|x\|$ denotes the l2-norm of z. However, as precision increases, the step size parameter is expected to be smaller (due to finer quantization), and the step size updates are expected to be larger (due to the accumulation of updates from more quantized items when computing its gradient). To address this, a gradient scale g is multiplied by the step size loss. For the weight step size, g is calculated as $1/\sqrt{N_W Q_P}$, and for the activation step size, g is calculated as $1/\sqrt{N_W Q_P}$, where N_W is the number of weights in a layer and N_f is the number of features in a layer.

2.2.4 Training

LSQ trains the model quantizers by making the step sizes learnable parameters, with the loss gradient computed using the quantizer gradient mentioned earlier. In contrast, other model parameters can be trained with conventional techniques. A common method of training quantized networks [48] is employed where full precision weights are stored and updated, while quantized weights and activations are used for forward and backward passes. The gradient through the quantizer round function is calculated using the straight-through estimator [9] so that

$$\frac{\partial \hat{v}}{\partial v} = \begin{cases} 1, & \text{if } -Q_N < v/s < Q_p, \\ 0, & \text{otherwise}, \end{cases} \tag{2.12}$$

and stochastic gradient descent is used to update parameters.

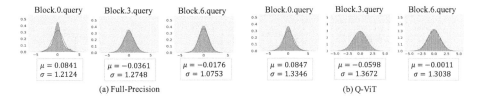

FIGURE 2.3

The histogram of query values **q** (shadow) along with the PDF curve of Gaussian distribution $N(\mu, \sigma^2)$ [195], for three selected layers in DeiT-T and 4-bit fully quantized DeiT-T (baseline). μ and σ^2 are the statistical mean and variance of the values.

For ease of training, the input to the matrix multiplication layers is set to $\hat{v}$, mathematically equivalent to the inference operations described earlier. The input activations and weights are set to 2, 3, 4, or 8 bits for all matrix multiplication layers except the first and last, which are always set to 8 bits. This standard practice in quantized networks has been shown to improve performance significantly. All other parameters are represented using FP32. Quantized networks are initialized using weights from a trained full-precision model with a similar architecture before being fine-tuned in the quantized space.

2.3 Q-ViT: Accurate and Fully Quantized Low-Bit Vision Transformer

Inspired by the success of natural language processing (NLP), transformer-based models have shown great power in various computer vision (CV) tasks, such as image classification [60] and object detection [31]. Pre-trained with large-scale data, these models usually have many parameters. For example, 632M parameters consume 2528 MB of memory usage and 162G FLOPs in the ViT-H model, which is expensive in both memory and computation during inference. This limits the deployment of these models on resource-limited platforms. Therefore, compressed transformers are urgently needed for real applications.

Quantization-aware training (QAT) [158] methods perform quantization during back-propagation and achieve much less performance drop with a higher compression rate in general. QAT is effective for CNN models [159] for CV tasks. However, QAT methods still need to be explored for low-bit quantization of vision transformers. Therefore, we first build a fully quantized ViT baseline, a straightforward yet effective solution based on standard techniques. Our study discovers that the performance drop of fully quantized ViT lies in the information distortion among the attention mechanism in the forward process and the ineffective optimization for eliminating the distribution difference through distillation in the backward propagation. First, the ViT attention mechanism aims to model long-distance dependencies [227, 60]. However, our analysis shows that a direct quantization method leads to information distortion and a significant distribution variation for the query module between the quantized ViT and its full-precision counterpart. For example, as shown in Fig. 2.3, the variance difference is 0.4409 (1.2124 *vs.* 1.6533) for the first block [1]. This

---

[1] supports the Gaussian distribution hypothesis citeqin2022bibert

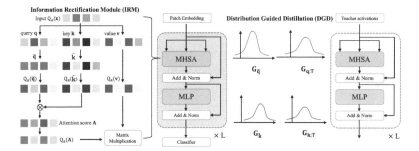

FIGURE 2.4
Overview of Q-ViT, applying Information Rectification Module (IRM) for maximizing representation information and Distribution Guided Distillation (DGD) for accurate optimization.

inevitably deteriorates the attention module's representation capability in capturing the input's global dependency. Second, the distillation for the fully quantized ViT baseline utilizes a distillation token (following [224]) to directly supervise the quantized ViT classification output. However, we found that such a simple supervision could be more effective, which is coarse-grained because of the large gap between the quantized attention scores and their full-precision counterparts.

To address the issues above, a fully quantized ViT (Q-ViT) [136] is developed by retaining the distribution of quantized attention modules as that of full-precision counterparts (see the overview in Fig. 2.4). Accordingly, we propose to modify the distorted distribution over quantized attention modules through an Information Rectification Module (IRM) based on information entropy maximization in the forward process. In the backward process, we present a distribution-guided distillation (DGD) scheme to eliminate the distribution variation through attention similarity loss between the quantized ViT and the full-precision counterpart.

2.3.1   Baseline of Fully Quantized ViT

First, we build a baseline to study fully quantized ViT since it has never been proposed in previous work. A straightforward solution is quantifying the representations (weights and activations) in ViT architecture in the forward propagation and applying distillation to the optimization in the backward propagation.

Quantized ViT architecture.   We briefly introduce the technology of neural network quantization. We first introduce a general asymmetric activation quantization and symmetric weight quantization scheme as

$$Q_a(x) = \lfloor \text{clip}\{(x-z)/\alpha_x, -Q_n^x, Q_p^x\} \rceil \quad Q_w(\mathbf{w}) = \lfloor \text{clip}\{\mathbf{w}/\alpha_{\mathbf{w}}, -Q_n^{\mathbf{w}}, Q_p^{\mathbf{w}}\} \rceil \tag{2.13}$$
$$\hat{x} = Q_a(x) \times \alpha_x + z, \qquad\qquad \hat{\mathbf{w}} = Q_w(\mathbf{w}) \times \alpha_{\mathbf{w}}.$$

Here, $\text{clip}\{y, r_1, r_2\}$ returns y with values below r_1 set as r_1 and values above r_2 set as r_2, and $\lfloor y \rceil$ rounds y to the nearest integer. With quantization of activations on signed a bits and weights to signed b bits, $Q_n^x = 2^{a-1}, Q_p^x = 2^{a-1} - 1$ and $Q_n^{\mathbf{w}} = 2^{b-1}, Q_p^{\mathbf{w}} = 2^{b-1} - 1$. In general, the forward and backward propagation of the quantization function in the quantized network is formulated as

$$\text{Forward:} \quad \text{Q-Linear}(x) = \hat{x} \cdot \hat{\mathbf{w}} = \alpha_x \alpha_{\mathbf{w}}((Q_a(x) + z/\alpha_x) \otimes Q_w(\mathbf{w})),$$

$$\text{Backward:} \quad \frac{\partial \mathcal{J}}{\partial x} = \frac{\partial \mathcal{J}}{\partial \hat{x}} \frac{\partial \hat{x}}{\partial x} = \begin{cases} \dfrac{\partial \mathcal{J}}{\partial \hat{x}} & \text{if } x \in [-Q_n^x, Q_p^x] \\ 0 & \text{otherwise} \end{cases},$$

$$\frac{\partial \mathcal{J}}{\partial \mathbf{w}} = \frac{\partial \mathcal{J}}{\partial x} \frac{\partial x}{\partial \hat{\mathbf{w}}} \frac{\partial \hat{\mathbf{w}}}{\partial \mathbf{w}} = \begin{cases} \dfrac{\partial \mathcal{J}}{\partial x} \dfrac{\partial x}{\partial \hat{\mathbf{w}}} & \text{if } \mathbf{w} \in [-Q_n^{\mathbf{w}}, Q_p^{\mathbf{w}}] \\ 0 & \text{otherwise} \end{cases}, \tag{2.14}$$

where $\mathcal{J}$ is the loss function, $Q(\cdot)$ is applied in forward propagation. At the same time, the straight-through estimator (STE) [9] is used to retain the gradient derivation in backward propagation. $\otimes$ denotes the matrix multiplication with efficient bit-wise operations.

The input images are first encoded as patches and pass through several transformer blocks. This transformer block consists of two components: Multi-Head Self-Attention (MHSA) and Multi-Layer Perceptron (MLP). The computation of attention weight depends on the corresponding query $\mathbf{q}$, key $\mathbf{k}$ and value $\mathbf{v}$, and the quantized computation in one attention head is

$$\mathbf{q} = \text{Q-Linear}_q(x), \mathbf{k} = \text{Q-Linear}_k(x), \mathbf{v} = \text{Q-Linear}_v(x), \tag{2.15}$$

where Q-Linear$_q$, Q-Linear$_k$, Q-Linear$_v$ denote the three quantized linear layers for $\mathbf{q}, \mathbf{k}, \mathbf{v}$, respectively. Thus, the attention weight is formulated as

$$\mathbf{A} = \frac{1}{\sqrt{d}}(Q_a(\mathbf{q}) \otimes Q_a(\mathbf{k})^\top),$$

$$Q_{\mathbf{A}} = Q_a(\text{softmax}(\mathbf{A})). \tag{2.16}$$

Training for Quantized ViT. Knowledge distillation is an essential supervision approach for training QNNs, which bridges the performance gap between quantized models and their full-precision counterparts. The usual practice is to use distillation with attention, as described in [224]

$$\mathcal{L}_{\text{dist}} = \frac{1}{2}\mathcal{L}_{\text{CE}}(\psi(Z_q), y) + \frac{1}{2}\mathcal{L}_{\text{CE}}(\psi(Z_q), y_t),$$

$$y_t = \arg\max_c Z_t(c). \tag{2.17}$$

2.3.2   Performance Degeneration of Fully Quantized ViT Baseline

Intuitively, in the fully quantized ViT baseline, the information representation ability depends mainly on the architecture based on the transformer, such as the attention weight in the MHSA module. However, the performance improvement brought about by such an architecture is severely limited by the quantized parameters, while the rounded and discrete quantization also significantly affects the optimization. The phenomenon identifies that the fully quantized ViT baseline bottleneck comes from architecture and optimization for forward and backward propagation.

Architecture bottleneck. We replace each module with the full-precision counterpart, respectively, and compare the accuracy drop as shown in Fig. 2.5. We find that quantizing query, key, value, and attention weight, *that is,* softmax($\mathbf{A}$) in Eq. (2.16) to 2 bits brings the most significant drop in accuracy between all parts of ViT, up to 10.03%. Although the quantized MLP layers and the quantized weights of the linear layers in MHSA result in

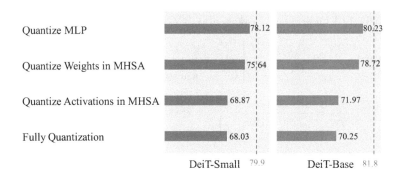

FIGURE 2.5
Analysis of bottlenecks from an architecture perspective. We report the accuracy of 2-bit quantized DeiT-S and DeiT-B on the ImageNet data set to replace the full precision structure.

only a drop of 1.78% and 4.26%, respectively. And once the query, key, value, and attention weights are quantized, even with all weights of linear layers in the MHSA module in full precision, the performance drops (10.57%) are still significant. Thus, improving the attention structure is critical to solving the performance drop problem of quantized ViT.

Optimization bottleneck. We calculate l2-norm distances between each attention weight among different blocks of the DeiT-S architecture as shown in Fig. 2.6. The MHSA modules in full-precision ViT with different depths learn different representations from images. As mentioned in [197], lower ViT layers pay more attention to global representations both locally and globally. However, fully quantized ViT (blue lines in Fig. 2.6) fails to learn accurate distances from the attention map. Therefore, it requires a new design to use full-precision teacher information better.

2.3.3 Information Rectification in Q-Attention

To address the information distortion of quantized representations in forward propagation, we propose an efficient Q-Attention structure based on information theory, which statistically maximizes the entropy of the representation and revives the attention mechanism in the fully quantized ViT. Since the representations with extremely compressed bit width in fully quantized ViT have limited capabilities, the ideal quantized representation should preserve the given full-precision counterparts as much as possible, which means that the mutual information between quantized and full-precision representations should be maximized, as mentioned in [195].

We further show the statistical results that the query and key value distribution in ViT architectures intended to follow Gaussian distributions under distilling supervision, whose histograms are bell-shaped [195]. For example, in Fig. 2.3 and Fig. 2.7, we have shown the query and key distributions and their corresponding Probability Density Function (PDF) using the calculated mean and standard deviation for each MHSA layer. Therefore, the query and key distributions in the MHSA modules of the full-precision counterparts are formulated as follows.

$$\mathbf{q} \sim \mathcal{N}(\mu(\mathbf{q}), \sigma(\mathbf{q})), \quad \mathbf{k} \sim \mathcal{N}(\mu(\mathbf{k}), \sigma(\mathbf{k})). \tag{2.18}$$

Since weight and activation with a highly compressed bit width in fully quantized ViT have limited capabilities, the ideal quantization process should preserve the corresponding

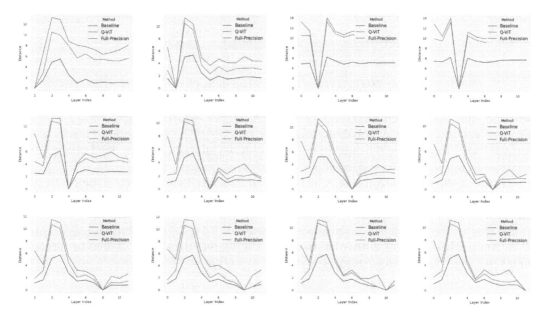

FIGURE 2.6
Attention-distance comparison for full-precision DeiT-Small, fully quantized DeiT-Small baseline, and Q-ViT for the same input. Q-ViT shows similar behavior with the full-precision model, while the baseline suffers indistinguishable attention distance for information degradation.

full-precision counterparts as much as possible; thus, the mutual information between quantized and full-precision representations [195]. As shown in [171], for the Gaussian distribution, the quantizers with the maximum output entropy (MOE) and the minimum average error (MAE) are approximately the same within a multiplicative constant. Therefore, minimizing the error between the full precision and the quantized values is equivalent to maximizing the information entropy of the quantized values. Thus, when the deterministic quantization function is applied to quantized ViT, this objective is equivalent to maximizing the information entropy $\mathcal{H}(Q_\mathbf{x})$ of the quantized representation $Q_\mathbf{x}$ [171] in Eq.(2.16),

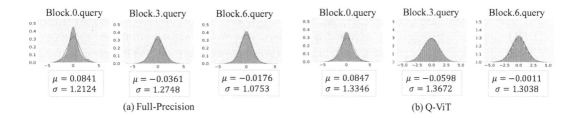

FIGURE 2.7
The histogram of query and key values $\mathbf{q}, \mathbf{k}$ (shadow) along with the PDF curve of Gaussian distribution $N(\mu, \sigma^2)$ [195], for three selected layers in DeiT-T and 4-bit Q-ViT. μ and σ^2 are the statistical mean and variance of the values.

which is defined as

$$\mathcal{H}(Q_a(\mathbf{x})) = -\sum_{q_\mathbf{x}} p(q_\mathbf{x}) \log p(q_\mathbf{x}) = \frac{1}{2} \log 2\pi e \sigma_\mathbf{x}^2,$$

$$\max \mathcal{H}(Q_a(\mathbf{x})) = \frac{n \ln 2}{2^n}, \quad \text{when } p(q_\mathbf{x}) = \frac{1}{2^n}, \tag{2.19}$$

where $q_\mathbf{x}$ are the random quantized variables in $Q_a(\mathbf{x})$ (which is $Q_a(\mathbf{q})$ or $Q_a(\mathbf{k})$ under different conditions) with probability mass function $p(\cdot)$. The information entropy in the quantization process should be maximized to retain the information contained in the MHSA modules from their full-precision counterparts.

However, direct application of a quantization function that converts values into finite fixed points brings about irreversible disturbance to the distributions and the information entropy $\mathcal{H}(Q_a(\mathbf{q}))$ and $\mathcal{H}(Q_a(\mathbf{k}))$ degenerates to a much lower level than its full precision counterparts. To mitigate the information degradation from the quantization process in the attention mechanism, an Information Rectification Module (IRM) is proposed to effectively maximize the information entropy of quantized attention weights.

$$Q_a(\tilde{\mathbf{q}}) = Q_a\left(\frac{\mathbf{q} - \mu(\mathbf{q}) + \beta_\mathbf{q}}{\gamma_\mathbf{q}\sqrt{\sigma^2(\mathbf{q}) + \epsilon_\mathbf{q}}}\right), \quad Q_a(\tilde{\mathbf{k}}) = Q_a\left(\frac{\mathbf{k} - \mu(\mathbf{k}) + \beta_\mathbf{k}}{\gamma_\mathbf{k}\sqrt{\sigma^2(\mathbf{k}) + \epsilon_\mathbf{k}}}\right), \tag{2.20}$$

where $\gamma_\mathbf{q}, \beta_\mathbf{q}$ and $\gamma_\mathbf{k}, \beta_\mathbf{k}$ are the learnable parameters to modify the distribution of $\tilde{\mathbf{q}}$, while $\epsilon_\mathbf{q}$ and $\epsilon_\mathbf{k}$ are constants that prevent the denominator from being 0. The learning rates of the learnable $\gamma_\mathbf{q}, \beta_\mathbf{q}$ and $\gamma_\mathbf{k}, \beta_\mathbf{k}$ are the same as for the entire network. Thus, after IRM, the information entropy $\mathcal{H}(Q_a(\tilde{\mathbf{q}}))$ and $\mathcal{H}(Q_a(\tilde{\mathbf{k}}))$ is formulated as

$$\mathcal{H}(Q(\tilde{\mathbf{q}})) = \frac{1}{2} \log 2\pi e[\gamma_\mathbf{q}^2(\sigma_\mathbf{q}^2 + \epsilon_\mathbf{q})], \quad \mathcal{H}(Q(\tilde{\mathbf{k}})) = \frac{1}{2} \log 2\pi e[\gamma_\mathbf{k}^2(\sigma_\mathbf{k}^2 + \epsilon_\mathbf{k})]. \tag{2.21}$$

Then, to revive the attention mechanism to capture critic elements by maximizing information entropy, the learnable parameters $\gamma_\mathbf{q}, \beta_\mathbf{q}$ and $\gamma_\mathbf{k}, \beta_\mathbf{k}$ reshape the distributions of the query and key values to achieve the maximum state of information. In a nutshell, in our IRM-Attention structure, the information entropy of quantized attention weight is maximized to alleviate its severe information distortion and revive the attention mechanism.

2.3.4 Distribution Guided Distillation Through Attention

To address the attention distribution mismatch that occurred in the fully quantized ViT baseline in backward propagation, we further propose a distribution-guided distillation (DGD) scheme with apposite distilled activations and well-designed similarity matrices to effectively utilize teacher knowledge, which optimizes fully quantized ViT more accurately.

As an optimization technique based on element-level comparison of activation, distillation allows the quantized ViT to mimic the full-precision teacher model about output logits. However, we find that the distillation procedure used in the previous ViT and fully quantized ViT baseline (Section 2.3.1) is unable to deliver meticulous supervision to attention weights (shown in Fig. 2.6), leading to insufficient optimization. To solve the optimization insufficiency in the distillation of the fully quantized ViT, we propose the Distribution-Guided Distillation (DGD) method in Q-ViT. We first build patch-based similarity pattern matrices for distilling the upstream query and key instead of attention following [226], which is formulated as

$$\tilde{G}_{\mathbf{q}_h}^l = \tilde{\mathbf{q}}_h^l \cdot (\tilde{\mathbf{q}}_h^l)^\top, \quad G_{\mathbf{q}_h}^{(l)} = \tilde{G}_{\mathbf{q}_h}^l / \|\tilde{G}_{\mathbf{q}_h}^l\|_2,$$

$$\tilde{G}_{\mathbf{k}_h}^l = \tilde{\mathbf{k}}_h^l \cdot (\tilde{\mathbf{k}}_h^l)^\top, \quad G_{\mathbf{k}_h}^{(l)} = \tilde{G}_{\mathbf{k}_h}^l / \|\tilde{G}_{\mathbf{k}_h}^l\|_2, \tag{2.22}$$

where $\|\cdot\|_2$ denotes ℓ_2 normalization and l, h are the layer index and the head index. Previous work shows that matrices constructed in this way are regarded as specific patterns that reflect the semantic understanding of the network [226]. And the patches encoded from the input images contain a high-level understanding of parts, objects, and scenes [83]. Thus, such a semantic-level distillation target guides and meticulously supervises quantized ViT. The corresponding $\tilde{G}^l_{\mathbf{q}_h;T}$ and $\tilde{G}^l_{\mathbf{k}_h;T}$ are constructed in the same way by the teacher's activation. Thus, combining the original distillation loss in Eq. (2.17), the final distillation loss is formulated as

$$\mathcal{L}_{\mathrm{DGD}} = \sum_{l \in [1,L]} \sum_{h \in [1,H]} \|\tilde{G}^l_{\mathbf{q}_h;T} - \tilde{G}^l_{\mathbf{q}_h}\|_2 + \|\tilde{G}^l_{\mathbf{k}_h;T} - \tilde{G}^l_{\mathbf{k}_h}\|_2,$$

$$\mathcal{L}_{\mathrm{distillation}} = \mathcal{L}_{\mathrm{dist}} + \mathcal{L}_{\mathrm{DGD}},$$

(2.23)

where L and H denote the number of ViT layers and heads. With the proposed Distribution-Guided Distillation, Q-ViT retains the distribution over query and key from the full-precision counterparts (as shown in Fig. 2.7).

Our DGD scheme first provides the distribution-aware optimization direction by processing appropriate distilled parameters. Then it constructs similarity matrices to eliminate scale differences and numerical instability, thereby improving fully quantized ViT by accurate optimization.

2.3.5 Ablation Study

Datasets. The experiments are carried out on the ILSVRC12 ImageNet classification dataset [204]. The ImageNet dataset is more challenging because of its large scale and greater diversity. There are 1000 classes and 1.2 million training images, and 50k validation images. Our experiments use the classic data augmentation method described in [224].

Experimental settings. In our experiments, we initialize the weights of the quantized model with the corresponding pre-trained full-precision model. The quantized model is trained for 300 epochs with a batch size of 512 and a base learning rate $2e-4$. We do not use the warm-up scheme. We apply the LAMB [275] optimizer with the weight decay set to 0 for all experiments. Other training settings follow DeiT [224] or Swin Transformer [154]. Note that we use 8-bit for the patch embedding (first) layer and the classification (last) layer following [61].

Backbone. We evaluate our quantization method on two popular implementations of vision transformers: DeiT [224] and Swin Transformer [154]. The DeiT-S, DeiT-B, Swin-T, and Swin-S are adopted as the backbone models, whose Top-1 accuracy on the ImageNet dataset are 79.9%, 81.8%, 81.2%, and 83.2%, respectively. For a fair comparison, we utilize the official implementation of DeiT and Swin Transformer.

We give quantitative results of the proposed IRM and DGD in Table 2.1. As shown in Table 2.1, the fully quantized ViT baseline suffers a severe performance drop on the classification task (0.2%, 2.1%, and 11.7% with 2/3/4 bits, respectively). IRM and DGD improve performance when used alone, and the two techniques enhance performance considerably when combined. For example, IRM improves the 2-bit baseline by 1.7%, and DGD achieves a 2.3% performance improvement. When IRM and DGD are combined, a performance improvement is achieved at 3.8%.

In conclusion, the two techniques can promote each other to improve Q-ViT and close the performance gap between the fully quantized ViT and the full-precision counterpart.

TABLE 2.1
Evaluating the components of Q-ViT based on the ViT-S backbone.

Method	#Bits	Top-1	#Bits	Top-1	#Bits	Top-1
Full-precision	32-32	79.9	-	-	-	-
Baseline	4-4	79.7	3-3	77.8	2-2	68.2
+IRM	4-4	80.2	3-3	78.2	2-2	69.9
+DGD	4-4	80.4	3-3	78.5	2-2	70.5
+IRM+DGD (Q-ViT)	4-4	**80.9**	3-3	**79.0**	2-2	**72.0**

2.4 Q-DETR: An Efficient Low-Bit Quantized Detection Transformer

Drawing inspiration from the achievements in natural language processing (NLP), object detection using transformers (DETR) has emerged as a new approach for training an end-to-end detector using a transformer encoder-decoder [31]. In contrast to earlier methods [201, 153] that heavily rely on convolutional neural networks (CNNs) and necessitate additional post-processing steps such as non-maximum suppression (NMS) and hand-designed sample selection, DETR tackles object detection as a direct set prediction problem.

Despite this attractiveness, DETR usually has many parameters and float-pointing operations (FLOPs). For instance, 39.8M parameters comprise 159 MB memory usage and 86G FLOPs in the DETR model with ResNet-50 backbone [84] (DETR-R50). This leads to unacceptable memory and computation consumption during inference and challenges deployments on devices with limited resources.

Therefore, substantial efforts on network compression have been made toward efficient online inference [264, 260]. Quantization is particularly popular for deploying AI chips by representing a network in low-bit formats. Yet prior post-training quantization (PTQ) for DETR [161] derives quantized parameters from pre-trained real-valued models, which often restricts the model performance in a sub-optimized state due to the lack of fine-tuning on the training data. In particular, the performance drastically drops when quantized to ultra-low bits (4 bits or less). Alternatively, quantization-aware training (QAT) [158, 259] performs quantization and fine-tuning on the training dataset simultaneously, leading to trivial performance degradation even with significantly lower bits. Though QAT methods have been proven to be very effective in compressing CNNs [159, 61] for computer vision tasks, an exploration of low-bit DETR remains untouched.

In this paper, we first build a low-bit DETR baseline, a straightforward solution based on common QAT techniques [61]. Through an empirical study of this baseline, we observe significant performance drops on the VOC [62] dataset. For example, a 4-bit quantized DETR-R50 using LSQ [61] only achieves 76.9% AP_{50}, leaving a 6.4% performance gaps compared with the real-valued DETR-R50. We find that the incompatibility of existing QAT methods mainly stems from the unique attention mechanism in DETR, where the spatial dependencies are first constructed between the object queries and encoded features. Then a feed-forward network feeds the co-attended object queries into box coordinates and class labels. A simple application of existing QAT methods on DETR leads to query information distortion, and therefore the performance severely degrades. Figure 2.8 exhibits an example of information distortion in query features of 4-bit DETR-R50, where we can see significant distribution variation of the query modules in quantized DETR and real-valued version. The query information distortion causes the inaccurate focus of spatial attention, which can be verified by following [169] to visualize the spatial attention weight maps in 4-bit and real-valued DETR-R50 in Fig. 2.9. We can see that the quantized DETR-R50 bear's

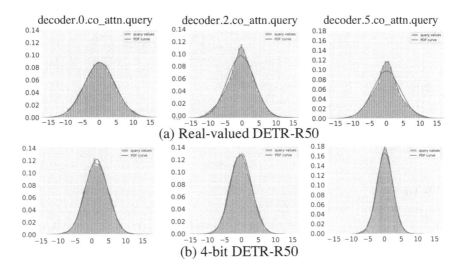

FIGURE 2.8
The histogram of query values $\mathbf{q}$ (blue shadow) and corresponding PDF curves (red curve) of Gaussian distribution [136], $w.r.t$ the cross attention of different decoder layers in (a) real-valued DETR-R50, and (b) 4-bit quantized DETR-R50 (baseline). Gaussian distribution is generated from the statistical mean and variance of the query values. The query in quantized DETR-R50 bears information distortion compared with the real-valued one. Experiments are performed on the VOC dataset [62].

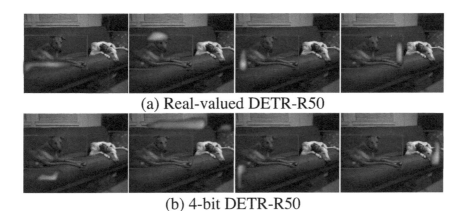

FIGURE 2.9
Spatial attention weight maps in the last decoder of (a) real-valued DETR-R50, and (b) 4-bit quantized DETR-R50. The rectangle denotes the ground-truth bounding box. Following [169], the highlighted area denotes the large attention weights in the selected four heads in compliance with bound prediction. Compared to its real-valued counterpart that focuses on the ground-truth bounds, quantized DETR-R50 deviates significantly.

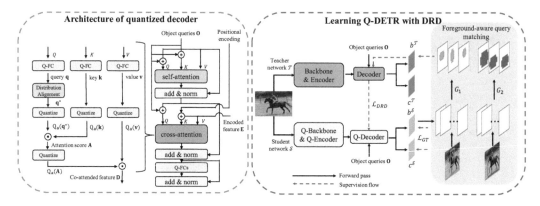

FIGURE 2.10
Overview of the proposed Q-DETR framework. We introduce the distribution rectification distillation method (DRD) to refine the performance of Q-DETR. From left to right, we respectively show the detailed decoder architecture of Q-DETR and the learning framework of Q-DETR. The Q-Backbone, Q-Encoder, and Q-Decoder denote quantized architectures, respectively.

inaccurate object localization. Therefore, a more generic method for DETR quantization is necessary.

To tackle the issue above, we propose an efficient low-bit quantized DETR (Q-DETR) [257] by rectifying the query information of the quantized DETR as that of the real-valued counterpart. Figure 2.10 provides an overview of our Q-DETR, mainly accomplished by a distribution rectification knowledge distillation method (DRD). We find ineffective knowledge transferring from the real-valued teacher to the quantized student primarily because of the information gap and distortion. Therefore, we formulate our DRD as a bi-level optimization framework established on the information bottleneck principle (IB). Generally, it includes an inner-level optimization to maximize the self-information entropy of student queries and an upper-level optimization to minimize the conditional information entropy between student and teacher queries. At the inner level, we conduct a distribution alignment for the query guided by its Gaussian-alike distribution, as shown in Fig. 2.8, leading to an explicit state in compliance with its maximum information entropy in the forward propagation. At the upper level, we introduce a new foreground-aware query matching that filters out low-qualified student queries for exact one-to-one query matching between student and teacher, providing valuable knowledge gradients to push minimum conditional information entropy in the backward propagation.

2.4.1 Quantized DETR Baseline

We first construct a baseline to study the low-bit DETR since no relevant work has been proposed. To this end, we follow LSQ+ [13] to introduce a general framework of asymmetric activation quantization and symmetric weight quantization:

$$
\begin{aligned}
\boldsymbol{x}_q &= \lfloor \text{clip}\{ \frac{(\boldsymbol{x} - z)}{\alpha_x}, Q_n^x, Q_p^x \} \rceil, \quad \mathbf{w}_q = \lfloor \text{clip}\{ \frac{\mathbf{w}}{\alpha_{\mathbf{w}}}, Q_n^{\mathbf{w}}, Q_p^{\mathbf{w}} \} \rceil, \\
Q_a(x) &= \alpha_x \circ \boldsymbol{x}_q + z, \qquad\qquad Q_w(x) = \alpha_{\mathbf{w}} \circ \mathbf{w}_q,
\end{aligned}
\tag{2.24}
$$

where clip$\{y, r_1, r_2\}$ clips the input y with value bounds r_1 and r_2; the $\lfloor y \rceil$ rounds y to its nearest integer; the $\circ$ denotes the channel-wise multiplication. And $Q_n^x = -2^{a-1}, Q_p^x =$

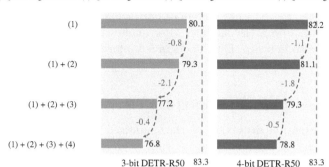

FIGURE 2.11
Performance of 3/4-bit quantized DETR-R50 on VOC with different quantized modules.

$2^{a-1} - 1$, $Q_n^{\mathbf{w}} = -2^{b-1}, Q_p^{\mathbf{w}} = 2^{b-1} - 1$ are the discrete bounds for a-bit activations and b-bit weights. x generally denotes the activation in this paper, including the input feature map of convolution and fully-connected layers and input of multi-head attention modules. Based on this, we first give the quantized fully-connected layer as:

$$\text{Q-FC}(\boldsymbol{x}) = Q_a(\boldsymbol{x}) \cdot Q_w(\mathbf{w}) = \alpha_x \alpha_{\mathbf{w}} \circ (\boldsymbol{x}_q \odot \mathbf{w}_q + z/\alpha_x \circ \mathbf{w}_q), \qquad (2.25)$$

where $\cdot$ denotes the matrix multiplication and $\odot$ denotes the matrix multiplication with efficient bit-wise operations. The straight-through estimator (STE) [9] is used to retain the derivation of the gradient in backward propagation.

In DETR [31], the visual features generated by the backbone are augmented with position embedding and fed into the transformer encoder. Given an encoder output $\mathbf{E}$, DETR performs co-attention between object queries $\mathbf{O}$ and the visual features $\mathbf{E}$, which are formulated as:

$$\mathbf{q} = \text{Q-FC}(\mathbf{O}), \quad \mathbf{k}, \mathbf{v} = \text{Q-FC}(\mathbf{E})$$
$$\mathbf{A}_i = \text{softmax}(Q_a(\mathbf{q})_i \cdot Q_a(\mathbf{k})_i^\top / \sqrt{d}), \qquad (2.26)$$
$$\mathbf{D}_i = Q_a(\mathbf{A})_i \cdot Q_a(\mathbf{v})_i,$$

where $\mathbf{D}$ is the multi-head co-attention module, *i.e.*, the co-attended feature for the object query. The d denotes the feature dimension in each head. More FC layers transform the decoder's output features of each object query for the final output. Given box and class predictions, the Hungarian algorithm [31] is applied between predictions and ground-truth box annotations to identify the learning targets of each object query.

2.4.2 Challenge Analysis

Intuitively, the performance of the quantized DETR baseline largely depends on the information representation capability mainly reflected by the information in the multi-head attention module. Unfortunately, such information is severely degraded by the quantized weights and inputs in the forward pass. Also, the rounded and discrete quantization significantly affect the optimization during backpropagation.

We conduct the quantitively ablative experiments by progressively replacing each module of the real-valued DETR baseline with a quantized one and compare the average precision (AP) drop on the VOC dataset [62] as shown in Fig. 2.11. We find that quantizing the MHA decoder module to low bits, *i.e.*, (1)+(2)+(3), brings the most significant accuracy drops of accuracy among all parts of the DETR methods, up to 2.1% in the 3-bit DETR-R50. At the same time, other parts of DETR show comparative robustness to the quantization function. Consequently, the critical problem of improving the quantized DETR methods is restoring the information in MHA modules after quantization. Other qualitative results in Fig. 2.8 and Fig. 2.9 also indicate that the degraded information representation is the main obstacle to a better quantized DETR.

2.4.3   Information Bottleneck of Q-DETR

To address the information distortion of the quantized DETR, we aim to improve the representation capacity of the quantized networks in a knowledge distillation framework. Generally, we utilize a real-valued DETR as a teacher and a quantized DETR as a student, distinguished with superscripts $\mathcal{T}$ and $\mathcal{S}$.

Our Q-DETR pursues the best tradeoff between performance and compression, which is precisely the goal of the information bottleneck (IB) method through quantifying the mutual information that the intermediate layer contains about the input (less is better) and the desired output (more is better) [210, 223]. In our case, the intermediate layer comes from the student, while the desired output includes the ground-truth labels as well as the queries of the teacher for distillation. Thus, the objective target of our Q-DETR is:

$$\min_{\theta^{\mathcal{S}}} I(X; \mathbf{E}^{\mathcal{S}}) - \beta I(\mathbf{E}^{\mathcal{S}}, \mathbf{q}^{\mathcal{S}}; \boldsymbol{y}^{GT}) - \gamma I(\mathbf{q}^{\mathcal{S}}; \mathbf{q}^{\mathcal{T}}), \qquad (2.27)$$

where $\mathbf{q}^{\mathcal{T}}$ and $\mathbf{q}^{\mathcal{S}}$ represent the queries in the teacher and student DETR methods as predefined in Eq. (2.26); β and γ are the Lagrange multipliers [210]; $\theta^{\mathcal{S}}$ is the parameters of the student; and $I(\cdot)$ returns the mutual information of two input variables. The first item $I(X; \mathbf{E}^{\mathcal{S}})$ minimizes information between input and visual features $\mathbf{E}^{\mathcal{S}}$ to extract task-oriented hints [240]. The second item $I(\mathbf{E}^{\mathcal{S}}, \mathbf{q}^{\mathcal{S}}; \boldsymbol{y}^{GT})$ maximizes information between extracted visual features and ground-truth labels for better object detection. Common network training and detection loss constraints can easily accomplish these two items, such as proposal classification and coordinate regression.

The core issue of this paper is to solve the third item $I(\mathbf{q}^{\mathcal{S}}; \mathbf{q}^{\mathcal{T}})$, which attempts to address the information distortion in student query via introducing teacher query as a priori knowledge. To accomplish our goal, we first expand the third item and reformulate it as:

$$I(\mathbf{q}^{\mathcal{S}}; \mathbf{q}^{\mathcal{T}}) = H(\mathbf{q}^{\mathcal{S}}) - H(\mathbf{q}^{\mathcal{S}}|\mathbf{q}^{\mathcal{T}}), \qquad (2.28)$$

where $H(\mathbf{q}^{\mathcal{S}})$ returns the self information entropy expected to be maximized while $H(\mathbf{q}^{\mathcal{S}}|\mathbf{q}^{\mathcal{T}})$ is the conditional entropy expected to be minimized. It is challenging to optimize the above maximum and minimum items simultaneously. Instead, we make a compromise to reformulate Eq. (2.28) as a bi-level issue [152, 46] that alternately optimizes the two items, which is explicitly defined as:

$$\min_{\theta} H(\mathbf{q}^{\mathcal{S}^*}|\mathbf{q}^{\mathcal{T}}),$$
$$\text{s.t.} \quad \mathbf{q}^{\mathcal{S}^*} = \arg\max_{\mathbf{q}^{\mathcal{S}}} H(\mathbf{q}^{\mathcal{S}}). \qquad (2.29)$$

Such an objective involves two sub-problems, including an inner-level optimization to derive the current optimal query $\mathbf{q}^{\mathcal{S}^*}$ and an upper-level optimization to conduct knowledge transfer from the teacher to the student. Below, we show that the two sub-problems can be solved in the forward and backward network propagation.

2.4.4   Distribution Rectification Distillation

Inner-level optimization. We first detail the maximization of self-information entropy. According to the definition of self information entropy, $H(\mathbf{q}^{\mathcal{S}})$ can be implicitly expanded as:

$$H(\mathbf{q}^{\mathcal{S}}) = -\int_{\mathbf{q}_i^{\mathcal{S}} \in \mathbf{q}^{\mathcal{S}}} p(\mathbf{q}_i^{\mathcal{S}}) \log p(\mathbf{q}_i^{\mathcal{S}}). \qquad (2.30)$$

However, an explicit form of $H(\mathbf{q}^{\mathcal{S}})$ can only be parameterized with a regular distribution $p(\mathbf{q}_i^{\mathcal{S}})$. Luckily, the statistical results in Fig. 2.8 show that the query distribution tends to follow a Gaussian distribution, also observed in [136]. This enables us to solve the inner-level optimization in a distribution alignment fashion. To this end, we first calculate the mean $\mu(\mathbf{q}^{\mathcal{S}})$ and variance $\sigma(\mathbf{q}^{\mathcal{S}})$ of query $\mathbf{q}^{\mathcal{S}}$ whose distribution is then modeled as $\mathbf{q}^{\mathcal{S}} \sim \mathcal{N}(\mu(\mathbf{q}^{\mathcal{S}}), \sigma(\mathbf{q}^{\mathcal{S}}))$. Then, the self-information entropy of the student query can proceed as:

$$\begin{aligned}
H(\mathbf{q}^{\mathcal{S}}) &= -\mathbb{E}[\log \mathcal{N}(\mu(\mathbf{q}^{\mathcal{S}}), \sigma(\mathbf{q}^{\mathcal{S}}))] \\
&= -\mathbb{E}[\log[(2\pi\sigma(\mathbf{q}^{\mathcal{S}})^2)^{\frac{1}{2}} \exp(-\frac{(\mathbf{q}_i^{\mathcal{S}} - \mu(\mathbf{q}^{\mathcal{S}}))^2}{2\sigma(\mathbf{q}^{\mathcal{S}})^2})]] \\
&= \frac{1}{2}\log 2\pi\sigma(\mathbf{q}^{\mathcal{S}})^2.
\end{aligned} \qquad (2.31)$$

The above objective reaches its maximum of $H(\mathbf{q}^{\mathcal{S}^*}) = (1/2)\log 2\pi e[\sigma(\mathbf{q}^{\mathcal{S}})^2 + \epsilon_{\mathbf{q}^{\mathcal{S}}}]$ when $\mathbf{q}^{\mathcal{S}^*} = [\mathbf{q}^{\mathcal{S}} - \mu(\mathbf{q}^{\mathcal{S}})]/[\sqrt{\sigma(\mathbf{q}^{\mathcal{S}})^2 + \epsilon_{\mathbf{q}^{\mathcal{S}}}}]$ where $\epsilon_{\mathbf{q}^{\mathcal{S}}} = 1e^{-5}$ is a small constant added to prevent a zero denominator. The mean and variance might be inaccurate in practice due to query data bias. To solve this, we use the concepts in batch normalization (BN) [207, 102] where a learnable shifting parameter $\beta_{\mathbf{q}^{\mathcal{S}}}$ is added to move the mean value. A learnable scaling parameter $\gamma_{\mathbf{q}^{\mathcal{S}}}$ is multiplied to move the query to the adaptive position. In this situation, we rectify the information entropy of the query in the student as follows:

$$\mathbf{q}^{\mathcal{S}^*} = \frac{\mathbf{q}^{\mathcal{S}} - \mu(\mathbf{q}^{\mathcal{S}})}{\sqrt{\sigma(\mathbf{q}^{\mathcal{S}})^2 + \epsilon_{\mathbf{q}^{\mathcal{S}}}}} \gamma_{\mathbf{q}^{\mathcal{S}}} + \beta_{\mathbf{q}^{\mathcal{S}}}, \qquad (2.32)$$

in which case the maximum self-information entropy of student query becomes $H(\mathbf{q}^{\mathcal{S}^*}) = (1/2)\log 2\pi e[(\sigma_{\mathbf{q}^{\mathcal{S}}}^2 + \epsilon_{\mathbf{q}^{\mathcal{S}}})/\gamma_{\mathbf{q}^{\mathcal{S}}}^2]$. Therefore, in the forward propagation, we can obtain the current optimal query $\mathbf{q}^{\mathcal{S}^*}$ via Eq. (2.32), after which, the upper-level optimization is further executed as detailed in the following contents.

Upper-level optimization. We continue minimizing the conditional information entropy between the student and the teacher. Following DETR [31], we denote the ground-truth labels by $\boldsymbol{y}^{GT} = \{c_i^{GT}, b_i^{GT}\}_{i=1}^{N_{gt}}$ as a set of ground-truth objects where N_{gt} is the number of foregrounds, c_i^{GT} and b_i^{GT} respectively represent the class and coordinate (bounding box) for the i-th object. In DETR, each query is associated with an object. Therefore, we can obtain N objects for teacher and student as well, denoted as $\boldsymbol{y}^{\mathcal{S}} = \{c_j^{\mathcal{S}}, b_j^{\mathcal{S}}\}_{j=1}^N$ and $\boldsymbol{y}^{\mathcal{T}} = \{c_j^{\mathcal{T}}, b_j^{\mathcal{T}}\}_{j=1}^N$.

The minimization of the conditional information entropy requires the student and teacher objects to be in a one-to-one matching. However, it is problematic for DETR due primarily to the sparsity of prediction results and the instability of the query's predictions [129]. To solve this, we propose a foreground-aware query matching to rectify "well-matched" queries. Concretely, we match the ground-truth bounding boxes with this student to find the maximum coincidence as:

$$G_i = \max_{1 \le j \le N} \text{GIoU}(b_i^{GT}, b_j^{\mathcal{S}}), \qquad (2.33)$$

where GIoU($\cdot$) is the generalized intersection over union function [202]. Each G_i reflects the "closeness" of student proposals to the i-th ground-truth object. Then, we retain highly qualified student proposals around at least one ground truth to benefit object recognition [235] as:

$$b_j^{\mathcal{S}} = \begin{cases} b_j^{\mathcal{S}}, & \text{GIoU}(b_i^{GT}, b_j^{\mathcal{S}}) > \tau G_i, \ \forall \ i \\ \varnothing, & \text{otherwise,} \end{cases} \tag{2.34}$$

where τ is a threshold controlling the proportion of distilled queries. After removing object-empty ($\varnothing$) queries in $\tilde{q}^{\mathcal{S}}$, we form a distillation-desired query set of students denoted as $\tilde{q}^{\mathcal{S}}$ associated with its object set $\tilde{y}^{\mathcal{S}} = \{\tilde{c}_j^{\mathcal{S}}, \tilde{b}_j^{\mathcal{S}}\}_{j=1}^{\tilde{N}}$. Correspondingly, we can obtain a teacher query set $\tilde{y}^{\mathcal{T}} = \{\tilde{c}_j^{\mathcal{T}}, \tilde{b}_j^{\mathcal{T}}\}_{j=1}^{\tilde{N}}$. For the j-th student query, its corresponding teacher query is matched as:

$$\tilde{c}_j^{\mathcal{T}}, \tilde{b}_j^{\mathcal{T}} = \arg\max_{\tilde{c}_k^{\mathcal{T}}, \tilde{b}_k^{\mathcal{T}}} \sum_{k=1}^{N} \mu_1 \, \text{GIoU}(\tilde{b}_j^{\mathcal{S}}, b_k^{\mathcal{T}}) - \mu_2 \|\tilde{b}_j^{\mathcal{S}} - b_k^{\mathcal{T}}\|_1, \tag{2.35}$$

where $\mu_1 = 2$ and $\mu_2 = 5$ control the matching function, values of which is to follow [31].

Finally, the upper-level optimization after rectification in Eq. (2.29) becomes:

$$\min_{\theta} H(\check{\mathbf{q}}^{\mathcal{S}^*} | \tilde{\mathbf{q}}^{\mathcal{T}}). \tag{2.36}$$

Optimizing Eq. (2.36) is challenging. Alternatively, we minimize the norm distance between $\check{\mathbf{q}}^{\mathcal{S}^*}$ and $\tilde{\mathbf{q}}^{\mathcal{T}}$, optima of which, *i.e.*, $\check{\mathbf{q}}^{\mathcal{S}^*} = \tilde{\mathbf{q}}^{\mathcal{T}}$, is exactly the same with that in Eq. (2.36). Thus, the final loss for our distribution rectification distillation loss becomes:

$$\mathcal{L}_{DRD}(\check{\mathbf{q}}^{\mathcal{S}^*}, \tilde{\mathbf{q}}^{\mathcal{T}}) = \mathbb{E}[\|\tilde{\mathbf{D}}^{\mathcal{S}^*} - \tilde{\mathbf{D}}^{\mathcal{T}}\|_2], \tag{2.37}$$

where we use the Euclidean distance of co-attented feature $\tilde{\mathbf{D}}$ (see Eq. 2.26) containing the information query $\tilde{\mathbf{q}}$ for optimization.

In backward propagation, the gradient updating drives the student queries toward their teacher hints. Therefore, we accomplish our distillation. The overall training losses for our Q-DETR model are:

$$\mathcal{L} = \mathcal{L}_{GT}(y^{GT}, y^{\mathcal{S}}) + \lambda \mathcal{L}_{DRD}(\check{\mathbf{q}}^{\mathcal{S}^*}, \tilde{\mathbf{q}}^{\mathcal{T}}), \tag{2.38}$$

where L_{GT} is the common detection loss for missions such as proposal classification and coordinate regression [31], and λ is a trade-off hyper-parameter.

2.4.5   Ablation Study

Datasets. We first conduct the ablative study and hyper-parameter selection on the PASCAL VOC dataset [62], which contains natural images from 20 different classes. We use the VOC `trainval2012`, and VOC `trainval2007` sets to train our model, which contains approximately 16k images, and the VOC `test2007` set to evaluate our Q-DETR, which contains 4952 images. We report COCO-style metrics for the VOC dataset: AP, AP_{50} (default VOC metric), and AP_{75}. We further conduct the experiments on the COCO 2017 [145] object detection tracking. Specifically, we train the models on COCO `train2017` and evaluate the models on COCO `val2017`. We list the average precision (AP) for IoUs$\in$ [0.5 : 0.05 : 0.95], designated as AP, using COCO's standard evaluation metric. For further analyzing our method, we also list AP_{50}, AP_{75}, AP_s, AP_m, and AP_l.

   Implementation Details. Our Q-DETR is trained with the DETR [31] and SMCA-DETR [70] framework. We select the ResNet-50 [84] and modify it with Pre-Activation structures and RPReLU [158] function following [155]. PyTorch [185] is used for implementing Q-DETR. We run the experiments on 8 NVIDIA Tesla A100 GPUs with 80 GB

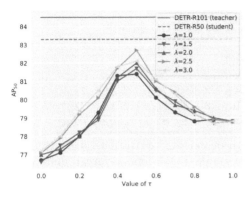 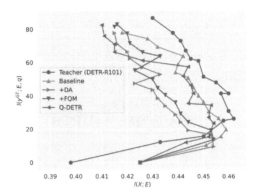

(a) Effect of τ and λ.   (b) Mutual information curves.

FIGURE 2.12
(a) We select τ and λ using 4-bit Q-DETR-R50 on VOC. (b) The mutual information curves of $I(X; \mathbf{E})$ and $I(\boldsymbol{y}^{GT}; \mathbf{E}, \mathbf{q})$ (Eq. 2.27) on the information plane. The red curves represent the teacher model (DETR-R101). The orange, green, red, and purple lines represent the 4-bit baseline, 4-bit baseline + DA, 4-bit baseline + FQM, and 4-bit baseline + DA + FQM (4-bit Q-DETR).

memory. We use ImageNet ILSVRC12 [123] to pre-train the backbone of a quantized student. The training protocol is the same as the employed frameworks [31, 70]. Specifically, we use a batch size of 16. AdamW [164] is used to optimize the Q-DETR, with the initial learning rate of $1e^{-4}$. We train for 300/500 epochs for the Q-DETR on VOC/COCO dataset, and the learning rate is multiplied by 0.1 at the 200/400-th epoch, respectively. Following the SMCA-DETR, we train the Q-SMCA-DETR for 50 epochs, and the learning rate is multiplied by 0.1 at the 40th epoch on both the VOC and COCO datasets. We utilize a multi-distillation strategy, saving the encoder and decoder network as real-valued at the first stage. Then we train the fully quantized DETR at the second stage, where we load the weight from the checkpoint of the first stage. We select real-valued DETR-R101 (84.5% AP_{50} on VOC and 43.5% AP on COCO) and SMCA-DETR-R101 (85.3% AP_{50} on VOC and 44.4% AP on COCO) as teacher network.

Hyper-parameter selection. As mentioned, we select hyper-parameters τ and λ in this part using the 4-bit Q-DETR model. We show the model performance (AP_{50}) with different setups of hyper-parameters $\{\tau, \lambda\}$ in Fig. 2.12 (a), where we conduct ablative experiments on the baseline + DA (AP_{50}=78.8%). As can be seen, the performances increase first and then decrease with the increase of τ from left to right. Since τ controls the proportion of selected distillation-desired queries, we show that the full-imitation ($\tau = 0$) performs worse than the vanilla baseline with no distillation ($\tau = 1$), showing query selection is necessary. The figure also shows that the performances increase first and then decrease with the increase of τ from left to right. The Q-DETR performs better with τ set as 0.5 and 0.6. With the varying value of λ, we find $\{\lambda, \tau\} = \{2.5, 0.6\}$ boost the performance of Q-DETR most, achieving 82.7% AP on VOC `test2007`. Based on the ablative study above, we set hyper-parameters τ and λ as 0.6 and 2.5, respectively, for the experiments in this paper.

Effectiveness of components. We show quantitative component improvements in Q-DETR in Table 2.2. As shown in Table 2.2, the quantized DETR baseline suffers a severe performance drop on AP_{50} (13.6%, 6.5%, and 5.3% with 2/3/4-bit, respectively). DA and FQM improve the performance when used alone, and the two techniques further boost the performance considerably when combined. For example, the DA improves the 2-bit baseline

TABLE 2.2

Evaluating the components of Q-DETR-R50 on the VOC dataset.

Method	#Bits	AP_{50}	#Bits	AP_{50}	#Bits	AP_{50}
Real-valued	32-32-32	83.3	-	-	-	-
Baseline	4-4-8	78.0	3-3-8	76.8	2-2-8	69.7
+DA	4-4-8	78.8	3-3-8	78.0	2-2-8	71.6
+FQM	4-4-8	81.5	3-3-8	80.9	2-2-8	74.9
+DA+FQM (Q-DETR)	4-4-8	**82.7**	3-3-8	**82.1**	2-2-8	**76.4**

Note: #Bits (W-A-Attention) denotes the bit-width of weights, activations, and attention activations. DA denotes the distribution alignment module. FQM denotes foreground-aware query matching.

by 1.9%, and the FQM achieves a 5.2% performance improvement. While combining the DA and FQM, the performance improvement achieves 6.7%.

Information analysis. We further show the information plane following [238] in Fig. 2.12. We adopt the test AP_{50} to quantify $I(\boldsymbol{y}^{GT}; \mathbf{E}, \mathbf{q})$. We employ a reconstruction decoder to decode the encoded feature $\mathbf{E}$ to reconstruct the input and quantify $I(X; \mathbf{E})$ using the ℓ_1 loss. As shown in Fig. 2.12, the curve of the larger teacher DETR-R101 is usually on the right of the curve of small student models, which indicates a greater ability of information representation. Likewise, the purple line (Q-DETR-R50) is usually on the right of the three left curves, showing the information representation improvements with the proposed methods.

3

Algorithms for Binary Neural Networks

3.1 Overview

The most extreme quantization in the quantization area is binarization, which is the focus of this book. Data can only have one of two potential values during binarization, which is a 1-bit quantization: -1 (or 0) or $+1$. Both weight and activation can be represented by a single bit in network compression without consuming a lot of memory. In addition, binarization replaces costly matrix multiplication operations with lighter bitwise XNOR and Bitcount operations. Therefore, compared to alternative compression techniques, binary neural networks (BNNs) have a variety of hardware-friendly advantages, such as significant acceleration, memory savings, and power efficiency. The usefulness of binarization has been demonstrated by ground-breaking work like BNN [99] and XNOR-Net [199], with XNOR-Net being able to speed up CPUs by 58% and save up to 32 bytes of RAM for a 1-bit convolution layer. Following the BNN paradigm, a lot of research has been done on this topic in recent years from the field of computer vision and machine learning [84, 201, 153], and it has been used for a variety of everyday tasks including image classification [48, 199, 159, 196, 267, 259], detection [263, 240, 264, 260], point cloud processing [194, 261], object reidentification [262], etc. By transforming a layer from full precision to 1-bit, the binarization approach intuitively makes it simple to verify the significance of a layer. If performance suffers noticeably after binarizing a particular layer, we can infer that this layer is on the network's sensitive path. From the perspective of explainable machine learning, it is also essential to determine if full-precision and binarized models operate similarly.

Numerous researchers have sought to shed light on the behaviors of model binarization, as well as the relationships between the robustness of the model and the architecture of deep neural networks, in addition to concentrating on the methods of model binarization. This may aid in approaching solutions to fundamental queries of what network topology is preferable and how the deep network functions. It is crucial to thoroughly explore BNN studies because they will help us better understand the behaviors and architectures of effective and reliable deep learning models. Some outstanding prior art reveals how BNN's components work. For example, Bi-Real Net [159] incorporates more shortcuts (Bi-Real) to mitigate the information loss caused by binarization. This structure functions similarly to the ResNet shortcut [84], which helps to explain why commonly used shortcuts can somewhat improve the performance of deep neural networks. One thing that can be observed by looking at the activations is that more specific information from the shallow layer can be transmitted to the deeper layer during forward propagation. On the other hand, to avoid the gradient vanishing problem, gradients can be directly propagated backward using the shortcut. By building numerous weak classifier groups, some ensemble approaches [301] improve BNN performance but occasionally run into overfitting issues. Based on analysis and testing with BNNs, they demonstrated that the number of neurons trumps bit width

DOI: 10.1201/9781003376132-3

and that real-valued neurons may not even be required in deep neural networks, which is comparable to the idea behind biological neural networks.

Additionally, an efficient method to examine the interpretability of deep neural networks is to reduce the bit width of a particular layer and examine its impact on accuracy. Numerous works [199, 159] investigate how sensitive various layers are to binarization. In common BNNs, the first and last layers should, by default, be kept at higher precision. This means that these layers are more crucial for predicting neural networks. This section attempts to state the nature of binary neural networks by introducing some representative work.

3.2   BNN: Binary Neural Network

Given an N-layer CNN model, we denote its weight set as $\mathbf{W} = \{\mathbf{w}^n\}_{n=1}^N$ and the input feature map set as $\mathbf{A} = \{\mathbf{a}_{in}^n\}_{n=1}^N$. The $\mathbf{w}^n \in \mathbb{R}^{C_{out}^n \times C_{in}^n \times K^n \times K^n}$ and $\mathbf{a}_{in}^n \in \mathbb{R}^{C_{in}^n \times W_{in}^n \times H_{in}^n}$ are the convolutional weight and the input feature map in the n-th layer, where C_{in}^n, C_{out}^n and K^n, respectively, represent the input channel number, the output channel number, and the kernel size. In addition, W_{in}^n and H_{in}^n are the width and height of the feature maps. Then, the convolutional outputs $\mathbf{a}_{out}^n$ can be technically formulated as:

$$\mathbf{a}_{out}^n = \mathbf{w}^n \otimes \mathbf{a}_{in}^n, \tag{3.1}$$

where $\otimes$ represents the convolution operation. In this book, we omit the non-linear function for simplicity. Following the prior works [48, 99], BNN intends to represent $\mathbf{w}^n$ and $\mathbf{a}^n$ in a binary discrete set as:

$$\mathbb{B} := \{-1(0), +1\}.$$

Thus, the 1-bit format of $\mathbf{w}^n$ and $\mathbf{a}^n$ is respectively $\mathbf{b}^{\mathbf{w}^n} \in \mathbb{B}^{C_{out}^n \times C_{in}^n \times K^n \times K^n}$ and $\mathbf{b}^{\mathbf{a}_{in}^n} \in \mathbb{B}^{C_{in}^n \times W_{in}^n \times H_{in}^n}$ such that the efficient XNOR and Bit-count instructions can approximate the floating-point convolutional outputs as:

$$\mathbf{a}_{out}^n \approx \mathbf{b}^{\mathbf{w}^n} \odot \mathbf{b}^{\mathbf{a}_{in}^n}, \tag{3.2}$$

where $\circ$ represents channel-wise multiplication and $\odot$ denotes XNOR and Bit-count instructions.

However, this quantization mode will cause the output amplitude to increase dramatically, different from the full precision convolution calculation, and cause the homogenization of characteristics [199]. Several novel objects are proposed to address this issue, which will be introduced in the following.

3.3   XNOR-Net: Imagenet Classification Using Binary Convolutional Neural Networks

The scaling factor was first proposed by XNOR-Net [199] to solve this problem. The weights and the inputs to the convolutional and fully connected layers in XNOR-Nets are approximated with binary values $\mathbb{B}$.

The XNOR-Net binarization approach seeks to identify the most accurate convolutional approximations. Specifically, XNOR-Net employs a scaling factor, which plays a vital role in the learning of BNNs, and improves the forward pass of BNNs as:

$$\mathbf{a}_{out}^n \approx \boldsymbol{\alpha}^n \circ (\mathbf{b}^{\mathbf{w}^n} \odot \mathbf{b}^{\mathbf{a}_{in}^n}), \tag{3.3}$$

where $\boldsymbol{\alpha}^n = \{\alpha_1^n, \alpha_2^n, ..., \alpha_{C_{out}^n}^n\} \in \mathbb{R}_+^{C_{out}^n}$ is known as the channel-wise scaling factor vector to mitigate the output gap between Eq. (3.1) and its approximation of Eq. (3.3). We denote $\mathcal{A} = \{\boldsymbol{\alpha}^n\}_{n=1}^N$. Since the weight values are binary, XNOR-Net can implement the convolution with additions and subtractions. In the following, we state the XNOR operation for a specific convolution layer, thus omitting the superscript n for simplicity. Most existing implementations simply follow earlier studies [199, 159] to optimize $\mathcal{A}$ based on non-parametric optimization as:

$$\boldsymbol{\alpha}^*, \mathbf{b}^{\mathbf{w}*} = \arg\min_{\boldsymbol{\alpha}, \mathbf{b}^{\mathbf{w}}} J(\boldsymbol{\alpha}, \mathbf{b}^{\mathbf{w}}), \tag{3.4}$$

$$J(\boldsymbol{\alpha}, \mathbf{b}^{\mathbf{w}}) = \|\mathbf{w} - \boldsymbol{\alpha}^n \circ \mathbf{b}^{\mathbf{w}}\|_2^2. \tag{3.5}$$

By expanding Eq. 3.5, we have:

$$J(\boldsymbol{\alpha}, \mathbf{b}^{\mathbf{w}}) = \boldsymbol{\alpha}^2 (\mathbf{b}^{\mathbf{w}})^\top \mathbf{b}^{\mathbf{w}} - 2\boldsymbol{\alpha} \circ \mathbf{w}^\top \mathbf{b}^{\mathbf{w}} + \mathbf{w}^\top \mathbf{w} \tag{3.6}$$

where $\mathbf{b}^{\mathbf{w}} \in \mathbb{B}$. Thus, $(\mathbf{b}^{\mathbf{w}})^\top \mathbf{b}^{\mathbf{w}} = C_{in} \times K \times K$. $\mathbf{w}^\top \mathbf{w}$ is also a constant due to $\mathbf{w}$ being a known variable. Thus, Eq. 3.6 can be rewritten as:

$$J(\boldsymbol{\alpha}, \mathbf{b}^{\mathbf{w}}) = \boldsymbol{\alpha}^2 \times C_{in} \times K \times K - 2\boldsymbol{\alpha} \circ \mathbf{w}^\top \mathbf{b}^{\mathbf{w}} + constant. \tag{3.7}$$

The optimal solution can be achieved by maximizing the following constrained optimization:

$$\mathbf{b}^{\mathbf{w}*} = \arg\max_{\mathbf{b}^{\mathbf{w}}} \mathbf{w}^\top \mathbf{b}^{\mathbf{w}}, s.t. \quad \mathbf{b}^{\mathbf{w}} \in \mathbb{B}, \tag{3.8}$$

which can be solved by the sign function:

$$\mathbf{b}^{\mathbf{w}_i} = \begin{cases} +1 & \mathbf{w}_i \geq 0 \\ -1 & \mathbf{w}_i < 0 \end{cases}$$

which is the optimal solution and is also widely used as a general solution to BNNs in the following numerous works [159]. To find the optimal value for the scaling factor $\boldsymbol{\alpha}^*$, we take the derivative of $J(\cdot)$ w.r.t. $\boldsymbol{\alpha}$ and set it to zero as:

$$\boldsymbol{\alpha}^* = \frac{\mathbf{w}^\top \mathbf{b}^{\mathbf{w}}}{C_{in}^n \times K^n \times K^n}. \tag{3.9}$$

By replacing $\mathbf{b}^{\mathbf{w}}$ with the sign function, we have that a closed-form solution of $\boldsymbol{\alpha}$ can be derived via the channel-wise absolute mean (CAM) as:

$$\alpha_i = \frac{\|\mathbf{w}_{i,:,:,:}\|_1}{C_{in} \times K \times K} \tag{3.10}$$

$\alpha_i = \frac{\|\mathbf{w}_{i,:,:,:}\|_1}{M}$. Therefore, the optimal estimation of a binary weight filter can be achieved simply by taking the sign of weight values. The optimal scaling factor is the average of the absolute weight values.

Based on the explicitly solved $\boldsymbol{\alpha}^*$, the training objective of the XNOR-Net-like BNNs is given in a bilevel form:

$$\begin{aligned} \mathbf{W}^* &= \arg\min_{\mathbf{W}} \mathcal{L}(\mathbf{W}; \mathcal{A}^*), \\ s.t. \quad &\arg\min_{\boldsymbol{\alpha}^n, \mathbf{b}^{\mathbf{w}^n}} J(\boldsymbol{\alpha}, \mathbf{b}^{\mathbf{w}}), \end{aligned} \tag{3.11}$$

which is also known as hard binarization [159]. In the following, we show some variants of such a binarization function.

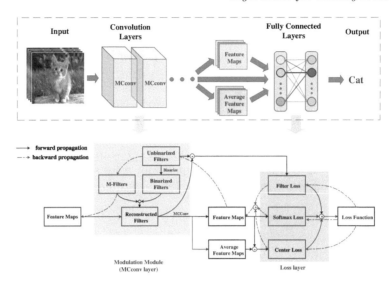

FIGURE 3.1
The overall frameworks of Modulated Convolutional Networks (MCNs).

3.4   MCN: Modulated Convolutional Network

In [199], XNOR-Network is presented where both the weights and inputs attached to the convolution are approximated with binary values, which allow an efficient implementation of convolutional operations, *i.e.*, particularly by reconstructing unbinarized filters with a single scaling factor and a binary filter. It has been theoretically and quantitatively demonstrated that simplifying the convolution procedure via binarized filters and approximating the original unbinarized filters is a very promising solution for CNNs compression.

However, the performance of binarized models generally drops significantly compared with using the original filters. It is mainly due to the following reasons: 1) The binarization of CNNs could be solved based on discrete optimization, which has long been neglected in previous works. 2) Existing methods do not consider quantization loss, filter loss, and intraclass compactness in the same backpropagation pipeline. 3) Rather than a single binarized filter, a set of binarized filters can better approximate the full-precision convolution.

As a promising solution, Modulated Convolutional Network (MCN) [236] is proposed as a novel binarization architecture to tackle these challenges toward highly accurate yet robust compression of CNNs. Unlike existing work that uses a single scaling factor in compression [199, 159], we introduce modulation filters (M-Filters) into CNNs to better approximate convolutional filters. The proposed M-Filters can help the network fuse the feature in a unified framework, significantly improving the network performance. To this end, a simple and specific modulation process is designed that is replicable at each layer and can be easily implemented. A complex modulation is also bounded as in [283]. In addition, we further consider the intraclass compactness in the loss function and obtain modulated convolutional networks (MCNs) [1]. Figure 3.1 shows the architecture of MCN. MCNs are designed based on binarized convolutional and modulation filters (M-Filters). M-Filters are mainly designed to approximate unbinarized convolutional filters in the end-to-end framework. Since an M-Filter (matrix) can be shared at each layer, the model size of MCNs is marginally in-

---

[1]The work has been commercialized.

creased. In particular, to alleviate the disturbance caused by the binarized process, a center loss is designed to incorporate the intraclass compactness with the quantization loss and filter loss. The red arrows are used to show the back-propagation process. By considering filter loss, center loss, and softmax loss in a unified framework, we achieve much better performance than state-of-the-art binarized models. Most importantly, our MCNs model is highly compressed and performs similarly to the well-known full-precision Resnets and WideResnets.

As shown in Fig. 3.1, M-Filters and weights can be jointly optimized end-to-end, resulting in a compact and portable learning architecture. Due to the low model complexity, such an architecture is less prone to overfitting and is suitable for resource-constrained environments. Specifically, our MCNs reduce the required storage space of a full-precision model by a factor of 32 while achieving the best performance compared to the existing binarized filter-based CNNs, even approximating full-precision filters. In addition, the number of model parameters to be optimized is significantly reduced, thus generating a computationally efficient CNNs model.

3.4.1 Forward Propagation with Modulation

We first elaborate on the MCNs as vanilla BNNs with only binarized weight. We design specific convolutional filters used in our MCNs. We deploy the 3D filter across all layers of size $K \times W \times W$ (one filter), which has K planes, and each of the planes is a $W \times W$-sized 2D filter. To use such filters, we extend the input channels of the network, e.g., from RGB to RRRR or (RGB+X) with $K = 4$ and X denotes any channel. Note that we only use one channel of gray-level images. Doing so allows us to implement our MCNs in existing deep-learning platforms quickly. After this extension, we directly deploy our filters in the convolution process, whose details concerning the MCNs convolution are illustrated in Fig. 3.2(b).

To reconstruct unbinarized filters, we introduce a modulated process based on M-Filters and binarized filters. An M-Filter is a matrix that serves as the weight of binarized filters, which is also the size of $K \times W \times W$. Let M_j be the j-th plane of an M-Filter. We define the operation $\circledcirc$ for a given layer as follows:

$$\hat{C}_i \circ M = \sum_{j}^{K} \hat{C}_i * M_{j}^{'}, \tag{3.12}$$

where $M_{j}^{'} = (M_j, ..., M_j)$ is a 3D matrix built based on K copies of the 2D matrix M_j with $j = 1, ..., K$. $*$ is the element-wise multiplication operator, also termed the Schur product operation. In Eq. 3.12, M is a learned weight matrix used to reconstruct convolutional filters C_i based on $\hat{C}_i$ and the operation $\circ$. And it leads to the filter loss in Eq. 3.18. An example of filter modulation is shown in Fig. 3.2(a). In addition, the operation $\circ$ results in a new matrix (named reconstructed filter), i.e., $\hat{C}_i * M_{j}^{'}$, which is elaborated in the following. We define:

$$Q_{ij} = \hat{C}_i * M_{j}^{'}, \tag{3.13}$$

$$Q_i = \{Q_{i1}, ..., Q_{iK}\}. \tag{3.14}$$

In testing, Q_i is not predefined but is calculated based on Eq. 3.13. An example is shown in Fig. 3.2(a). Q_i is introduced to approximate the unbinarized filters $\mathbf{w}_i$ to alleviate the information loss problem caused by the binarized process. In addition, we further require $M \geq 0$ to simplify the reconstructed process.

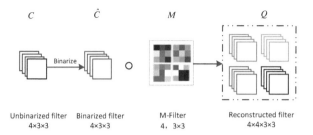

(a) Modulation process based on an M-Filter.

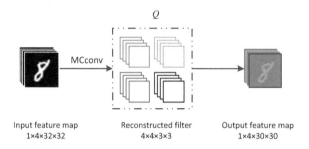

(b) MCNs Convolution (MCconv).

FIGURE 3.2

(a) The modulation process based on an M-Filter to obtain a reconstructed Filter Q. (b) An example of MCNs convolution with $K = 4$ planes. The number of planes of the M-Filter is the same as the number of channels of the feature map. This chapter defines a feature map as a 3D matrix with four channels.

In MCNs, reconstructed filters Q^l in the lth layer are used to calculate output feature maps F^{l+1} as:

$$F^{l+1} = MCconv(F^l, Q^l), \tag{3.15}$$

where $MCconv$ denotes the convolution operation implemented as a new module. A simple example of the forward convolutional process is described in Fig. 3.2(b), where there is one input feature map with one generated output feature map. In MCconv, the channels of one output feature map are generated as follows:

$$F_{h,k}^{l+1} = \sum_{i,g} F_g^l \otimes Q_{ik}^l, \tag{3.16}$$

$$F_h^{l+1} = (F_{h,1}^{l+1}, ..., F_{h,K}^{l+1}), \tag{3.17}$$

where $\otimes$ denotes the convolution operation; $F_{h,k}^{l+1}$ is the kth channel of the hth feature map in the $(l+1)$th convolutional layer. F_g^l denotes the gth feature map in the lth convolutional layer. In Fig. 3.2(b), $h = 1$ and $g = 1$, where after MCconv with one reconstructed filter, the number of channels in the output feature map is the same as that in the input feature map.

Figure 3.3 illustrates another example of MCNs convolution with multiple feature maps. An output feature map is the sum of the convolution between 10 input feature maps and 10 reconstructed filters in the corresponding group. For example, for the first output feature

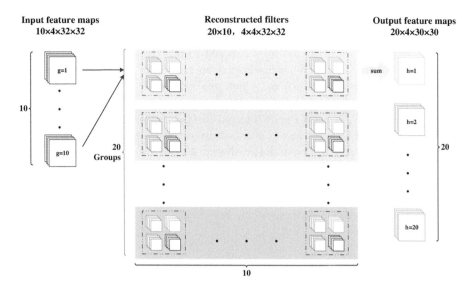

FIGURE 3.3
MCNs Convolution (MCconv) with multiple feature maps. There are 10 and 20 feature maps in the input and the output, respectively. The reconstructed filters are divided into 20 groups, and each group contains 10 reconstructed filters, corresponding to the number of feature maps and MC feature maps, respectively.

map, $h = 1, i = 1, ..., 10, g = 1, ..., 10$, and for the second output feature map, $h = 2, i = 11, ..., 20, g = 1, ..., 10$.

When the first convolutional layer is considered, the input size of the network is 32×32 [2]. First, each image channel is copied $K = 4$ times, resulting in the new input of size $4 \times 32 \times 32$ to the entire network.

It should be noted that the number of input and output channels in every feature map is the same, so MCNs can be easily implemented by simply replicating the same MCconv module at each layer.

3.4.2 Loss Function of MCNs

To constrain CNNs to have binarized weights, we introduce a new loss function in MCNs. Two aspects are considered: unbinarized convolutional filters are reconstructed based on binarized filters; the intra-class compactness is incorporated based on output features. We further introduce the variables used in this section: C_i^l are unbinary filters of the lth convolutional layer, $l \in \{1, ..., N\}$; $\hat{C}_i^l$ denote binarized filters corresponding to C_i^l; M^l denotes the modulation filter (M-Filter) shared by all C_i^l in the lth convolutional layer and M_j^l represents the jth plane of M^l; $\circ$ is a new plane-based operation (Eq. 3.12) which is defined in the next section. We then have the first part of the loss function for minimization:

$$L_M = \frac{\theta}{2} \sum_{i,l} \|C_i^l - \hat{C}_i^l \circ M^l\|^2 +$$

$$\frac{\lambda}{2} \sum_m \|f_m(\hat{C}, \vec{M}) - \overline{f}(\hat{C}, \vec{M})\|^2, \tag{3.18}$$

---

[2]We only use one channel of gray-level images ($3 \times 32 \times 32$)

where θ and λ are hyper parameters, $\vec{M} = \{M^1, ..., M^N\}$ are M-Filters, and $\hat{C}$ is the binarized filter set across all layers. Operation $\circ$ defined in Eq. 3.12 is used to approximate unbinarized filters based on binarized filters and M-Filters, leading to filter loss as the first term on the right of Eq. 3.18. The second term on the right is similar to the center loss used to evaluate intraclass compactness, which deals with the feature variation caused by the binarization process. $f_m(\hat{C}, \vec{M})$ denotes the feature map of the last convolutional layer for the mth sample, and $\overline{f}(\hat{C}, \vec{M})$ denotes the class-specific mean feature map of previous samples. We note that the center loss is successfully deployed to handle feature variations. We only keep the binarized filters and the shared M-Filters (quite small) to reduce the storage space to calculate the feature maps after training. We consider the conventional loss and then define a new loss function $L_{S,M} = L_S + L_M$, where L_S is the conventional loss function, e.g., softmax loss.

Again, we consider the quantization process in our loss $L_{S,M}$, and obtain the final minimization objective as:

$$L(C, \hat{C}, M) = L_{S,M} + \frac{\theta}{2}\|\widehat{C}^{[k]} - C - \eta\delta_{\widehat{C}}^{[k]}\|^2, \qquad (3.19)$$

where θ is shared with Eq. 3.18 to reduce the number of parameters. $\delta_{\widehat{C}}^{[k]}$ is the gradient of $L_{S,M}$ with respect to $\widehat{C}^{[k]}$. Unlike conventional methods (such as XNOR), where only the filter reconstruction is considered in the weight calculation, our discrete optimization method provides a comprehensive way to calculate binarized CNNs by considering filter loss, softmax loss, and feature compactness in a unified framework.

3.4.3   Back-Propagation Updating

In MCNs, unbinarized filters C_i and M-Filters M must be learned and updated. These two types of filters are jointly learned. In each convolutional layer, MCNs sequentially update unbinarized filters and M-Filters.

Updating unbinarized filters: The gradient $\delta_{\hat{C}}$ corresponding to C_i is defined as

$$\delta_{\hat{C}} = \frac{\partial L}{\partial \hat{C}_i} = \frac{\partial L_S}{\partial \hat{C}_i} + \frac{\partial L_M}{\partial \hat{C}_i} + \theta(\widehat{C}^{[k]} - C^{[k]} - \eta_1\delta_{\widehat{C}}^{[k]}), \qquad (3.20)$$

$$C_i \leftarrow C_i - \eta_1\delta_{\hat{C}}, \qquad (3.21)$$

where L, L_S, and L_M are loss functions, and η_1 is the learning rate. Furthermore, we have the following.

$$\frac{\partial L_S}{\partial \hat{C}_i} = \frac{\partial L_S}{\partial Q} \cdot \frac{\partial Q}{\partial \hat{C}_i} = \sum_j \frac{\partial L_S}{\partial Q_{ij}} \cdot M_j', \qquad (3.22)$$

$$\frac{\partial L_M}{\partial \hat{C}_i} = \theta \sum_j (C_i - \hat{C}_i \circ M_j) \circ M_j, \qquad (3.23)$$

Updating M-Filters: We further update the M-Filter M with C fixed. δ_M is defined as the gradient of M, and we have:

$$\delta_M = \frac{\partial L}{\partial M} = \frac{\partial L_S}{\partial M} + \frac{\partial L_M}{\partial M}, \qquad (3.24)$$

$$M \leftarrow |M - \eta_2\delta_M|, \qquad (3.25)$$

Algorithm 1 MCN training. L is the loss function, Q is the reconstructed filter, λ_1 and λ_2 are decay factors, and N is the number of layers. Update() updates the parameters based on our update scheme.

Input: a minibatch of inputs and their labels, unbinarized filters C, modulation filters M, learning rates η_1 and η_2, corresponding to C and M, respectively.

Output: updated unbinarized filters C^{t+1}, updated modulation filters M^{t+1}, and updated learning rates η_1^{t+1} and η_2^{t+1}.

1: {1. Computing gradients with aspect to the parameters:}
2: {1.1. Forward propagation:}
3: **for** $k = 1$ to N **do**
4:     $\hat{C} \leftarrow$ Binarize(C)
5:     Computing Q via Eq. 3.13 $\sim$ 3.14
6:     Convolutional features calculation using Eq. 3.15 $\sim$ 3.17
7: **end for**
8: {1.2. Backward propagation:}
9: {Note that the gradients are not binary.}
10: Computing $\delta_Q = \frac{\partial L}{\partial Q}$
11: **for** $k = N$ to 1 **do**
12:     Computing $\delta_{\hat{C}}$ using Eq. 3.20, Eq. 3.22 $\sim$ 3.23
13:     Computing δ_M using Eq. 3.24, Eq. 3.26 $\sim$ 3.27
14: **end for**
15: {Accumulating the parameters gradients:}
16: **for** $k = 1$ to N **do**
17:     $C^{t+1} \leftarrow$ Update$(\delta_{\hat{C}}, \eta_1)$ (using Eq. 3.21)
18:     $M^{t+1} \leftarrow$ Update(δ_M, η_2) (using Eq. 3.25)
19:     $\eta_1^{t+1} \leftarrow \lambda_1 \eta_1$
20:     $\eta_2^{t+1} \leftarrow \lambda_2 \eta_2$
21: **end for**

---

where η_2 is the learning rate. Furthermore, we have the following.

$$\frac{\partial L_S}{\partial M} = \frac{\partial L_S}{\partial Q} \cdot \frac{\partial Q}{\partial M} = \sum_{i,j} \frac{\partial L_S}{\partial Q_{ij}} \cdot \hat{C}_i, \tag{3.26}$$

Based on Eq. 3.18 and we have:

$$\frac{\partial L_M}{\partial M} = -\theta \sum_{i,j} (C_i - \hat{C}_i \circ M_j) \cdot \hat{C}_i. \tag{3.27}$$

Details about the derivatives concerning center loss can be found in [245]. These derivations show that MCNs can be learned with the BP algorithm. The quantization process leads to a new loss function via a simple projection function, which never affects the convergence of MCNs. We describe our algorithm in Algorithm 1.

3.4.4 Parameters Evaluation

θ **and** λ**:** There are θ and λ in Eq. 3.18, which are related to the filter loss and center loss. The effect of parameters θ and λ is evaluated in CIFAR-10 for a 20-layer MCN with width 16-16-32-64, the architecture detail of which can be found in [281] and is also shown in Fig. 3.6. The Adadelta optimization algorithm [282] is used during the training process,

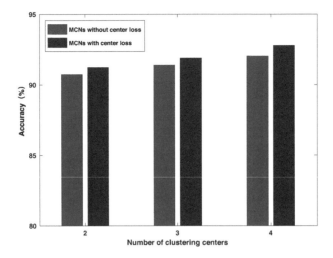

FIGURE 3.4
Accuracy with different numbers of clustering centers for 20-layer MCNs with width 16-16-32-64.

with a batch size of 128. Using different values of θ, the performance of MCNs is shown in Fig. 3.7. First, only the effect of θ is evaluated. Then the center loss is implemented based on a fine-tuning process. Performance is observed to be stable with variations θ and λ.

The number of clustering centers: We show the quantization with $U = 2, 3, 4$ denoting the numbers of clustering centers. In this experiment, we investigate the effect of varying the number of clustering centers in MCNs based on CIFAR-10.

The results are shown in Fig. 3.4, where accuracy increases with more clustering centers and center loss can also be used to improve performance. However, to save storage space and to compare with other binary networks, we use two clustering centers for MCNs in all the following experiments.

Our binarized networks can save storage space by 32 in convolutional layers compared with the corresponding full-precision networks, where 4 bytes (32 bits) represent a real value. Since MCNs only contain one fully connected layer that is not binarized, the storage of the whole network is significantly reduced.

The architecture parameter K: The number of planes for each M-Filter, i.e., K, is also evaluated. As revealed by the results in Fig. 3.5, more planes in each M-filter involved in reconstructing the unbinarized filters yield better performance. For example, when increasing K from 4 to 8, the performance is improved by 1.02%. For simplicity, we choose $K = 4$ in the following experiments.

The width of MCNs: CIFAR-10 is used to evaluate the effect of the width of Wide-ResNets with MCNs. The accuracy and number of parameters are compared with a recent binary CNN, LBCNN. The basic width of the stage (the number of convolution kernels per layer) is set to $16 - 16 - 32 - 64$. To compare with LBCNN, we set up 20-layer MCNs with basic block-c (in Fig. 3.9), whose depth is the same as in LBCNN. We also use other network widths to evaluate the effect of width on MCNs.

The results are shown in Table 3.1. The second column refers to the width of each layer of the MCNs, and a similar notation is also used in [281]. In the third column, we give the parameter amounts of MCNs and the 20-layer LBCNN with the best result. The fourth column shows the accuracy of baselines whose networks are trained based on the Wide-ResNets (WRNs) structure with the same depth and width as the MCNs. The last two

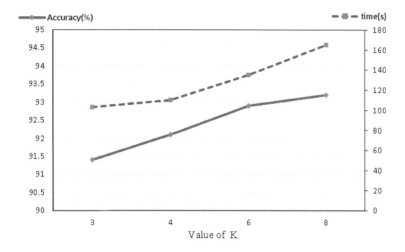

FIGURE 3.5
Accuracy with different K for 20-layer MCNs with width 16-16-32-64 on CIFAR-10.

columns show the accuracies of U-MCNs and MCNs, respectively. The performance in the last three columns shows that the accuracy of MCNs only decreases slightly when binarized filters are used. Note that with a fixed number of convolutional layers, the performance of MCNs increases with larger network width. At the same time, the number of parameters also increases. Compared to LBCNN, the parameters of the MCNs are much fewer (61 M vs. 17.2 M), but the performance of the MCNs is much better (92.96% vs. 95.30%). Also, the last three columns show that MCNs have achieved performance similar to U-MCNs and WRNs.

3.4.5 Model Effect

Learning convergence: The MCNs model is based on a binarized process implemented on the Torch platform (classification). For a 20-layer MCN with width 16-16-32-64 that is trained after 200 epochs, the training process takes about 3 hours with two 1080ti GPUs. We plot the training and testing accuracy of MCNs and U-MCNs in Fig. 3.10. The architecture of U-MCNs is the same as that of MCNs. Figure 3.10 clearly shows that MCNs (the blue curves) converge at speeds similar to those of their unbinarized counterpart (the red curves). **Runtime analysis**: We performed a run-time analysis to compare MCNs and LBCNN. The runtimes of MCNs and LBCNN for all CIFAR-10 test samples are 8.7 s and 160.6 s,

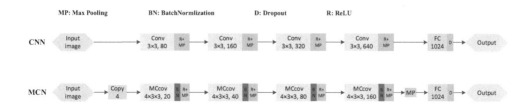

FIGURE 3.6
Network architectures of CNNs and MCNs.

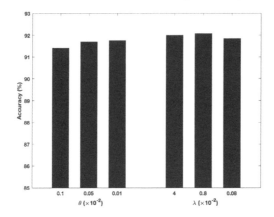

FIGURE 3.7
Accuracy with different θ and λ.

TABLE 3.1
Classification accuracy (%) on CIFAR-10 with 20-layer U-MCNs and MCNs.

Method	Kernel Stage	Size (MB)	WRNs	U-MCNs	**MCNs**	**MCNs-1**
	16 16-32-64	1.1	92.31	93.69	92.08	92.10
	16-32-64-128	4.3	–	94.88	93.98	93.94
MCNs	32-64-128-256	17.1	–	95.50	95.13	95.33
	64-64-128-256	17.2	95.75	95.72	95.30	95.34
LBCNN (q=384)	–	61	–	–	92.96	–

respectively, with similar accuracy (93.98% vs. 92.96%). When LBCNN has several parameters (4.3M) similar to those of the MCNs, the test run time of LBCNN becomes 16.2 s, which is still slower than our MCNs.

Visualization: We visualize MCconv features in Fig. 3.8 across different layers and the curves of elements in different M-Filters in Fig. 3.11. Similarly to conventional CNNs, the features of different layers capture rich and hierarchy information in Fig. 3.8. Based on the reconstructed filters Q corresponding to the M-Filters, we obtain convolutional features that appear diverse for different M-Filters. In summary, different MCconv layers and

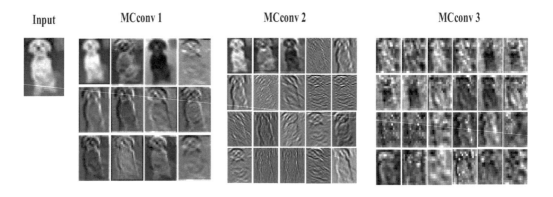

FIGURE 3.8
Example of output feature maps produced by Q from different layers.

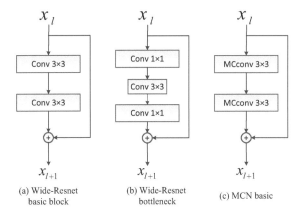

FIGURE 3.9
Residual blocks. (a) and (b) are for Wide-ResNets. (c) A basic block for MCNs.

M-Filters can capture the hierarchy and diverse information, which thus results in a high performance based on compressed models. Figure 3.11 show the curves of the elements in M-Filter 1 (M'_1), M-Filter 2 (M'_2), M-Filter 3 (M'_3), and M-Filter 4 (M'_4) (in Fig. 3.2(a) and Eq. 3.12) on the CIFAR experiment. The values of nine elements in each M-Filter are learned similarly to their averages (dotted lines). This validates that the special MCNs-1 with a single average element in each M'_j matrix is reasonable and compact without performance loss.

3.5 PCNN: Projection Convolutional Neural Networks

Modulated convolutional networks (MCNs) are presented in [237] to binarize kernels, achieving better results than the baselines. However, in the inference step, MCNs require

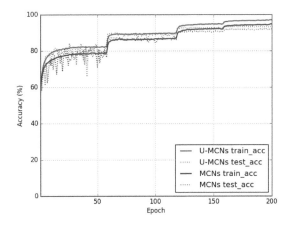

FIGURE 3.10
Training and testing curves.

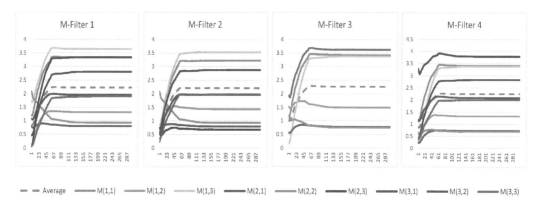

FIGURE 3.11
The curves of elements in M-Filter 1 (M_1'), M-Filter 2 (M_2'), M-Filter 3 (M_3'), and M-Filter 4 (M_4') (in Fig. 3.2(a) and Eq. 3.12) on the CIFAR experiment in the training process. The values of the nine elements in each M-Filter are learned similarly to their averages (dotted lines). This validates that the special MCNs-1 with a single average element in each M_j' matrix is reasonable and compact without large performance loss.

reconstructing full-precision convolutional filters from binarized filters, limiting their use in computationally limited environments. It has been theoretically and quantitatively demonstrated that simplifying the convolution procedure via binarized kernels and approximating the original unbinarized kernels is a very promising solution for DCNNs' compression.

Although prior BNNs significantly reduce storage requirements, they also generally have significant accuracy degradation compared to those using full-precision kernels and activations. This is mainly because CNN binarization could be solved by considering discrete optimization in the backpropagation (BP) process. Discrete optimization methods can often guarantee the quality of the solutions they find and lead to much better performance in practice [66, 119, 127]. Second, the loss caused by the binarization of CNNs has not been well studied.

We propose a new discrete backpropagation via projection (DBPP) algorithm to efficiently build our projection convolutional neural networks (PCNNs) [77] and obtain highly accurate yet robust BNNs. Theoretically, we achieve a projection loss by taking advantage of our DBPP algorithms' ability to perform discrete optimization on model compression. The advantages of the projection loss also lie in that it can be jointly learned with the conventional cross-entropy loss in the same pipeline as backpropagation. The two losses are simultaneously optimized in continuous and discrete spaces, optimally combined by the projection approach in a theoretical framework. They can enrich the diversity and thus improve modeling capacity. As shown in Fig.3.12, we develop a generic projection convolution layer that can be used in existing convolutional networks. Both the quantized kernels and the projection are jointly optimized in an end-to-end manner. Our project matrices are optimized but not for reference, resulting in a compact and efficient learning architecture. As a general framework, other loss functions (e.g., center loss) can also be used to further improve the performance of our PCNNs based on a progressive optimization method.

Discrete optimization is one of the hot topics in mathematics and is widely used to solve computer vision problems [119, 127]. Conventionally, the discrete optimization problem is solved by searching for an optimal set of discrete values concerning minimizing a loss function. This chapter proposes a new discrete backpropagation algorithm that uses a projection function to binarize or quantize the input variables in a unified framework. Due to the flex-

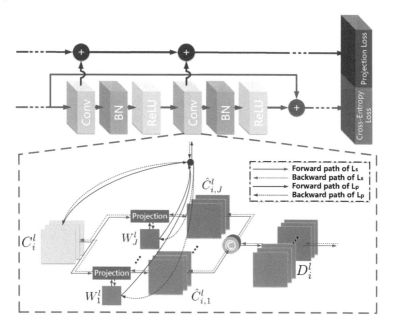

FIGURE 3.12

In PCNNs, a new discrete backpropagation via projection is proposed to build binarized neural networks in an end-to-end manner. Full-precision convolutional kernels C_i^l are quantized by projection as $\hat{C}_{i,j}^l$. Due to multiple projections, the diversity is enriched. The resulting kernel tensor D_i^l is used the same as in conventional ones. Both the projection loss L_p and the traditional loss L_s are used to train PCNNs. We illustrate our network structure *Basic Block Unit* based on ResNet, and more specific details are shown in the dotted box (projection convolution layer). ⓒ indicates the concatenation operation on the channels. Note that inference does not use projection matrices W_j^l and full-precision kernels C_i^l.

ible projection scheme, we obtain diverse binarized models with higher performance than the previous ones.

3.5.1 Projection

In our work, we define the quantization of the input variable as a projection onto a set;

$$\Omega := \{a_1, a_2, ..., a_U\}, \tag{3.28}$$

where each element a_i, $i = 1, 2, ..., U$ satisfies the constraint $a_1 < a_2 < ... < a_U$, and is the discrete value of the input variable. Then we define the projection of $x \in \mathbb{R}$ onto Ω as

$$P_\Omega(\omega, x) = \arg\min_{a_i} \|\omega \circ x - a_i\|, i \in \{1, ..., U\}, \tag{3.29}$$

where ω is a projection matrix and $\circ$ denotes the Hadamard product. Equation 3.29 indicates that the projection aims to find the closest discrete value for each continuous value x.

3.5.2 Optimization

Minimizing $f(x)$ based on the discrete optimization or integer programming method, whose variables are restricted to discrete values, becomes more challenging when training a large-scale problem on a huge data set [53]. We propose to solve the problem within the backpropagation framework by considering: 1) the inference process of the optimized model is based on the quantized variables, which means that the variable must be quantized in the forward pass (corresponding to the inference) during training, and the loss is calculated based on the quantized variables; the backpropagation is not necessarily to be quantized, which however needs to consider the relationship between quantized variables and their counterparts fully. Based on the above considerations, we propose that in the kth iteration, based on the projection in Eq. 3.29, $x^{[k]}$ is quantized to $\hat{x}^{[k]}$ in the forward pass as

$$\hat{x}^{[k]} = P_\Omega(\omega, x^{[k]}), \tag{3.30}$$

which is used to improve the backpropagation process by defining an objective as

$$\begin{aligned} &\min \quad f(\omega, x) \\ &\text{s.t.} \quad \hat{x}_j^{[k]} = P_\Omega^j(\omega_j, x), \end{aligned} \tag{3.31}$$

where $\omega_j, j \in \{1, ..., J\}$ is the jth projection matrix[3], and J is the total number of projection matrices. To solve the problem in (3.31), we define our update rule as

$$x \leftarrow x^{[k]} - \eta \delta_{\hat{x}}^{[k]}, \tag{3.32}$$

where the superscript $[k+1]$ is removed from x, $\delta_{\hat{x}}$ is the gradient of $f(\omega, x)$ with respect to $x = \hat{x}$, and η is the learning rate. The quantization process $\hat{x}^{[k]} \leftarrow x^{[k]}$, that is, $P_\Omega^j(\omega_j, x^{[k]})$, is equivalent to finding the projection of $\omega_j \circ (x + \eta \delta_{\hat{x}}^{[k]})$ onto Ω as

$$\hat{x}^{[k]} = \arg \min_{\hat{x}} \{\|\hat{x} - \omega_j \circ (x + \eta \delta_{\hat{x}}^{[k]})\|^2, \hat{x} \in \Omega\}. \tag{3.33}$$

Obviously, $\hat{x}^{[k]}$ is the solution to the problem in (3.33). So, by incorporating (3.33) into $f(\omega, x)$, we obtain a new formulation for (3.31) based on the Lagrangian method as

$$\min f(\omega, x) + \frac{\lambda}{2} \sum_j^J \|\hat{x}^{[k]} - \omega_j \circ (x + \eta \delta_{\hat{x}}^{[k]})\|^2. \tag{3.34}$$

The newly added part (right) shown in (3.34) is a quadratic function and is referred to as **projection loss**.

3.5.3   Theoretical Analysis

We take a close look at the projection loss in Eq. 3.34; we have

$$\hat{x}^{[k]} - \omega \circ (x + \eta \delta_{\hat{x}}^{[k]}) = \hat{x}^{[k]} - \omega \circ x - \omega \circ \eta \delta_{\hat{x}}^{[k]}. \tag{3.35}$$

In this case, we only consider one projection function, so the subscript j of ω_j is omitted for simplicity. For multiple projections, the analysis is given after that. In the forward step, only the discrete kernel values participate in the calculation, so their gradients can be obtained by

$$\frac{\partial f(\omega, \hat{x}^{[k]})}{\partial \hat{x}^{[k]}} = \omega \circ \delta_{\hat{x}}^{[k]}, \tag{3.36}$$

---

[3]Since the kernel parameters x are represented as a matrix, ω_j denotes a matrix as ω.

as ω and $\hat{x}$ are bilinear with each other as $\omega \circ \hat{x}^{[k]}$. In our discrete optimization framework, the discrete values of convolutional kernels are updated according to their gradients. Taking Eq. 3.36 into consideration, we derive the update rule for $\hat{x}^{[k+1]}$ as

$$\hat{x}^{[k+1]} = \hat{x}^{[k]} - \eta \frac{\partial f(\omega, \hat{x}^{[k]})}{\partial \hat{x}^{[k]}} = \hat{x}^{[k]} - \omega \circ \eta \delta_{\hat{x}}^{[k]}. \tag{3.37}$$

By plugging Eq. 3.37 into Eq. 3.35, we achieve a new objective function or a loss function that minimizes

$$||\hat{x}^{[k+1]} - \omega \circ x||, \tag{3.38}$$

to approximate

$$\hat{x} = \omega \circ x, x = \omega^{-1} \circ \hat{x}. \tag{3.39}$$

We further discuss multiple projections, based on Eq. 3.39 and projection loss in (3.34), and have

$$\min \frac{1}{2} \sum_{j}^{J} ||x - \omega_j^{-1} \circ \hat{x}_j||^2. \tag{3.40}$$

We set $g(x) = \frac{1}{2} \sum_{j}^{J} ||x - \omega_j^{-1} \circ \hat{x}_j||^2$ and calculate its derivative as $g'(x) = 0$, and we have

$$x = \frac{1}{J} \sum_{j}^{J} \omega_j^{-1} \circ \hat{x}_j, \tag{3.41}$$

which shows that multiple projections can better reconstruct the full kernels based on binaries counterparts.

3.5.4 Projection Convolutional Neural Networks

PCNNs, shown in Fig. 3.12, work using DBPP for model quantization. We accomplish this by reformulating our projection loss shown in (3.34) into the deep learning paradigm as

$$L_p = \frac{\lambda}{2} \sum_{l,i}^{L,I} \sum_{j}^{J} ||\hat{C}_{i,j}^{l,[k]} - \widetilde{W}_j^{l,[k]} \circ (C_i^{l,[k]} + \eta \delta_{\hat{C}_{i,j}^{l,[k]}})||^2, \tag{3.42}$$

where $C_i^{l,[k]}, l \in \{1, ..., L\}, i \in \{1, ..., I\}$ denotes the ith kernel tensor of the lth convolutional layer in the kth iteration. $\hat{C}_{i,j}^{l,[k]}$ is the quantized kernel of $C_i^{l,[k]}$ via projection $P_\Omega^{l,j}, j \in \{1, ..., J\}$ as

$$\hat{C}_{i,j}^{l,[k]} = P_\Omega^{l,j}(\widetilde{W}_j^{l,[k]}, C_i^{l,[k]}), \tag{3.43}$$

where $\widetilde{W}_j^{l,[k]}$ is a tensor, calculated by duplicating a learned projection matrix $W_j^{l,[k]}$ along the channels, which thus fits the dimension of $C_i^{l,[k]}$. $\delta_{\hat{C}_{i,j}^{l,[k]}}$ is the gradient at $\hat{C}_{i,j}^{l,[k]}$ calculated based on L_S, that is, $\delta_{\hat{C}_{i,j}^{l,[k]}} = \frac{\partial L_S}{\partial \hat{C}_{i,j}^{l,[k]}}$. The iteration index $[k]$ is omitted for simplicity.

In PCNNs, both the cross-entropy loss and projection loss are used to build the total loss as

$$L = L_S + L_P. \tag{3.44}$$

The proposed projection loss regularizes the continuous values converging onto Ω^N while minimizing the cross-entropy loss, illustrated in Fig. 4.15 and Fig. 3.25.

3.5.5   Forward Propagation Based on Projection Convolution Layer

For each full precision kernel C_i^l, the corresponding quantized kernels $\hat{C}_{i,j}^l$ are concatenated to construct the kernel D_i^l that actually participates in the convolution operation as

$$D_i^l = \hat{C}_{i,1}^l \oplus \hat{C}_{i,2}^l \oplus \cdots \oplus \hat{C}_{i,J}^l, \tag{3.45}$$

where $\oplus$ denotes the concatenation operation on the tensors. In PCNNs, the projection convolution is implemented based on D^l and F^l to calculate the next layer's feature map F^{l+1}.

$$F^{l+1} = Conv2D(F^l, D^l), \tag{3.46}$$

where $Conv2D$ is the traditional 2D convolution. Although our convolutional kernels are 3D-shaped tensors, we design the following strategy to fit the traditional 2D convolution as

$$F_{h,j}^{l+1} = \sum_{i,h} F_h^l \otimes D_{i,j}^l, \tag{3.47}$$

$$F_h^{l+1} = F_{h,1}^l \oplus \cdots \oplus F_{h,J}^l, \tag{3.48}$$

where $\otimes$ denotes the convolutional operation. $F_{h,j}^{l+1}$ is the jth channel of the hth feature map at the $(l+1)$th convolutional layer and F_h^l denotes the hth feature map at the lth convolutional layer. To be more precise, for example, when $h = 1$, for the jth channel of an output feature map, $F_{1,j}^{l+1}$ is the sum of the convolutions between all the h input feature maps and i corresponding quantized kernels. All channels of the output feature maps are obtained as $F_{h,1}^{l+1}, ..., F_{h,j}^{l+1}, ..., F_{h,J}^{l+1}$, and they are concatenated to construct the hth output feature map F_h^{l+1}.

It should be emphasized that we can utilize multiple projections to increase the diversity of convolutional kernels D^l. However, the single projection can perform much better than the existing BNNs. The essential is the use of DBPP, which differs from [147] based on a single quantization scheme. Within our convolutional scheme, there is no dimension disagreement on feature maps and kernels in two successive layers. Thus, we can replace the traditional convolutional layers with ours to binarize widely used networks, such as VGGs and ResNets. At inference time, we only store the set of quantized kernels D_i^l instead of the full-precision ones; that is, projection matrices W_j^l are not used for inference, achieving a reduction in storage.

3.5.6   Backward Propagation

According to Eq. 3.44, what should be learned and updated are the full-precision kernels C_i^l and the projection matrix W^l ($\widetilde{W}^l$) using the updated equations described below.

Updating C_i^l: We define δ_{C_i} as the gradient of the full-precision kernel C_i, and have

$$\delta_{C_i^l} = \frac{\partial L}{\partial C_i^l} = \frac{\partial L_S}{\partial C_i^l} + \frac{\partial L_P}{\partial C_i^l}, \tag{3.49}$$

$$C_i^l \leftarrow C_i^l - \eta_1 \delta_{C_i^l}, \tag{3.50}$$

where η_1 is the learning rate for the convolutional kernels. More specifically, for each item in Eq. 3.49, we have

$$\begin{aligned}
\frac{\partial L_S}{\partial C_i^l} &= \sum_j^J \frac{\partial L_S}{\partial \hat{C}_{i,j}^l} \frac{\partial P_{\Omega^N}^{l,j}(\widetilde{W}_j^l, C_i^l)}{\partial (\widetilde{W}_j^l \circ C_i^l)} \frac{\partial (\widetilde{W}_j^l \circ C_i^l)}{\partial C_i^l} \\
&= \sum_j^J \frac{\partial L_S}{\partial \hat{C}_{i,j}^l} \circ \mathbb{1}_{-1 \leq \widetilde{W}_j^l \circ C_i^l \leq 1} \circ \widetilde{W}_j^l,
\end{aligned} \tag{3.51}$$

$$\frac{\partial L_P}{\partial C_i^l} = \lambda \sum_j^J \left[\widetilde{W}_j^l \circ \left(C_i^l + \eta \delta_{\hat{C}_{i,j}^l} \right) - \hat{C}_{i,j}^l \right] \circ \widetilde{W}_j^l, \tag{3.52}$$

where $\mathbb{1}$ is the indicator function [199] widely used to estimate the gradient of the nondifferentiable function. More specifically, the output of the indicator function is 1 only if the condition is satisfied; otherwise, 0. **Updating W_j^l:** Likewise, the gradient of the projection parameter $\delta_{W_j^l}$ consists of the following two parts

$$\delta_{W_j^l} = \frac{\partial L}{\partial W_j^l} = \frac{\partial L_S}{\partial W_j^l} + \frac{\partial L_P}{\partial W_j^l}, \tag{3.53}$$

$$W_j^l \leftarrow W_j^l - \eta_2 \delta_{W_j^l}, \tag{3.54}$$

where η_2 is the learning rate for W_j^l. We also have the following.

$$
\begin{aligned}
\frac{\partial L_S}{\partial W_j^l} &= \sum_h^J \left(\frac{\partial L_S}{\partial \widetilde{W}_j^l} \right)_h \\
&= \sum_h^J \left(\sum_i^I \frac{\partial L_S}{\partial \hat{C}_{i,j}^l} \frac{\partial P_{\Omega^N}^{l,j}(\widetilde{W}_j^l, C_i^l)}{\partial(\widetilde{W}_j^l \circ C_i^l)} \frac{\partial(\widetilde{W}_j^l \circ C_i^l)}{\partial \widetilde{W}_j^l} \right)_h \\
&= \sum_h^J \left(\sum_i^I \frac{\partial L_S}{\partial \hat{C}_{i,j}^l} \circ \mathbb{1}_{-1 \leq \widetilde{W}_j^l \circ C_i^l \leq 1} \circ C_i^l \right)_h,
\end{aligned}
\tag{3.55}
$$

$$\frac{\partial L_P}{\partial W_j^l} = \lambda \sum_h^J \left(\sum_i^I \left[\widetilde{W}_j^l \circ \left(C_i^l + \eta \delta_{\hat{C}_{i,j}^l} \right) - \hat{C}_{i,j}^l \right] \circ \left(C_i^l + \eta \delta_{\hat{C}_{i,j}^l} \right) \right)_h, \tag{3.56}$$

where h indicates the hth plane of the tensor along the channels. It shows that the proposed algorithm can be trained from end to end, and we summarize the training procedure in Algorithm 13. In the implementation, we use the mean of W in the forward process but keep the original W in the backward propagation.

Note that in PCNNs for BNNs, we set $U = 2$ and $a_2 = -a_1$. Two binarization processes are used in PCNNs. The first is the kernel binarization, which is done based on the projection onto Ω^N, whose elements are calculated based on the mean absolute values of all full precision kernels per layer [199] as

$$\frac{1}{I} \sum_i^I \left(\|C_i^l\|_1 \right), \tag{3.57}$$

where I is the total number of kernels.

3.5.7 Progressive Optimization

Training 1-bit CNNs is a highly non-convex optimization problem, and initialization states will significantly impact the convergence. Unlike the method in [159] that a real-valued CNN model with the clip function pre-trained on ImageNet initializes the 1-bit CNNs models, we propose applying a progressive optimization strategy in training 1-bit CNNs. Although a real-valued CNN model can achieve high classification accuracy, we doubt the converging states between real-value and 1-bit CNNs, which may mistakenly guide the converging process of 1-bit CNNs.

Algorithm 2 Discrete backpropagation via projection

Input:
    The training dataset; the full-precision kernels C; the projection matrix W; the learning rates η_1 and η_2.

Output:
    The binary or ternary PCNNs are based on the updated C and W.
 1: Initialize C and W randomly;
 2: **repeat**
 3:    // Forward propagation
 4:    **for** $l = 1$ to L **do**
 5:       $\hat{C}_{i,j}^l \leftarrow P(W, C_i^l)$; // using Eq. 3.43 (binary) or Eq. 3.59 (ternary)
 6:       $D_i^l \leftarrow Concatenate(\hat{C}_{i,j})$; // using Eq. 3.45
 7:       Perform activation binarization; //using the sign function
 8:       Traditional 2D convolution; // using Eq. 3.46, 3.47 and 3.48
 9:    **end for**,
10:    Calculate cross-entropy loss L_S;
11:    // Backward propagation
12:    Compute $\delta_{\hat{C}_{i,j}^l} = \frac{\partial L_S}{\partial \hat{C}_{i,j}^l}$;
13:    **for** $l = L$ to 1 **do**
14:       // Calculate the gradients
15:       calculate $\delta_{C_i^l}$; // using Eq. 3.49, 3.51 and 3.52
16:       calculate $\delta_{W_j^l}$; // using Eq. 3.115, 3.116 and 3.56
17:       // Update the parameters
18:       $C_i^l \leftarrow C_i^l - \eta_1 \delta_{C_i^l}$; // Eq. 3.50
19:       $W_j^l \leftarrow W_j^l - \eta_2 \delta_{W_j^l}$; //Eq. 3.54
20:    **end for**
21:    Adjust the learning rates η_1 and η_2.
22: **until** the network converges

We believe that compressed ternary CNNs such as TTN [299] and TWN [130] have better initialization states for binary CNNs. Theoretically, the performance of models with ternary weights is slightly better than those with binary weights and far worse than those of real-valued ones. Still, they provide an excellent initialization state for 1-bit CNNs in our proposed progressive optimization framework. Subsequent experiments show that our PCNNs trained from a progressive optimization strategy perform better than those from scratch, even better than the ternary PCNNs from scratch.

The discrete set for ternary weights is a special case, defined as $\Omega := \{a_1, a_2, a_3\}$. We further require $a_1 = -a_3 = \Delta$ as Eq. 3.57 and $a_2 = 0$ to be hardware friendly [130]. Regarding the threshold for ternary weights, we follow the choice made in [229] as

$$\Delta^l = \sigma \times E(|C^l|) \approx \frac{\sigma}{I} \sum_{i}^{I} \left(\|C_i^l\|_1 \right), \tag{3.58}$$

where σ is a constant factor for all layers. Note that [229] applies to Eq. 3.58 on convolutional inputs or feature maps; we find it appropriate in convolutional weights as well. Consequently, we redefine the projection in Eq. 3.29 as

$$P_\Omega(\omega, x) = \arg\min_{a_i} \|\omega \circ x - 2a_i\|, i \in \{1, ..., U\}. \tag{3.59}$$

In our proposed progressive optimization framework, the PCNNs with ternary weights (ternary PCNNs) are first trained from scratch and then served as pre-trained models to progressively fine-tune the PCNNs with binary weights (binary PCNNs).

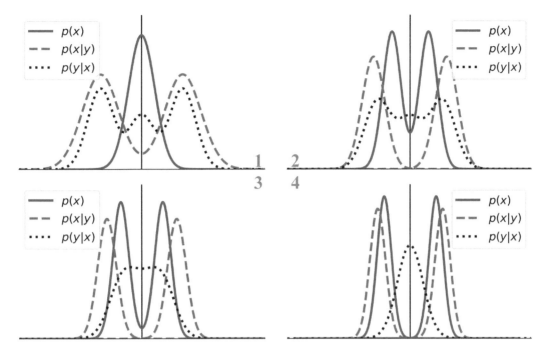

FIGURE 3.13

In our proposed progressive optimization framework, the two additional losses, projection loss, and center loss are simultaneously optimized in continuous and discrete spaces, optimally combined by the projection approach in a theoretical framework. The subfigure on the left explains the softmax function in the cross-entropy loss. The subfigure in the middle illustrates the process of progressively turning ternary kernel weights into binary ones within our projection approach. The subfigure on the right shows the function of center loss to force the learned feature maps to cluster together, class by class.

To alleviate the disturbance caused by the quantization process, intraclass compactness is further deployed based on the center loss function [245] to improve performance. Given the input features $x_i \in \mathbb{R}^d$ or Ω and the y_ith class center $c_{y_i} \in \mathbb{R}^d$ or Ω of the input features, we have

$$L_C = \frac{\gamma}{2} \sum_{i=1}^{m} \|x_i - c_{y_i}\|_2^2, \tag{3.60}$$

where m denotes the total number of samples or batch size, and γ is a hyperparameter to balance the center loss with other losses. More details on center loss can be found in [245]. By incorporating Eq. 3.60 into Eq. 3.110, the total loss is updated as

$$L = L_S + L_P + L_C. \tag{3.61}$$

We note that the center loss is successfully deployed to handle feature variations in the training and will be omitted in the inference, so there is no additional memory storage and computational cost. More intuitive illustrations can be found in Fig. 3.13, and a more detailed training procedure is described in Algorithm 3.

Algorithm 3 Progressive Optimization with Center Loss

Input: The training dataset; the full-precision kernels C; the pre-trained kernels ${}^tC$ from ternary
   PCNNs; the projection matrix W; the learning rates η_1 and η_2.
Output: The binary PCNNs are based on the updated C and W.
 1: Initialize W randomly but C from ${}^tC$;
 2: **repeat**
 3:    // Forward propagation
 4:    **for** $l = 1$ to L **do**
 5:       $\hat{C}^l_{i,j} \leftarrow P(W, C^l_i)$; // using Eq. 3.43
 6:       $D^l_i \leftarrow Concatenate(\hat{C}_{i,j})$; // using Eq. 3.45
 7:       Perform activation binarization; //using the sign function
 8:       Traditional 2D convolution; // using Eq. 3.46, 3.47 and 3.48
 9:    **end for**
10:    Calculate cross-entropy loss L_S;
11:    **if** using center loss **then**
12:       $L' = L_S + L_C$;
13:    **else**
14:       $L' = L_S$;
15:    **end if**
16:    // Backward propagation
17:    Compute $\delta_{\hat{C}^l_{i,j}} = \frac{\partial L'}{\partial \hat{C}^l_{i,j}}$;
18:    **for** $l = L$ to 1 **do**
19:       // Calculate the gradients
20:       calculate $\delta_{C^l_i}$; // using Eq. 3.49, 3.51 and 3.52
21:       calculate $\delta_{W^l_j}$; // using Eq. 3.115, 3.116 and 3.56
22:       // Update the parameters
23:       $C^l_i \leftarrow C^l_i - \eta_1 \delta_{C^l_i}$; // Eq. 3.50
24:       $W^l_j \leftarrow W^l_j - \eta_2 \delta_{W^l_j}$; //Eq. 3.54
25:    **end for**
26:    Adjust the learning rates η_1 and η_2.
27: **until** the network converges

3.5.8 Ablation Study

Parameter As mentioned above, the proposed projection loss, similar to clustering, can control quantization. We computed the distributions of the full-precision kernels and visualized the results in Figs. 3.14 and 3.15. The hyperparameter λ is designed to balance projection loss and cross-entropy loss. We vary it from $1e-3$ to $1e-5$ and finally set it to 0 in Fig. 3.14, where the variance increases as the number of λ. When $\lambda=0$, only one cluster is obtained, where the kernel weights are tightly distributed around the threshold $= 0$. This could result in instability during binarization because little noise may cause a positive weight to be negative and vice versa.

   We also show the evolution of the distribution of how projection loss works in the training process in Fig. 3.15. A natural question is: do we always need a large λ? As a discrete optimization problem, the answer is no, and the experiment in Table 3.4 can verify it, i.e., both the projection loss and the cross-entropy loss should be considered simultaneously with good balance. For example, when λ is set to $1e-4$, the accuracy is higher than those with other values. Thus, we fix λ to $1e-4$ in the following experiments.

Learning convergence For PCNN-22 in Table 3.2, the PCNN model is trained for 200 epochs and then used to perform inference. In Fig. 3.16, we plot training and test loss with $\lambda = 0$ and $\lambda = 1e-4$, respectively. It clearly shows that PCNNs with $\lambda = 1e-4$ (blue

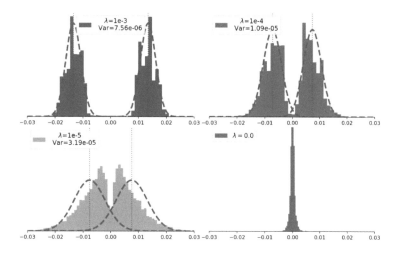

FIGURE 3.14

We visualize the distribution of kernel weights of the first convolution layer of PCNN-22. The variance increases when the ratio decreases λ, which balances projection loss and cross-entropy loss. In particular, when $\lambda = 0$ (no projection loss), only one group is obtained, where the kernel weights are distributed around 0, which could result in instability during binarization. In contrast, two Gaussians (with projection loss, $\lambda > 0$) are more powerful than the single one (without projection loss), which thus results in better BNNs, as also validated in Table 3.2.

curves) converge faster than PCNNs with $\lambda = 0$ (yellow curves) when the epoch number > 150.

Diversity visualization In Fig. 3.17, we visualize four channels of the binary kernels D_i^l in the first row, the feature maps produced by D_i^l in the second row, and the corresponding feature maps after binarization in the third row when $J=4$. This way helps illustrate the diversity of kernels and feature maps in PCNNs. Thus, multiple projection functions can capture diverse information and perform highly based on compressed models.

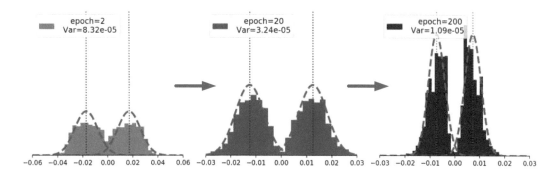

FIGURE 3.15

With λ fixed to $1e - 4$, the variance of the kernel weights decreases from the 2nd epoch to the 200th epoch, which confirms that the projection loss does not affect the convergence.

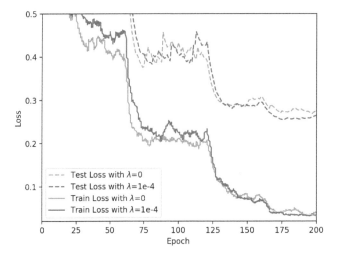

FIGURE 3.16
Training and testing curves of PCNN-22 when $\lambda=0$ and $1e-4$, which shows that the projection affects little on the convergence.

3.6   RBCN: Rectified Binary Convolutional Networks with Generative Adversarial Learning

Quantization approaches represent network weights and activations with fixed-point integers of low bit width, allowing computation with efficient bitwise operations. Binarization [199, 159] is an extreme quantization approach where both weights and activations are $+1$ or -1, represented by a single bit. This chapter designs highly compact binary neural networks (BNNs) from the perspective of quantization and network pruning.

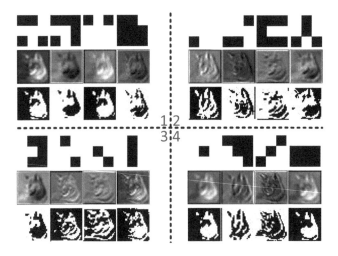

FIGURE 3.17
Illustration of binary kernels D_i^l (first row), feature maps produced by D_i^l (second row), and corresponding feature maps after binarization (third row) when $J=4$. This confirms the diversity in PCNNs.

TABLE 3.2

With different λ, the accuracy of PCNN-22 and PCNN-40 based on WRN-22 and WRN-40, respectively, on CIFAR10 dataset.

Model	λ			
	$1e-3$	$1e-4$	$1e-5$	0
PCNN-22	91.92	92.79	92.24	91.52
PCNN-40	92.85	93.78	93.65	92.84

Despite the progress made in 1-bit quantization and network pruning, few works have combined the two in a unified framework to reinforce each other. It is necessary to introduce pruning techniques into 1-bit CNNs since not all filters and kernels are equally important or worth quantizing in the same way. One potential solution is to prune the network and perform a 1-bit quantization over the remaining weights to produce a more compressed network. However, this solution does not consider the difference between binarized and full precision parameters during pruning. Therefore, a promising alternative is to prune the quantized network. However, designing a unified framework to combine quantization and pruning is still an open question.

To address these issues, we introduce a rectified binary convolutional network (RBCN) [148] to train a BNN, in which a novel learning architecture is presented in a GAN framework. Our motivation is based on the fact that GANs can match two data distributions (the full-precision and 1-bit networks). This can also be viewed as distilling/exploiting the full precision model to benefit its 1-bit counterpart. For training RBCN, the primary process for binarization is illustrated in Fig. 6.10, where the full-precision model and the 1-bit model (generator) provide "real" and "fake" feature maps to the discrimina-

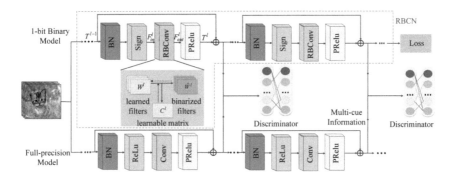

FIGURE 3.18

This figure shows the framework for integrating the Rectified Binary Convolutional Network (RBCN) with Generative Adversarial Network (GAN) learning. The full precision model provides "real" feature maps, while the 1-bit model (as a generator) provides "fake" feature maps to discriminators trying to distinguish "real" from "fake." Meanwhile, the generator tries to make the discriminators work improperly. When this process is repeated, both the full-precision feature maps and kernels (across all convolutional layers) are sufficiently employed to enhance the capacity of the 1-bit model. Note that (1) the full precision model is used only in learning but not in inference; (2) after training, the full precision learned filters W are discarded, and only the binarized filters $\hat{W}$ and the shared learnable matrices C are kept in RBCN for the calculation of the feature maps in inference.

tors. The discriminators try to distinguish the "real" from the "fake," and the generator tries to make the discriminators unable to work well. The result is a rectified process and a unique architecture with a more precise estimation of the full precision model. Pruning is also explored to improve the applicability of the 1-bit model in practical applications in the GAN framework. To accomplish this, we integrate quantization and pruning into a unified framework.

3.6.1   Loss Function

The rectification process combines full precision kernels and feature maps to rectify the binarization process. It includes kernel approximation and adversarial learning. This learnable kernel approximation leads to a unique architecture with a precise estimation of the convolutional filters by minimizing kernel loss. Discriminators $D(\cdot)$ with filters Y are introduced to distinguish feature maps R of the full precision model from those T of RBCN. The RBCN generator with filters W and matrices C is trained with Y using knowledge of the supervised feature maps R. In summary, W, C and Y are learned by solving the following optimization problem:

$$\arg \min_{W,\hat{W},C} \max_{Y} \mathscr{L} = \mathscr{L}_{Adv}(W,\hat{W},C,Y) + \mathscr{L}_S(W,\hat{W},C) + \mathscr{L}_{Kernel}(W,\hat{W},C), \quad (3.62)$$

where $\mathscr{L}_{Adv}(W,\hat{W},C,Y)$ is the adversarial loss as

$$\mathscr{L}_{Adv}(W,\hat{W},C,Y) = log(D(R;Y)) + log(1 - D(T;Y)), \quad (3.63)$$

where $D(\cdot)$ consists of a series of basic blocks, each containing linear and LeakyRelu layers. We also have multiple discriminators to rectify the binarization training process.

In addition, $\mathscr{L}_{Kernel}(W,\hat{W},C)$ denotes the kernel loss between the learned full precision filters W and the binarized filters $\hat{W}$ and is defined as:

$$\mathscr{L}_{Kernel}(W,\hat{W},C) = \lambda_1/2||W - C\hat{W}||^2, \quad (3.64)$$

where λ_1 is a balance parameter. Finally, $\mathscr{L}_S$ is a traditional problem-dependent loss, such as softmax loss. The adversarial, kernel, and softmax loss are regularizations on $\mathscr{L}$.

For simplicity, the update of the discriminators is omitted in the following description until Algorithm 13. We also have omitted $log(\cdot)$ and rewritten the optimization in Eq. 6.79 as in Eq. 3.65 for simplicity.

$$\min_{W,\hat{W},C} \mathscr{L}_S(W,\hat{W},C) + \lambda_1/2 \sum_l \sum_i ||W_i^l - C^l\hat{W}_i^l||^2 + \sum_l \sum_i ||1 - D(T_i^l;Y)||^2. \quad (3.65)$$

where i represents the ith channel and l represents the lth layer. In Eq. 3.65, the objective is to obtain W, $\hat{W}$ and C with Y fixed, which is why the term $D(R;Y)$ in Eq. 6.79 can be ignored. The update process for Y is found in Algorithm 13. The advantage of our formulation in Eq. 3.65 lies in that the loss function is trainable, which means it can be easily incorporated into existing learning frameworks.

3.6.2   Learning RBCNs

In RBCNs, convolution is implemented using W^l, C^l and F_{in}^l to calculate output feature maps F_{out}^l as

$$F_{out}^l = RBConv(F_{in}^l;\hat{W}^l,C^l) = Conv(F_{in}^l,\hat{W}^l \odot C^l), \quad (3.66)$$

where $RBConv$ denotes the convolution operation implemented as a new module, F_{in}^l and F_{out}^l are the feature maps before and after convolution, respectively. W^l are full precision filters, the values of $\hat{W}^l$ are 1 or -1, and $\odot$ is the operation of the element-by-element product.

During the backward propagation process of RBCNs, the full precision filters W and the learnable matrices C are required to be learned and updated. These two sets of parameters are jointly learned. We update W first and then C in each convolutional layer.

Update W: Let $\delta_{W_i^l}$ be the gradient of the full precision filter W_i^l. During backpropagation, the gradients are first passed to $\hat{W}_i^l$ and then to W_i^l. Thus,

$$\delta_{W_i^l} = \frac{\partial \mathscr{L}}{\partial W_i^l} = \frac{\partial \mathscr{L}}{\partial \hat{W}_i^l} \frac{\partial \hat{W}_i^l}{\partial W_i^l}, \tag{3.67}$$

where

$$\frac{\partial \hat{W}_i^l}{\partial W_i^l} = \begin{cases} 2 + 2W_i^l, & -1 \leq W_i^l < 0, \\ 2 - 2W_i^l, & 0 \leq W_i^l < 1, \\ 0, & \text{otherwise}, \end{cases} \tag{3.68}$$

which is an approximation of $2\times$ the Dirac delta function [159]. Furthermore,

$$\frac{\partial \mathscr{L}}{\partial \hat{W}_i^l} = \frac{\partial \mathscr{L}_S}{\partial \hat{W}_i^l} + \frac{\partial \mathscr{L}_{Kernel}}{\partial \hat{W}_i^l} + \frac{\partial \mathscr{L}_{Adv}}{\partial \hat{W}_i^l}, \tag{3.69}$$

and

$$W_i^l \leftarrow W_i^l - \eta_1 \delta_{W_i^l}, \tag{3.70}$$

where η_1 is the learning rate. Then,

$$\frac{\partial \mathscr{L}_{Kernel}}{\partial \hat{W}_i^l} = -\lambda_1 (W_i^l - C^l \hat{W}_i^l) C^l, \tag{3.71}$$

$$\frac{\partial \mathscr{L}_{Adv}}{\partial \hat{W}_i^l} = -2(1 - D(T_i^l; Y)) \frac{\partial D}{\partial \hat{W}_i^l}. \tag{3.72}$$

Update C: We further update the learnable matrix C^l with W^l fixed. Let δ_{C^l} be the gradient of C^l. Then we have

$$\delta_{C^l} = \frac{\partial \mathscr{L}_S}{\partial C^l} + \frac{\partial \mathscr{L}_{Kernel}}{\partial C^l} + \frac{\partial \mathscr{L}_{Adv}}{\partial C^l}, \tag{3.73}$$

and

$$C^l \leftarrow C^l - \eta_2 \delta_{C^l}, \tag{3.74}$$

where η_2 is another learning rate. Furthermore,

$$\frac{\partial \mathscr{L}_{Kernel}}{\partial C^l} = -\lambda_1 \sum_i (W_i^l - C^l \hat{W}_i^l) \hat{W}_i^l, \tag{3.75}$$

$$\frac{\partial \mathscr{L}_{Adv}}{\partial C^l} = -\sum_i 2(1 - D(T_i^l; Y)) \frac{\partial D}{\partial C^l}. \tag{3.76}$$

These derivations show that the rectified process is trainable in an end-to-end manner. The complete training process is summarized in Algorithm 13, including how to update the discriminators. As described in line 17 of Algorithm 13, we independently update other parameters while fixing the convolutional layer's parameters to enhance each layer's feature maps' variety. This way, we speed up the training convergence and fully explore the potential of 1-bit networks. In our implementation, all the values of C^l are replaced by their average during the forward process. A scalar, not a matrix, is involved in inference, thus speeding up computation.

3.6.3   Network Pruning

We further prune the 1-bit CNNs to increase model efficiency and improve the flexibility of RBCNs in practical scenarios. This section considers the optimization pruning process, including changing the loss function and updating the learnable parameters.

3.6.3.1   Loss Function

After binarizing the CNNs, we prune the resulting 1-bit CNNs under the generative adversarial learning framework using the method described in [142]. We used a soft mask to remove the corresponding structures, such as filters, while obtaining close to the baseline accuracy. The discriminator $D_p(\cdot)$ with weights Y_p is introduced to distinguish the output of the baseline network R_p from those T_p of the pruned 1-bit network. The pruned network with weights W_p, $\hat{W}_p$, C_p and a soft mask M_p, is learned together with Y_p using knowledge of the supervised features of the baseline. W_p, $\hat{W}_p$, C_p, M_p and Y_p are learned by solving the optimization problem as follows:

$$\arg \min_{W_p,\hat{W}_p,C_p,M_p} \max_{Y_p} \mathscr{L}_p = \mathscr{L}_{Adv\_p}(W_p,\hat{W}_p,C_p,M_p,Y_p) + \mathscr{L}_{Kernel\_p}(W_p,\hat{W}_p,C_p)$$
$$\mathscr{L}_{S\_p}(W_p,\hat{W}_p,C_p) + \mathscr{L}_{Data\_p}(W_p,\hat{W}_p,C_p,M_p) + \mathscr{L}_{Reg\_p}(M_p,Y_p), \tag{3.77}$$

where $\mathscr{L}_p$ is the pruning loss function, and the forms of $\mathscr{L}_{Adv\_p}(W_p,\hat{W}_p,C_p,M_p,Y_p)$ and $\mathscr{L}_{Kernel\_p}(W_p,\hat{W}_p,C_p)$ are

$$\mathscr{L}_{Adv\_p}(W_p,\hat{W}_p,C_p,M_p,Y_p) = log(D_p(R_p;Y_p)) + log(1 - D_p(T_p;Y_p)), \tag{3.78}$$

$$\mathscr{L}_{Kernel\_p}(W_p,\hat{W}_p,C_p) = \lambda_1/2||W_p - C_p\hat{W}_p||^2. \tag{3.79}$$

$\mathscr{L}_{S\_p}$ is a traditional problem-dependent loss such as softmax loss. $\mathscr{L}_{Data\_p}$ is the data loss between the output features of the baseline and the pruned network and is used to align the output of these two networks. The data loss can then be expressed as the MSE loss.

$$\mathscr{L}_{Data\_p}(W_p,\hat{W}_p,C_p,M_p) = \frac{1}{2n}||R_p - T_p||^2, \tag{3.80}$$

where n is the size of the minibatch.

$\mathscr{L}_{Reg\_p}(M_p,Y_p)$ is a regularizer on W_p,$\hat{W}_p$,M_p and Y_p, which can be split into two parts as follows:

$$\mathscr{L}_{Reg\_p}(M_p,Y_p) = \mathscr{R}_\lambda(M_p) + \mathscr{R}(Y_p), \tag{3.81}$$

where $\mathscr{R}(Y_p) = log(D_p(T_p;Y_p))$, $\mathscr{R}_\lambda(M_p)$ is a sparsity regularizer form with parameters λ and $\mathscr{R}_\lambda(M_p) = \lambda||M_p||_{l_1}$.

As with the process in binarization, the update of the discriminators is omitted in the following description until Algorithm 2. We have also omitted $log(\cdot)$ for simplicity and rewritten the optimization of Eq. 3.77 as

$$\min_{W_p,\hat{W}_p,C_p,M_p} \lambda_1/2 \sum_l \sum_i ||W_{p,i}^l - C^l\hat{W}_{p,i}^l||^2 + \sum_l \sum_i ||1 - D(T_{p,i}^l;Y)||^2$$
$$+ \mathscr{L}_{S\_p}(W_p,\hat{W}_p,C_p) + \frac{1}{2n}||R_p - T_p||^2 + \lambda||M_p||_{l_1}. \tag{3.82}$$

3.6.3.2   Learning Pruned RBCNs

In pruned RBCNs, the convolution is implemented as

$$F_{out,p}^l = RBConv(F_{in,p}^l; \hat{W}_p^l \circ M_p^l, C_p^l) = Conv(F_{in,p}^l, (\hat{W}_p \circ M_p^l) \odot C_p^l), \tag{3.83}$$

where $\circ$ is an operator that obtains the pruned weight with mask M_p. The other part of the forward propagation in the pruned RBCNs is the same as in the RBCNs.

In pruned RBCNs, what needs to be learned and updated are full precision filters W_p, learnable matrices C_p, and soft mask M_p. In each convolutional layer, these three sets of parameters are jointly learned.

Update M_p. M_p is updated by FISTA [141] with the initialization of $\alpha_{(1)} = 1$. Then we obtain the following.

$$\alpha_{(k+1)} = \frac{1}{2}(1 + \sqrt{1 + 4\alpha_{(k)}^2}), \tag{3.84}$$

$$y_{(k+1)} = M_{p,(k)} + \frac{a_{(k)} - 1}{a_{(k+1)}}(M_{p,(k)} - M_{p,(k-1)}), \tag{3.85}$$

$$M_{p,(k+1)} = prox_{\eta_{(k+1)}\lambda\|\cdot\|_1}(y_{(k+1)} - \eta_{k+1}\frac{\partial(\mathscr{L}_{Adv\_p} + \mathscr{L}_{Data\_p})}{\partial(y_{(k+1)})}), \tag{3.86}$$

where η_{k+1} is the learning rate in iteration $k + 1$ and $prox_{\eta_{(k+1)}\lambda\|\cdot\|_1}(z_i) = sign(z_i) \cdot (|z_i| - \eta_0\lambda)_+$, more details can be found in [142].

Update W_p. Let $\delta_{W_{p,i}^l}$ be the gradient of the full precision filter $W_{p,i}^l$. During backpropagation, the gradients pass to $\hat{W}_{p,i}^l$ first and then to $W_{p,i}^l$. Furthermore,

$$\delta_{W_{p,i}^l} = \frac{\partial\mathscr{L}_p}{\partial\hat{W}_{p,i}^l} = \frac{\partial\mathscr{L}_{S\_p}}{\partial\hat{W}_{p,i}^l} + \frac{\partial\mathscr{L}_{Adv\_p}}{\partial\hat{W}_{p,i}^l} + \frac{\partial\mathscr{L}_{Kernel\_p}}{\partial\hat{W}_{p,i}^l} + \frac{\partial\mathscr{L}_{Data\_p}}{\partial\hat{W}_{p,i}^l}, \tag{3.87}$$

and

$$W_{p,i}^l \leftarrow W_{p,i}^l - \eta_{p,1}\delta_{W_{p,i}^l}, \tag{3.88}$$

where $\eta_{p,1}$ is the learning rate, $\frac{\partial\mathscr{L}_{Kernel\_p}}{\partial\hat{W}_{p,i}^l}$ and $\frac{\partial\mathscr{L}_{Adv\_p}}{\partial\hat{W}_{p,i}^l}$ are

$$\frac{\partial\mathscr{L}_{Kernel\_p}}{\partial\hat{W}_{p,i}^l} = -\lambda_1(W_{p,i}^l - C_p^l\hat{W}_{p,i}^l)C_p^l, \tag{3.89}$$

$$\frac{\partial\mathscr{L}_{Adv\_p}}{\partial\hat{W}_{p,i}^l} = -2(1 - D(T_{p,i}^l; Y_p))\frac{\partial D_p}{\partial\hat{W}_{p,i}^l}. \tag{3.90}$$

And

$$\frac{\partial\mathscr{L}_{Data\_p}}{\partial\hat{W}_{p,i}^l} = -\frac{1}{n}(R_p - T_p)\frac{\partial T_p}{\partial\hat{W}_{p,i}^l}, \tag{3.91}$$

Update C_p. We further update the learnable matrix C_p^l with W_p^l and M_p^l fixed. Let $\delta_{C_p^l}$ be the gradient of C_p^l. Then we have

$$\delta_{C_p^l} = \frac{\partial\mathscr{L}_p}{\partial\hat{C}_p^l} = \frac{\partial\mathscr{L}_{S\_p}}{\partial\hat{C}_p^l} + \frac{\partial\mathscr{L}_{Adv\_p}}{\partial\hat{C}_p^l} + \frac{\partial\mathscr{L}_{Kernel\_p}}{\partial\hat{C}_p^l} + \frac{\partial\mathscr{L}_{Data\_p}}{\partial\hat{C}_p^l}, \tag{3.92}$$

and

$$C_p^l \leftarrow C_p^l - \eta_{p,2}\delta_{C_p^l}. \tag{3.93}$$

and $\frac{\partial\mathscr{L}_{Kernel\_p}}{\partial C_p^l}$ and $\frac{\partial\mathscr{L}_{Adv\_p}}{\partial C_p^l}$ are

$$\frac{\partial\mathscr{L}_{Kernel\_p}}{\partial C_p^l} = -\lambda_1\sum_i(W_{p,i}^l - C_p^l\hat{W}_{p,i}^l)\hat{W}_{p,i}^l, \tag{3.94}$$

$$\frac{\partial \mathcal{L}_{Adv\_p}}{\partial C_p^l} = -\sum_i 2(1 - D_p(T_{p,i}^l; Y_p))\frac{\partial D_p}{\partial C_p^l}. \tag{3.95}$$

Furthermore,

$$\frac{\partial \mathcal{L}_{Data\_p}}{\partial C_p^l} = \frac{1}{n}\sum_i (R_p - T_p)\frac{\partial T_p}{\partial C_p^l}. \tag{3.96}$$

The complete training process is summarized in Algorithm 4, including the update of the discriminators.

Algorithm 4 Pruned RBCN

Input: The training dataset, the pre-trained 1-bit CNNs model, the feature maps R_p from the pre-trained model, the pruning rate, and the hyper-parameters, including the initial learning rate, weight decay, convolution stride, and padding size.

Output: The pruned RBCN with updated parameters W_p, $\hat{W}_p$, M_p and C_p.

1: **repeat**
2:      Randomly sample a mini-batch;
3:      // Forward propagation
4:      Training a pruned architecture // Using Eq.17-22
5:      **for all** $l = 1$ to L convolutional layer **do**
6:          $F_{out,p}^l = Conv(F_{in,p}^l, (\hat{W}_p^l \circ M_p) \odot C_p^l)$;
7:      **end for**
8:      // Backward propagation
9:      **for all** $l = L$ to 1 **do**
10:         Update the discriminators $D_p^l(\cdot)$ by ascending their stochastic gradients:
11:         $\nabla_{D_p^l}(log(D_p^l(R_p^l; Y_p)) + log(1 - D_p^l(T_p^l; Y_p)) + log(D_p^l(T_p; Y_p)))$;
12:         Update soft mask M_p by **FISTA** // Using Eq. 24-26
13:         Calculate the gradients $\delta_{W_p^l}$; // Using Eq. 27-31
14:         $W_p^l \leftarrow W_p^l - \eta_{p,1}\delta_{W_p^l}$; // Update the weights
15:         Calculate the gradient $\delta_{C_p^l}$; // Using Eq. 32-36
16:         $C_p^l \leftarrow C_p^l - \eta_{p,2}\delta_{C_p^l}$; // Update the learnable matrix
17:     **end for**
18: **until** the maximum epoch
19: $\hat{W} = sign(W)$.

3.6.4   Ablation Study

This section studies the performance contributions of the kernel approximation, the GAN, and the update strategy (we fix the parameters of the convolutional layers and update the other layers). CIFAR100 and ResNet18 with different kernel stages are used.

1) We replace the convolution in Bi-Real Net with our kernel approximation (*RBConv*) and compare the results. As shown in the column of "Bi" and "R" in Table 3.3, RBCN achieves an improvement in accuracy 1.62% over Bi-Real Net (56.54% vs. 54.92%) using the same network structure as in ResNet18. This significant improvement verifies the effectiveness of the learnable matrices.

2) Using GAN makes RBCN improve 2.59% (59.13% vs. 56.54%) with the kernel stage of 32-32-64-128, which shows that GAN can help mitigate the problem of being trapped in poor local minima.

TABLE 3.3

Performance contributions of the components in RBCNs on CIFAR100, where Bi=Bi-Real Net, R=*RBConv*, G=GAN, and B=update strategy.

	Kernel Stage	Bi	R	R+G	R+G+B
RBCN	32-32-64-128	54.92	56.54	59.13	**61.64**
RBCN	32-64-128-256	63.11	63.49	64.93	**65.38**
RBCN	64-64-128-256	63.81	64.13	65.02	**66.27**

Note: The numbers in bold represent the best results.

3) We further improve RBCNs by updating the BN layers with W and C fixed after each epoch (line 17 in Algorithm 13). This further increases our accuracy by 2.51% (61.64% vs. 59.13%) in CIFAR100 with 32-32-64-128.

3.7   BONN: Bayesian Optimized Binary Neural Network

First, we briefly introduce Bayesian learning. Bayesian learning is a paradigm for constructing statistical models based on the Bayes Theorem, providing practical learning algorithms and helping us understand other learning algorithms. Bayesian learning shows its signifi-

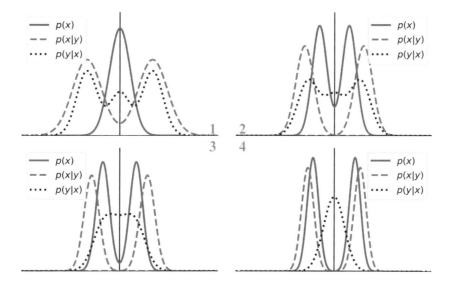

FIGURE 3.19

The evolution of the prior $p(\boldsymbol{x})$, the distribution of the observation $\boldsymbol{y}$, and the posterior $p(\boldsymbol{x}|\boldsymbol{y})$ during learning, where $\boldsymbol{x}$ is the latent variable representing the full-precision parameters and $\boldsymbol{y}$ is the quantization error. Initially, the parameters $\boldsymbol{x}$ are initialized according to a single-mode Gaussian distribution. When our learning algorithm converges, the ideal case is that (i) $p(\boldsymbol{y})$ becomes a Gaussian distribution $\mathcal{N}(0, \nu)$, which corresponds to the minimum reconstruction error, and (ii) $p(\boldsymbol{x}|\boldsymbol{y}) = p(\boldsymbol{x})$ is a Gaussian mixture distribution with two modes where the binarized values $\hat{\boldsymbol{x}}$ and $-\hat{\boldsymbol{x}}$ are located.

cant advantages in solving probabilistic graphical models. It can help achieve information exchange between the perception task and the inference task, conditional dependencies on high-dimensional data, and effective uncertainty modeling. [14, 124] have been extensively studied in Bayesian neural networks (BayesNNs). More recent developments establishing the efficacy of BayesNNs can be found in [215, 139] and the references therein. Estimating the posterior distribution is a vital part of Bayesian inference and represents the information on the uncertainties for both the data and the parameters. However, an exact analytical solution for the posterior distribution is intractable, as the number of parameters is large and the functional form of a neural network does not lend itself to exact integration [16]. Several approaches have been proposed for solving posterior distributions of weights of BayesNNs, based on optimization-based techniques such as variational inference (VI) and sampling-based approaches, such as Markov Chain Monte Carlo (MCMC). MCMC techniques are typically used to obtain sampling-based estimates of the posterior distribution. BayesNNs with MCMC have not seen widespread adoption due to the computational cost of time and storage on a large dataset [120].

In contrast to MCMC, VI tends to converge faster and has been applied to many popular Bayesian models, such as factorial and topic models [15]. The basic idea of VI is that it first defines a family of variational distributions and then minimizes the Kullback-Leibler (KL) divergence concerning the variational family. Many recent works have discussed the application of variational inference to BayesNNs, *e.g.*, [16, 216].

Despite the progress made in 1-bit or network pruning, little work has combined quantization and pruning in a unified framework to reinforce each other. However, it is necessary to introduce pruning techniques into 1-bit CNNs. Not all filters and kernels are equally essential and worth quantizing in the same way, as validated subsequently in our experiments. One potential solution is to prune the network first and then perform a 1-bit quantization on the remaining network to have a more compressed network. However, such a solution does not consider the difference between the binarized and full-precision parameters during pruning. Instinctively, 1-bit CNNs tend to be easily pruned, as CNNs are more redundant before and after binarization [150]. Thus, one promising alternative is to conduct pruning over BNNs. However, it remains an open problem to design a unified framework to calculate a 1-bit network first and then prune it. In particular, due to the deterioration of the representation ability in 1-bit networks, the backpropagation process can be susceptible to parameter updates, making existing optimization schemes [77] fail.

To address this problem, we use Bayesian learning, a well-established global optimization scheme [174],[16], to prune 1-bit CNNs. First, Bayesian learning binarizes the full-precision kernels to two quantization values (centers) to obtain 1-bit CNNs. The quantization error is minimized when the full-precision kernels follow a Gaussian mixture model, with each Gaussian centered on its corresponding quantization value. Given two centers for 1-bit CNNs, two Gaussians that form the mixture model are used to model the full-precision kernels. Subsequently, the Bayesian learning framework establishes a new pruning operation to prune 1-bit CNNs. In particular, we divide the filters into two groups, assuming that those in one group follow the same Gaussian distribution. Then, their average is used to replace the weights of the filters in this group. Figure 3.20 illustrates the general framework where three innovative elements are introduced to the learning procedure of 1-bit CNNs with compression: (1) minimizing the reconstruction error of the parameters before and after quantization, (2) Modeling the parameter distribution as a Gaussian mixture with two modes centered on the binarized values, and (3) pruning the quantized network by maximizing a posterior probability. Further analysis led to our three new losses and the corresponding learning algorithms, referred to as *Bayesian kernel loss*, *Bayesian feature loss*, and *Bayesian pruning loss*. These three losses can be jointly applied with the conventional cross-entropy loss within the same back-propagation pipeline. The advantages of Bayesian

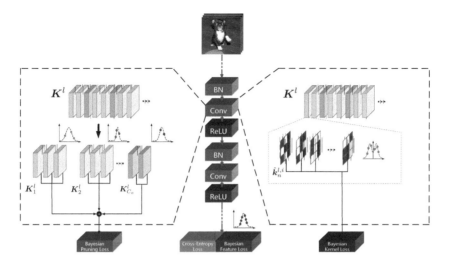

FIGURE 3.20
By considering the prior distributions of the kernels and features in the Bayesian framework, we achieve three new Bayesian losses to optimize the 1-bit CNNs. The Bayesian kernel loss improves the layerwise kernel distribution of each convolution layer, the Bayesian feature loss introduces the intraclass compactness to alleviate the disturbance induced by the quantization process, and the Bayesian pruning loss centralizes channels following the same Gaussian distribution for pruning. The Bayesian feature loss is applied only to the fully connected layer.

learning are intrinsically inherited during model quantization and pruning. The proposed losses can also comprehensively supervise the 1-bit CNN training process concerning kernel and feature distributions. Finally, a new direction on 1-bit CNN pruning is explored further to improve the compressed model's applicability in practical applications.

3.7.1 Bayesian Formulation for Compact 1-Bit CNNs

The state-of-the-art methods [128, 199, 77] learn 1-bit CNNs by involving optimization in continuous and discrete spaces. In particular, training a 1-bit CNN involves three steps: a forward pass, a backward pass, and a parameter update through gradient calculation. Binarized weights ($\hat{x}$) are only considered during the forward pass (inference) and gradient calculation. After updating the parameters, we have the total precision weights (x). As revealed in [128, 199, 77], how to connect $\hat{x}$ with x is the key to determining the performance of a quantized network. In this chapter, we propose to solve it in a probabilistic framework to learn optimal 1-bit CNNs.

3.7.2 Bayesian Learning Losses

Bayesian kernel loss: Given a network weight parameter x, its quantized code should be as close to its original (full precision) code as possible, so that the quantization error is minimized. We then define:

$$y = w^{-1} \circ \hat{x} - x, \tag{3.97}$$

where $x, \hat{x} \in \mathbf{R}^n$ are the full precision and quantized vectors, respectively, $w \in \mathbf{R}^n$ denotes the learned vector to reconstruct x, $\circ$ represents the Hadamard product, and $y \sim G(0, \nu)$

is the reconstruction error that is assumed to obey a Gaussian prior with zero mean and variance ν. Under the most probable $\boldsymbol{y}$ (corresponding to $\boldsymbol{y} = \boldsymbol{0}$ and $\boldsymbol{x} = \boldsymbol{w}^{-1} \circ \hat{\boldsymbol{x}}$, *i.e.*, the minimum reconstruction error), we maximize $p(\boldsymbol{x}|\boldsymbol{y})$ to optimize $\boldsymbol{x}$ for quantization (*e.g.*, 1-bit CNNs) as:

$$\max p(\boldsymbol{x}|\boldsymbol{y}), \tag{3.98}$$

which can be solved based on Bayesian learning that uses Bayes' theorem to determine the conditional probability of a hypothesis given limited observations. We note that the calculation of BNNs is still based on optimizing $\boldsymbol{x}$, as shown in Fig. 3.19, where the binarization is performed based on the sign function. Equation 3.98 is complicated and difficult to solve due to the unknown w^{-1} as shown in Eq. 3.97. From a Bayesian learning perspective, we resolve this problem via Maximum A posteriori (MAP):

$$\begin{aligned} \max p(\boldsymbol{x}|\boldsymbol{y}) &= \max p(\boldsymbol{y}|\boldsymbol{x})p(\boldsymbol{x}) \\ &= \min ||\hat{\boldsymbol{x}} - \boldsymbol{w} \circ \boldsymbol{x}||_2^2 - 2\nu \log(p(\boldsymbol{x})), \end{aligned} \tag{3.99}$$

where

$$p(\boldsymbol{y}|\boldsymbol{x}) \propto \exp(-\frac{1}{2\nu}||\boldsymbol{y}||_2^2) \propto \exp(-\frac{1}{2\nu}||\hat{\boldsymbol{x}} - \boldsymbol{w} \circ \boldsymbol{x}||_2^2). \tag{3.100}$$

In Eq. 3.100, we assume that all components of the quantization error $\boldsymbol{y}$ are i.i.d., thus resulting in a simplified form. As shown in Fig. 3.19, for 1-bit CNNs, $\boldsymbol{x}$ is usually quantized to two numbers with the same absolute value. We neglect the overlap between the two numbers, and thus $p(\boldsymbol{x})$ is modeled as a Gaussian mixture with two modes:

$$\begin{aligned} p(\boldsymbol{x}) &= \frac{1}{2}(2\pi)^{-\frac{N}{2}} \det(\boldsymbol{\Psi})^{-\frac{1}{2}} \left\{ \exp\left(-\frac{(\boldsymbol{x} - \boldsymbol{\mu})^T \boldsymbol{\Psi}^{-1}(\boldsymbol{x} - \boldsymbol{\mu})}{2}\right) \right. \\ &\quad + \left. \exp\left(-\frac{(\boldsymbol{x} + \boldsymbol{\mu})^T \boldsymbol{\Psi}^{-1}(\mathbf{x} + \boldsymbol{\mu})}{2}\right) \right\} \\ &\approx \frac{1}{2}(2\pi)^{-\frac{N}{2}} \det(\boldsymbol{\Psi})^{-\frac{1}{2}} \left\{ \exp\left(-\frac{(\boldsymbol{x}_+ - \boldsymbol{\mu}_+)^T \boldsymbol{\Psi}_+^{-1}(\boldsymbol{x}_+ - \boldsymbol{\mu}_+)}{2}\right) \right. \\ &\quad + \left. \exp\left(-\frac{(\boldsymbol{x}_- + \boldsymbol{\mu}_-)^T \boldsymbol{\Psi}_-^{-1}(\boldsymbol{x}_- + \boldsymbol{\mu}_-)}{2}\right) \right\}, \end{aligned} \tag{3.101}$$

where $\boldsymbol{x}$ is divided into $\boldsymbol{x}_+$ and $\boldsymbol{x}_-$ according to the signs of the elements in $\boldsymbol{x}$, and N is the dimension of $\boldsymbol{x}$. Accordingly, Eq. 3.99 can be rewritten as:

$$\begin{aligned} \min ||\hat{\boldsymbol{x}} - \boldsymbol{w} \circ \boldsymbol{x}||_2^2 &+ \nu(\boldsymbol{x}_+ - \boldsymbol{\mu}_+)^T \boldsymbol{\Psi}_+^{-1}(\boldsymbol{x}_+ - \boldsymbol{\mu}_+) \\ &+ \nu(\boldsymbol{x}_- + \boldsymbol{\mu}_-)^T \boldsymbol{\Psi}_-^{-1}(\boldsymbol{x}_- + \boldsymbol{\mu}_-) + \nu \log(\det(\boldsymbol{\Psi})), \end{aligned} \tag{3.102}$$

where $\boldsymbol{\mu}_-$ and $\boldsymbol{\mu}_+$ are solved independently. $\det(\boldsymbol{\Psi})$ is accordingly set to be the determinant of the matrix $\boldsymbol{\Psi}_-$ or $\boldsymbol{\Psi}_+$. We call Eq. 3.102 the Bayesian kernel loss.

Bayesian feature loss: We also design a Bayesian feature loss to alleviate the disturbance caused by the extreme quantization process in 1-bit CNNs. Considering the intraclass compactness, the features $\boldsymbol{f}_m$ of the m-th class supposedly follow a Gaussian distribution with the mean $\boldsymbol{c}_m$ as revealed in the center loss [245]. Similarly to the Bayesian kernel loss, we define $y_f^m = \boldsymbol{f}_m - \boldsymbol{c}_m$ and $y_f^m \sim \mathcal{N}(\boldsymbol{0}, \boldsymbol{\sigma}_m)$, and we have:

$$\min ||\boldsymbol{f}_m - \boldsymbol{c}_m||_2^2 + \sum_{n=1}^{N_f} \left[\sigma_{m,n}^{-2}(f_{m,n} - c_{m,n})^2 + \log(\sigma_{m,n}^2) \right], \tag{3.103}$$

which is called the Bayesian feature loss. In Eq. 3.103, $\sigma_{m,n}$, $f_{m,n}$, and $c_{m,n}$ are the n-th elements of $\boldsymbol{\sigma}_m$, $\boldsymbol{f}_m$, and $\boldsymbol{c}_m$, respectively. We take the latent distributions of kernel weights and features into consideration in the same framework and introduce Bayesian losses to improve the capacity of 1-bit CNNs.

3.7.3 Bayesian Pruning

After binarizing CNNs, we pruned 1-bit CNNs under the same Bayesian learning framework. Different channels might follow a similar distribution, based on which similar channels are combined for pruning. From the mathematical aspect, we achieve a Bayesian formulation of BNN pruning by directly extending our basic idea in [78], which systematically calculates compact 1-bit CNNs. We represent the kernel weights of the l-th layer $\boldsymbol{K}^l$ as a tensor $\in \mathbf{R}^{C_o^l \times C_i^l \times H^l \times W^l}$, where C_o^l and C_i^l denote the numbers of output and input channels, respectively, and H^l and W^l are the height and width of the kernels, respectively. For clarity, we define

$$\boldsymbol{K}^l = [\boldsymbol{K}_1^l, \boldsymbol{K}_2^l, ..., \boldsymbol{K}_{C_o^l}^l], \tag{3.104}$$

where $\boldsymbol{K}_i^l$, $i = 1, 2, ..., C_o^l$, is a 3-dimensional filter $\in \mathbf{R}^{C_i^l \times H^l \times W^l}$. For simplicity, l is omitted from the remainder of this section. To prune 1-bit CNNs, we assimilate similar filters into the same one based on a controlling learning process. To do this, we first divide $\boldsymbol{K}$ into different groups using the K-means algorithm and then replace the filters of each group by their average during optimization. This process assumes that $\boldsymbol{K}_i$ in the same group follows the same Gaussian distribution during training. Then the pruning problem becomes how to find the average $\overline{\boldsymbol{K}}$ to replace all $\boldsymbol{K}_i$'s, which follows the same distribution. It leads to a similar problem as in Eq. 3.99. It should be noted that the learning process with a Gaussian distribution constraint is widely considered in [82].

Accordingly, Bayesian learning is used to prune 1-bit CNNs. We denote $\boldsymbol{\epsilon}$ as the difference between a filter and its mean, *i.e.*, $\boldsymbol{\epsilon} = \boldsymbol{K} - \overline{\boldsymbol{K}}$, following a Gaussian distribution for simplicity. To calculate $\overline{\boldsymbol{K}}$, we minimize $\boldsymbol{\epsilon}$ based on MAP in our Bayesian framework, and we have

$$\overline{\boldsymbol{K}} = \arg\max_{\boldsymbol{K}} p(\boldsymbol{K}|\boldsymbol{\epsilon}) = \arg\max_{\boldsymbol{K}} p(\boldsymbol{\epsilon}|\boldsymbol{K})p(\boldsymbol{K}), \tag{3.105}$$

$$p(\boldsymbol{\epsilon}|\boldsymbol{K}) \propto \exp(-\frac{1}{2\nu}||\boldsymbol{\epsilon}||_2^2) \propto \exp(-\frac{1}{2\nu}||\boldsymbol{K} - \overline{\boldsymbol{K}}||_2^2), \tag{3.106}$$

and $p(\boldsymbol{K})$ is similar to Eq. 3.101 but with one mode. Thus, we have

$$\begin{aligned} \min ||\boldsymbol{K} - \overline{\boldsymbol{K}}||_2^2 &+ \nu(\boldsymbol{K} - \overline{\boldsymbol{K}})^T \boldsymbol{\Psi}^{-1} (\boldsymbol{K} - \overline{\boldsymbol{K}}) \\ &+ \nu \log(\det(\boldsymbol{\Psi})), \end{aligned} \tag{3.107}$$

which is called the Bayesian pruning loss. In summary, our Bayesian pruning solves the problem more generally, assuming that similar kernels follow a Gaussian distribution and will finally be represented by their centers for pruning. From this viewpoint, we can obtain a more general pruning method, which is more suitable for binary neural networks than the existing ones. Moreover, we take the latent distributions of kernel weights, features, and filters into consideration in the same framework and introduce Bayesian losses and Bayesian pruning to improve the capacity of 1-bit CNNs. Comparative experimental results on model pruning also demonstrate the superiority of our BONNs [287] over existing pruning methods.

3.7.4 BONNs

We employ the three Bayesian losses to optimize 1-bit CNNs, which form our Bayesian Optimized 1-bit CNNs (BONNs). To do this, we reformulate the first two Bayesian losses for 1-bit CNNs as

$$
\begin{aligned}
L_B = \frac{\lambda}{2} \sum_{l=1}^{L} \sum_{i=1}^{C_o^l} \sum_{n=1}^{C_i^l} \{ & \|\hat{\boldsymbol{k}}_n^{l,i} - \boldsymbol{w}^l \circ \boldsymbol{k}_n^{l,i}\|_2^2 \\
& + \nu(\boldsymbol{k}_{n+}^{l,i} - \boldsymbol{\mu}_{i+}^l)^T (\boldsymbol{\Psi}_{i+}^l)^{-1} (\boldsymbol{k}_{n+}^{l,i} - \boldsymbol{\mu}_{i+}^l) \\
& + \nu(\boldsymbol{k}_{n-}^{l,i} + \boldsymbol{\mu}_{i-}^l)^T (\boldsymbol{\Psi}_{i-}^l)^{-1} (\boldsymbol{k}_{n-}^{l,i} + \boldsymbol{\mu}_{i-}^l) \\
& + \nu \log(\det(\boldsymbol{\Psi}^l))\} + \frac{\theta}{2} \sum_{m=1}^{M} \{ \|\boldsymbol{f}_m - \boldsymbol{c}_m\|_2^2 \\
& + \sum_{n=1}^{N_f} \left[\sigma_{m,n}^{-2} (f_{m,n} - c_{m,n})^2 + \log(\sigma_{m,n}^2) \right] \},
\end{aligned}
\tag{3.108}
$$

where $\boldsymbol{k}_n^{l,i}, l \in \{1, ..., L\}, i \in \{1, ..., C_o^l\}, n \in \{1, ..., C_i^l\}$, is the vectorization of the i-th kernel matrix at the l-th convolutional layer, $\boldsymbol{w}^l$ is a vector used to modulate $\boldsymbol{k}_n^{l,i}$, and $\boldsymbol{\mu}_i^l$ and $\boldsymbol{\Psi}_i^l$ are the mean and covariance of the i-th kernel vector at the l-th layer, respectively. And we term L_B the Bayesian optimization loss. Furthermore, we assume that the parameters in the same kernel are independent. Thus $\boldsymbol{\Psi}_i^l$ becomes a diagonal matrix with the identical value $(\sigma_i^l)^2$, where $(\sigma_i^l)^2$ is the variance of the i-th kernel of the l-th layer. In this case, the calculation of the inverse of $\boldsymbol{\Psi}_i^l$ is sped up, and all the elements of $\boldsymbol{\mu}_i^l$ are identical and equal to μ_i^l. Note that in our implementation, all elements of $\boldsymbol{w}^l$ are replaced by their average during the forward process. Accordingly, only a scalar instead of a matrix is involved in the inference, and thus the computation is significantly accelerated.

After training 1-bit CNNs, Bayesian pruning loss L_P is then used for the optimization of feature channels, which can be written as:

$$
\begin{aligned}
L_P = \sum_{l=1}^{L} \sum_{j=1}^{J_l} \sum_{i=1}^{I_j} \{ & \|\boldsymbol{K}_{i,j}^l - \overline{\boldsymbol{K}}_j^l\|_2^2 \\
& + \nu(\boldsymbol{K}_{i,j}^l - \overline{\boldsymbol{K}}_j^l)^T (\boldsymbol{\Psi}_j^l)^{-1} (\boldsymbol{K}_{i,j}^l - \overline{\boldsymbol{K}}_j^l) + \nu \log(\det(\boldsymbol{\Psi}_j^l))\},
\end{aligned}
\tag{3.109}
$$

where J_l is the number of Gaussian clusters (groups) of the l-th layer, and $\boldsymbol{K}_{i,j}^l$, $i = 1, 2, ..., I_j$, are those $\boldsymbol{K}_i^l$'s that belong to the j-th group. In our implementation, we define $J_l = \text{int}(C_o^l \times \epsilon)$, where ϵ is a predefined pruning rate. In this chapter, we use one ϵ for all layers. Note that when the j-th Gaussian just has one sample $\boldsymbol{K}_{i,j}^l, \overline{\boldsymbol{K}}_j^l = \boldsymbol{K}_{i,j}^l$ and $\boldsymbol{\Psi}_j$ is a unit matrix.

In BONNs, the cross-entropy loss L_S, the Bayesian optimization loss L_B, and the Bayesian pruning loss L_P are aggregated together to build the total loss as:

$$
L = L_S + L_B + \zeta L_P,
\tag{3.110}
$$

where ζ is 0 in binarization training and becomes 1 in pruning. The loss of Bayesian kernels constrains the distribution of the convolution kernels to a symmetric Gaussian mixture with two modes. It simultaneously minimizes the quantization error through the $\|\hat{\boldsymbol{k}}_n^{l,i} - \boldsymbol{w}^l \circ \boldsymbol{k}_n^{l,i}\|_2^2$ term. Meanwhile, the Bayesian feature loss modifies the distribution of the features to reduce intraclass variation for better classification. The Bayesian pruning loss converges kernels similar to their means and thus compresses the 1-bit CNNs further.

3.7.5   Forward Propagation

In forward propagation, the binarized kernels and activations accelerate the convolution computation. The reconstruction vector is essential for 1-bit CNNs as described in Eq. 3.97,

---

Algorithm 5 Optimizing 1-bit CNNs with Bayesian Learning

Input:

    The full-precision kernels $\boldsymbol{k}$, the reconstruction vector $\boldsymbol{w}$, the learning rate η, regularization parameters λ, θ and variance ν, and the training dataset.

Output:

    The BONN with the updated $\boldsymbol{k}, \boldsymbol{w}, \boldsymbol{\mu}, \boldsymbol{\sigma}, \boldsymbol{c}_m, \boldsymbol{\sigma}_m$.

  1: Initialize $\boldsymbol{k}$ and $\boldsymbol{w}$ randomly, and then estimate $\boldsymbol{\mu}, \boldsymbol{\sigma}$ based on the average and variance of $\boldsymbol{k}$, respectively;

  2: **repeat**

  3:     // Forward propagation

  4:     **for** $l = 1$ to L **do**

  5:         $\hat{\boldsymbol{k}}_i^l = \boldsymbol{w}^l \circ \text{sign}(\boldsymbol{k}_i^l), \forall i$; // Each element of $\boldsymbol{w}^l$ is replaced by the average of all elements $\overline{w}^l$.

  6:         Perform activation binarization; // Using the sign function

  7:         Perform 2D convolution with $\hat{\boldsymbol{k}}_i^l, \forall i$;

  8:     **end for**

  9:     // Backward propagation

 10:     Compute $\delta_{\hat{\boldsymbol{k}}_i^l} = \frac{\partial L_S}{\partial \hat{\boldsymbol{k}}_i^l}, \forall l, i$;

 11:     **for** $l = L$ to 1 **do**

 12:         Calculate $\delta_{\boldsymbol{k}_i^l}, \delta_{\boldsymbol{w}^l}, \delta_{\mu_i^l}, \delta_{\sigma_i^l}$; // using Eqs. 3.112~3.119

 13:         Update parameters $\boldsymbol{k}_i^l, \boldsymbol{w}^l, \mu_i^l, \sigma_i^l$ using SGD;

 14:     **end for**

 15:     Update $\boldsymbol{c}_m, \boldsymbol{\sigma}_m$;

 16: **until** convergence

---

where $\boldsymbol{w}$ denotes a learned vector to reconstruct the full precision vector and is shared in a layer. As mentioned in Section 3.2, during forward propagation, $\boldsymbol{w}^l$ becomes a scalar $\overline{w}^l$ in each layer, where $\overline{w}^l$ is the mean of $\boldsymbol{w}^l$ and is calculated online. The convolution process is represented as

$$\boldsymbol{O}^{l+1} = ((\overline{w}^l)^{-1}\hat{\boldsymbol{K}}^l) * \hat{\boldsymbol{O}}^l = (\overline{w}^l)^{-1}(\hat{\boldsymbol{K}}^l * \hat{\boldsymbol{O}}^l), \tag{3.111}$$

where $\hat{\boldsymbol{O}}^l$ denotes the binarized feature map of the l-th layer, and O^{l+1} is the feature map of the $(l+1)$-th layer. As in Eq. 3.111 depicts, the actual convolution is still binary, and O^{l+1} is obtained by simply multiplying $(\overline{w}^l)^{-1}$ and the binarization convolution. For each layer, only one floating-point multiplication is added, which is negligible for BONNs.

In addition, we consider the Gaussian distribution in the forward process of Bayesian pruning, which updates every filter in one group based on its mean. Specifically, we replace each filter $\boldsymbol{K}_{i,j}^l = (1 - \gamma)\boldsymbol{K}_{i,j}^l + \gamma\overline{\boldsymbol{K}}_j^l$ during pruning.

3.7.6   Asynchronous Backward Propagation

To minimize Eq. 3.108, we update $\boldsymbol{k}_n^{l,i}, \boldsymbol{w}^l, \mu_i^l, \sigma_i^l, \boldsymbol{c}_m$, and $\boldsymbol{\sigma}_m$ using stochastic gradient descent (SGD) in an asynchronous manner, which updates $\boldsymbol{w}$ instead of $\overline{w}$ as elaborated below.

Updating $\boldsymbol{k}_n^{l,i}$: We define $\delta_{\boldsymbol{k}_n^{l,i}}$ as the gradient of the full-precision kernel $\boldsymbol{k}_n^{l,i}$, and we have:

$$\delta_{\boldsymbol{k}_n^{l,i}} = \frac{\partial L}{\partial \boldsymbol{k}_n^{l,i}} = \frac{\partial L_S}{\partial \boldsymbol{k}_n^{l,i}} + \frac{\partial L_B}{\partial \boldsymbol{k}_n^{l,i}}. \tag{3.112}$$

For each term in Eq. 3.112, we have:

$$
\begin{aligned}
\frac{\partial L_S}{\partial \boldsymbol{k}_n^{l,i}} &= \frac{\partial L_S}{\partial \hat{\boldsymbol{k}}_n^{l,i}} \frac{\partial \hat{\boldsymbol{k}}_n^{l,i}}{\partial (\boldsymbol{w}^l \circ \boldsymbol{k}_n^{l,i})} \frac{\partial (\boldsymbol{w}^l \circ \boldsymbol{k}_n^{l,i})}{\partial \boldsymbol{k}_n^{l,i}} \\
&= \frac{\partial L_S}{\partial \hat{\boldsymbol{k}}_n^{l,i}} \circ \mathbb{1}_{-1 \le \boldsymbol{w}^l \circ \boldsymbol{k}_n^{l,i} \le 1} \circ \boldsymbol{w}^l,
\end{aligned}
\tag{3.113}
$$

$$
\begin{aligned}
\frac{\partial L_B}{\partial \boldsymbol{k}_n^{l,i}} &= \lambda \{ \boldsymbol{w}^l \circ \left[\boldsymbol{w}^l \circ \boldsymbol{k}_n^{l,i} - \hat{\boldsymbol{k}}_n^{l,i} \right] \\
&\quad + \nu [(\boldsymbol{\sigma}_i^l)^{-2} \circ (\boldsymbol{k}_{i+}^l - \boldsymbol{\mu}_{i+}^l) \\
&\quad + (\boldsymbol{\sigma}_i^l)^{-2} \circ (\boldsymbol{k}_{i-}^l + \boldsymbol{\mu}_{i-}^l)],
\end{aligned}
\tag{3.114}
$$

where $\mathbb{1}$ is the indicator function that is widely used to estimate the gradient of nondifferentiable parameters [199], and $(\boldsymbol{\sigma}_i^l)^{-2}$ is a vector whose elements are all equal to $(\sigma_i^l)^{-2}$.
Updating $\boldsymbol{w}^l$: Unlike the forward process, $\boldsymbol{w}$ is used in backpropagation to calculate the gradients. This process is similar to the way to calculate $\hat{\boldsymbol{x}}$ from $\boldsymbol{x}$ asynchronously. Specifically, $\delta_{\boldsymbol{w}^l}$ is composed of the following two parts:

$$
\delta_{\boldsymbol{w}^l} = \frac{\partial L}{\partial \boldsymbol{w}^l} = \frac{\partial L_S}{\partial \boldsymbol{w}^l} + \frac{\partial L_B}{\partial \boldsymbol{w}^l}.
\tag{3.115}
$$

For each term in Eq. 3.115, we have:

$$
\begin{aligned}
\frac{\partial L_S}{\partial \boldsymbol{w}^l} &= \sum_{i=1}^{I_l} \sum_{n=1}^{N_{I_l}} \frac{\partial L_S}{\partial \hat{\boldsymbol{k}}_n^{l,i}} \frac{\partial \hat{\boldsymbol{k}}_n^{l,i}}{\partial (\boldsymbol{w}^l \circ \boldsymbol{k}_n^{l,i})} \frac{\partial (\boldsymbol{w}^l \circ \boldsymbol{k}_n^{l,i})}{\partial \boldsymbol{w}^l} \\
&= \sum_{i=1}^{I_l} \sum_{n=1}^{N_{I_L}} \frac{\partial L_S}{\partial \hat{\boldsymbol{k}}_n^{l,i}} \circ \mathbb{1}_{-1 \le \boldsymbol{w}^l \circ \boldsymbol{k}_n^{l,i} \le 1} \circ \boldsymbol{k}_n^{l,i},
\end{aligned}
\tag{3.116}
$$

$$
\frac{\partial L_B}{\partial \boldsymbol{w}^l} = \lambda \sum_{i=1}^{I_l} \sum_{n=1}^{N_{I_l}} (\boldsymbol{w}^l \circ \boldsymbol{k}_n^{l,i} - \hat{\boldsymbol{k}}_n^{l,i}) \circ \boldsymbol{k}_n^{l,i}.
\tag{3.117}
$$

Updating μ_i^l and σ_i^l: Note that we use the same μ_i^l and σ_i^l for each kernel (see Section 3.2). So, the gradients here are scalars. The gradients $\delta_{\mu_i^l}$ and $\delta_{\sigma_i^l}$ are calculated as:

$$
\begin{aligned}
\delta_{\mu_i^l} &= \frac{\partial L}{\partial \mu_i^l} = \frac{\partial L_B}{\partial \mu_i^l} \\
&= \frac{\lambda \nu}{C_i^l \times H^l \times W^l} \sum_{n=1}^{C_i^l} \sum_{p=1}^{H^l \times W^l} \begin{cases} (\sigma_i^l)^{-2} (\mu_i^l - k_{n,p}^{l,i}), & k_{n,p}^{l,i} \ge 0, \\ (\sigma_i^l)^{-2} (\mu_i^l + k_{n,p}^{l,i}), & k_{n,p}^{l,i} < 0, \end{cases}
\end{aligned}
\tag{3.118}
$$

$$
\begin{aligned}
\delta_{\sigma_i^l} &= \frac{\partial L}{\partial \sigma_i^l} = \frac{\partial L_B}{\partial \sigma_i^l} \\
&= \frac{\lambda \nu}{C_i^l \times H^l \times W^l} \sum_{n=1}^{C_i^l} \sum_{p=1}^{H^l \times W^l} \begin{cases} -(\sigma_i^l)^{-3}(k_{n,p}^{l,i} - \mu_i^l)^2 + (\sigma_i^l)^{-1}, & k_{n,p}^{l,i} \ge 0, \\ -(\sigma_i^l)^{-3}(k_{n,p}^{l,i} + \mu_i^l)^2 + (\sigma_i^l)^{-1}, & k_{n,p}^{l,i} < 0, \end{cases}
\end{aligned}
\tag{3.119}
$$

where $k_{n,p}^{l,i}, p \in \{1, ..., H^l \times W^l\}$, denotes the p-th element of $\boldsymbol{k}_n^{l,i}$. In the fine-tuning process, we update $\boldsymbol{c}_m$ using the same strategy as center loss [245]. The update of $\sigma_{m,n}$ based on L_B is straightforward and is not elaborated here for brevity.

Algorithm 6 Pruning 1-bit CNNs with Bayesian learning

Input:

The pre-trained 1-bit CNN model with parameters $\boldsymbol{K}$, the reconstruction vector $\boldsymbol{w}$, the learning rate η, regularization parameters λ, θ, variance ν and convergence rate γ and the training dataset.

Output:

The pruned BONN with updated $\boldsymbol{K}$, $\boldsymbol{w}$, $\boldsymbol{\mu}$, $\boldsymbol{\sigma}$, $\boldsymbol{c}_m$, $\boldsymbol{\sigma}_m$.

1: **repeat**
2:    // Forward propagation
3:    **for** $l = 1$ to L **do**
4:       $\boldsymbol{K}_{i,j}^l = (1 - \gamma)\boldsymbol{K}_{i,j}^l + \gamma\overline{\boldsymbol{K}}_j^l$;
5:       $\hat{\boldsymbol{k}}_i^l = \boldsymbol{w}^l \circ \mathrm{sign}(\boldsymbol{k}_i^l), \forall i$; // Each element of $\boldsymbol{w}^l$ is replaced by the average of all elements $\overline{w}^l$.

6:       Perform activation binarization; // Using the sign function
7:       Perform 2D convolution with $\hat{\boldsymbol{k}}_i^l, \forall i$;
8:    **end for**
9:    // Backward propagation
10:   Compute $\delta_{\hat{\boldsymbol{k}}_i^l} = \frac{\partial L_S}{\partial \hat{\boldsymbol{k}}_i^l}, \forall l, i$;
11:   **for** $l = L$ to 1 **do**
12:      Calculate $\delta_{\boldsymbol{k}_i^l}, \delta_{\boldsymbol{w}^l}, \delta_{\mu_i^l}, \delta_{\sigma_i^l}$; // using Eqs. 3.115~3.120
13:      Update parameters $\boldsymbol{k}_i^l, \boldsymbol{w}^l, \mu_i^l, \sigma_i^l$ using SGD;
14:   **end for**
15:   Update $\boldsymbol{c}_m, \boldsymbol{\sigma}_m$;
16: **until** Filters in the same group are similar enough

Updating $\boldsymbol{K}_{i,j}^l$: In pruning, we aim to converge the filters to their mean gradually. So we replace each filter $\boldsymbol{K}_{i,j}^l$ with its corresponding mean $\overline{\boldsymbol{K}}_{i,j}^l$. The gradient of the mean is represented as follows:

$$
\begin{aligned}
\frac{\partial L}{\partial \boldsymbol{K}_{i,j}^l} &= \frac{\partial L_S}{\partial \boldsymbol{K}_{i,j}^l} + \frac{\partial L_B}{\partial \boldsymbol{K}_{i,j}^l} + \frac{\partial L_P}{\partial \boldsymbol{K}_{i,j}^l} \\
&= \frac{\partial L_S}{\partial \overline{\boldsymbol{K}}_j^l}\frac{\partial \overline{\boldsymbol{K}}_j^l}{\partial \boldsymbol{K}_{i,j}^l} + \frac{\partial L_B}{\partial \overline{\boldsymbol{K}}_j^l}\frac{\partial \overline{\boldsymbol{K}}_j^l}{\partial \boldsymbol{K}_{i,j}^l} + \frac{\partial L_P}{\partial \boldsymbol{K}_{i,j}^l} \\
&= \frac{1}{I_j}\Big(\frac{\partial L_S}{\partial \overline{\boldsymbol{K}}_j^l} + \frac{\partial L_B}{\partial \overline{\boldsymbol{K}}_j^l}\Big) + 2(\boldsymbol{K}_{i,j}^l - \overline{\boldsymbol{K}}_j) \\
&\quad + 2\nu(\boldsymbol{\Psi}_j^l)^{-1}(\boldsymbol{K}_{i,j}^l - \overline{\boldsymbol{K}}_j),
\end{aligned}
\tag{3.120}
$$

where $\overline{\boldsymbol{K}}_j^l = \frac{1}{I_j}\sum_{i=1}^{I_j} \boldsymbol{K}_{i,j}^l$ that is used to update the filters in a group by mean $\overline{\boldsymbol{K}}_j^l$. We leave the first filter in each group to prune redundant filters and remove the others. However, such an operation changes the distribution of the input channel of the batch norm layer, resulting in a dimension mismatch for the next convolutional layer. To solve the problem, we keep the size of the batch norm layer, whose values correspond to the removed filters, set to zero. In this way, the removed information is retained to the greatest extent. In summary, we show that the proposed method is trainable from end to end. The learning procedure is detailed in Algorithms 5 and 6.

TABLE 3.4

With different λ and θ, we evaluate the accuracies of BONNs based on WRN-22 and WRN-40 on CIFAR-10/100. When varying λ, the Bayesian feature loss is not used ($\theta = 0$). However, when varying θ, we choose the optimal loss weight ($\lambda = 1e - 4$) for the Bayesian kernel loss.

Hyper-param.		WRN-22 (BONN)		WRN-40 (BONN)	
		CIFAR-10	CIFAR-100	CIFAR-10	CIFAR-100
	$1e - 3$	85.82	59.32	85.79	58.84
λ	$1e - 4$	**86.23**	**59.77**	**87.12**	**60.32**
	$1e - 5$	85.74	57.73	86.22	59.93
	0	84.97	55.38	84.61	56.03
	$1e - 2$	**87.34**	60.31	87.23	60.83
θ	$1e - 3$	86.49	60.37	87.18	**61.25**
	$1e - 4$	86.27	**60.91**	**87.41**	61.03
	0	86.23	59.77	87.12	60.32

3.7.7   Ablation Study

Hyper-Parameter Selection In this section, we evaluate the effects of hyperparameters on BONN performance, including λ and θ. The Bayesian kernel loss and the Bayesian feature loss are balanced by λ and θ, respectively, to adjust the distributions of kernels and features in a better form. WRN-22 and WRN-40 are used. The implementation details are given below.

As shown in Table 3.4, we first vary λ and set θ to zero to validate the influence of Bayesian kernel loss on kernel distribution. The utilization of Bayesian kernel loss effectively improves the accuracy on CIFAR-10. However, the accuracy does not increase with λ, indicating we need not a larger λ but a proper λ to reasonably balance the relationship between the cross-entropy and the Bayesian kernel loss. For example, when λ is set to $1e - 4$, we obtain an optimal balance and the best classification accuracy.

The hyperparameter θ dominates the intraclass variations of the features, and the effect of the Bayesian feature loss on the features is also investigated by changing θ. The results illustrate that the classification accuracy varies similarly to λ, verifying that Bayesian feature loss can lead to a better classification accuracy when a proper θ is chosen.

We also evaluate the convergence performance of our method over its comparative counterparts in terms of ResNet-18 on ImageNet ILSVRC12. As plotted in Fig. 3.22, the XNOR-Net training curve oscillates vigorously, which is suspected to be triggered by a suboptimal learning process. On the contrary, our BONN achieves better training and test accuracy.

Effectiveness of Bayesian Binarization on ImageNet ILSVRC12 We experimented by examining how each loss affects performance better to understand Bayesian losses on the large-scale ImageNet ILSVRC12 dataset. Based on the experiments described earlier, if used, we set λ to $1e - 4$ and θ to $1e - 3$. As shown in Table 3.5, both the Bayesian kernel loss and Bayesian feature loss can independently improve the accuracy on ImageNet. When applied together, the Top-1 accuracy reaches the highest value of 59.3%. As shown in Fig. 3.21, we visualize the feature maps across the ResNet-18 model on the ImageNet dataset. They indicate that our method can extract essential features for accurate classification.

TABLE 3.5

Effect of Bayesian losses on the ImageNet data set. The backbone is ResNet-18.

Bayesian kernel loss	✗	✔	✗	✔
Bayesian feature loss	✗	✗	✔	✔
Accuracy Top-1	56.3	58.3	58.4	**59.3**
Top-5	79.8	80.8	80.8	**81.6**

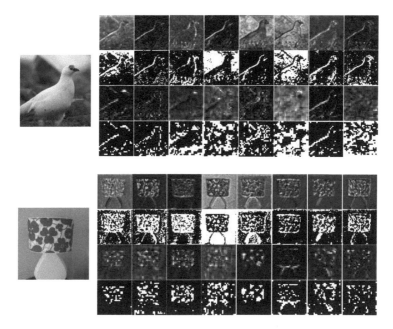

FIGURE 3.21

The images on the left are the input images chosen from the ImageNet ILSVRC12 dataset. Right images are feature maps and binary feature maps from different layers of BONNs. The first and third rows are feature maps for each group, while the second and fourth rows are corresponding binary feature maps. Although binarization of the feature map causes information loss, BONNs could extract essential features for accurate classification.

Weight Distribution Figure 3.23 further illustrates the distribution of the kernel weights, with λ fixed to $1e-4$. During the training process, the distribution gradually approaches the two-mode GMM, as assumed previously, confirming the effectiveness of the Bayesian kernel loss in a more intuitive way. We also compare the kernel weight distribution between XNOR-Net and BONN. As shown in Fig. 3.24, the kernel weights learned in XNOR-Net are tightly distributed around the threshold value, but those in BONN are regularized in a

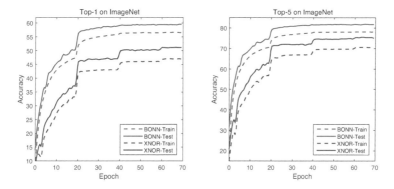

FIGURE 3.22

Training and test accuracies on ImageNet when $\lambda = 1e-4$ shows the superiority of the proposed BONN over XNOR-Net. The backbone of the two networks is ResNet-18.

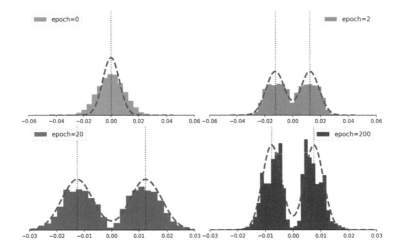

FIGURE 3.23

We demonstrate the kernel weight distribution of the first binarized convolution layer of BONNs. Before training, we initialize the kernels as a single-mode Gaussian distribution. From the 2-th epoch to the 200-th epoch, with λ fixed to $1e-4$, the distribution of the kernel weights becomes more and more compact with two modes, which confirms that the Bayesian kernel loss can regularize the kernels into a promising distribution for binarization.

two-mode GMM style. Figure 3.25 shows the evolution of the binarized values during the training process of XNOR-Net and BONN. The two different patterns indicate that the binarized values learned in BONN are more diverse.

Effectiveness of Bayesian Feature Loss on Real-Valued Models: We apply our Bayesian feature loss on real-value models, including ResNet-18 and ResNet-50 [84]. We retrain these two backbones with our Bayesian feature loss for 70 epochs. We set the hyperparameter θ to $1e-3$. The SGD optimizer has an initial learning rate set to 0.1. We use

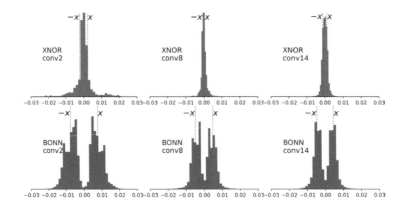

FIGURE 3.24

The weight distributions of XNOR and BONN are based on WRN-22 (2nd, 8th, and 14th convolutional layers) after 200 epochs. The weight distribution difference between XNOR and BONN indicates that the kernels are regularized across the convolutional layers with the proposed Bayesian kernel loss.

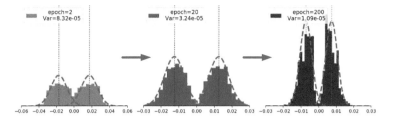

FIGURE 3.25
Evolution of the binarized values, $|x|$s, during the XNOR and BONN training process. They are both based on WRN-22 (2nd, 3rd, 8th, and 14th convolutional layers), and the curves do not share the same y-axis. The binarized values of XNOR-Net tend to converge to small and similar values, but these of BONN are learned diversely.

a learning rate schedule that decreases to 10% every 30 epochs. As shown in Table 3.6, our Bayesian feature loss can further boost the performance of models with real values by a clear margin. Specifically, our method promotes the performance of ResNet-18 and ResNet-50 by 0.6% and 0.4% Top-1 accuracies, respectively.

3.8 RBONN: Recurrent Bilinear Optimization for a Binary Neural Network

We first briefly introduce the bilinear models in deep learning. Under certain circumstances, bilinear models can be used in CNNs. An important application, network pruning, is among the hottest topics in the deep learning community [142, 162]. Vital feature maps and related channels are pruned using bilinear models [162]. Iterative methods, *e.g.*, the Fast Iterative Shrinkage-Thresholding Algorithm (FISTA) [141] and the Accelerated Proximal Gradient (APG) [97] can be used to prune bilinear-based networks. Many deep learning applications, such as fine-grained categorization [146, 133], visual question answering (VQA) [278], and person re-identification [214], are promoted by embedding bilinear models into CNNs, which model pairwise feature interactions and fuse multiple features with attention.

Previous methods [77, 148] compute scaling factors by approximating the weight filter with real value $\mathbf{w}$ such that $\mathbf{w} \approx \alpha \circ \mathbf{b^w}$, where $\alpha \in \mathbb{R}_+$ is the scaling factor (vector) and $\mathbf{b^w} = \text{sign}(\mathbf{w})$ to enhance the representation capability of BNNs. In essence, the approximation

TABLE 3.6
Effect of Bayesian feature loss on the ImageNet data set. The core is ResNet-18 and ResNet-50 with real value.

Model		ResNet-18		ResNet-50	
Bayesian feature loss		✗	✓	✗	✓
Accuracy	Top-1	69.3	**69.9**	76.6	**77.0**
	Top-5	89.2	**89.8**	92.4	**92.7**

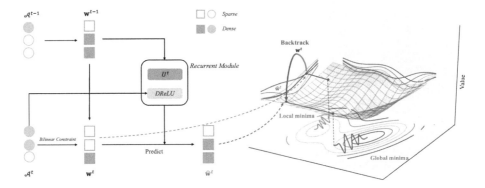

FIGURE 3.26
An illustration of the RBONN framework. Conventional gradient-based algorithms assume that hidden variables in bilinear models are independent, which causes an insufficient training of $\mathbf{w}$ due to neglecting the relationship with $\mathcal{A}$ as shown in the loss surface (right part). Our RBONN can help $\mathbf{w}$ escape from local minima and achieve a better solution.

can be considered a bilinear optimization problem with the objective function as

$$\arg\min_{\mathbf{w},\alpha} G(\mathbf{w},\alpha) = \|\mathbf{w} - \alpha \circ \mathbf{b}^{\mathbf{w}}\|_2^2 + R(\mathbf{w}),$$

or

$$\arg\min_{\mathbf{w},\mathcal{A}} G(\mathbf{w},\mathcal{A}) = \|\mathbf{b}^{\mathbf{w}} - \mathcal{A}\mathbf{w}\|_2^2 + R(\mathbf{w}), \qquad (3.121)$$

where $\mathcal{A} = diag(\frac{1}{\alpha_1}, \cdots, \frac{1}{\alpha_N})$, N is the number of elements in α. $\circ$ denotes the channel-wise multiplication, and $R(\cdot)$ represents regularization, typically the norm ℓ_1 or ℓ_2. $G(\mathbf{w},\mathcal{A})$ includes a bilinear form of $\mathcal{A}\mathbf{w}$ widely used in the field of computer vision [52, 162, 97]. Note that the bilinear function is $\mathcal{A}\mathbf{w}$ rather than $G(\mathbf{w},\mathcal{A})$ in Equation 6.34. Eq. 6.34 is rational for BNNs with $\mathcal{A}$ and $\mathbf{w}$ as bilinear coupled variables, since $\mathbf{w}$ is the variable and $\mathbf{b}^{\mathbf{w}}$ is just the sign of $\mathbf{w}$.

We introduce a recurrent bilinear optimization for binary neural networks (RBONNs) [259] by learning the coupled scaling factor and real-valued weight end-to-end. More specifically, recurrent optimization can efficiently backtrack weights, which will be trained more sufficiently than conventional methods. To this end, a Density-ReLU (DReLU) is introduced to activate the optimization process based on the density of the variable $\mathcal{A}$. In this way, we achieve a controlled learning process with a backtracking mechanism by considering the interaction of variables, thus avoiding the local minima and reaching the performance limit of BNNs, as shown in Fig. 3.26.

However, such bilinear constraints will lead to an asynchronous convergence problem and directly affect the learning process of $\mathcal{A}$ and $\mathbf{w}$. We can know that the variable with a slower convergence speed (usually $\mathbf{w}$) is **not as sufficiently** trained as another faster one. Moreover, BNNs are based on nonconvex optimization and will suffer more from the local minima problem due to such an asynchronous convergence. A powerful example is that $\mathbf{w}$ will tendentiously fall into the local optimum with low magnitude when the magnitude of $\mathcal{A}$ is much larger than 0 (due to $\mathbf{b}^{\mathbf{w}} \in \{-1, +1\}$). On the contrary, $\mathbf{w}$ will have a large magnitude and thus slowly converge when elements of $\mathcal{A}$ are close to 0.

3.8.1   Bilinear Model of BNNs

We formulate the optimization of BNNs as follows.

$$\underset{\mathbf{w},\mathcal{A}}{\arg\min} L_S(\mathbf{w},\mathcal{A}) + \lambda G(\mathbf{w},\mathcal{A}), \tag{3.122}$$

where λ is the hyper-parameter. G contains the bilinear part as mentioned in Eq. 6.34. $\mathbf{w}$ and $\mathcal{A}$ formulate a pair of coupled variables. Thus, the conventional gradient descent method can be used to solve the bilinear optimization problem as

$$\mathcal{A}^{t+1} = |\mathcal{A}^t - \eta_1 \frac{\partial L}{\partial \mathcal{A}^t}|, \tag{3.123}$$

$$\begin{aligned}
(\frac{\partial L}{\partial \mathcal{A}^t})^T &= (\frac{\partial L_S}{\partial \mathcal{A}^t})^T + \lambda(\frac{\partial G}{\partial \mathcal{A}^t})^T, \\
&= (\frac{\partial L_S}{\partial \mathbf{a}_{out}^t} \frac{\partial \mathbf{a}_{out}^t}{\partial \mathcal{A}^t})^T + \lambda \mathbf{w}^t (\mathcal{A}^t \mathbf{w}^t - \mathbf{b}^{\mathbf{w}^t})^T, \\
&= (\frac{\partial L_S}{\partial \mathbf{a}_{out}^t})^T (\mathbf{b}^{\mathbf{a}_{in}^t} \odot \mathbf{b}^{\mathbf{w}^t})(\mathcal{A}^t)^{-2} + \lambda \mathbf{w}^t \hat{G}(\mathbf{w}^t, \mathcal{A}^t),
\end{aligned} \tag{3.124}$$

where η_1 is the learning rate, $\hat{G}(\mathbf{w}^t, \mathcal{A}^t) = (\mathcal{A}^t \mathbf{w}^t - \mathbf{b}^{\mathbf{w}^t})^T$. The conventional gradient descent algorithm for bilinear models iteratively optimizes one variable while keeping the other fixed. This is a suboptimal solution due to ignoring the relationship between the two hidden variables in optimization. For example, when $\mathbf{w}$ approaches zero due to the sparsity regularization term $R(\mathbf{w})$, $\mathcal{A}$ will have a larger magnitude due to G (Eq. 6.34). Consequently, both the first and second values of Eq. 6.70 will be dramatically suppressed, causing the gradient vanishing problem for $\mathcal{A}$. Contrarily, if $\mathcal{A}$ changes little during optimization, $\mathbf{w}$ will also suffer from the vanished gradient problem due to the supervision of G, causing a local minimum. Due to the coupling relationship of $\mathbf{w}$ and $\mathcal{A}$, the gradient calculation for $\mathbf{w}$ is challenging.

3.8.2   Recurrent Bilinear Optimization

We solve the problem in Eq. 6.34 from a new perspective that $\mathbf{w}$ and $\mathcal{A}$ are coupled. We aim to prevent $\mathcal{A}$ from becoming denser and $\mathbf{w}$ from becoming sparser, as analyzed above. Firstly, based on the chain rule and its notations in [187], we have the scalar form of the update rule for $\widehat{\mathbf{w}}_{i,j}$ as

$$\begin{aligned}
\widehat{\mathbf{w}}_{i,j}^{t+1} &= \mathbf{w}_{i,j}^t - \eta_2 \frac{\partial L_S}{\partial \mathbf{w}_{i,j}^t} - \eta_2 \lambda (\frac{\partial G}{\partial \mathbf{w}_{i,j}^t} + Tr((\frac{\partial G}{\partial \mathcal{A}^t})^T \frac{\partial \mathcal{A}^t}{\partial \mathbf{w}_{i,j}^t})), \\
&= \mathbf{w}_{i,j}^{t+1} - \eta_2 \lambda Tr(\mathbf{w}^t \hat{G}(\mathbf{w}^t, \mathcal{A}^t) \frac{\partial \mathcal{A}^t}{\partial \mathbf{w}_{i,j}^t}),
\end{aligned} \tag{3.125}$$

which is based on $\mathbf{w}_{i,j}^{t+1} = \mathbf{w}_{i,j}^t - \eta_2 \frac{\partial L}{\partial \mathbf{w}_{i,j}^t}$. $\hat{\mathbf{w}}^{t+1}$ denotes $\mathbf{w}$ in the $t+1$-th iteration when considering the coupling of $\mathbf{w}$ and $\mathcal{A}$. When computing the gradient of the coupled variable $\mathbf{w}$, the gradient of its coupled variable $\mathcal{A}$ should also be considered using the chain rule. Vanilla $\mathbf{w}^{t+1}$ denotes the computed $\mathbf{w}$ at $t+1$-th iteration without considering the coupling relationship. Here, we denote $I = C_{out}$ and $J = C_{in} \times K \times K$ for simplicity. With writing $\mathbf{w}$ in a row vector $[\mathbf{w}_1, \cdots, \mathbf{w}_I]^T$ and writing $\hat{G}$ in a column vector $[\hat{g}_1, \cdots, \hat{g}_I]$ and using $i = 1, \cdots, I$ and $j = 1, \cdots, J$, we can see that $\mathcal{A}_{i,i}$ and $\mathbf{w}_{nj}$ are independent when $\forall n \neq j$.

Omitting superscript $\cdot^t$, we have the i-th component of $\frac{\partial \mathcal{A}}{\partial \mathbf{w}}$ as

$$
\left(\frac{\partial \mathcal{A}}{\partial \mathbf{w}}\right)_i =
\begin{bmatrix}
0 & \dots & \cdot & \dots & 0 \\
\cdot & & \cdot & & \cdot \\
\frac{\partial \mathcal{A}_{i,i}}{\partial \mathrm{w}_{i,1}} & \dots & \frac{\partial \mathcal{A}_{i,i}}{\partial \mathrm{w}_{i,j}} & \dots & \frac{\partial \mathcal{A}_{i,i}}{\partial \mathrm{w}_{i,J}} \\
\cdot & & \cdot & & \cdot \\
0 & \dots & \cdot & \dots & 0
\end{bmatrix},
\tag{3.126}
$$

we can derive

$$
\mathbf{w}\hat{G}(\mathbf{w}, \mathcal{A}) =
\begin{bmatrix}
\mathbf{w}_1 \hat{g}_1 & \dots & \mathbf{w}_1 \hat{g}_i & \dots & \mathbf{w}_1 \hat{g}_I \\
\cdot & & \cdot & & \cdot \\
\cdot & & \cdot & & \cdot \\
\cdot & & \cdot & & \cdot \\
\mathbf{w}_I \hat{g}_1 & \dots & \mathbf{w}_I \hat{g}_i & \dots & \mathbf{w}_I \hat{g}_I
\end{bmatrix}.
\tag{3.127}
$$

Combining Eq. 3.126 and Eq. 3.127, we get

$$
\mathbf{w}\hat{G}(\mathbf{w}, \mathcal{A})\left(\frac{\partial \mathcal{A}}{\partial \mathbf{w}}\right)_i =
\begin{bmatrix}
\mathbf{w}_1 \hat{g}_i \frac{\partial \mathcal{A}_{i,i}}{\partial \mathrm{w}_{i,1}} & \dots & \cdot & \dots & \mathbf{w}_1 \hat{g}_i \frac{\partial \mathcal{A}_{i,i}}{\partial \mathrm{w}_{i,j}} \\
\cdot & & \cdot & & \cdot \\
\mathbf{w}_i \hat{g}_i \frac{\partial \mathcal{A}_{i,i}}{\partial \mathrm{w}_{i,1}} & \dots & \cdot & \dots & \mathbf{w}_i \hat{g}_i \frac{\partial \mathcal{A}_{i,i}}{\partial \mathrm{w}_{i,J}} \\
\cdot & & \cdot & & \cdot \\
\mathbf{w}_I \hat{g}_i \frac{\partial \mathcal{A}_{i,i}}{\partial \mathrm{w}_{i,1}} & \dots & \cdot & \dots & \mathbf{w}_I \hat{g}_i \frac{\partial \mathcal{A}_{i,i}}{\partial \mathrm{w}_{i,J}}
\end{bmatrix}.
\tag{3.128}
$$

After that, the i-th component of the trace item in Eq. 6.72 is then calculated by:

$$
Tr[\mathbf{w}\hat{G}(\frac{\partial \mathcal{A}}{\partial \mathbf{w}})_i] = \mathbf{w}_i \hat{g}_i \sum_{j=1}^{J} \frac{\partial \mathcal{A}_{i,i}}{\partial \mathrm{w}_{i,j}}
\tag{3.129}
$$

Combining Eq. 6.72 and Eq. 3.129, we can get

$$
\hat{\mathbf{w}}^{t+1} = \mathbf{w}^{t+1} - \eta_2 \lambda
\begin{bmatrix}
\hat{g}_1^t \sum_{j=1}^{J} \frac{\partial \mathcal{A}_{1,1}^t}{\partial \mathrm{w}_{1,j}^t} \\
\cdot \\
\cdot \\
\cdot \\
\hat{g}_I^t \sum_{j=1}^{J} \frac{\partial \mathcal{A}_{I,I}^t}{\partial \mathrm{w}_{I,j}^t}
\end{bmatrix}
\circledast
\begin{bmatrix}
\mathbf{w}_1^t \\
\cdot \\
\cdot \\
\cdot \\
\mathbf{w}_I^t
\end{bmatrix}
\tag{3.130}
$$

$$
= \mathbf{w}^{t+1} + \eta_2 \lambda \boldsymbol{d}^t \circledast \mathbf{w}^t,
$$

where η_2 is the learning rate of the real value weight filters $\mathbf{w}_i$, $\circledast$ denotes the Hadamard product. We take $\boldsymbol{d}^t = -[\hat{g}_1^t \sum_{j=1}^{J} \frac{\partial \mathcal{A}_{1,1}^t}{\partial \mathrm{w}_{1,j}^t}, \cdots, \hat{g}_I^t \sum_{j=1}^{J} \frac{\partial \mathcal{A}_{I,I}^t}{\partial \mathrm{w}_{I,j}^t}]^T$, which is unsolvable and undefined in the backpropagation of BNNs. To address this issue, we employ a recurrent model to approximate $\boldsymbol{d}^t$ and have

$$
\hat{\mathbf{w}}^{t+1} = \mathbf{w}^{t+1} + U^t \circ DReLU(\mathbf{w}^t, \mathcal{A}^t),
\tag{3.131}
$$

and

$$
\mathbf{w}^{t+1} \leftarrow \hat{\mathbf{w}}^{t+1},
\tag{3.132}
$$

where we introduce a hidden layer with channel-wise learnable weights $U \in \mathbb{R}_+^{C_{out}}$ to recurrently backtrack the $\mathbf{w}$. We present $DReLU$ to supervise such an optimization process to realize a controllable recurrent optimization. Channel-wise, we implement $DReLU$ as

$$
DReLU(\mathbf{w}_i, \mathcal{A}_i) =
\begin{cases}
\mathbf{w}_i & if\ (\neg D(\mathbf{w}_i')) \wedge D(\mathcal{A}_i) = 1, \\
0 & otherwise,
\end{cases}
\tag{3.133}
$$

Algorithm 7 RBONN training.

Input: a minibatch of inputs and their labels, real-valued weights $\mathbf{w}$, recurrent model weights U, scaling factor matrix $\mathcal{A}$, learning rates η_1, η_2 and η_3.

Output: updated real-valued weights $\mathbf{w}^{t+1}$, updated scaling factor matrix $\mathcal{A}^{t+1}$, and updated recurrent model weights U^{t+1}.

1: **while** Forward propagation **do**
2:    $\mathbf{b}^{\mathbf{w}^t} \leftarrow \text{sign}(\mathbf{w}^t)$.
3:    $\mathbf{b}^{\mathbf{a}^t_{in}} \leftarrow \text{sign}(\mathbf{a}^t_{in})$.
4:    Features calculation using Eq. 6.36
5:    Loss calculation using Eq. 6.68
6: **end while**
7: **while** Backward propagation **do**
8:    Computing $\frac{\partial L}{\partial \mathcal{A}^t}$, $\frac{\partial L}{\partial \mathbf{w}^t}$, and $\frac{\partial L}{\partial U^t}$ using Eq. 6.70, 6.72, and 3.136.
9:    Update $\mathcal{A}^{t+1}$, $\mathbf{w}^{t+1}$, and U^{t+1} according to Eqs. 6.69, 6.44, and 6.50, respectively.
10: **end while**

---

where $\mathbf{w}' = diag(\|\mathbf{w}_1\|_1, \cdots, \|\mathbf{w}_{C_{out}}\|_1)$. And we judge when asynchronous convergence occurs in optimization based on $(\neg D(\mathbf{w}'_i)) \wedge D(\mathcal{A}_i) = 1$, where the density function is defined as

$$D(\boldsymbol{x}_i) = \begin{cases} 1 & if \ \ ranking(\sigma(\boldsymbol{x})_i) > \mathcal{T}, \\ 0 & otherwise, \end{cases} \tag{3.134}$$

where $\mathcal{T}$ is defined by $\mathcal{T} = int(C_{out} \times \tau)$. τ is the hyperparameter that denotes the threshold. $\sigma(\boldsymbol{x})_i$ denotes the i-th eigenvalue of diagonal matrix $\boldsymbol{x}$, and $\boldsymbol{x}_i$ denotes the i-th row of matrix $\boldsymbol{x}$. Finally, we define the optimization of U as

$$U^{t+1} = |U^t - \eta_3 \frac{\partial L}{\partial U^t}|, \tag{3.135}$$

$$\frac{\partial L}{\partial U^t} = \frac{\partial L_S}{\partial \mathbf{w}^t} \circ DReLU(\mathbf{w}^{t-1}, \mathcal{A}^t), \tag{3.136}$$

where η_3 is the learning rate of U. We elaborate on the RBONN training process outlined in Algorithm 13.

3.8.3   Discussion

In this section, we first review the related methods on "gradient approximation" of BNNs, then further discuss the difference of RBONN with the related methods and analyze the effectiveness of the proposed RBONN.

In particular, BNN [99] directly unitizes the Straight-Through-Estimator in the training stage to calculate the gradient of weights and activations as

$$\frac{\partial \mathbf{b}^{\mathbf{w}_{i,j}}}{\partial \mathbf{w}_{i,j}} = 1_{|\mathbf{w}_{i,j}| < 1}, \frac{\partial \mathbf{b}^{\mathbf{a}_{i,j}}}{\partial \mathbf{a}_{i,j}} = 1_{|\mathbf{a}_{i,j}| < 1} \tag{3.137}$$

which suffers from an obvious gradient mismatch between the gradient of the binarization function. Intuitively, the Bi-Real Net [159] designs an approximate binarization function that can help alleviate the gradient mismatch in backward propagation as

$$\frac{\partial \mathbf{b}^{\mathbf{a}_{i,j}}}{\partial \mathbf{a}_{i,j}} = \begin{cases} 2 + 2\mathbf{a}_{i,j}, & -1 \leq \mathbf{a}_{i,j} < 0, \\ 2 - 2\mathbf{a}_{i,j}, & 0 \leq \mathbf{a}_{i,j} < 1, \\ 0, & otherwise, \end{cases} \tag{3.138}$$

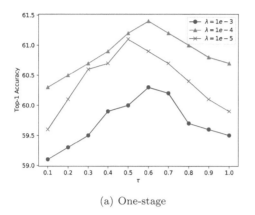

(a) One-stage

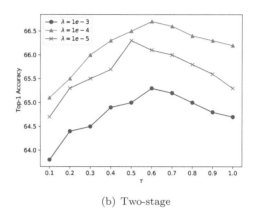

(b) Two-stage

FIGURE 3.27
Effect of hyperparameters λ and τ on one- and two-stage training using 1-bit ResNet-18.

which is termed the ApproxSign function and is used for the backpropagation gradient calculation of the activation. Compared to the traditional STE, ApproxSign has a shape similar to that of the original binarization function sign, and thus the activation gradient error can be controlled to some extent. Similarly, CBCN [149] applies an approximate function to address the gradient mismatch from the sign function. MetaQuant [38] introduces Metalearning to learn the gradient error of weights using a neural network. IR-Net [196] includes a self-adaptive Error Decay Estimator (EDE) to reduce the gradient error in training, which considers different requirements on different stages of the training process and balances the update ability of parameters and reduction of gradient error. RBNN [140] proposes a training-aware approximation of the sign function for gradient backpropagation.

In summary, prior art focuses on approximating the gradient derived from $\frac{\partial \mathbf{b}^a}{\partial \mathbf{a}_{i,j}}$ or $\frac{\partial \mathbf{b}^w}{\partial \mathbf{w}_{i,j}}$. Unlike other approaches, our approach focuses on a different perspective of the gradient approximation, *i.e.*, gradient from $\frac{\partial G}{\partial \mathbf{w}_{i,j}}$. Our goal is to decouple $\mathcal{A}$ and $\mathbf{w}$ to improve the gradient calculation of $\mathbf{w}$. RBONN manipulates $\mathbf{w}$'s gradient from its bilinear coupling variable $\mathcal{A}$ ($\frac{\partial G(\mathcal{A})}{\partial \mathbf{w}_{i,j}}$). More specifically, our RBONN can be combined with the prior art by comprehensively considering $\frac{\partial L_S}{\partial \mathbf{a}_{i,j}}$, $\frac{\partial L_S}{\partial \mathbf{w}_{i,j}}$ and $\frac{\partial G}{\partial \mathbf{w}_{i,j}}$ in the backpropagation process.

3.8.4   Ablation Study

Hyper-parameter λ and τ. The most important hyper-parameter of RBONN are λ and τ, which control the proportion of L_R and the threshold of backtracking in recurrent bilinear optimization. On ImageNet for 1-bit ResNet-18, the effect of hyperparameters λ and τ is evaluated under one- and two-stage training. The performance of RBONN is demonstrated in Fig. 3.27, where λ ranges from $1e-3$ to $1e-5$ and τ ranges from 1 to 0.1. As observed, with λ reducing, performance improves at first before plummeting. The same trend emerges when we increase τ in both implementations. As demonstrated in Fig. 3.27, when λ is set to $1e-4$ and τ is set to 0.6, 1-bit ResNet-18 generated by our RBONN gets the best performance. As

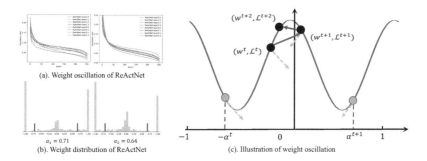

(a). Weight oscillation of ReActNet

(b). Weight distribution of ReActNet

(c). Illustration of weight oscillation

FIGURE 3.28
(a) We show the epoch-wise weight oscillation of ReActNet. (b) We randomly select two channels of the first 1-bit layer in ReActNet [158]. The distribution is with three peaks centering around $\{-1, 0, +1\}$, which magnifies the non-parametric scaling factor (red line). (c) We illustrate the weight oscillation caused by such inappropriate scale calculation, where $\mathbf{w}$ and $\mathcal{L}$ indicate the latent weight and network loss function (blue line), respectively.

a result, we apply this set of hyperparameters to the remaining experiments in this chapter. Note that the recurrent model does not affect when τ is set to 1.

3.9   ReBNN: Resilient Binary Neural Network

Conventional BNNs [199, 158] are often sub-optimized due to their intrinsic frequent weight oscillation during training. We first identify that the weight oscillation mainly originates from the non-parametric scaling factor. Figure 3.28(a) shows the epoch-wise oscillation[4] of ReActNet, where the weight oscillation exists even when the network is convergent. As shown in Fig. 3.28(b), the conventional ReActNet [158] possesses a channel-wise tri-modal distribution in the 1-bit convolution layers, whose peaks, respectively, center around $\{-1, 0, +1\}$. This distribution leads to a magnified scaling factor α, and thus the quantized weights $\pm\alpha$ are much larger than the small weights around 0, which might cause the weight oscillation. As illustrated in Fig. 3.28(c), In BNNs, the real-valued latent tensor is binarized by the sign function and scaled by the scaling factor (the orange dot) in forward propagation. In backward propagation, the gradient is calculated based on the quantized value $\pm\alpha$ (indicated by the yellow dotted line). However, the gradient of small latent weights is misleading when weights around ±1 magnify the scaling factor, such as ReActNet (Fig. 3.28(a)). Then the update is conducted on the latent value (the black dot), leading to the latent weight oscillation. With minimal representation states, such latent weights with small magnitudes frequently oscillate during non-convex optimization.

We aim to introduce a Resilient Binary Neural Network (ReBNN) [258] to address the problem above. The intuition of our work is to relearn the channel-wise scaling factor and the latent weights in a unified framework. Consequently, we propose parameterizing the scaling factor and introducing a weighted reconstruction loss to build an adaptive training objective.

---

[4]A toy example of weight oscillation: From iteration t to $t+1$, a misleading weight update occurs causing an oscillation from −1 to 1, and from iteration t to $t+2$ causes an oscillation from 1 to −1.

We further show that the oscillation is factually controlled by the balanced parameter attached to the reconstruction loss, providing a theoretical foundation for parameterizing it in backpropagation. The oscillation only occurs when the gradient has a magnitude large enough to change the sign of the latent weight. Consequently, we calculate the balanced parameter based on the maximum magnitude of the weight gradient during each iteration, leading to resilient gradients and effectively mitigating the weight oscillation.

3.9.1   Problem Formulation

Most existing implementations simply follow previous studies [199, 159] to optimize $\mathcal{A}$ and latent weights $\mathbf{W}$ based on a nonparametric bilevel optimization as:

$$\mathbf{W}^* = \arg\min_{\mathbf{W}} \mathcal{L}(\mathbf{W}; \mathcal{A}^*), \tag{3.139}$$

$$\text{s.t. } \boldsymbol{\alpha}^{n*} = \arg\min_{\boldsymbol{\alpha}^n} \|\mathbf{w}^n - \boldsymbol{\alpha}^n \circ \mathbf{b}^{\mathbf{w}^n}\|_2^2, \tag{3.140}$$

where $\mathcal{L}(\cdot)$ represents the training loss. Consequently, a closed-form solution of $\boldsymbol{\alpha}^n$ can be derived by channelwise absolute mean (CAM) as $\alpha_i^n = \frac{\|\mathbf{w}_{i,:,:,:}^n\|_1}{M^n}$ and $M^n = C_{in}^n \times K^n \times K^n$. For ease of representation, we use $\mathbf{w}_i^n$ as an alternative to $\mathbf{w}_{i,:,:,:}^n$ in the following. The latent weight $\mathbf{w}^n$ is updated using a standard gradient backpropagation algorithm, and its gradient is calculated as:

$$\delta_{\mathbf{w}_i^n} = \frac{\partial \mathcal{L}}{\partial \mathbf{w}_i^n} = \frac{\partial \mathcal{L}}{\partial \hat{\mathbf{w}}_i^n} \frac{\partial \hat{\mathbf{w}}_i^n}{\partial \mathbf{w}_i^n} = \alpha_i^n \frac{\partial \mathcal{L}}{\partial \hat{\mathbf{w}}_i^n} \circledast \mathbf{1}_{|\mathbf{w}_i^n| \leq 1}, \tag{3.141}$$

where $\circledast$ denotes the Hadmard product and $\hat{\mathbf{w}}^n = \boldsymbol{\alpha}^n \circ \mathbf{b}^{\mathbf{w}^n}$.

Discussion. Equation (3.141) shows weight gradient mainly comes from the nonparametric α_i^n and the gradient $\frac{\partial \mathcal{L}}{\partial \hat{\mathbf{w}}_i^n}$. $\frac{\partial \mathcal{L}}{\partial \hat{\mathbf{w}}_i^n}$ is automatically solved in backpropagation and becomes smaller with network convergence; however, α_i^n is often magnified by the trimodal distribution [158]. Therefore, the weight oscillation originates mainly from α_i^n. Given a single weight $\mathbf{w}_{i,j}^n (1 \leq j \leq M^n)$ centering around zero, the gradient $\frac{\partial \mathcal{L}}{\partial \mathbf{w}_{i,j}^n}$ is misleading, due to the significant gap between $\mathbf{w}_{i,j}^n$ and $\alpha_i^n \mathbf{b}^{\mathbf{w}_{i,j}^n}$. Consequently, bilevel optimization leads to frequent weight oscillations. To address this issue, we reformulate traditional bilevel optimization using a Lagrange multiplier and show that a learnable scaling factor is a natural training stabilizer.

3.9.2   Method

We first give the learning objective as follows:

$$\arg\min_{\mathbf{W},\mathcal{A}} \mathcal{L}(\mathbf{W}, \mathcal{A}) + \mathcal{L}_R(\mathbf{W}, \mathcal{A}), \tag{3.142}$$

where $\mathcal{L}_R(\mathbf{W}, \mathcal{A})$ is a weighted reconstruction loss and is defined as:

$$\mathcal{L}_R(\mathbf{W}, \mathcal{A}) = \frac{1}{2} \sum_{n=1}^{N} \sum_{i=1}^{C_{out}} \gamma_i^n \|\mathbf{w}_i^n - \alpha_i^n \mathbf{b}^{\mathbf{w}_i^n}\|_2^2, \tag{3.143}$$

in which γ_i^n is a balanced parameter. Based on the objective, the weight gradient in Eq. (3.141) becomes:

$$
\begin{aligned}
\delta_{\mathbf{w}_i^n} &= \frac{\partial \mathcal{L}}{\partial \mathbf{w}_i^n} + \gamma_i^n(\mathbf{w}_i^n - \alpha_i^n \mathbf{b}^{\mathbf{w}_i^n}) \\
&= \alpha_i^n(\frac{\partial \mathcal{L}}{\partial \hat{\mathbf{w}}_i^n} \circledast \mathbf{1}_{|\mathbf{w}_i^n| \le 1} - \gamma_i^n \mathbf{b}^{\mathbf{w}_i^n}) + \gamma_i^n \mathbf{w}_i^n.
\end{aligned}
\tag{3.144}
$$

The $\mathcal{S}_i^n(\alpha_i^n, \mathbf{w}_i^n) = \gamma_i^n(\mathbf{w}_i^n - \alpha_i^n \mathbf{b}^{\mathbf{w}_i^n})$ is an additional term added in the backpropagation process. We add this element because too small α_i^n diminishes the gradient $\delta_{\mathbf{w}_i^n}$ and causes a constant weight $\mathbf{w}_i^n$. In what follows, we state and prove the proposition that $\delta_{\mathbf{w}_{i,j}^n}$ is a resilient gradient for a single weight $\mathbf{w}_{i,j}^n$. Sometimes we omit the subscript i, j and the superscript n for an easy representation.

Proposition 1. *The additional term* $\mathcal{S}(\alpha, \mathbf{w}) = \gamma(\mathbf{w} - \alpha \mathbf{b^w})$ *achieves a resilient training process by suppressing frequent weight oscillation. Its balanced factor* γ *can be considered the parameter that controls the appearance of the weight oscillation.*

Proof: We prove the proposition by contradiction. For a single weight $\mathbf{w}$ centering around zero, the straight-through-estimator $\mathbf{1}_{|\mathbf{w}| \le 1} = 1$. Thus, we omit it in the following. Based on Eq. (3.144), with a learning rate η, the weight updating process is formulated as:

$$
\begin{aligned}
\mathbf{w}^{t+1} &= \mathbf{w}^t - \eta \delta_{\mathbf{w}^t} \\
&= \mathbf{w}^t - \eta[\alpha^t(\frac{\partial \mathcal{L}}{\partial \hat{\mathbf{w}}^t} - \gamma \mathbf{b}^{\mathbf{w}^t}) + \gamma \mathbf{w}^t] \\
&= (1 - \eta\gamma)\mathbf{w}^t - \eta\alpha^t(\frac{\partial \mathcal{L}}{\partial \hat{\mathbf{w}}^t} - \gamma \mathbf{b}^{\mathbf{w}^t}) \\
&= (1 - \eta\gamma)\big[\mathbf{w}^t - \frac{\eta\alpha^t}{(1 - \eta\gamma)}(\frac{\partial \mathcal{L}}{\partial \hat{\mathbf{w}}^t} - \gamma \mathbf{b}^{\mathbf{w}^t})\big],
\end{aligned}
\tag{3.145}
$$

where t denotes the t-th training iteration and η represents the learning rate. Different weights share different distances from the quantization level ± 1. Therefore, their gradients should be modified according to their scaling factors and current learning rate. We first assume the initial state $\mathbf{b}^{\mathbf{w}^t} = -1$, and the analysis process applies to the case of initial state $\mathbf{b}^{\mathbf{w}^t} = 1$. The oscillation probability from iteration t to $t+1$ is the following:

$$
P(\mathbf{b}^{\mathbf{w}^t} \ne \mathbf{b}^{\mathbf{w}^{t+1}})\big|_{\mathbf{b}^{\mathbf{w}^t} = -1} \le P(\frac{\partial \mathcal{L}}{\partial \hat{\mathbf{w}}^t} \le -\gamma).
\tag{3.146}
$$

Similarly, the oscillation probability from iteration $t+1$ to $t+2$ is as follows:

$$
P(\mathbf{b}^{\mathbf{w}^{t+1}} \ne \mathbf{b}^{\mathbf{w}^{t+2}})\big|_{\mathbf{b}^{\mathbf{w}^{t+1}} = 1} \le P(\frac{\partial \mathcal{L}}{\partial \hat{\mathbf{w}}^{t+1}} \ge \gamma).
\tag{3.147}
$$

Thus, the sequential oscillation probability from iteration t to $t+2$ is as follows:

$$
\begin{aligned}
&P((\mathbf{b}^{\mathbf{w}^{t+1}} \ne \mathbf{b}^{\mathbf{w}^{t+2}}) \cap (\mathbf{b}^{\mathbf{w}^{t+1}} \ne \mathbf{b}^{\mathbf{w}^{t+2}}))|_{\mathbf{b}^{\mathbf{w}^t} = -1} \\
&\le P((\frac{\partial \mathcal{L}}{\partial \hat{\mathbf{w}}^t} \le -\gamma) \cap (\frac{\partial \mathcal{L}}{\partial \hat{\mathbf{w}}^{t+1}} \ge \gamma)),
\end{aligned}
\tag{3.148}
$$

which denotes that the weight oscillation occurs only if the magnitudes of $\frac{\partial \mathcal{L}}{\partial \hat{\mathbf{w}}^t}$ and $\frac{\partial \mathcal{L}}{\partial \hat{\mathbf{w}}^{t+1}}$ are more significant than γ. **As a result, its attached factor γ can be considered a parameter used to control the occurrence of the weight oscillation.**

However, if the conditions in Eq. (3.148) are met, with Eq. (3.145) concluded, the gradient of $\hat{\mathbf{w}}^{t+1}$ is formulated as:

$$\frac{\partial \mathcal{L}}{\partial \hat{\mathbf{w}}^{t+1}} = \frac{\partial \mathcal{L}}{\partial \hat{\mathbf{w}}^t} - \eta \frac{\partial^2 \mathcal{L}}{\partial (\hat{\mathbf{w}}^t)^2} \geq \gamma,$$

$$\eta \frac{\partial^2 \mathcal{L}}{\partial (\hat{\mathbf{w}}^t)^2} \leq \frac{\partial \mathcal{L}}{\partial \hat{\mathbf{w}}^t} - \gamma \leq -2\gamma. \tag{3.149}$$

Note that η and γ are two positive variables, thus the second-order gradient $\frac{\partial^2 \mathcal{L}}{\partial (\hat{\mathbf{w}}^t)^2} < 0$ holds always. Consequently, $\mathcal{L}(\hat{\mathbf{w}}^{t+1})$ can only be local maxima rather than a minimum, which raises a contradiction to convergence in the training process. Such a contradiction indicates that the training algorithm will be convergent until no oscillation occurs due to the additional term $\mathcal{S}(\alpha, \mathbf{w})$. Therefore, we complete our proof. $\square$

Our proposition and proof reveal that the balanced parameter γ is a "threshold." A minimal "threshold" fails to mitigate the frequent oscillation effectively, while a too-large threshold suppresses the necessary sign inversion and hinders the gradient descent process. To solve this, we devise the learning rule of γ as:

$$\gamma_i^{n,t+1} = \frac{1}{M^n} \|\mathbf{b}^{\mathbf{w}_i^{n,t}} \circledast \mathbf{b}^{\mathbf{w}_i^{n,t+1}} - \mathbf{1}\|_0 \cdot \max_{1 \leq j \leq M^n} (|\frac{\partial \mathcal{L}}{\partial \hat{\mathbf{w}}_{i,j}^{n,t}}|), \tag{3.150}$$

where the first element $\frac{1}{M^n} \|\mathbf{b}^{\mathbf{w}_i^{n,t}} \circledast \mathbf{b}^{\mathbf{w}_i^{n,t+1}} - \mathbf{1}\|_0$ denotes the proportion of weights with change of sign. The second item $\max_{1 \leq j \leq M^n} (|\frac{\partial \mathcal{L}}{\partial \hat{\mathbf{w}}_{i,j}^{n,t}}|)$ is derived from Eq. (3.148), denoting the gradient with the greatest magnitude of the t-th iteration. In this way, we suppress the frequent weight oscillation with a resilient gradient.

We further optimize the scaling factor as follows:

$$\delta_{\alpha_i^n} = \frac{\partial \mathcal{L}}{\partial \alpha_i^n} + \frac{\partial \mathcal{L}_R}{\partial \alpha_i^n}. \tag{3.151}$$

The gradient derived from the softmax loss can be easily calculated based on backpropagation. Based on Eq. (6.88), it is easy to derive:

$$\frac{\partial \mathcal{L}_R}{\partial \alpha_i^n} = \gamma_i^n (\mathbf{w}_i^n - \alpha_i^n \mathbf{b}^{\mathbf{w}_i^n}) \circledast \mathbf{b}^{\mathbf{w}_i^n}. \tag{3.152}$$

3.9.3   Ablation Study

Since our ReBNN does not introduce additional hyperparameters, we first evaluate the different calculations of γ. Then we show how our ReBNN achieves a resilient training process. In the ablation study, we used the ResNet-18 backbone initialized from the first stage training with W32A1 following [158].

Calculation of γ: We compare the different calculations of γ in this part. As shown in Table 3.7, the performances increase first and then decrease when the value of constant γ. Considering that the magnitude of the gradient varies in both layer and channel senses, a subtle γ can hardly be manually set as a global value. We further compare the gradient-based calculation. As shown in the bottom lines, we first use $\max_{1 \leq j \leq M^n} (|\frac{\partial \mathcal{L}}{\partial \hat{\mathbf{w}}_{i,j}^{n,t}}|)$, the maximum intrachannel gradient. of the last iteration, which performs similarly to the constant $1e-4$. This indicates that only using the maximum intra-channel gradient may suppress necessary

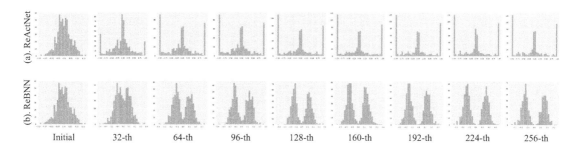

FIGURE 3.29
The evolution of latent weight distribution of (a) ReActNet and (b) ReBNN. We select the first channel of the first binary convolution layer to show the evolution. The model is initialized from the first stage training with W32A1 following [158]. We plot the distribution every 32 epochs.

sign flip, thus hindering the training. Inspired by this, we use Eq. (3.150) to calculate γ and improve performance by 0.6%, showing that considering the proportion of the weight oscillation allows for the necessary sign flip and leads to more effective training. We also show the training loss curves in Fig. 3.30(b). As plotted, the $\mathcal{L}$ curves almost demonstrate the training sufficiency degrees. Therefore, we conclude that ReBNN with γ calculated by Eq. (3.150) achieves the lowest training loss and an efficient training process. Note that the loss may not be minimal at each training iteration. Still, our method is just a reasonable version of gradient descent algorithms, which can be used to solve the optimization problem as a general one. We empirically prove ReBNN's capability of mitigating the weight oscillation, leading to better convergence.

Resilient training process: This section shows the evolution of the latent weight distribution. We plot the distribution of the first binary convolution layer's first channel per 32 epochs in Fig. 3.29. As seen, our ReBNN can efficiently redistribute the BNNs toward resilience. Conventional ReActNet [158] possesses a tri-model distribution, which is unstable due to the scaling factor with large magnitudes. In contrast, our ReBNN is constrained by the balanced parameter γ during training, thus leading to a resilient bi-modal distribution with fewer weights centering around zero. We also plot the ratios of sequential weight oscillation of ReBNN and ReActNet for the 1-st, 8-th, and 16-th binary convolution layers

TABLE 3.7
We compare different calculation methods of γ, including constants that vary from 0 to $1e-2$ and gradient-based calculation.

Value of γ	Top-1	Top-5
0	65.8	86.3
$1e-5$	66.2	86.7
$1e-4$	66.4	86.7
$1e-3$	66.3	86.8
$1e-2$	65.9	86.5
$\max_{1 \leq j \leq M^n}(\lvert \frac{\partial \mathcal{L}}{\partial \hat{\mathbf{w}}_{i,j}^{n,t}} \rvert)$	66.3	86.2
Eq. (3.150)	**66.9**	**87.1**

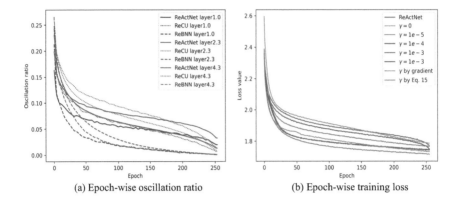

(a) Epoch-wise oscillation ratio   (b) Epoch-wise training loss

FIGURE 3.30

(a) Epoch-wise weight oscillation ratio of ReActNet (solid), ReCU (dotted), and ReBNN (dashed). (b) Comparing the loss curves of ReActNet and our ReBNN with different calculations of γ.

of ResNet-18. As shown in Fig. 3.30(a), the dashed lines gain much lower magnitudes than the solid (ReActNet) and dotted (ReCU [267]) lines with the same color, validating the effectiveness of our ReBNN in suppressing the consecutive weight oscillation. Besides, the sequential weight oscillation ratios of ReBNN are gradually decreased to 0 as the training converges.

4

Binary Neural Architecture Search

4.1 Background

Deep convolutional neural networks (DCNNs) have dominated as the best performers on various computer vision tasks such as image classification [84], instance segmentation [163], and object detection [220] due to the great success of deep network architecture design. With the increasing demand for architecture engineering, instead of designing complex architectures manually, neural architecture search (NAS) is among the best approaches for many tasks by generating delicate neural architectures.

Thanks to the rapid development of deep learning, significant gains in performance have been realized in a wide range of computer vision tasks, most of which are manual-designed network architectures [123, 211, 84, 92]. The neural architecture search (NAS) approach has recently attracted increased attention. The goal is to find automatic ways to design neural architectures to replace conventional hand-crafted ones. Existing NAS approaches need to explore a huge search space and can be roughly divided into three approaches: evolution-based, reinforcement-learning-based, and one-shot-based.

To implement the architecture search within a short period, researchers try to reduce the cost of evaluating each searched candidate. Early efforts include sharing weights between searched and newly generated networks [27]. Later, this method was generalized to a more elegant framework called one-shot architecture search [20, 28, 151, 188, 254]. In these approaches, an over-parameterized network or super-network covering all candidate operations is trained only once, and the final architecture is obtained by sampling from this super-network. For example, [20] trained the overparameterized network using a Hyper-Net [81], and [188] proposed to share parameters among Child models to avoid retraining each candidate from scratch. DARTS [151] introduces a differentiable framework and thus combines the search and evaluation stages into one. Despite its simplicity, researchers have found some drawbacks and proposed improved approaches over DARTS [254, 39]. PDARTS [39] presents an efficient algorithm that allows the depth of searched architectures to grow gradually during the training procedure, significantly reducing search time. ProxylessNAS [29] adopted the differentiable framework and proposed to search architectures on the target task instead of adopting the conventional proxy-based framework.

Binary neural architecture search replaces the real-valued weights and activations with binarized ones, which consumes much less memory and computational resources to search binary networks and provides a more promising way to efficiently find network architectures. These methods can be categorized into *direct binary architecture search* and *auxiliary binary architecture search*. Direct binary architecture search yields binary architectures directly from well-designed binary search spaces. As the first art in this field, $BNAS_1$ [36] effectively reduces search time by channel sampling and search space pruning in the early training stages for a differentiable NAS. $BNAS_2$ [114] utilizes diversity in the early search to learn better performing binary architectures. BMES [189] learns an efficient binary MobileNet [90] architecture through evolution-based search. However, the accuracy of the direct

binary architecture search can be improved by the auxiliary binary architecture search [24].
BATS [24] designs a new search space specially tailored for the binary network and incorporates it into the DARTS framework.

Unlike the aforementioned methods, our work is driven by the performance discrepancy between the 1-bit neural architecture and its real-valued counterpart. We introduce tangent propagation to explore the accuracy discrepancy and further accelerate the search process by applying the GGN to the Hessian matrix in optimization. Furthermore, we introduce a novel decoupled optimization to address asynchronous convergence in such a differentiable NAS process, leading to better performed 1-bit CNNs. The overall framework leads to a novel and effective BNAS process.

To introduce the advances of the NAS area, we separately introduce the representative works in the NAS and binary NAS in the following.

4.2   ABanditNAS: Anti-Bandit for Neural Architecture Search

Low search efficiency has prevented NAS from its practical use, and the introduction of adversarial optimization and a larger search space further exacerbates the issue. Early work directly regards network architecture search as a black-box optimization problem in a discrete search space and takes thousands of GPU days. To reduce the search space, a common idea is to adopt a cell-based search space [307]. However, when it comes to searching in a huge and complicated search space, prior cell-based works may still suffer from memory issues and are computationally intensive with the number of meta-architecture. For example, DARTS [151] can only optimize over a small subset of 8 cells, which are then stacked to form a deep network of 20. We reformulate NAS as a multi-armed bandit problem with a vast search space to increase search efficiency. The multi-armed bandit algorithm targets predicting the best arm in a sequence of trials to balance the result and its uncertainty. Likewise, NAS aims to get the best operation from an operation pool at each edge of the model with finite optimization steps, similar to the multi-armed bandit algorithm. They are both exploration and exploitation problems. Therefore, we tried to introduce the multi-armed bandit algorithm into NAS. In addition, the multi-armed bandit algorithm avoids the gradient descent process and provides good search speed for NAS. Unlike traditional Upper Confidence Bound (UCB) bandit algorithms that prefer to sample using UCB and focus on exploration, we propose Anti-Bandit to further exploit both UCB and Lower Confidence Bound (LCB) to balance exploration and exploitation. We achieve an accuracy-bias trade-off during the search process for the operation performance estimation. Using the test performance to identify the optimal architecture quickly is desirable. With the help of the Anti-Bandit algorithm, our Anti-Bandit NAS (ABanditNAS) [34] can handle the vast and complicated search space, where the number of operations that define the space can be 9^{60}!

Specifically, our proposed Anti-Bandit algorithm uses UCB to reduce search space, and LCB guarantees that every arm is thoroughly tested before abandoning it, as shown in Figure 4.1. Based on the observation that the early optimal operation is not necessarily the optimal one in the end, and the worst operations in the early stage usually have worse performance in the end [291], we pruned the operations with the worst UCB, after enough trials selected by the worst LCB. This means that the operations we finally reserve are certainly a near-optimal solution. The more tests that are conducted, the closer UCB and LCB are to the average value. Therefore, LCB tends to increase and UCB decreases with increasing sampling times. Specifically, operations with poor performance in the early stages, such as parameterized operations, will receive more opportunities but are abandoned once

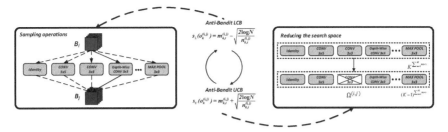

FIGURE 4.1
ABanditNAS is divided into two steps: sampling using LCB and abandoning using UCB.

they are confirmed to be bad. Meanwhile, when well trained, weight-free operations will be compared only with parameterized operations. On the other hand, with the operation pruning process, the search space becomes smaller and smaller, leading to an efficient search process.

4.2.1 Anti-Bandit Algorithm

Our goal is to search for network architectures effectively and efficiently. However, a dilemma exists for NAS about whether to maintain a network structure that offers significant rewards (exploitation) or to investigate further other network structures (exploration). Based on probability theory, the multi-armed bandit can solve the aforementioned exploration-versus-exploitation dilemma, which makes decisions among competing choices to maximize their expected gain. Specifically, we propose an anti-bandit that chooses and discards the arm k in the trial based on

$$\tilde{r}_k - \tilde{\delta}_k \leq r_k \leq \tilde{r}_k + \tilde{\delta}_k, \tag{4.1}$$

where r_k, $\tilde{r}_k$ and $\tilde{\delta}_k$ are the true reward, the average reward, and the estimated variance obtained from arm k. $\tilde{r}_k$ is the value term that favors actions that historically perform well, and $\tilde{\delta}_k$ is the exploration term that gives actions an exploration bonus. $\tilde{r}_k - \tilde{\delta}_k$ and $\tilde{r}_k + \tilde{\delta}_k$ can be interpreted as the lower and upper bounds of a confidence interval,

The traditional UCB algorithm, which optimistically substitutes $\tilde{r}_k + \tilde{\delta}$ for r_k, emphasizes exploration; however, ignores exploitation. Unlike the UCB bandit, we further exploited the LCB and UCB to balance exploration and exploitation. A smaller LCB usually has little expectations but significant variance and should be given a larger chance to be sampled for more trials. Then, based on the observation that the worst operations in the early stage usually have worse performance at the end [291], we use UCB to prune the operation with the worst performance and reduce the search space. In summary, we adopt LCB, $\tilde{r}_k - \tilde{\delta}$, to sample the arm, which should be further optimized, and use UCB, $\tilde{r}_k + \tilde{\delta}$, to abandon the operation with the minimum value. Because the variance is bounded and converges, the operating estimate value is always close to the true value and gradually approaches the true value as the number of trials increases. Our anti-bandit algorithm overcomes the limitations of an exploration-based strategy, including levels of understanding and suboptimal gaps. The definitions of the value term and the variance term and the proof of our proposed method are shown below.

Definition 1. If an operation on arm k has been recommended n_k times, $reward_i$ is the reward on arm k on all trails. The value term of anti-bandit is defined as follows

$$\tilde{r}_k = \frac{\sum reward_i}{n_k}. \tag{4.2}$$

The value of selecting an operation $\tilde{r_k}$ is the expected reward $\sum reward_i$ we receive when we take an operation from the possible set of operations. If n_k approaches infinity, $\tilde{r_k}$ approaches the actual value of the operation r_k. However, the number of operations n_k cannot be infinite. Therefore, we should approximate the actual value as closely as possible through the variance.

Definition 2. There exists a difference between the estimated probability $\tilde{r_k}$ and the actual probability r_k, and we can estimate the variance concerning the value

$$\tilde{\delta}_k = \sqrt{\frac{2\ln N}{n}}, \tag{4.3}$$

where N is the total number of trails.

Proof. Suppose $X \in [0, 1]$ represents the theoretical value of each independently distributed operation. n is the number of times the arm has been played up to trial, and p_i is the actual value of the operation in the ith trail. Furthermore, we define $p = \frac{\sum_i p_i}{n}$ and $q = 1 - p$. Since the variance boundary of independent operations can represent the global variance boundary (see the Appendix), based on Markov's inequality, we can arrive at below :

$$\begin{aligned}
P[X > p + \delta] &= P[\sum_i (X_i - p_i) > \delta] \\
&= P[e^{\lambda \sum_i (X_i - p_i)} > e^{\lambda\delta}] \\
&\leq \frac{E[e^{\lambda \sum_i (X_i - p_i)}]}{e^{\lambda\delta}}.
\end{aligned} \tag{4.4}$$

Since we can get $1 + x \leq e^x \leq 1 + x + x^2$ when $0 \leq |x| \leq 1$), $E[e^{\lambda \sum_i (X_i - p_i)}]$ in Eq. 4.4 can be further approximated as follows:

$$\begin{aligned}
E[e^{\lambda \sum_i (X_i - p_i)}] &= \prod_i E[e^{\lambda(X_i - p_i)}] \\
&\leq \prod_i E[1 + \lambda(X_i - p_i) + \lambda^2(X_i - p_i)^2] \\
&= \prod_i (1 + \lambda^2 v_i^2) \\
&\leq e^{\lambda^2 v^2},
\end{aligned} \tag{4.5}$$

where v denotes the variance of X. Combining Eq. 4.4 and Eq. 4.5 gives $P[X > p + \delta] \leq \frac{e^{\lambda^2 v^2}}{e^{\lambda\delta}}$. Since λ is a positive constant, it can be obtained by the transformation of the values $P[X > p + \delta] \leq e^{-2n\delta^2}$. According to the symmetry of the distribution, we have $P[X < p - \delta] \leq e^{-2n\delta^2}$. Finally, we get the following inequality:

$$P[|X - p| \leq \delta] \geq 1 - 2e^{-2n\delta^2}. \tag{4.6}$$

We need to decrease δ as operating recommendations increase. Therefore, we choose $\sqrt{\frac{2\ln N}{n}}$ as $\tilde{\delta}$. That is to say, $p - \sqrt{\frac{2\ln N}{n}} \leq X \leq p + \sqrt{\frac{2\ln N}{n}}$ is implemented at least with probability $1 - \frac{2}{N^4}$. The variance value will gradually decrease as the trail progresses, and $\tilde{r_k}$ will gradually approach r_k. Equation 4.7 shows that we can achieve a probability of 0.992 when the number of the trail gets 4.

$$\sqrt{1 - \frac{2}{N^4}} = \begin{cases} 0.857 & N=2 \\ 0.975 & N=3 \\ 0.992 & N=4. \end{cases} \tag{4.7}$$

According to Eq. 4.6, the variance in the anti-bandit algorithm is bounded, and the lower/upper confidence bounds can be estimated as

$$\tilde{r_k} - \sqrt{\frac{2 \ln N}{n}} \leq r_k \leq \tilde{r_k} + \sqrt{\frac{2 \ln N}{n}}. \tag{4.8}$$

4.2.2 Search Space

Following [307, 151, 291], we search for computation cells as the building blocks of the final architecture. A cell is a fully connected directed acyclic graph (DAG) of M nodes, *i.e.*, $\{B_1, B_2, ..., B_M\}$ as shown in Fig. 4.13. Here, each node is a specific tensor (*e.g.*, a feature map in convolutional neural networks), and each directed edge (i, j) between B_i and B_j denotes an operation $o^{(i,j)}(.)$, which is sampled from $\Omega^{(i,j)} = \{o_1^{(i,j)}, ..., o_K^{(i,j)}\}$. $\{\Omega^{(i,j)}\}$ is the search space of a cell. Each node B_j takes its dependent nodes as input and can be obtained by $B_j = \Sigma_{i<j} o^{(i,j)}(B_i)$. The constraint $i < j$ here is to avoid cycles in a cell. Each cell takes the output of the last cell as input. For brevity, we denote by B_0 the last node of the previous cell and the first node of the current cell. Unlike existing approaches that use only normal and reduction cells, we search for v ($v > 2$) cells instead. For general NAS search, we follow [151] and take seven normal operations, *i.e.*, 3×3 max pooling, 3×3 average pooling, skip connection (identity), 3×3 convolution with rate 2, 5×5 convolution with rate 2, 3×3 depth-wise separable convolution, and 5×5 depth-wise separable convolution. Considering adversarially robust optimization for NAS, we introduce two additional operations, the 3×3 Gabor filter and denoising block, for model defense. Therefore, the size of the entire search space is $K^{|\mathcal{E}_\mathcal{M}| \times v}$, where $\mathcal{E}_\mathcal{M}$ is the set of possible edges with M intermediate nodes in the fully connected DAG. In the case with $M = 4$ and $v = 6$, together with the input node, the total number of cell structures in the search space is $9^{(1+2+3+4) \times 6} = 9^{10 \times 6}$. Here, we briefly introduce the two additional operations.

Gabor filter. Gabor filters [69, 68] containing frequency and orientation representations can characterize the spatial frequency structure in images while preserving spatial relationships. This operation provides superb robustness for the network [191]. Gabor filters are defined as: $\exp(-\frac{x'^2 + \gamma^2 y'^2}{2\sigma^2}) \cos(2\pi \frac{x'}{\lambda} + \psi)$. Here, $x' = x \cos \theta + y \sin \theta$ and $y' = -x \sin \theta + y \cos \theta$. σ, γ, λ, ψ, and θ are learnable parameters. Note that the symbols used here apply only to the Gabor filter and are different from the symbols used in the rest of this chapter. Figure 4.2(b) shows an example of Gabor filters.

Denoising block. As described in [253], adversarial perturbations on images will introduce noise in the features. Therefore, denoising blocks can improve adversarial robustness by denoising features. Following this, we add the nonlocal mean denoising block [22] as shown in Fig. 4.2(c) to the search space to denoise the features. Calculate a denoised feature map z of an input feature map x by taking a weighted mean of the spatial locations of the features in general $\mathcal{L}$ as $z_p = \frac{1}{C(x)} \sum_{\forall q \in \mathcal{L}} f(x_p, x_q) \cdot x_q$, where $f(x_p, x_q)$ is a feature-dependent weighting function and $C(x)$ is a normalization function.

4.2.3 Anti-Bandit Strategy for NAS

As described in [274, 291], the validation accuracy ranking of different network architectures is not a reliable indicator of the final quality of the architecture. However, the experimental results suggest that if an architecture performs poorly at the beginning of training, there is little hope that it can be part of the final optimal model [291]. As training progresses, this observation becomes more and more specific. On the basis of this observation, we derive a simple but effective training strategy. During training and the increasing epochs,

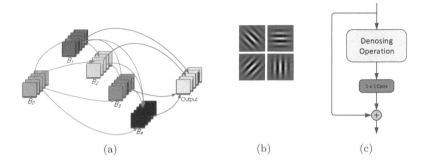

(a)   (b)   (c)

FIGURE 4.2
(a) A cell containing four intermediate nodes B_1, B_2, B_3, B_4 that apply sampled operations on the input node B_0. B_0 is from the output of the last cell. The output node concatenates the outputs of the four intermediate nodes. (b) Gabor Filter. (c) A generic denoising block. Following [253], it wraps the denoising operation with a 1×1 convolution and an identity skip connection [84].

we progressively abandon the worst-performing operation and sample the operations with little expectations but a significant variance for each edge. Unlike [291], which uses the performance as the evaluation metric to decide which operation should be pruned, we use the anti-bandit algorithm described in Section 4.2.1 to make a decision.

Following UCB in the bandit algorithm, we obtain the initial performance for each operation on every edge. Specifically, we sample one of the K operations in $\Omega^{(i,j)}$ for every edge, then obtain the validation accuracy a, which is the initial performance $m_{k,0}^{(i,j)}$ by adversarially training the sampled network for one epoch and finally assigning this accuracy to all the sampled operations.

By considering the confidence of the kth operation using Eq. 4.8, the LCB is calculated by

$$s_L(o_k^{(i,j)}) = m_{k,t}^{(i,j)} - \sqrt{\frac{2\log N}{n_{k,t}^{(i,j)}}}, \qquad (4.9)$$

where N is the total number of samples, $n_{k,t}^{(i,j)}$ refers to the number of times the kth operation of the edge (i,j) has been selected and t is the epoch index. The first item in Eq. 4.9 is the value term (see Eq. 4.2) which favors the operations that look good historically, and the second is the exploration term (see Eq. 4.3) which allows operations to get an exploration bonus that grows with $\log N$. The selection probability for each operation is defined as

$$p(o_k^{(i,j)}) = \frac{\exp\{-s_L(o_k^{(i,j)})\}}{\sum_m \exp\{-s_L(o_m^{(i,j)})\}}. \qquad (4.10)$$

The minus sign in Eq. 4.10 means that we prefer to sample operations with a smaller confidence. After sampling one operation for every edge based on $p(o_k^{(i,j)})$, we obtain the validation accuracy a by training adversarially the sampled network for one epoch, and then update the performance $m_{k,t}^{(i,j)}$ that historically indicates the validation accuracy of all the sampled operations $o_k^{(i,j)}$ as

$$m_{k,t}^{(i,j)} = (1-\lambda)m_{k,t-1}^{(i,j)} + \lambda * a, \qquad (4.11)$$

where λ is a hyperparameter.

Finally, after $K * T$ samples where T is a hyperparameter, we calculate the confidence with the UCB according to Eq. 4.8 as

$$s_U(o_k^{(i,j)}) = m_{k,t}^{(i,j)} + \sqrt{\frac{2 \log N}{n_{k,t}^{(i,j)}}}. \tag{4.12}$$

The operation with minimal UCB for every edge is abandoned. This means that operations that are given more opportunities but result in poor performance are removed. With this pruning strategy, the search space is significantly reduced from $|\Omega^{(i,j)}|^{10 \times 6}$ to $(|\Omega^{(i,j)}| - 1)^{10 \times 6}$, and the reduced space becomes

$$\Omega^{(i,j)} \leftarrow \Omega^{(i,j)} - \{\underset{o_k^{(i,j)}}{\arg\min}\, s_U(o_k^{(i,j)})\}, \forall (i,j). \tag{4.13}$$

The reduction procedure is repeated until the optimal structure is obtained, where only one operation is left on each edge.

Complexity Analysis. There are $\mathcal{O}(K^{|\mathcal{E}_\mathcal{M}| \times v})$ combinations in the search space discovery process with v types of different cells. In contrast, ABanditNAS reduces the search space for every $K * T$ epoch. Therefore, the complexity of the proposed method is the following.

$$\mathcal{O}(T \times \sum_{k=2}^{K} k) = \mathcal{O}(TK^2). \tag{4.14}$$

4.2.4 Adversarial Optimization

The goal of adversarial training [167] is to learn networks that are robust to adversarial attacks. Given a network f_θ parameterized by θ, a dataset (x_e, y_e), a loss function l and a threat model Δ, the learning problem can be formulated as the following optimization problem: $\min_\theta \sum_e \max_{\delta \in \Delta} l\big(f_\theta(x_e + \delta), y_e\big)$, where δ is the adversarial perturbation. In this chapter, we consider the typical l_∞ threat model [167], $\Delta = \{\delta : \|\delta\|_\infty \leq \epsilon\}$ for some $\epsilon > 0$. Here, $\| \cdot \|_\infty$ is the l_∞ norm distance metric and ϵ is the adversarial manipulation budget. The adversarial training procedure uses attacks to approximate inner maximization over Δ, followed by some variation of gradient descent on model parameters θ. For example, one of the earliest versions of adversarial training uses the Fast Gradient Sign Method (FGSM) [75] to approximate the inner maximization. This could be seen as a relatively inaccurate approximation of inner maximization for l_∞ perturbations, and it has the closed-form solution: $\theta = \epsilon \cdot \text{sign}\big(\nabla_x l(f(x), y)\big)$. A better approximation of inner maximization is to take multiple smaller FGSM steps of size α instead. However, the number of gradient computations caused by the multiple steps is proportional to $\mathcal{O}(EF)$ in a single epoch, where E is the size of the data set and F is the number of steps taken by the adversary PGD. This is F times higher than standard training with $\mathcal{O}(E)$ gradient computations per epoch, and adversarial training is typically F times slower. To accelerate adversarial training, we combine FGSM with random initialization [247] for our ABanditNAS. Our ABanditNAS with adversarial training is summarized in Algorithm 8.

4.2.5 Analysis

Effect on the hyperparameter λ. The hyper-parameter λ balances the performance between the past and the current. Different values of λ result in similar search costs. The performance of the structures searched by ABanditNAS with different values of λ is used

---

Algorithm 8 ABanditNAS with adversarial training

Input: Training data, validation data, searching hyper-graph, adversarial perturbation δ, adversarial manipulation budget ϵ, $K = 9$, hyper-parameters α, $\lambda = 0.7$, $T = 3$. **Output:** The remaining optimal structure,

 1: $t = 0$; $c = 0$
 2: Get initial performance $m_{k,0}^{(i,j)}$
 3: **while** $(K > 1)$ **do**
 4:      $c \leftarrow c + 1$
 5:      $t \leftarrow t + 1$
 6:      Calculate $s_L(o_k^{(i,j)})$ using Eq. 4.9
 7:      Calculate $p(o_k^{(i,j)})$ using Eq. 4.10
 8:      Select an architecture by sampling one operation based on $p(o_k^{(i,j)})$ from $\Omega^{(i,j)}$ for every edge
         # Train the selected architecture adversarially:
 9:      **for** $e = 1, ..., E$ **do**
10:          $\delta = \text{Uniform}(-\epsilon, \epsilon)$
11:          $\delta \leftarrow \delta + \alpha \cdot \text{sign}\left(\nabla_x l\big(f(x_e + \delta), y_e\big)\right)$
12:          $\delta = \max\left(\min(\delta, \epsilon), -\epsilon\right)$
13:          $\theta \leftarrow \theta - \nabla_\theta l\big(f_\theta(x_e + \delta), y_e\big)$
14:      **end for**
15:      Get the accuracy a on the validation data Update the performance $m_{k,t}^{(i,j)}$ using Eq. 4.11
16:      **if** $c = K * T$ **then**
17:          Calculate $s_U(o_k^{(i,j)})$ using Eq. 4.12
18:          Update the search space $\{\Omega^{(i,j)}\}$ using Eq. 4.13
19:          $c = 0$
20:          $K \leftarrow K - 1$
21:      **end if**
22: **end while**

---

to find the best λ. We train the structures in the same setting. From Fig. 4.3, we can see that when $\lambda = 0.7$, ABanditNAS is most robust.

Effect on the search space. We test the performance of ABanditNAS with different search spaces. In this part, we adopt the same experimental setting as the general NAS. The search space of the general NAS has 7 operations. We incrementally add the Gabor filter, denoising block, 1×1 dilated convolution with rate 2 and 7×7 dilated convolution with rate 2, until the number of operations in the search space reaches 11. In Table 4.1, # Search Space represents the number of operations in the search space. Although the difficulty of searching increases with increasing search space, ABanditNAS can effectively select the appropriate operations. Each additional operation has little effect on search efficiency, demonstrating the efficiency of our search method. When the number of operations in the search space is 9, the classification accuracy of the model searched by ABanditNAS exceeds all the methods with the same level of search cost.

4.3   CP-NAS: Child-Parent Neural Architecture Search for 1-bit CNNs

Comparatively speaking, 1-bit CNNs based on handcrafted architectures have been extensively researched. Binarized filters have been used in conventional CNNs to compress deep models [199, 99, 159], showing up to 58 times speedup and 32 times memory

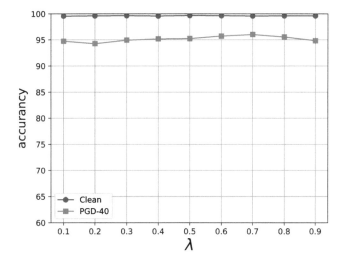

FIGURE 4.3
Performances of structures searched by ABanditNAS with different hyper-parameter values λ.

savings, which is widely considered as one of the most efficient ways to perform computing on embedded devices with low computational cost. In [199], the XNOR network is presented, where the weights and inputs attached to the convolution are approximated with binarized values. This efficiently implements convolutional operations by reconstructing the unbinarized filters with a single scaling factor. In [77], a projection convolutional neural network (PCNN) is proposed to implement binarized neural networks (BNNs) based on a simple back-propagation algorithm. [287] proposes Bayesian optimized 1-bit CNNs, taking advantage of Bayesian learning to significantly improve the performance of extreme 1-bit CNNs. Binarized models show advantages in reduction in computational cost and memory savings. However, they suffer from poor performance in practical applications. There still remains a gap between 1-bit weights/activations and full-precision counterparts, which motivates us to explore the potential relationship between 1-bit and full-precision models to evaluate binarized networks performance based on NAS. This section introduces a Child-Parent model to efficiently search for a binarized network architecture in a unified framework.

The search strategy for the Child-Parent model consists of three steps shown in Fig. 4.4. First, we sample the operations without replacement and construct two classes of subnetworks that share the same architecture, i.e., binarized networks (child) and full-precision networks (parent). Second, we train both subnetworks and obtain the performance indicator of the corresponding operations by calculating the child network accuracy and the accuracy

TABLE 4.1
The performance of ABanditNAS with different search spaces on CIFAR10.

Architecture	# Search Space	Accuracy (%)	# Params (M)	Search Cost (GPU days)	Search Method
ABanditNAS	7	97.13	3.0	**0.09**	Anti-Bandit
ABanditNAS	8	97.47	3.3	0.11	Anti-Bandit
ABanditNAS	9	97.52	4.1	0.13	Anti-Bandit
ABanditNAS	10	97.53	**2.7**	0.15	Anti-Bandit
ABanditNAS	11	**97.66**	3.7	0.16	Anti-Bandit

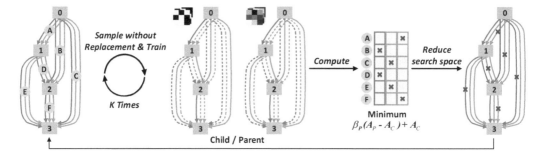

FIGURE 4.4

The main framework of the proposed Child-Parent search strategy. In a loop, we first sample the operation without replacement for each edge of the search space and then train the child and parent models generated by the same architecture simultaneously. Second, we use the Eqs. 4.15 and 4.28 to compute the evaluation indicator calculated by the accuracy of both models on the validation data set. Until all operations are selected, we remove the operation on each edge with the worst performance.

loss between child and parent networks. It is observed that the worst operations in the early stage usually have worse performance in the end. On the basis of this observation, we then remove the operation with the worst performance according to the performance indicator. This process is repeated until only one operation is left on each edge. We reformulate the traditional loss function as a kernel-level Child-Parent loss for binarized optimization of child-parent model.

4.3.1 Child-Parent Model for Network Binarization

Network binarization calculates neural networks with 1-bit weights and activations to fit the full-precision network and can significantly compress deep convolutional neural networks (CNNs). Previous work [287] usually investigates the binarization problem by exploring the full-precision model to guide the optimization of binarized models. Based on the investigation, we reformulate NAS-based network binarization as a Child-Parent model as shown in Fig. 4.5. The child and parent models are the binarized model and the full-precision counterpart, respectively.

Conventional NAS is inefficient due to the complicated reward computation in network training, where the evaluation of a structure is usually done after the network training converges. There are also some methods to perform the evaluation of a cell during network training. [292] points out that the best choice in the early stages is not necessarily the final optimal one; however, the worst operation in the early stages usually performs poorly in the end. And this phenomenon will become more and more significant as training progresses. On the basis of this observation, we propose a simple yet effective operation-removing process, which is the key task of the proposed CP-model.

Intuitively, the difference between the ability of children and parents and how much children can independently handle their problems are two main aspects that should be considered to define a reasonable performance evaluation measure. Our Child-Parent model introduces a similar performance indicator to improve search efficiency. The performance indicator includes two parts, the performance loss between the binarized network (child) and the full-precision network (parent), and the performance of the binarized network (child).

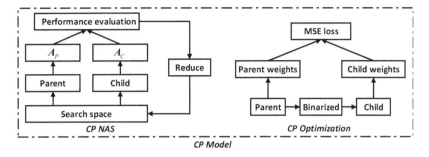

FIGURE 4.5
The main framework of the Child-Parent model. The Child-Parent model focuses on binarized architecture search (left) and binarized optimization (right).

Thus, we can define it for each operation of the sampled network as

$$z_{k,t}^{(i,j)} = \beta_P(A_{P,t} - A_{C,t}) + A_{C,t} \tag{4.15}$$

where $A_{P,t}$ and $A_{C,t}$ represents the network performance calculated by the accuracy of the full-precision model (Parent) and the binarized model (Child) on the validation dataset, and β_P is the hyperparameter to control performance loss. i,j represents the index of the node to generate the edge (i,j) shown in Fig. 4.6, k is the operation index of the corresponding edge and t represents the tth sampling process. Note that we used the performance of the sampled network to evaluate the performance of the corresponding selected operations.

CP-NAS [304] not only uses the accuracy on the validation dataset to guide the search process directly but also considers the information of the full-precision model to investigate better the full potential of the binarized model that can ultimately be reached. Additional details are provided in the following section.

As shown in Fig. 4.5, unlike the traditional teacher-student model [87], which transfers the generalization ability of the first model to a smaller model by using the class probabilities as "soft targets," the child-parent model focuses on the performance measure that is particularly suitable for NAS-based network binarization. Furthermore, the loss function for the teacher-student model is constrained to the feature map or the output, while ours focuses on the kernel weights.

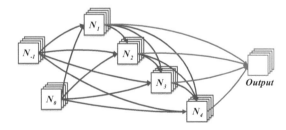

FIGURE 4.6
The cell architecture for CP-NAS. A cell includes 2 input nodes, 4 intermediate nodes, and 14 edges.

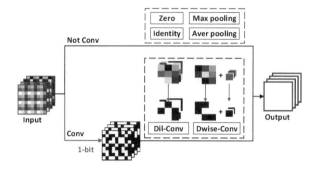

FIGURE 4.7
The operations of each edge. Each edge has 4 convolutional operations, including 2 types of binarized convolution with $3*3$ or $5*5$ receptive fields and 4 non-convolutional operations.

4.3.2 Search Space

We search for computation cells as the building blocks of the final architecture. As in [305, 306, 151], we construct the network with a predefined number of cells, and each cell is a fully connected directed acyclic graph (DAG) $\mathcal{G}$ with M nodes, $\{N_1, N_2, ..., N_M\}$. For simplicity, we assume that each cell only takes the outputs of the two previous cells as input and each input node has pre-defined convolutional operations for preprocessing. Each node N_j is obtained by $N_j = \sum_{i<j} o^{(i,j)}(N_i)$. N_i is the node dependent on N_j with the constraints $i < j$ to avoid cycles in a cell. We also define the nodes N_{-1} and N_0 without input as the first two nodes of a cell. Each node is a specific tensor as a feature map, and each directed edge (i,j) denotes an operation $o^{(i,j)}(.)$, which is sampled from the following $K = 8$ operations:

- no connection (zero)
- skip connection (identity)
- 3×3 dilated convolution with rate 2
- 5×5 dilated convolution with rate 2

- 3×3 max pooling
- 3×3 average pooling
- 3×3 depth-wise separable convolution
- 5×5 depth-wise separable convolution

We replace the separable convolution in depth with a binarized form, as shown in Fig. 4.7 and 4.8. Optimizing BNNs is more challenging than conventional CNNs [77, 199], as binarization adds additional burdens to NAS.

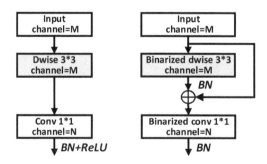

FIGURE 4.8
Compared to the origin separable convolution in depth (left), a new binarized separable convolution in depth is designed for CP-NAS (right).

Algorithm 9 Child-Parent NAS

Input: Training data, Validation data
Parameter: Searching hyper-graph: $\mathcal{G}$, $K = 8$, $selection(o_k^{(i,j)}) = 0$ for all edges
Output: Optimal structure α

1: **while** $(K > 1)$ **do**
2:    **for** $t = 1, ..., T$ epoch **do**
3:      **for** $e = 1, ..., K$ epoch **do**
4:        Select an architecture by sampling (without replacement) one operation from $\mathcal{O}^{(i,j)}$ for every edge;
5:        Construct the Child model and Parent model with the same selected architecture, and then train both models to get the accuracy on the validation data; Use Eq.4.15 to compute the performance and assign that to all the sampled operations;
6:      **end for**
7:    **end for**
8:    Update $e(o_k^{(i,j)})$ using Eq. 4.28;
9:    Reduce the search space $\{\mathcal{O}^{(i,j)}\}$ with the worst performance evaluation by $e(o_k^{(i,j)})$;
10:    $K = K - 1$;
11: **end while**
12: **return** solution

4.3.3 Search Strategy for CP-NAS

As shown in Fig. 4.4, we randomly sample one operation from the K operations in $\mathcal{O}^{(i,j)}$ for every edge and then obtain the performance based on Eq. 4.15 by training the sampled parent and child networks for one epoch. Finally, we assign this performance to all the sampled operations. These steps are performed K times by sampling without replacement, giving each operation exactly one accuracy for every edge for fairness.

We repeat the complete sampling process T times. Thus, each operation for every edge has T performance $\{z_{k,1}^{(i,j)}, z_{k,2}^{(i,j)}, ..., z_{k,T}^{(i,j)}\}$ calculated by Eq. 4.15. Furthermore, to reduce the undesired fluctuation in the performance evaluation, we normalize the performance of K operations for each edge to obtain the final evaluation indicator as

$$e(o_k^{(i,j)}) = \frac{exp\{\bar{z}_k^{(i,j)}\}}{\sum_{k'} exp\{\bar{z}_{k'}^{(i,j)}\}}, \tag{4.16}$$

where $\bar{z}_k^{(i,j)} = \frac{1}{T} \sum_t z_{k,t}^{(i,j)}$. Along with increasing epochs, we progressively abandon the worst evaluation operation from each edge until there is only one operation for each edge.

4.3.4 Optimization of the 1-Bit CNNs

Inspired by XNOR and PCNN, we reformulate our unified framework's binarized optimization as Child-Parent optimization.

To binarize the weights and activations of CNNs, we introduce the kernel-level Child-Parent loss for binarized optimization in two respects. First, we minimize the distribution between the full-precision and corresponding binarized filters. Second, we minimize the intraclass compactness based on the output features. We then have a loss function, as

$$\mathcal{L}_{\hat{H}} = \sum_{c,l} \text{MSE}(H_c^l, \hat{H}_c^l) + \frac{\lambda}{2} \sum_s \|f_{C,s}(\hat{H}) - \overline{f}_{C,s}(H)\|^2, \tag{4.17}$$

where λ is a hyperparameter to balance the two terms. H_c^l is the cth full-precision filter of the lth convolutional layer and $\hat{H}_c^l$ denotes its corresponding reconstructed filter; MSE($\cdot$) represents the mean square error (MSE) loss. The second term minimizes the intraclass compactness since the binarization process causes feature variations. $f_{C,s}(\hat{H})$ denotes the feature map of the last convolutional layer for the sth sample, and $\overline{f}_{C,s}(\hat{H})$ denotes the class-specific mean feature map for the corresponding samples. Combining $\mathcal{L}_{\hat{H}}$ with the conventional loss $\mathcal{L}_{CE}$, we obtain the final loss:

$$\mathcal{L} = \mathcal{L}_{CE} + \mathcal{L}_{\hat{H}}. \tag{4.18}$$

The $\mathcal{L}$ and its derivatives are easily calculated directly using the efficient automatic derivatives package.

4.3.5 Ablation Study

We tested different β_P for our method on the CIFAR-10 dataset, as shown on the right side of Fig. 4.9. We can see that when β_P increases, the precision increases at first but decreases when $\beta_P \geq 2$. It validates that the performance loss between the Child and Parent models is a significant measure for the 1-bit CNNs search. When β_P increases, CP-NAS tends to select the architecture with fewer convolutional operations, and the imbalance between two elements in our CP model leads to a performance drop.

We also compare the architectures obtained by CP-NAS, Random, PC (PC-DARTs), and BNAS† as shown in Fig. 4.9. Unlike the case of the full-precision model, Random and PC-DARTs lack the necessary guidance, which has poor performance for binarized architecture search. Both BNAS† and CP-NAS have the evaluation indicator for operation selection. Differently, our CP-NAS also uses performance loss, which can outperform the other three strategies.

Efficiency. As shown in XNOR, the 1-bit CNNs are very efficient and promising for resource-limited devices. Our CP-NAS achieves a performance comparable to that of the full precision hand-crafted model with up to an estimated 11 times memory saving and 58 times speed up, which is worth further research and will benefit extensive edge computing applications.

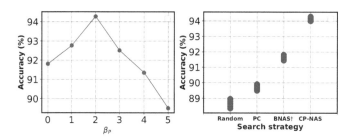

FIGURE 4.9
The result (right) for different β_P on CIFAR-10. The 1-bit CNNs result (left) for different search strategies on CIFAR-10, including random search, PC (PC-DARTs), BNAS†, CP-NAS. We approximately implement BNAS† by setting β_P as 0 in CP-NAS, which means that we only use the performance measure for the operation selection.

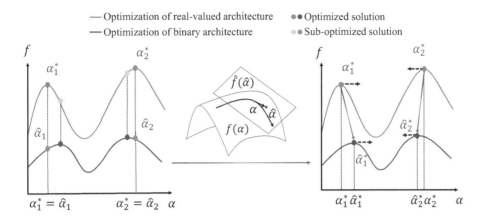

FIGURE 4.10
Motivation for DCP-NAS. We first show directly binarizing real-valued architecture to 1-bit is sub-optimal. Thus we use tangent propagation (middle) to find an optimized 1-bit neural architecture along the tangent direction, leading to a better-performed 1-bit neural architecture.

4.4 DCP-NAS: Discrepant Child-Parent Neural Architecture Search for 1-Bit CNNs

Based on CP-NAS introduced above, the real-valued models converge much faster than the 1-bit models, as revealed in [157], which motivates us to use the tangent direction of the Parent supernet (real-valued model) as an indicator of the optimization direction for the Child supernet (1-bit model). We assume that all the possible 1-bit neural architectures can be learned from the tangent space of the Parent model, based on which we introduce a *Discrepant Child-Parent Neural Architecture Search* (DCP-NAS) [135] method to produce an optimized 1-bit CNN. Specifically, as shown in Fig. 4.10, we use the Parent model to find a tangent direction to learn the 1-bit Child through tangent propagation rather than directly binarizing the Parent-to-Child relationship. Since the tangent direction is based on second-order information, we further accelerate the search process by Generalized Gauss-Newton matrix (GGN), leading to an efficient search process. Furthermore, a coupling relationship exists between weights and architecture parameters in such DARTS-based [151] methods, leading to an asynchronous convergence and an insufficient training process. To overcome this obstacle, we propose a decoupled optimization for training the Child-Parent model, leading to an effective and optimized search process. The overall framework of our DCP-NAS is shown in Fig. 4.11.

4.4.1 Preliminary

Neural architecture search Given a conventional CNN model, we denote $\mathbf{w} \in \mathcal{W}$ and $\mathcal{W} = \mathbb{R}_{C_{out} \times C_{in} \times K \times K}$ and $\mathbf{a}_{in} \in \mathbb{R}_{C_{in} \times W \times H}$ as its weights and feature maps in the specific layer. C_{out} and C_{in} represent the output and input channels of the specific layer. (W, H) is the width and height of the feature maps and K is the kernel size. Then we have

$$\mathbf{a}_{out} = \mathbf{a}_{in} \otimes \mathbf{w}, \tag{4.19}$$

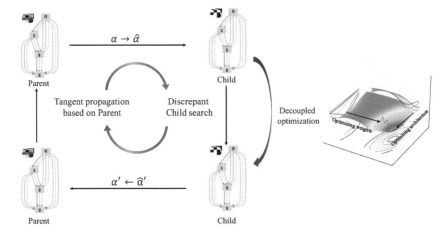

FIGURE 4.11
The main framework of the proposed DCP-NAS, where α and $\hat{\alpha}$ denote real-valued and binary architecture, respectively. We first conduct the real-valued NAS in a single round and generate the corresponding tangent direction. Then we learn a discrepant binary architecture via tangent propagation. In this process, real-valued and binary networks inherit architectures from their counterparts, in turn.

where $\otimes$ is the convolution operation. We omit the batch normalization (BN) and activation layers for simplicity. Based on this, a normal NAS problem is given as

$$\max_{\mathbf{w}\in\mathcal{W},\alpha\in\mathcal{A}} f(\mathbf{w},\alpha), \tag{4.20}$$

where $f : \mathcal{W}\times\mathcal{A} \rightarrow \mathbb{R}$ is a differentiable objective function *w.r.t.* the network weight $\mathbf{w} \in \mathcal{W}$ and the architecture space $\mathcal{A} \in \mathbb{R}_{M\times E}$, where E and M denote the number of edges and operators, respectively. Considering that minimizing $f(\mathbf{w},\alpha)$ is a black-box optimization, we relax the objective function to $\tilde{f}(\mathbf{w},\alpha)$ as the objective of NAS

$$\min_{\mathbf{w}\in\mathcal{W},\alpha\in\mathcal{A}} \mathcal{L}_{\text{NAS}} = -\tilde{f}(\mathbf{w},\alpha)$$
$$= -\sum_{n=1}^{N} p_n(\mathcal{X})\log(p_n(\mathbf{w},\alpha)), \tag{4.21}$$

where N denotes the number of classes and $\mathcal{X}$ is the input data. $\tilde{f}(\mathbf{w},\alpha)$ represents the performance of a specific architecture with real value weights, where $p_n(\mathcal{X})$ and $p_n(\mathbf{w},\alpha)$ denote the true distribution and the distribution of network prediction, respectively.

Binary neural architecture search The 1-bit model aims to quantize $\hat{\mathbf{w}}$ and $\hat{\mathbf{a}}_{in}$ into $\mathbf{b}^{\hat{\mathbf{w}}} \in \{-1,+1\}_{C_{out}\times C_{in}\times K\times K}$ and $\mathbf{b}^{\hat{\mathbf{a}}_{in}} \in \{-1,+1\}_{C_{in}\times H\times W}$ using the efficient XNOR and Bit-count operations to replace full precision operations. Following [48], the forward process of the 1-bit CNN is

$$\hat{\mathbf{a}}_{out} = \beta \circ \mathbf{b}^{\hat{\mathbf{a}}_{in}} \odot \mathbf{b}^{\hat{\mathbf{w}}}, \tag{4.22}$$

where $\odot$ is the XNOR, and bit count operations and $\circ$ denotes channelwise multiplication. $\beta = [\beta_1, \cdots, \beta_{C_{out}}] \in \mathbb{R}_{C_{out}}^{+}$ is the vector consisting of channel-wise scale factors. $\mathbf{b} = \text{sign}(\cdot)$ denotes the binarized variable using the sign function, which returns one if the input is greater than zero and -1 otherwise. It then enters several non-linear layers, *e.g.*,

BN layer, non-linear activation layer, and max-pooling layer. We omit these for the sake of simplification. Then, the output $\hat{\mathbf{a}}_{out}$ is binarized to $\mathbf{b}^{\hat{\mathbf{a}}_{out}}$ by the sign function. The fundamental objective of BNNs is to calculate $\hat{\mathbf{w}}$. We want it to be as close as possible before and after binarization to minimize the binarization effect. Then, we define the reconstruction error following [77] as

$$\mathcal{L}_R(\hat{\mathbf{w}}, \beta) = \|\hat{\mathbf{w}} - \beta \circ \mathbf{b}^{\hat{\mathbf{w}}}\|_2^2. \quad (4.23)$$

Based on the above derivation, the vanilla direct BNAS [36, 114] can be defined as

$$\max_{\hat{\mathbf{w}} \in \mathcal{W}, \hat{\alpha} \in \mathcal{A}, \beta \in \mathbb{R}^+} f_{\mathbf{b}}(\hat{\mathbf{w}}, \hat{\alpha}, \beta), \quad (4.24)$$

where $\mathbf{b}^{\hat{\mathbf{w}}} = \text{sign}(\hat{\mathbf{w}})$ is used for inference and $\hat{\alpha}$ is a neural architecture with binary weights. Prior to direct BNAS [36] learning the BNAS from such an objective as

$$\max_{\hat{\mathbf{w}} \in \mathcal{W}, \hat{\alpha} \in \mathcal{A}, \beta \in \mathbb{R}^+} \tilde{f}_{\mathbf{b}}(\hat{\mathbf{w}}, \hat{\alpha}, \beta) = \sum_{n=1}^{N} \hat{p}_n(\hat{\mathbf{w}}, \hat{\alpha}, \beta) \log(\hat{p}_n(\mathcal{X})), \quad (4.25)$$

where we use notations similar to those of Eq. 4.21. Equation 4.25 means that the vanilla direct BNAS only focuses on the binary search space under the supervision of cross-entropy loss, which is less effective due to the search process being not exhaustive [24].

4.4.2   Redefine Child-Parent Framework for Network Binarization

Network binarization calculates neural networks with 1-bit weights and activations to fit the full-precision network, which can significantly compress the CNNs. Prior work [287] usually investigates the binarization problem by exploring the full-precision model to guide the optimization of binarized models. Based on the investigation, we reformulate NAS-based network binarization as a Child-Parent model as shown in Fig. 4.12. The Child and Parent models are the binarized and full-precision counterparts, respectively.

Conventional NAS is inefficient due to the complicated reward computation in network training, where the evaluation of a structure is usually done after the network training converges. There are also some methods to evaluate a cell during the training of the network. [292] points out that the best choice in the early stages is not necessarily the final optimal one. However, the worst operation in the early stages usually has a bad performance. This phenomenon will become more and more significant as the training goes on. Based on this observation, we propose a simple yet effective operation-removing process, which is the crucial task of the proposed CP model.

Intuitively, the representation difference between the Children and Parents, and how many Children can independently handle their problems are two main aspects that should be considered to define a reasonable performance evaluation measure. Based on this analysis, we introduce the Child-Parent framework for binary NAS, which defines the objective as

$$\hat{\mathbf{w}}^*, \hat{\alpha}^*, \beta^* = \underset{\hat{\mathbf{w}} \in \hat{\mathcal{W}}, \alpha \in \mathcal{A}, \beta \in \mathbb{R}^+}{\text{argmin}} \mathcal{L}_{\text{CP-NAS}}(\tilde{f}^P(\mathbf{w}, \alpha), \ \tilde{f}_{\mathbf{b}}^C(\hat{\mathbf{w}}, \hat{\alpha}, \beta))$$

$$= \underset{\hat{\mathbf{w}} \in \hat{\mathcal{W}}, \alpha \in \mathcal{A}, \beta \in \mathbb{R}^+}{\text{argmin}} \tilde{f}^P(\mathbf{w}, \alpha) - \tilde{f}_{\mathbf{b}}^C(\hat{\mathbf{w}}, \hat{\alpha}, \beta), \quad (4.26)$$

where $\tilde{f}^P(\mathbf{w}, \alpha)$ denotes the performance of the real-valued parent model as predefined in Eq. 4.21. $\tilde{f}_{\mathbf{b}}^C$ is further defined as $\tilde{f}_{\mathbf{b}}^C(\hat{\mathbf{w}}, \alpha, \beta) = \sum_{n=1}^{N} \hat{p}_n(\hat{\mathbf{w}}, \alpha, \beta) \log(\hat{p}_n(\mathcal{X}))$ following Eq. 4.25. As shown in Eq. 4.26, we propose $\mathcal{L}$ to estimate the performance of candidate

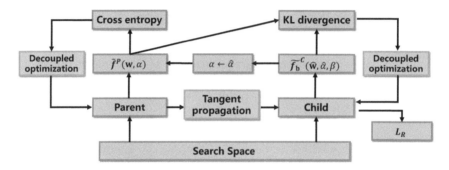

FIGURE 4.12
The main framework of the Discrepant Child-Parent model. In orange, we show the critical novelty of DCP-NAS, *i.e.*, tangent propagation and decoupled optimization.

architectures with binarized weights and activations, which consider both real-valued architectures and binarized architectures.

4.4.3 Search Space

We search for computation cells as the building blocks of the final architecture. As in [305, 307, 151] and Fig. 4.13, we construct the network with a predefined number of cells, and each cell is a fully connected directed acyclic graph (DAG) $\mathcal{G}$ with N nodes. For simplicity, we assume that each cell only takes the outputs of the two previous cells as input, and each input node has pre-defined convolutional operations for preprocessing. Each node j is obtained by

$$\mathbf{a}^{(j)} = \sum_{i<j} o^{(i,j)}(\mathbf{a}^{(i)})$$
$$o^{(i,j)}(\mathbf{a}^i) = \mathbf{w}^{(i,j)} \otimes \mathbf{a}^i, \tag{4.27}$$

where i is the dependent nodes of j with the constraints $i < j$ to avoid cycles in a cell, and $\mathbf{a}^j$ is the output of the node j. $\mathbf{w}^{(i,j)}$ denotes the weights of the convolution operation between the i-th and j-th nodes, and $\otimes$ denotes the convolution operation. Each node is a specific tensor like a feature map, and each directed edge (i, j) denotes an operation $o^{(i,j)}(.)$, which is sampled from the following $M = 8$ operations:

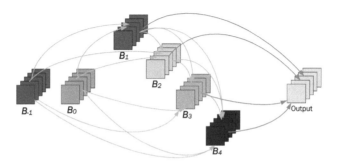

FIGURE 4.13
The cell architecture for DCP-NAS. One cell includes 2 input nodes, 4 intermediate nodes, and 14 edges.

- no connection (zero)
- skip connection (identity)
- 3×3 dilated convolution with rate 2
- 5×5 dilated convolution with rate 2
- 3×3 max pooling
- 3×3 average pooling
- 3×3 depth-wise separable convolution
- 5×5 depth-wise separable convolution

We replace the separable convolution depth-wise with a binarized form, *i.e.*, binarized weights and activations. Skip connection is an identity mapping in NAS, instead of an additional shortcut. Optimizing BNNs is more challenging than conventional CNNs [77, 199], as binarization adds additional burdens to NAS. Following [151], to reduce the undesirable fluctuation in performance evaluation, we normalize the architecture parameter of the M operations for each edge to obtain the final architecture indicator as

$$\hat{o}_m^{(i,j)}(\mathbf{a}^{(j)}) = \frac{exp\{\alpha_m^{(i,j)}\}}{\sum_{m'} exp\{\alpha_{m'}^{(i,j)}\}} o_m^{(i,j)}(\mathbf{a}^{(j)}) \tag{4.28}$$

4.4.4 Tangent Propagation for DCP-NAS

In this section, we propose the generation of the tangent direction based on the Parent model and then present the tangent propagation to search for the optimized architecture in the binary NAS effectively. As shown in Fig. 4.12, the novelty of DCP-NAS introduces tangent propagation and decoupled optimization, leading to a practical discrepancy-based search framework. The main motivation of DCP-NAS is to "fine-tune" the Child model architecture based on the real-valued Parent rather than directly binarizing the Parent. Thus, we first take advantage of the Parent model to generate
the tangent direction from the architecture gradient of the model as

$$\frac{\partial \tilde{f}^C(\mathbf{w}, \alpha)}{\partial \alpha} = \sum_{n=1}^{N} \frac{\partial p_n(\mathbf{w}, \alpha)}{\partial \alpha}, \tag{4.29}$$

where $\tilde{f}(\mathbf{w}, \alpha)$ is predefined in Eq. 4.21.

Then we conduct the second step, *i.e.*, tangent propagation for the child model.

For each epoch of binary NAS in our DCP-NAS, we inherit weights from the real-valued architecture $\hat{\alpha} \leftarrow \alpha$ and enforce the binary network to learn distributions similar to those of real-valued networks.

$$\max_{\hat{\mathbf{w}} \in \mathcal{W}, \hat{\alpha} \in \mathcal{A}, \beta \in \mathbb{R}^+} G(\hat{\mathbf{w}}, \hat{\alpha}, \beta) = \tilde{f}^P(\mathbf{w}, \alpha) log \frac{\tilde{f}^P(\mathbf{w}, \alpha)}{\tilde{f}_{\mathbf{b}}^C(\hat{\mathbf{w}}, \hat{\alpha}, \beta)}$$
$$= \sum_{n=1}^{N} p_n(\mathbf{w}, \alpha) \log(\frac{\hat{p}_n(\hat{\mathbf{w}}, \hat{\alpha}, \beta)}{p_n(\mathbf{w}, \alpha)}), \tag{4.30}$$

where the KL divergence is used to supervise the binary search process. $G(\hat{\mathbf{w}}, \hat{\alpha}, \beta)$ calculates the similarity of the output logits between the real value network $p(\cdot)$ and the binary network $\hat{p}(\cdot)$, where the teacher's output is already given.

To further optimize the binary architecture, we constrain the gradient of binary NAS using the tangent direction as

$$\min_{\hat{\alpha} \in \mathcal{A}} \mathbf{D}(\hat{\alpha}) = \|\frac{\partial \tilde{f}^P(\mathbf{w}, \alpha)}{\partial \alpha} - \frac{\partial G(\hat{\mathbf{w}}, \hat{\alpha}, \beta)}{\partial \hat{\alpha}}\|_2^2 \tag{4.31}$$

We use Eqs. 4.30 – 4.31 to jointly learn the DCP-NAS and rewrite the objective function in Eq. 4.26 as

$$
\begin{aligned}
\mathcal{L}_{\text{DCP-NAS}}(\tilde{f}^P(\mathbf{w}, \alpha), \ \ \tilde{f}^C_{\mathbf{b}}(\hat{\mathbf{w}}, \hat{\alpha}, \beta)) \\
= -G(\hat{\mathbf{w}}, \hat{\alpha}, \beta) + \lambda \mathbf{D}(\hat{\alpha}) + \mu \mathcal{L}_R(\hat{\mathbf{w}}, \beta).
\end{aligned} \tag{4.32}
$$

Then we optimize the binary architecture $\hat{\alpha}$ along the tangent direction of the real-valued model, which inherits from the real-valued one. Note that when we set $\lambda = 0$, the Eq. 4.32 is equivalent to the objective of the original CP-NAS [304]. As revealed in [157], the real-valued weights converge faster than the binarized ones. Motivated by this observation, the tangent direction of the Parent supernet can be used to approximate the optimization direction of the more slowly converged Child supernet. To conclude, in Eq. 4.31, we improve the optimization of the Child architecture based on the tangent direction of the Parent architecture, which leads the Child supernet to be trained more efficiently.

Considering that binary weights are learned by KL divergence, we optimize our DCP-NAS as

$$
\begin{aligned}
\nabla_{\hat{\alpha}} \mathcal{L}_{\text{DCP-NAS}}(\tilde{f}^P(\mathbf{w}, \alpha), \ \ \tilde{f}^C_{\mathbf{b}}(\hat{\mathbf{w}}, \hat{\alpha}, \beta)) \\
= -\frac{\partial G(\hat{\mathbf{w}}, \hat{\alpha}, \beta)}{\partial \hat{\alpha}} + \lambda \frac{\partial \mathbf{D}(\hat{\alpha})}{\partial \hat{\alpha}} \\
= -\frac{\partial G(\hat{\mathbf{w}}, \hat{\alpha}, \beta)}{\partial \hat{\alpha}} + 2\lambda \left(\frac{\partial G(\hat{\mathbf{w}}, \hat{\alpha}, \beta)}{\partial \hat{\alpha}} - \frac{\partial \tilde{f}^P(\mathbf{w}, \alpha)}{\partial \alpha} \right) \frac{\partial^2 G(\hat{\mathbf{w}}, \hat{\alpha}, \beta)}{\partial \hat{\alpha}^2} \\
= -\frac{\partial G(\hat{\mathbf{w}}, \hat{\alpha}, \beta)}{\partial \hat{\alpha}} + 2\lambda \left(\frac{\partial G(\hat{\mathbf{w}}, \hat{\alpha}, \beta)}{\partial \hat{\alpha}} - \frac{\partial \tilde{f}^P(\mathbf{w}, \alpha)}{\partial \alpha} \right) \mathbf{H}_G(\hat{\alpha}),
\end{aligned} \tag{4.33}
$$

$$
\nabla_{\hat{\mathbf{w}}} \mathcal{L}_{\text{DCP-NAS}}(\tilde{f}^P(\mathbf{w}, \alpha), \ \ \tilde{f}^C_{\mathbf{b}}(\hat{\mathbf{w}}), \hat{\alpha}, \beta) = -\frac{\partial G(\hat{\mathbf{w}}, \hat{\alpha}, \beta)}{\partial \mathbf{b}^{\hat{\mathbf{w}}}} \frac{\partial \mathbf{b}^{\hat{\mathbf{w}}}}{\partial \hat{\mathbf{w}}}, \tag{4.34}
$$

where

$$
\frac{\partial \mathbf{b}^{\hat{\mathbf{w}}}}{\partial \hat{\mathbf{w}}} = \mathbf{1}_{|\hat{\mathbf{w}}| \leq 1}. \tag{4.35}
$$

and λ is a hyperparameter; $\mathbf{H}_{\tilde{f}_{\mathbf{b}}}(\hat{\alpha}) = \frac{\partial^2 \tilde{f}_{\mathbf{b}}(\hat{\mathbf{w}}, \hat{\alpha})}{\partial \hat{\alpha}^2}$ denotes the Hessian matrix. The DCP-NAS process is outlined in Fig. 4.12.

We minimize the difference between the gradient (tangent direction) $\frac{\partial G(\hat{\mathbf{w}}, \hat{\alpha}, \beta)}{\partial \hat{\alpha}}$ and the gradient (tangent direction) $\frac{\partial \tilde{f}^P(\mathbf{w}, \alpha)}{\partial \alpha}$, to search the architectures (both real-valued NAS and binary NAS) in the same direction to generate a better 1-bit architecture. Note that α inherits from $\hat{\alpha}$ at the beginning of each real value NAS iteration, indicating that we only utilize w and α of real value NAS for heuristic optimization direction for 1-bit NAS instead of looking for a better architecture for real value networks. Since a better tangent direction $\frac{\partial \tilde{f}^P(\mathbf{w}, \alpha)}{\partial \alpha}$ is achieved, DCP-NAS can have a more suitable $\hat{\alpha}$ for binary networks. We note that α is different from $\hat{\alpha}$, which is not an optimized architecture for real-valued weights but an optimized architecture for 1-bit weights.

The expression above contains an expensive matrix gradient computation in its second term. Thus, we introduce a first-order approximation of the Hessian matrix to accelerate search efficiency in Section 4.4.5.

4.4.5   Generalized Gauss-Newton Matrix (GGN) for Hessian Matrix

Since the Hessian matrix is computationally expensive, this section mainly tries to accelerate the calculation of the aforementioned Hessian matrix by deriving a second-order expansion based on Eq. 4.34.

In the following, we prove that the Hessian matrix of the loss function is directly related to the expectation of the covariance of the gradient. Taking the loss function as the negative logarithm of the likelihood, let $\mathcal{X}$ be a set of input data from the network and $p(\mathcal{X}; \hat{\mathbf{w}}, \hat{\alpha})$ be the predicted distribution on $\mathcal{X}$ under the parameters of the network are $\hat{\mathbf{w}}$ and $\hat{\alpha}$, *i.e.*, output logits of the head layer.

By omitting $\hat{\mathbf{w}}$ for simplicity, Fisher's information on the set of probability distributions $P = \{p_n(\mathcal{X}; \hat{\alpha}), n \in N\}$ can be described by a matrix whose value in the i-th row and the j-th column.

$$I_{i,j}(\hat{\alpha}) = \mathbb{E}_{\mathcal{X}}\left[\frac{\partial \log p_n(\mathcal{X}; \hat{\alpha})}{\partial \hat{\alpha}_i} \frac{\partial \log p_n(\mathcal{X}; \hat{\alpha})}{\partial \hat{\alpha}_j}\right]. \tag{4.36}$$

Recall that N denotes the number of classes described in Eq. 4.21. It is then trivial to prove that the Fisher information of the probability distribution set P approaches a scaled version of the Hessian of log-likelihood as

$$I_{i,j}(\hat{\alpha}) = -\mathbb{E}_{\mathcal{X}}\left[\frac{\partial^2 \log p_n(\mathcal{X}; \hat{\alpha})}{\partial \hat{\alpha}_i \partial \hat{\alpha}_j}\right]. \tag{4.37}$$

Let $H_{i,j}$ denote the second-order partial derivatives $\frac{\partial^2}{\partial \hat{\alpha}_i \partial \hat{\alpha}_j}$. Note that the first derivative of log-likelihood is

$$\frac{\partial \log p_n(\mathcal{X}; \hat{\alpha})}{\partial \hat{\alpha}_i} = \frac{\partial p_n(\mathcal{X}; \hat{\alpha})}{p_n(\mathcal{X}; \hat{\alpha})\partial \hat{\alpha}_i}, \tag{4.38}$$

The second derivative is

$$\mathbf{H}_{i,j} \log p_n(\mathcal{X}; \hat{\alpha}) = \frac{\mathbf{H}_{i,j} p_n(\mathcal{X}; \hat{\alpha})}{p_n(\mathcal{X}; \hat{\alpha})} - \frac{\partial p_n(\mathcal{X}; \hat{\alpha})}{p_n(\mathcal{X}; \hat{\alpha})\partial \hat{\alpha}_i} \frac{\partial p_n(\mathcal{X}; \hat{\alpha})}{p_n(\mathcal{X}; \hat{\alpha})\partial \hat{\alpha}_j}. \tag{4.39}$$

Considering that

$$\mathbb{E}_{\mathcal{X}}\left(\frac{\mathbf{H}_{i,j} p_n(\mathcal{X}; \hat{\alpha})}{p_n(\mathcal{X}; \hat{\alpha})}\right) = \int \frac{\mathbf{H}_{i,j} p_n(\mathcal{X}; \hat{\alpha})}{p_n(\mathcal{X}; \hat{\alpha})} p_n(\mathcal{X}; \hat{\alpha}) d\mathcal{X}$$
$$= \mathbf{H}_{i,j} \int p_n(\mathcal{X}; \hat{\alpha}) d\mathcal{X} = 0, \tag{4.40}$$

we take the expectation of the second derivative and then obtain the following.

$$\mathbb{E}_{\mathcal{X}}(\mathbf{H}_{i,j} \log p_n(\mathcal{X}; \hat{\alpha})) = -\mathbb{E}_{\mathcal{X}}\left\{\frac{\partial p_n(\mathcal{X}; \hat{\alpha})}{p_n(\mathcal{X}; \hat{\alpha})\partial \hat{\alpha}_i} \frac{\partial p_n(\mathcal{X}; \hat{\alpha})}{p_n(\mathcal{X}; \hat{\alpha})\partial \hat{\alpha}_j}\right\}$$
$$= -\mathbb{E}_{\mathcal{X}}\left\{\frac{\partial p_n(\mathcal{X}; \hat{\alpha})}{\partial \hat{\alpha}_i} \frac{\partial p_n(\mathcal{X}; \hat{\alpha})}{\partial \hat{\alpha}_j}\right\}. \tag{4.41}$$

Thus, an equivalent substitution for the Hessian matrix $\mathbf{H}_{\tilde{f}_{\mathbf{b}}}(\hat{\alpha})$ in Eq. 4.32 is the product of two first-order derivatives. This concludes the proof that we can use the covariance of gradients to represent the Hessian matrix for efficient computation.

4.4.6 Decoupled Optimization for Training the DCP-NAS

In this section, we first describe the coupling relationship between the weights and the architecture parameters in the DCP-NAS. Then we present the decoupled optimization during backpropagation of the sampled supernet to fully and effectively optimize these two coupling parameters.

Coupled models for DCP-NAS Combing Eq. 4.27 and Eq. 4.28, we first show how parameters in DCP-NAS are formulated in a coupling relationship as

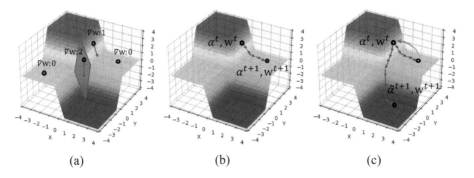

(a)   (b)   (c)

FIGURE 4.14
The loss landscape illustration of supernet. (a) The gradient of current weights with different α, (b) the vanilla α^{t+1} with backpropagation, (c) $\tilde{\alpha}^{t+1}$ with the decoupled optimization.

$\mathbf{a}^{(j)} = \sum_{i<j} \text{softmax}(\alpha_m^{(i,j)})(\mathbf{w}^{(i,j)} \otimes \mathbf{a}^{(i)})$, where $\mathbf{w}^{(i,j)} = [[\mathbf{w}_m]] \in \mathbb{R}_{M \times 1}, \mathbf{w}_m \in \mathbb{R}_{C_{out} \times C_{in} \times K_m \times K_m}$ denotes the weights of all candidate operations between the i-th and j-th nodes and K_m denotes the kernel size of the m-th operation. Specifically, for pooling and identity operations, K_m equals the downsample size and the size of the feature map, $\mathbf{w}_m$ equals $\mathbf{1}/(K_m \times K_m)$ and $\mathbf{1}$, respectively. For each intermediate node, its output $\mathbf{a}^{(j)}$ is jointly determined by $\alpha_m^{(i,j)}$ and $\mathbf{w}_m^{(i,j)}$, while $\mathbf{a}^{(i)}$ is independent of both $\alpha_m^{(i,j)}$ and $\mathbf{w}_m^{(i,j)}$. As shown in Figs. 4.14 (a) and (b), with different α, the gradient of the corresponding $\mathbf{w}$ can be varied and sometimes difficult to optimize, possibly trapped in local minima. However, by decoupling α and $\mathbf{w}$, the supernet can jump out of the local minima and be optimized with better convergence.

Based on the deviation and analysis above, we propose our objective for optimizing the neural architecture search process

$$\arg\min_{\alpha,\mathbf{w}} \mathcal{L}(\mathbf{w}, \alpha) = \begin{cases} \mathcal{L}_{\text{NAS}} + reg(\mathbf{w}), & \text{for Parent model} \\ \mathcal{L}_{\text{DCP-NAS}} + reg(\mathbf{w}), & \text{for Child model} \end{cases} \quad (4.42)$$

where $\alpha \in \mathbb{R}_{E \times M}, \mathbf{w} \in \mathbb{R}_{M \times 1}$, and $reg(\cdot)$ denotes the regularization item. Following [151, 265], the weights $\mathbf{w}$ and the architectural parameters α are optimized sequentially, in which $\mathbf{w}$ and α are updated independently. However, optimizing $\mathbf{w}$ and α independently is improper due to their coupling relationship. We consider the searching and training process of differentiable Chile-Parent neural architecture search as a coupling optimization problem and solve the problem using a new backtracking method. Details will be shown in Section 4.4.6.

Decoupled Optimization for Child-Parent model From a new perspective, we reconsider the coupling relation between $\mathbf{w}$ and α. The derivative calculation process of $\mathbf{w}$ should consider its coupling parameters α. Based on the chain rule [187] and its notation, we have the following.

$$\begin{aligned} \tilde{\alpha}^{t+1} &= \alpha^t + \eta_1\left(-\frac{\partial \mathcal{L}(\alpha^t, \mathbf{w}^t)}{\partial \alpha^t} + \eta_2 Tr[(\frac{\partial \mathcal{L}(\alpha^t, \mathbf{w}^t)}{\partial \mathbf{w}^t})^T \frac{\partial \mathbf{w}^t}{\partial \alpha^t}]\right) \\ &= \alpha^{t+1} + \eta_1 \eta_2 Tr[(\frac{\partial \mathcal{L}(\alpha^t, \mathbf{w}^t)}{\partial \mathbf{w}^t})^T \frac{\partial \mathbf{w}^t}{\partial \alpha^t}], \end{aligned} \quad (4.43)$$

where η_1 represents the learning rate, η_2 represents the backtracking coefficient, and $\tilde{\alpha}^{t+1}$ denotes the value after the backtracking of vanilla α^{t+1}. In contrast, vanilla α^{t+1} is calculated from the backpropagation rule and the corresponding optimizer in the neural network.

$Tr(\cdot)$ represents the trace of a matrix. However, the item $\frac{\partial \mathbf{w}^t}{\partial \alpha^t}$ of Eq. 4.43 is undefined and unsolvable based on the normal backpropagation process. To address this problem, we propose a decoupled optimization method as follows. In the following, we omit the superscript $\cdot^t$ and define $\tilde{\mathcal{L}}$ as

$$\tilde{\mathcal{L}} = (\frac{\partial \mathcal{L}(\alpha, \mathbf{w})}{\partial \mathbf{w}})^T / \alpha, \tag{4.44}$$

which considers the coupling optimization problem as in Eq. 4.42. Note that $R(\cdot)$ is only considered when backtracking. Thus, we have

$$\frac{\partial \mathcal{L}(\alpha, \mathbf{w})}{\partial \mathbf{w}} = Tr[\alpha \tilde{\mathcal{L}} \frac{\partial \mathbf{w}}{\partial \alpha}]. \tag{4.45}$$

For simplifying the derivation, we rewrite $\tilde{\mathcal{L}}$ as $[\tilde{g}_1, \tilde{g}_e, \cdots, \tilde{g}_E]$, where each $\tilde{g}_e$ is a column vector. Assuming that $\mathbf{w}_m$ and $\alpha_{i,j}$ are independent when $m \; != j$, $\alpha_{i,j}$ denotes a specific element in the matrix α, we have

$$(\frac{\partial \mathbf{w}}{\partial \alpha})_m = \begin{bmatrix} 0 & \cdots & \frac{\partial \mathbf{w}_m}{\partial \alpha_{1,m}} & \cdots & 0 \\ \cdot & & \cdot & & \cdot \\ 0 & \cdots & \frac{\partial \mathbf{w}_m}{\partial \alpha_{e,m}} & \cdots & 0 \\ \cdot & & \cdot & & \cdot \\ 0 & \cdots & \frac{\partial \mathbf{w}_m}{\partial \alpha_{E,m}} & \cdots & 0 \end{bmatrix}_{E \times M} \tag{4.46}$$

and with rewritten α as a column vector $[\alpha_1, \alpha_e, \cdots, \alpha_E]^T$ with each α_e is a row vector, we have

$$\alpha \tilde{\mathcal{L}} = \begin{bmatrix} \alpha_1 \tilde{g}_1 & \cdots & \alpha_1 \tilde{g}_e & \cdots & \alpha_1 \tilde{g}_E \\ \cdot & & \cdot & & \cdot \\ \alpha_e \tilde{g}_1 & \cdots & \alpha_e \tilde{g}_e & \cdots & \alpha_e \tilde{g}_E \\ \cdot & & \cdot & & \cdot \\ \alpha_E \tilde{g}_1 & \cdots & \alpha_E \tilde{g}_e & \cdots & \alpha_E \tilde{g}_E \end{bmatrix}_{E \times E}. \tag{4.47}$$

Combing Eq. 4.46 and Eq. 4.47, the matrix in the trace item of Eq. 4.44 can be written as

$$\alpha \tilde{\mathcal{L}}(\frac{\partial \mathbf{w}}{\partial \alpha})_m = \begin{bmatrix} 0 & \cdots & \alpha_1 \sum_{e'=1}^{E} \tilde{g}_{e'} \frac{\partial \mathbf{w}_m}{\partial \alpha_{e',m}} & \cdots & 0 \\ \cdot & & \cdot & & \cdot \\ 0 & \cdots & \alpha_e \sum_{e'=1}^{E} \tilde{g}_{e'} \frac{\partial \mathbf{w}_m}{\partial \alpha_{e',m}} & \cdots & 0 \\ \cdot & & \cdot & & \cdot \\ 0 & \cdots & \alpha_E \sum_{e'=1}^{E} \tilde{g}_{e'} \frac{\partial \mathbf{w}_m}{\partial \alpha_{e',m}} & \cdots & 0 \end{bmatrix}_{E \times M}. \tag{4.48}$$

Thus the whole matrix $\alpha \tilde{\mathcal{L}} \frac{\mathbf{w}}{\alpha}$ is with the size of $E \times M \times M$. After the above derivation, we compute the e-th component of the trace item in Eq. 4.44 as

$$Tr[\alpha \tilde{\mathcal{L}}(\frac{\partial \mathbf{w}}{\partial \alpha})]_e = \alpha_e \sum_{m=1}^{M} \sum_{e'=1}^{E} \tilde{g}_{e'} \frac{\mathbf{w}_m}{\partial \alpha_{e',m}} \tag{4.49}$$

Noting that in the vanilla propagation process, $\alpha^{t+1} = \alpha^t - \eta_1 \frac{\partial \mathcal{L}(\alpha^t)}{\partial \alpha^t}$, thus combining Eq. 4.49 we have

$$\tilde{\alpha}^{t+1} = \alpha^{t+1} - \eta \begin{bmatrix} \sum_{m=1}^{M} \sum_{e'=1}^{E} \tilde{g}_{e'} \frac{\partial \mathbf{w}_m}{\partial \alpha_{e',m}} \\ \cdot \\ \sum_{m=1}^{M} \sum_{e'=1}^{E} \tilde{g}_{e'} \frac{\partial \mathbf{w}_m}{\partial \alpha_{e',m}} \\ \cdot \\ \sum_{m=1}^{M} \sum_{e'=1}^{E} \tilde{g}_{e'} \frac{\partial \mathbf{w}_m}{\partial \alpha_{e',m}} \end{bmatrix} \circledast \begin{bmatrix} \alpha_1 \\ \cdot \\ \alpha_e \\ \cdot \\ \alpha_E \end{bmatrix} \tag{4.50}$$

$$= \alpha^{t+1} + \eta \psi^t \circledast \alpha^t,$$

Algorithm 10 Search process of DCP-NAS

Input: Training data, validation data
Parameter: Searching hyper-graph: $\mathcal{G}$, $M = 8$, $e(o_m^{(i,j)}) = 0$ for all edges
Output: Optimized $\hat{\alpha}^*$.

1: **while** DCP-NAS **do**
2:     **while** Training real-valued Parent **do**
3:         Search a temporary real-valued architecture $p(\mathbf{w}, \alpha)$.
4:         Decoupled optimization from Eqs. 4.43 to 4.53.
5:         Generate the tangent direction $\frac{\partial \tilde{f}(\mathbf{w}, \alpha)}{\partial \alpha}$ from Eqs. 4.21 to 4.29.
6:     **end while**
7:     Architecture inheriting $\hat{\alpha} \leftarrow \alpha$.
8:     **while** Training 1-bit Child **do**
9:         Calculate the learning objective from Eqs. 4.26 to 4.32.
10:        Tangent propagation from Eqs. 4.33 to 4.41 and decoupled optimization from Eqs. 4.43 to 4.53.
11:        Obtain the $\hat{p}(\hat{\mathbf{w}}, \hat{\alpha})$.
12:    **end while**
13:    Architecture inheriting $\alpha \leftarrow \hat{\alpha}$.
14: **end while**
15: **return** Optimized architecture $\hat{\alpha}^*$.

---

where $\circledast$ represents the Hadamard product and $\eta = \eta_1 \eta_2$. We take $\psi^t = -[\sum_{m=1}^{M} \sum_{e'=1}^{E} \tilde{g}_{e'} \frac{\partial \mathbf{w}_m}{\partial \alpha_{e',m}}, \cdots, \sum_{m=1}^{M} \sum_{e'=1}^{E} \tilde{g}_{e'} \frac{\partial \mathbf{w}_m}{\partial \alpha_{e',m}}]^T$. Note that, $\frac{\partial \mathbf{w}}{\partial \alpha}$ is unsolvable and has no explicit form in NAS, which causes an unsolvable ψ^t. Thus we introduce a learnable parameter $\tilde{\psi}^t$ for approximating ψ^t, which back-propagation process is calculated as

$$\tilde{\psi}^{t+1} = |\tilde{\psi}^t - \eta_\psi \frac{\partial \mathcal{L}}{\partial \tilde{\psi}^t}|. \tag{4.51}$$

Eq. 4.50 shows that our method is based on a projection function to solve the optimization coupling problem by the learnable parameter $\tilde{\psi}^t$. In this method, we consider the influence of α^t and backtrack the optimized state in the $(t+1)$-th step to form $\tilde{\alpha}^{t+1}$. However, the key point in optimization is where and when the backtracking should be applied. Thus, we define the update rule as

$$\tilde{\alpha}_m^{t+1} = \begin{cases} P(\alpha_{:,m}^{t+1}, \alpha_{:,m}^t), & \text{if } ranking(R(\mathbf{w}_m)) > \tau \\ \tilde{\alpha}_{:,m}^{t+1}, & \text{otherwise} \end{cases} \tag{4.52}$$

where $P(\alpha_{:,m}^{t+1}, \alpha_{:,m}^t) = \alpha_{:,m}^{t+1} + \eta \tilde{\psi}^t \circledast \alpha_{:,m}^t$ and the subscript $\cdot_m$ denotes a specific edge. $R(\mathbf{w}_m)$ denotes the norm constraint of $\mathbf{w}_m$ and is further defined as

$$R(\mathbf{w}_m) = \|\mathbf{w}_m\|_2^2, \quad \forall m = 1, \cdots, M, \tag{4.53}$$

where τ denotes the threshold for deciding whether or not to backtrack. We further define the threshold as follows.

$$\tau = \lfloor \epsilon \cdot M \rfloor \tag{4.54}$$

where ϵ denotes a hyperparameter to control the percentage of edge backtracking. With backtracking α, the supernet can learn to jump out of the local minima. The general process of DCP-NAS is described in Algorithm 10. Note that the decoupled optimization can be

TABLE 4.2
Effect of with/without the reconstruction error and the
tangent direction constraint on the ImageNet data set. The
architecture used for the experiments is DCP-NAS-L.

Tangent direction ($\mathbf{D}(\hat{\alpha})$)		✗	✓	✗	✓
Reconstruction error ($\mathcal{L}_R(\hat{\mathbf{w}}, \beta)$)		✗	✗	✓	✓
Accuracy	Top-1	66.7	68.3	68.2	**72.4**
	Top-5	83.3	85.0	85.1	**89.2**

used for both parent and child models. When applied to the Child model, the $\mathbf{w}$ here denotes
the reconstructed weights from the binarized weights, *that is,*, $\mathbf{w} = \beta \circ \mathbf{b}^{\hat{\mathbf{w}}}$.

4.4.7 Ablation Study

Effectiveness of Tangent Propagation In this section, we evaluate the effects of the
tangent propagation on the performance of DCP-NAS, the hyperparameter used in this
section includes λ, μ. Furthermore, we also discuss the effectiveness of the reconstruction
error. The implementation details are given below.

For searching for a better binary neural architecture, λ and μ are used to balance the
KL divergence $\tilde{f}(\hat{\mathbf{w}}, \hat{\alpha}, \beta)$ to supervise the Child, the reconstruction error for binary weights
$\mathcal{L}_R(\hat{\mathbf{w}}, \beta)$ and the constraint in the tangent direction $\mathbf{D}(\hat{\alpha})$. We evaluated λ and μ on the
ImageNet data set with the DCP-NAS-L architecture. To better understand tangent prop-
agation on the large-scale ImageNet ILSVRC12 dataset, we experimented to examine how
the tangent direction constraint affects performance. Based on the experiments described
above, we first set λ to $5e - 3$ and μ to 0.2 if they are used. As shown in Table 4.2, both

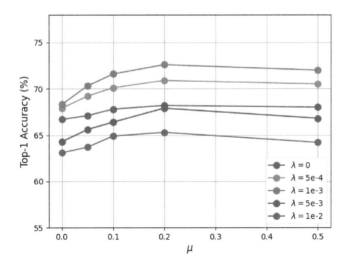

FIGURE 4.15
With different λ and μ, we evaluated the Top-1 accuracies of DCP-NAS-L
on ImageNet.

TABLE 4.3

Search efficiency for different search strategies on ImageNet, including previous NAS in both the real-valued and 1-bit search space, random search, and our DCP-NAS.

Method		T.P.	GGN	D.O.	Top-1 Acc.	Search Cost
Real-valued NAS	PNAS	-	-	-	74.2	225
	DARTS	-	-	-	73.1	4
	PC-DARTS	-	-	-	75.8	3.8
Direct BNAS	$BNAS_1$	-	-	-	64.3	2.6
	$BNAS_2$-H	-	-	-	63.5	-
	Random Search				51.3	4.4
Auxiliary BNAS	CP-NAS	-	-	-	66.5	2.8
	DCP-NAS-L	✔	✘	✘	71.4	27.9
	DCP-NAS-L	✔	✔	✘	71.2	2.9
	DCP-NAS-L	✔	✘	✔	**72.6**	27.9
	DCP-NAS-L	✔	✔	✔	72.4	**2.9**

Note: T.P. and D.O. denote Tangent Propagation and Decoupled Optimization, respectively.

the tangent direction constraint and the reconstruction error can improve the accuracy on ImageNet. When applied together, the Top-1 accuracy reaches the highest value of 72.4%. Then we conduct experiments with various values of λ and μ as shown in Figure 4.15. We observe that with a fixed value of μ, the accuracy of Top-1 increases in the beginning with increasing λ, but decreases when λ is greater than 1e-3. When λ becomes larger, DCP-NAS tends to select the binary architecture with a gradient similar to that of its real-valued counterpart. To some extent, the 1-bit model's accuracy is neglected, leading to a performance drop. Another phenomenon of performance variation is that the accuracy of Top-1 increases first and then decreases with increasing μ while λ contains fixed values. Too much attention paid to minimizing the distance between 1-bit parameters and their counterparts may introduce a collapse of the representation ability to 1-bit models and severely degenerate the performance of DCP-NAS.

To better understand the acceleration rate of applying the Generalized Gauss-Newton (GGN) matrix in the search process, we conducted experiments to examine the search cost with and without GGN. As shown in Table 4.3, we compare the searching efficiency and the accuracy of the architecture obtained by Random Search (random selection), Real-valued NAS methods, Binarized NAS methods, CP-NAS, DCP-NAS without GGN method, and DCP-NAS with GGN applied. In a random search, the 1-bit supernet randomly samples and trains an architecture in each epoch, then assigns the expectation of all performance to each corresponding edge and operations, and returns the architecture with the highest score, which lacks the necessary guidance in the search process and therefore has poor performance for binary architecture search. Notably, our DCP-NAS without GGN is highly computationally consumed for the second-order gradient, which is necessarily computed in the tangent propagation. Note that directly optimizing two supernets is computationally redundant. However, the introduction of GGN for the Hessian matrix significantly accelerates the search process, reducing the search cost to almost 10% with a negligible accuracy vibration. As shown in Table 4, with the use of GGN, our method reduces the search cost from 29 to 2.9, which is more efficient than DARTS. Additionally, our DCP-NAS achieves a

TABLE 4.4

Results of the comparison on the ImageNet dataset with DCP-NAS of the distance calculation method used to constrain the gradient of binary NAS in the tangent direction, *i.e.*, Eq. 4.31. We use the small size of the model, *that is,* DCP-NAS-S, to evaluate the searched architecture.

Method	Accuracy(%)		Memory (MBits)	Search Cost
	Top1	Top5		
Cosine similarity	62.5	83.9	4.2	2.9
L1-norm	62.7	84.3	4.3	2.9
F-norm	**63.0**	**84.5**	4.2	2.9

much smaller performance gap between real-valued NAS with a lower search cost by a clear margin. We conduct ablative experiments for different architecture discrepancy calculation methods to further clarify the tangent propagation. As shown in Table 4.4, F-norm applied in Eq. 4.31 achieves the best performance, while the cosine similarity and the L1-norm are not as effective as the F-norm.

5

Applications in Natural Language Processing

5.1 Background

We first overview the background of three aspects of this section: quantization-aware training for the low-bit language model, post-training quantization for the low-bit language model, and binary language model.

5.1.1 Quantization-Aware Training (QAT) for Low-Bit Large Language Models

Large pre-trained language models have achieved remarkable success in various natural language processing tasks resorting to the increasing model size and computation overhead [227, 54, 21], which make it prohibitive to deploy these language models on many resource-constrained devices. To make the deployment of existing language models possible, various model compression techniques have been proposed, such as pruning [64, 172, 244], knowledge distillation [107, 217], weight-sharing [51, 125, 98], dynamic computation with adaptive depth or width [88, 255, 298], and network quantization [285, 221, 195, 6]. Among these techniques, network quantization enjoys the merit of reducing the size of the model and the computation overhead without modifying the network architecture. It thus receives extensive favor, and many methods have been explored to quantify language models.

For now, most language model quantization methods follow quantization-aware training (QAT), in which the full-precision model is trained for an entire training process. In practice, such QAT-based methods usually perform better than other quantization paradigms, such as post-training quantization (PTQ).

5.1.2 Post-Training Quantization (PTQ) for Low-Bit Large Language Models

Despite QAT producing a satisfactory performance for large language models compared with post-training quantization (PTQ), which relies on a small calibration set to perform quantization, it often suffers from several issues. Specifically, QAT usually conducts end-to-end back-propagation training over the whole training set, which can be slow in training time, memory demanding, and data consuming. These issues can sometimes be prohibited for industrial language models.

Compared with the PTQ method, QAT mainly has drawbacks in three aspects: training time, memory demand, and data consumption. First, QAT conducts training over the entire training set, so it takes much more time than PTQ over the calibration set. Moreover, recent QAT methods [6, 285] further combine two-stage knowledge distillation [107], which can take nearly four times longer than FP model training. The slow training time undoubtedly affects the easiness of industrial language models. Second, conducting QAT on memory-limited devices is sometimes prohibited due to the increasing size of large language models. As demonstrated in [5], the QAT method [285] even consumes 8.3 GB more memory than FP when trained with knowledge distillation. On the contrary, PTQ methods can conduct quantization by only caching the intermediate results of each layer, which can be fed into memory-limited training devices. Third, the training set is sometimes inaccessible due to industry data security or privacy issues. In contrast, PTQ constructs the small calibration set by sampling only $1K \sim 4K$ instances from the whole training set.

In summary, PTQ is an appealing, efficient alternative in training time, memory overhead, and data consumption. Generally, instead of the whole training set, PTQ methods leverage only a small portion of training data to minimize the layer-wise reconstruction error incurred by quantization [101, 179, 180]. The layer-wise objective breaks down the end-to-end training, solving the quantization optimization problem in a more sample-efficient [297] and memory-saving way. Nonetheless, it is non-trivial to directly apply previous PTQ methods for language models such as BERT [54], as the performance drops sharply. For this reason, some efforts are investigated to improve performance.

5.1.3 Binary BERT Pre-Trained Models

Recent pre-trained BERT models have advanced the state-of-the-art performance in various natural language tasks [227, 55]. Nevertheless, deploying BERT models on resource-constrained edge devices is challenging due to the massive parameters and floating-point operations (FLOPs), limiting the application of pre-trained BERT models. To mitigate this, model compression techniques are widely studied and applied for deploying BERTs in resource-constrained and real-time scenarios, including knowledge distillation [206, 217, 106], parameter pruning [172, 64], low-rank approximation [166, 126], weight sharing [50, 126, 98], dynamic networks with adaptive depth and/or width [89, 255], and quantization [280, 208, 65, 285].

Among all these model compression approaches, quantization, which utilizes lower bit-width representation for model parameters, emerges as an efficient way to deploy compact BERT models on edge devices. Theoretically, it compresses the model by replacing each 32-bit floating-point parameter with a low-bit fixed-point representation. Existing attempts try to quantize pre-trained BERT [280, 208, 65] to even as low as ternary values (2-bit) with minor performance drop [285]. More aggressively, binarization of the weights and activations of BERT [6, 195, 222, 156, 40] could bring at most $32\times$ reduction in model sizes and replace most floating-point multiplications with additions, which significantly alleviate the huge parameter and FLOPs burden.

Network binarization is first proposed in [48] and has been extensively studied in the academia [199, 99, 159]. For BERT binarization, a general workflow is to binarize the representation in BERT architecture in the forward propagation and apply distillation to the optimization in the backward propagation. In detail, the forward and backward propagation of sign function in binarized network can be formulated as:

$$\text{Forward: } \text{sign}(x) = \begin{cases} 1 & \text{if } x \geq 0 \\ -1 & \text{otherwise} \end{cases}, \tag{5.1}$$

$$\text{Backward: } \frac{\partial C}{\partial x} = \begin{cases} \frac{\partial C}{\partial \, \text{sign}(x)} & \text{if } |x| \leq 1 \\ 0 & \text{otherwise} \end{cases}, \tag{5.2}$$

where x is the input and C is the cost function for the minibatch. $\text{sign}(\cdot)$ function is applied in the forward propagation while the straight-through estimator (STE) [9] is used to obtain the derivative in the backward propagation. In detail, for the weight of binarized linear layers, the common practice is to redistribute the weight to *zero-mean* for retaining representation information [199] and applies scaling factors to minimize quantization errors [199]. The activation is binarized by the sign without re-scaling for computational efficiency. Thus, the computation can be expressed as

$$
\text{bi-linear}(\mathbf{X}) = \alpha_{\mathbf{w}}(\text{sign}(\mathbf{X}) \otimes \text{sign}(\mathbf{W} - \mu(\mathbf{W}))),
$$
$$
\alpha_{\mathbf{w}} = \frac{1}{n}\|\mathbf{W}\|_{\ell 1},
$$
(5.3)

where $\mathbf{W}$ and $\mathbf{X}$ denote full-precision weight and activation, $\mu(\cdot)$ denotes the mean value, $\alpha_{\mathbf{w}}$ is the scaling factors for weight, and $\otimes$ denotes the matrix multiplication with bitwise xnor and bitcount. Besides, the quantization of activation $\mathbf{X}$ in Eq. (5.3) is set to higher bit-widths in some works to boost the performance of binarized BERT [6, 222].

The input data first passes through a quantized embedding layer before being fed into the transformer blocks [285, 6]. And each transformer block consists of two main components are the Multi-Head Attention (MHA) module and the Feed-Forward Network (FFN). The computation of MHA depends on queries $\mathbf{Q}$, keys $\mathbf{K}$, and values $\mathbf{V}$, which are derived from hidden states $\mathbf{H} \in \mathbb{R}^{N \times D}$. N represents the length of the sequence, and D represents the dimension of features. For a specific transformer layer, the computation in an attention head can be expressed as

$$
\mathbf{Q} = \text{bi-linear}_Q(\mathbf{H}),
$$
$$
\mathbf{K} = \text{bi-linear}_K(\mathbf{H}),
$$
(5.4)
$$
\mathbf{V} = \text{bi-linear}_V(\mathbf{H}),
$$

where bi-linear$_Q$, bi-linear$_K$, and bi-linear$_V$ represent three different binarized linear layers for $\mathbf{Q}, \mathbf{K},$ and $\mathbf{V}$, respectively. Then the attention score $\mathbf{A}$ is computed as follows:

$$
\mathbf{A} = \frac{1}{\sqrt{D}}\left(\mathbf{B_Q} \otimes \mathbf{B_K}^{\top}\right),
$$
(5.5)
$$
\mathbf{B_Q} = \text{sign}(\mathbf{Q}), \quad \mathbf{B_K} = \text{sign}(\mathbf{K}),
$$

where $\mathbf{B_Q}$ and $\mathbf{B_K}$ are the binarized query and key, respectively. Note that the obtained attention weight is then truncated by attention mask, and each row in $\mathbf{A}$ can be regarded as a k-dim vector, where k is the number of unmasked elements. Then attention weights $\mathbf{B_A^s}$ are binarized as

$$
\mathbf{B_A^s} = \text{sign}(\text{softmax}(\mathbf{A})).
$$
(5.6)

Despite the appealing properties of network binarization for relieving the massive parameters and FLOPs, it is technically hard from an optimization perspective for BERT binarization. As illustrated in Fig. 5.1, the performance for quantized BERT drops mildly from 32-bit to as low as 2-bit, *i.e.*, around 0.6% ↓ on MRPC and 0.2% ↓ on MNLI-m of the GLUE benchmark [230]. However, when reducing the bit-width to one, the performance drops sharply, *i.e.*, $\sim$ 3.8% ↓ and $\sim$ 0.9% ↓ on the two tasks. In summary, binarization of BERT brings severe performance degradation compared with other weight bit-widths. Therefore, BERT binarization remains a challenging yet valuable task for academia and industries. This section surveys existing works and advances for binarizing BERT pre-trained models.

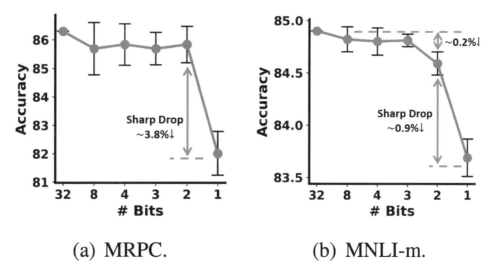

(a) MRPC.   (b) MNLI-m.

FIGURE 5.1
Performance of quantized BERT with varying weight bit-widths and 8-bit activation on MRPC and MNLI-m.

5.2 Fully Quantized Transformer for Machine Translation

Prato *et al.* introduce FullyQT, an all-inclusive quantization strategy for the Transformer. Also, it is the first work to show that it is possible to avoid any loss in translation quality with a fully quantized transformer [190]. Their method contains four parts: the quantization scheme, the choice of quantized layer, tensor bucketing, and a unique design for zeros.

5.2.1 Quantization Scheme

The quantization scheme was uniform, meaning that the step size between two quantized values is constant. This choice, which is an additional constraint, was made for practical reasons. It simplifies all computations required during inference, enabling the exploitation of hardware resources more efficiently. Given an element x of a tensor X, uniform quantization scheme is defined as:

$$\mathcal{Q}(x) = \lfloor \frac{clamp(x; x_{min}, x_{max}) - x_{min}}{s} \rceil, \tag{5.7}$$

where x_{min} and x_{max} defines the endpoints of the quantization interval. The *clamp* function associates all values outside of the $[x_{max}, x_{max}]$ range to the closest endpoint, and $\lfloor \cdot \rceil$ represents rounding to the nearest integer.

The step size s is computed by:

$$s = \frac{x_{min} - x_{min}}{2^b - 1}, \tag{5.8}$$

where b is simply the bit precision.

When quantization is applied to weights, x_{min} and x_{max} are respectively $min(X)$ and $max(X)$. However, when quantization is applied to activations, those values are running

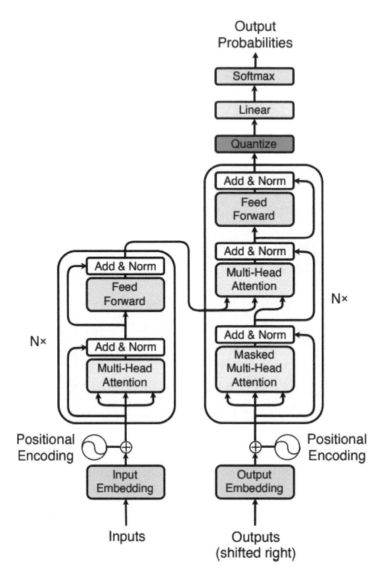

FIGURE 5.2
Fully quantized transformer.

estimates computed during training. For every forward pass, x_{min} and x_{max} variables are updated via an exponential moving average with a momentum of 0.9.

During backpropagation, the straight-through estimator [37] is used to Bypass the undifferentiable round function, and the gradients of clamped values are set to zero.

5.2.2 What to Quantize

They choose to quantize all operations, which can provide a computational speed gain at inference. The overview is presented in Fig. 5.2. In particular, they quantize all matrix multiplications, meaning that the inputs and weights of MatMuls will both be b-bit quantized. The model's divisions are also quantized as long as the numerator and denominator are

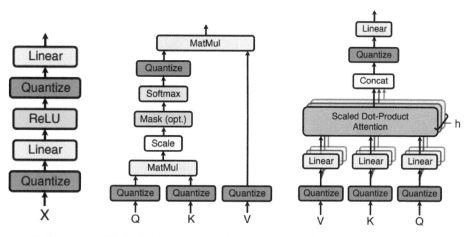

(a)   Feed-forward   (b) Scaled Dot-Product Attention.   (c) Multi-Head Self-Attention.
Networks.

FIGURE 5.3
(a) Feed-forward Networks. (b) Scaled Dot-Product Attention. (c) Multi-Head Self-Attention.

second or higher-dimension tensors. For all other operations, such as sums, the computational cost added by the quantization operation outweighs the benefit of operating with reduced precision. As a result, they do not quantize such operations. More precisely, all weights of the Transformer are quantized, excluding biases, due to the biases being summed with the INT32 output of matrix multiplications, which provide no additional computational efficiency from being quantized. Furthermore, the memory space of biases is insignificant compared to the weight matrices. The biases only represent less than 0.1% of total weights. As for positional embeddings, the authors quantized the embeddings once before training due to the fixed positional embeddings. The γ weights of LayerNorms are also quantized. For activations, the authors quantize the sum of the input embeddings with the positional encodings in both the encoder and decoder. The (Q, K, V) matrixs within the multi-head self-attention are quantized. Also, the softmax's numerator, the softmax's denominator, the softmax's output, and the scaled dot-product attention's output are quantized, as shown in Fig. 5.3(b) and Fig. 5.3(c). At the inference stage, the authors adopt the exponential function to replace the softmax to make the full-precision exponential function a low-bit format. For the position-wise feed-forward networks, they quantize the output of the ReLUs and the feed-forward themselves, as shown in Fig. 5.3(a). Finally, for all LayerNorms, we quantize the numerator $x - \mu$, the denominator $\sqrt{\sigma^2 + \epsilon}$, their quotient, and the output of the LayerNorm.

5.2.3   Tensor Bucketing

The authors adopt tensor bucketing, where they quantize subsets of the tensor with each set of quantization parameters instead of using a single set of quantization parameters per quantized tensor. Even though this adds more scalars, the memory cost is insignificant overall. Furthermore, the authors argue that the added flexibility can significantly alleviate the precision loss, thanks to all values being mapped to a single low numerical precision domain. This tensor bucketing method uses several subsets equal to the output dimension

TABLE 5.1
Performance of our quantization method on the WMT14 EN-DE and WMT14 EN-FR test set.

Model	Method	Precision	EN-DE				EN-FR			
			PPL	BLEU	Size (Gb)	Compr.	PPL	BLEU	Size (Gb)	Compr.
Base	Baseline	32-bit	4.95	26.46	2.02	1x	3.21	38.34	1.94	1x
	Default Approach	8-bit	74.04	0.21	0.52	3.91x	*nan*	0	0.50	3.91x
	Post-Quantization	8-bit	4.97	26.44	0.52	3.91x	3.26	38.30	0.50	3.91x
	FullyQT	8-bit	4.94	26.38	0.52	3.91x	3.23	**38.41**	0.50	3.91x
	Post-Quantization	6-bit	6.00	24.84	0.39	5.18x	3.98	35.02	0.37	5.17x
	FullyQT	6-bit	5.09	**26.98**	0.39	5.18x	3.38	37.07	0.37	5.17x
	FullyQT	4-bit	11.96	18.32	0.26	7.66x	48.21	1.59	0.25	7.64x
Big	Baseline	32-bit	4.38	**27.13**	6.85	1x	2.77	**40.54**	6.69	1x
	Post-Quantization	8-bit	4.27	26.55	1.74	3.95x	2.78	39.78	1.69	3.95x
	FullyQT	8-bit	4.57	26.96	1.74	3.95x	2.80	40.25	1.69	3.95x
	Post-Quantization	6-bit	5.12	24.86	1.31	5.24x	3.08	37.92	1.28	5.24x
	FullyQT	6-bit	4.78	26.76	1.31	5.24x	2.87	39.59	1.28	5.24x
	FullyQT	4-bit	33.11	10.22	0.88	7.79x	42.42	2.81	0.86	7.79x

for all weight matrices. For activations, they use tensor bucketing for the following tensors: the sum of input embeddings with the positional encoding, the Q, K, V inputs, the scaled dot-product attention's output, the feed-forward's output, the LayerNorm's numerator, quotient, and output.

5.2.4 Dealing with Zeros

Unlike the classic quantization method proposed in [104], they do not nudge the domain so that the zero value gets perfectly mapped. Specifically, the only zero values are the padding, the Softmax numerator, and output, the output of ReLU layers, and dropouts. Since padding does not affect the final output, they ignore these values when quantizing. For the quantization parameter, x_{min} for ReLUs and the Softmax's numerator and output are fixed to 0, guaranteeing the perfect value mapping. Finally, quantization is applied before any dropout operation.

In Table 5.1 shows the performance of the proposed method on the WMT14 EN-DE and WMT14 EN-FR. They compare results with two full-precision Transformers: base and big variants. Two other quantization approaches are evaluated. The first is the "default" approach, which naively quantizes every possible operation. The second approach applies the proposed quantization strategy post-training. In all cases except for post-quantization, BLEU was computed on the test set using the checkpoint which scored the highest accuracy on the validation set. Towards the end of training, they ran one validation epoch for every 100 training steps. Baselines and FullyQT 8-bit results were averaged over 5 trials. Standard deviation of the BLEU scores did not seem higher for any method and ranged between 0.09 and 0.51. Training with quantization was about twice as slow as with the baselines. As for post-training quantization, the BLEU score was computed on the test set using the best validation performance out of 20 trials. The default approach's nan in the EN-FR task is due to numerical instability. By quantizing every operation, zeros in the LayerNorm's denominator are more frequent.

In summary, this paper's contributions are as follows: (1) a uniform quantization scheme; (2) a detailed demonstration of the choice of quantized layer; (3) a tensor bucketing method for achieving higher precision; and (4) a special design for zeros.

5.3   Q-BERT: Hessian-Based Ultra Low-Precision Quantization of BERT

Shen *et al.* [209] proposes Q-BERT, a low precision uniform quantization method that utilizes the second order Hessian information. In particular, a Hessian-based mix-precision method and a new group-wise quantization scheme are introduced.

5.3.1   Hessian-Based Mix-Precision

Due to different encoder layers attending to different structures and exhibiting different sensitivity to quantization [45], the authors argue that assigning the same number of bits to all the layers is sub-optimal. Thus, they explore mixed-precision quantization, where more bits are assigned to more sensitive layers to retain performance. Previous method has developed a Hessian AWare Quantization (HAWQ) [59] to determine mixed-bits assignments for each layer. Its main idea is that the parameters in layers with higher Hessian spectrum (*i.e.*, larger top eigenvalues) are more sensitive to quantization and require higher precision than layers with small Hessian spectrum. However, they argue that the number of parameters for each encoder layer in a transformer-based model is larger, *e.g.*, 7M. Given that the Hessian of each layer is a matrix of size 7M $\times$7M, directly compute the second-order statistics is infeasible. However, the authors adopt a matrix-free power iteration method [270] to compute the Hessian spectrum, which does not require the explicit formation of the operator. The matrix-free power iteration method can provide the top eigenvalues, which are then used as the indicator of the sensitivity of a layer. The previous method [59] uses the averaged top eigenvalues for different training data as the indicator. More aggressive quantization is performed for layers with smaller top eigenvalues, corresponding to a flatter loss landscape. However, the authors find that assigning bits based only on the average top eigenvalues is infeasible for many NLP tasks, due to the top eigenvalues of Hessian for some layers exhibiting very high variance with respect to different portions of the input dataset. To address this, the following metric instead of just using mean value is adopted:

$$\Omega_i = |mean(\lambda_i)| + std(\lambda_i), \tag{5.9}$$

where λ_i is the distribution of the top eigenvalues of Hessian of layer i, calculated with 10% of training dataset. After Ω_i is computed, they sort them in descending order, and use it as a metric to relatively determine the quantization precision. Then, quantization-aware finetuning is performed based on the selected precision setting. The eigenvalue distribution of various datasets are provided in Fig. 5.5.

5.3.2   Group-Wise Quantization

For Bert-base, the dimension of each input token is 768 and each self-attention head has 4 dense matrices. Directly quantizing the 4 matrices in multi-head self-attention as an entirety with the same quantization range can significantly degrade the accuracy, since there are more than 2M parameters in total, and the weights corresponding to each neuron may lie in a different range of full-precision numbers. Although channel-wise quantization can be used to alleviate this problem in CNNs, each convolutional kernel can be treated as a single output channel with its own quantization range. However, because each dense matrix used in the transformer-based model adopts a single kernel, channel-wise quantization cannot be directly applied. Therefore, the authors propose group-wise quantization for attention-based models. In particular, each individual matrix W with respect to each head in one

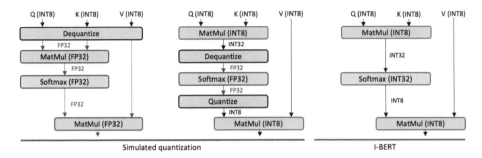

FIGURE 5.4
The overview of algorithm prproposed in [118].

dense matrix of multi-head self-attention is treated as a group. As a result, there will be 12 groups since there are 12 heads. Then, in each group, they bucket sequential output neurons together as sub-groups, *e.g.*, each N output neurons as one sub-group. Consequently, there are $12 \times \frac{64}{N}$ sub-group in total (the hidden dim in each head of Bert-base is $\frac{768}{12} = 64$). Now, each subgroup has its own quantization range. Fig. 5.6 presents an illustration. Here N_h

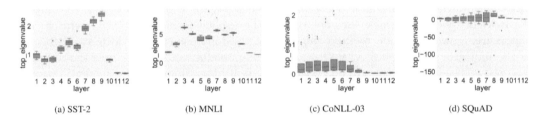

FIGURE 5.5
Top eigenvalue distributions for different encoder layers for various datasets including SST-2, MNLI, CoNNL-03, and SQuAD. The middle layers generally have higher mean values and larger variance than the others. The last three layers have the smallest variance and mean values among all layers.

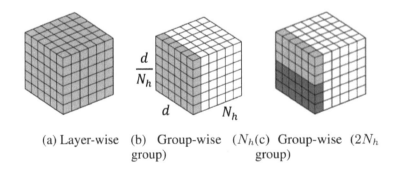

FIGURE 5.6
The overview of group-wise quantization method proposed in [209]. Here N_h (number of heads) value matrices W_v are concatenated together, resulting in a 3-d tensor. The same color denotes the same group with a shared quantization range.

TABLE 5.2

Quantization results for BERT-base on SST-2. Results are obtained with 128 groups in each layer.

Method	w-bits	e-bits	Acc	Size	Size-w/o-e
Baseline	32	32	93.00	415.4	324.5
Q-BERT	8	8	92.88	103.9	81.2
DirectQ	4	8	85.67	63.4	40.6
Q-BERT	4	8	**92.66**	63.4	40.6
DirectQ	3	8	82.86	53.2	30.5
Q-BERT	3	8	**92.54**	53.2	30.5
Q-BERT(MP)	2/4(MP)	8	**92.55**	53.2	30.5
DirectQ	2	8	80.62	43.1	20.4
Q-BERT	2	8	**84.63**	43.1	20.4
Q-BERT(MP)	2/3(MP)	8	**92.08**	**48.1**	**25.4**

Note: The quantization bits used for weights is abbreviated as "w-bits," embedding as "e-bits," model size in MB as "Size," and model size without embedding layer in MB as "Size-w/o-e." For simplicity and efficacy, all the models except for Baseline are using 8-bits activation. Here "MP" refers to mixed-precision quantization.

(number of heads) value matrices W_v are concatenated together, resulting in a 3-d tensor. For layer-wise quantization, as shown in Fig. 5.6(a), the entire 3-d tensor will be quantized into the same range of discrete numbers. A special case of group-wise quantization is that each dense matrix is a group, and every matrix can have its own quantization range as shown in Fig. 5.6(b). A more general case in Fig. 5.6(c) instead provides a more general case where each dense matrix with respect to output neuron is partitioned, and every continuous $\frac{d}{2N_h}$ output neurons is bucketed as a group.

The results of Q-BERT on the development set of SST-2 are presented Table 5.2. SST-2 is a movie review dataset with binary annotations, where the binary label indicates positive and negative reviews. It can be seen that Q-BERT outperform the baseline by a large margin over various bit pricsions.

5.4 I-BERT: Integer-Only BERT Quantization

Kim *et al.* [118] propose I-BERT to construct an integer-only BERT. Their motivation comes from the fact that previous quantization schemes for transformer-based language models use simulated quantization (fake quantization), where all or part of operations in the inference (*e.g.*, GELU, Softmax, and Layer Normalization) are carried out with floating point arithmetic. Such approaches are illustrated in the left side of Fig. 5.4. However, such approaches are hard to deploy in real-edge application scenarios where many neural accelerators or popular edge processors do not support floating-point arithmetic. To solve these challenges, an integer-only quantization for Bert is necessary. Specifically, the proposed I-BERT incorporates a series of novel integer-only quantization schemes for transformer-based language models including new kernels for the efficient and accurate integer-only computation of GELU and Softmax, a known algorithm [49] for integer calculation of square root is utilized to perform integer-only computation for LayerNorm. Finally, an integral framework is introduced by exploiting these approximations of GELU, Softmax, and LayerNorm. The illustration of I-BERT is presented in the right side of Fig. 5.4.

5.4.1 Integer-Only Computation of GELU and Softmax

For the integer-only computation of GELU and Softmax, they use a class of interpolating polynomials to approximate the function. Given the function value for a set of $n+1$ different data points $\{(x_0, f_0), ..., (x_n, f_n)\}$, the target is to find a polynomial of degree at most n that exactly matches the function value at these points. They argue that a unique polynomial of degree at most n passes through all the data points and proposes an analytic solution for the target polynomial.

5.4.2 Integer-Only Computation of LayerNorm

For integer-only LayerNorm, the challenge is that the input statistics (*i.e.*, μ, and σ) change rapidly along with training, and these values must be calculated dynamically during run-time. Computing μ is straightforward, however, evaluating σ requires the square-root function. To approximate the square-root function by integer-only calculation, the authors adopt an efficiently iterative algorithm proposed in [49]. Given any non-negative integer input n, based on the Newton's Method, the algorithm iteratively searches for the exact value of $\lfloor \sqrt{n} \rfloor$ and only requires integer arithmetic. Then, the rest of the non-linear operations in LayerNorm such as division and square are straightforwardly computed with integer arithmetic.

The integer-only quantization results for RoBERTa-Base/Large are presented in Table 5.3. As one can see, I-BERT consistently achieves comparable or slightly higher accuracy than the baseline. For RoBERTa-Base, I-BERT achieves higher accuracy for all cases (up to 1.4 for RTE), except for MNLI-m, QQP, and STS-B tasks. Also, a similar behavior on the RoBERTa-Large model can be observed, where I-BERT matches or outperforms the baseline accuracy for all the downstream tasks. On average, I-BERT outperforms the baseline by 0.3/0.5 for RoBERTa-Base/Large, respectively.

TABLE 5.3

I-BERT quantization result for RoBERTa-Base and RoBERTa-Large on the development set of the GLUE benchmark. Baseline is trained from the pre-trained models, and I-BERT is quantized and fine-tuned from the baseline.

		RoBERTa-Base									
Method	Precision	MNLI-m	MNLI-mm	QQP	QNLI	SST-2	CoLA	STS-B	MRPC	RTE	Avg.
Baseline	FP32	**87.8**	**87.4**	**90.4**	**92.8**	94.6	61.2	**91.1**	90.9	78.0	86.0
I-BERT	INT8	87.5	**87.4**	90.2	**92.8**	**95.2**	**62.5**	90.8	**91.1**	**79.4**	**86.3**
Diff		-0.3	0.0	-0.2	0.0	+0.6	+1.3	-0.3	+0.2	+1.4	+0.3
		RoBERTa-Large									
Method	Precision	MNLI-m	MNLI-mm	QQP	QNLI	SST-2	CoLA	STS-B	MRPC	RTE	Avg.
Baseline	FP32	90.0	89.9	92.8	94.1	96.3	68.0	**92.2**	91.8	86.3	89.0
I-BERT	INT8	**90.4**	**90.3**	**93.0**	**94.5**	**96.4**	**69.0**	92.2	**93.0**	**87.0**	**89.5**
Diff		+0.4	+0.4	+0.2	+0.4	+0.1	+1.0	0.0	+1.2	+0.7	+0.5

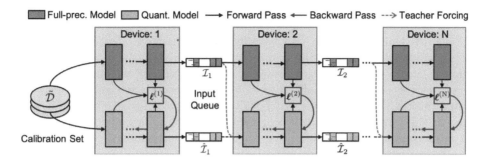

FIGURE 5.7
The overview of algorithm proposed in [5].

In summary, this paper's contributions are as follows: (1) new kernels for the efficient and accurate integer-only GELU and Softmax. That is, the GELU and Softmax are approximated with lightweight second-order polynomials, which can be evaluated with integer-only arithmetic; (2) integer-only LayerNorm computation by leveraging a known algorithm for integer calculation of square root [49]; and (3) a total integer-only quantization for language models by utilizing the proposed approximations of GELU, Softmax.

5.5 Toward Efficient Post-Training Quantization of Pre-Trained Language Models

Bai *et al.* [5] proposes MREM that aims at improving the performance of post-training quantization for language models, while simultaneously maintaining the training efficiency, memory overhead, and data accessibility equipped by post-training quantization. The algorithm overview proposed in [5] is presented in Fig. 5.7. As can be seen, the full-precision and quantized models are first partitioned into multiple modules, then put on different computing devices. Each module samples input tensor from its input queue, which makes them can be trained locally without waiting for their predecessors. Moreover, teacher forcing is applied to mitigate the issue of reconstruction error propagation on the quantized module.

5.5.1 Module-Wise Reconstruction Error Minimization

At first, the language models are partitioned into multiple modules, each consisting of multiple transformer layers. Then, they propose module-wise reconstruction error minimization (MREM) to optimize each module's model weight and quantization parameters, which permits sufficient optimization. Specifically, given a language model with L transformer layers, embedding layers and the classification head, the model is partitioned into N modules. Suppose the n-th module contains p transformer layers, then it include $[l_j, l_{j+1}, l_{j+2}, \ldots, l_{j+p-1}]$ transformer layers with l_j being the first layer of this module. The proposed MREM aims at minimizing the joint reconstruction errors between all intermediate output $\hat{f}_l$ of the quantized n-th module from its full-precision counterpart f_l as follows:

$$\mathcal{L}_n = \sum_{i=j}^{j+p-1} \|\hat{f}_{l_i} - f_{l_i}\|_2. \tag{5.10}$$

The learnable weights and quantization parameters in the n-th module are updated by minimizing the reconstruction errors. The proposed MREM can be optimized parallelly: given previously trained modules, only weights and quantization parameters in the current module are updated. Moreover, the number of modules N can be adjusted depending on the memory constraint of computing resources. The flexibility of the number of transformer layers ensures the proper trade-off between layer-wise correlation and memory overhead of training devices can be achieved. Although a similar block-wise objective is previously proposed in [137], it requires calculating second-order Hessian matrices for optimization, which can be computationally prohibitive for large language models.

5.5.2   Model Parallel Strategy

Second, a new model parallel strategy is designed to accelerate the training process of MREM. A common strategy is to optimize each module one by one. However, the training of this strategy still needs a long time. Motivated by this, the authors propose a model parallel strategy that allows all modules to be trained jointly without synchronizing with adjacent partition modules by allocating each partitioned module to the individual computing device. Specifically, every module is computed one after another in the first t_0 step to construct an input queue $\mathcal{I}$, which contains t_0 intermediate output results. For the n-th module, its input queue comes from the previous module, *i.e.*, $\mathcal{I}_{n-1}^t = \left\{ f_{n-1}^1, f_{n-1}^2, f_{n-1}^3, \ldots, f_{n-1}^{t_0} \right\}$. Then, parallel training takes place. Each module samples its input from the correspondingly input queue and optimizes the loss defined by Eq. (5.10). Meanwhile, the input queue is also updated with the first-in-first-out rule throughout the training. Once a module produces its output, the results will be fed into the following input queue. In the backward pass, the gradients can propagate locally within each module, without affecting its predecessors. As a result, such a design can avoid the load imbalance issue from straggler modules, bringing nearly the theoretical $N\times$ speed-up if deploying in N GPU. Such results are superior to previous data parallel [131] or model parallel [96] techniques.

5.5.3   Annealed Teacher Forcing

Third, the authors design an annealed teacher forcing for the parallel strategy. They find that the naive parallel training suffers from the propagation of reconstruction error since each quantized module passes the quantization error to its successors before being fully optimized. In particular, all modules get optimized simultaneously instead of sequentially in the parallel strategy. The next module takes the output from the input queue before its predecessor is fully optimized. Therefore, the predecessor's reconstruction error will propagate to the following modules before it is sufficiently minimized. To solve this problem, the proposed annealed teacher forcing is similar to the method in [246]. The full-precision module provides clean signals to the next quantized module. This breaks the reconstruction error propagation and further improves the performance of the parallel strategy. Specifically, the output f_n from the n-th full-precision module serves as the clean input to the $(n+1)$-th quantized module to substitute the original $\hat{f}_n$ that comes from the quantized module. As a result, f_n can stop the propagation of the accumulated error on the quantized module. Nevertheless, such an approach breaks the connection to previous quantized modules and may suffer from forward inconsistency between training and inference for the quantized model. To solve this problem, the actually input to $(n+1)$-th quantized module is the convex combination between the full-precision f_n and quantized $\hat{f}_n$ as follows:

$$\tilde{f}_n = \lambda f_n + (1 - \lambda)\hat{f}_n. \tag{5.11}$$

The hyperparameter λ controls the strength of teacher forcing. $\lambda = 1$ gives the full correction of reconstruction error but with forward inconsistency, *e.g.*, the connection between the current module and previous quantized modules is broken. While $\lambda = 0$ reduces forward inconsistency, it suffers from the propagated reconstruction error. To achieve a good trade-off between reconstruction error reduction and forward inconsistency elimination, a linear decay strategy for λ is proposed:

$$\lambda_t = max(1 - \frac{t}{T_0}, 0), \tag{5.12}$$

where T_0 is the preset maximum steps of the decay. In the beginning, a large λ is desired since each module is rarely optimized. Later, a small λ is preferred to transit to normal training such that the forward inconsistency can be bridged. The remaining $T - T_0$ steps stick to normal training so that each quantized module adapts to its own predecessors.

The comparsion between the proposed method and other existing state-of-the-art BERT quantization methods are presented in Table 5.4. From Table 5.4, both the proposed MREM-S and MREM-P outperform existing PTQ approaches in most cases, and even achieve results close to QAT approaches. For example, the "W4-E4-A8" quantized MREM-S and MREM-P have the averaged accuracies of 83.5% and 83.4% on MNLI respectively are on par with "W2/4-E8-A8" quantized Q-BERT. In terms of the "W2-E2-A8" quantized models, our MREM-S and MREM-P surpass GOBO by **11.7%** ↑ and **11.3%** ↑ on MNLI-m, respectively.

In summary, this paper's contributions are as follows: (1) module-wise reconstruction error minimization (MREM) that is a fast, memory-saving, and data-efficient approach to improve the post-training quantization for language models; (2) a new model parallel strategy based on MREM to accelerate post-training quantization with theoretical speed-up for distributed training; and (3) annealed teacher forcing to alleviate the propagation of reconstruction error and boost the performance.

TABLE 5.4
Results on the GLUE development set. "MREM-S" denotes sequential optimization.

Quantization	#Bits (W-E-A)	Size	PTQ	MNLI-m	QQP	QNLI	SST-2	CoLA	STS-B	MRPC	RTE	Avg.
-	*full-prec.*	418	-	84.9	91.4	92.1	93.2	59.7	90.1	86.3	72.2	83.9
Q-BERT	2-8-8	43	-	76.6	-	-	84.6	-	-	-	-	-
Q-BERT	2/4-8-8	53	-	83.5	-	-	92.6	-	-	-	-	-
Quant-Noise	PQ	38	-	83.6	-	-	-	-	-	-	-	-
TernaryBERT	2-2-8	28	-	83.3	90.1	91.1	92.8	55.7	87.9	87.5	72.9	82.7
GOBO	3-4-32	43	✓	83.7	-	-	-	-	88.3	-	-	-
GOBO	2-2-32	28	✓	71.0	-	-	-	-	82.7	-	-	-
MREM-S	4-4-8	50	✓	83.5	90.2	91.2	91.4	55.1	89.1	84.8	71.8	82.4
	2-2-8	28	✓	82.7	89.6	90.3	91.2	52.3	88.7	86.0	71.1	81.5
MREM-P	4-4-8	50	✓	83.4	90.2	91.0	91.5	54.7	89.1	86.3	71.1	82.2
	2-2-8	28	✓	82.3	89.4	90.3	91.3	52.9	88.3	85.8	72.9	81.6

Note: "MREM-P" denotes parallel optimization. "Size" refers to model storage in "MB". "PTQ" indicates whether the method belongs to post-training quantization. "Avg." denotes the average results of all tasks.

5.6 Outlier Suppression: Pushing the Limit of Low-Bit Transformer Language Models

Wei *et al.* [243] propose a new method to suppress the outliers existing in the language models and thus pushes the 6-bit post-training quantization (PTQ) and 4-bit quantization-aware training (QAT) accuracy of BERT to the full-precision level.

Previous works [17, 165] indicate that the Transformer-based models hold significantly large outliers (even close to 100). Moreover, these extreme outliers behave in structured patterns. That is, they mainly gather at a few embedding dimensions and even become larger on unique tokens. Due to these special outliers that can devastate the quantization performance, the existing method [17] chooses to bypass solutions such as a finer quantization granularity. However, this finer quantization granularity increases computation cost and unavoidably hinders the acceleration effect. In contrast, Wei *et al.* propose to suppress the outliers rather than walk around them. At first, an in-depth analysis is provided to investigate the inducement of the outliers and the impact of clipping the outliers.

5.6.1 Analysis

Specifically, the analysis presents two findings: (1) the scaling parameter in LayerNorm amplifies the outliers from embedding dimensions and (2) when clipping the outliers and evaluating the final performance, the importance of outliers is highly varied. For the first finding, the scaling parameter γ in the LayerNorm structure works as an outlier amplifier, which amplifies the outliers in the output. For token t at j-th embedding dimension, the LayerNorm is defined as follows:

$$\tilde{X}_{t,j} = \frac{X_{t,j} - \mu_t}{\sqrt{\sigma_t^2 + \epsilon}} \cdot \gamma_j + \beta_j, \tag{5.13}$$

where μ_t and σ_t^2 are the mean and variance of token t, respectively. Then, by observing the formula of LayerNorm, the multiplier γ plays a crucial part in amplifying the magnitude of the token t, as shown in Fig. 5.8 Thus, they propose to remove the amplification effect by extracting γ from Eq. (5.13) and use the Non-scaling LayerNorm Eq. (5.14):

$$X'_{t,j} = \frac{X_{t,j} - \mu_t}{\sqrt{\sigma_t^2 + \epsilon}} \cdot \gamma_j + \frac{\beta_j}{\gamma}, \tag{5.14}$$

Since the magnitude of the token t is shortening by extracting γ, the resulting X' behaves more friendly than $\tilde{X}$ for quantization.

For the second finding, they discover that the influence of final performance when clipping the outliers varies greatly. In particular, when clipping the outliers and evaluating the final performance, they find that the importance of outliers is highly varied. Take the outliers after GELU as an example. Fig. 5.9 shows that clipping the more aggressive outliers sharply (clipping signals in 10-100 to 10) even does not hurt the full-precision performance with accuracy still at 91.02. At the same time, the accuracy drops suddenly to 85.93 with too many outliers cut. In addition, though those less important outliers might present in a long tail form, they are only provided by a few tokens. In particular, unimportant outliers which can be clipped without even any accuracy drop in FP models only correspond to a few tokens. From the red points in Fig. 5.9, which represents the proportion of clipped tokens, it can be clearly seen that the more aggressive outliers though occupy a large range from 10 to 100 only matches with 3% tokens. Destroying those sharper outliers belonging to a few tokens will not affect the performance.

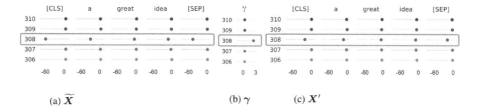

(a) $\widetilde{X}$ (b) γ (c) X'

FIGURE 5.8

Presentation of outliers over $\tilde{X}$, γ and X' of LayerNorm on BERT-SST-2. For example, at dimension 308, γ and $\tilde{X}$ both have sharper values. By excluding γ, it can be seen that X' holds milder distribution than $\tilde{X}$.

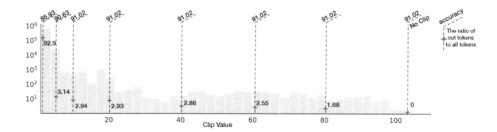

FIGURE 5.9

The distribution using (mean + 3 * std) is drawn as the left border, then enumerating the value to cut the tensor on RoBERTa-QNLI. The reflect the proportion of clipped tokens.

5.6.2   Gamma Migration

Specifically, the gamma migration produces a more quantization-friendly model by migrating the outlier amplifier γ into subsequent modules in an equivalent transformation and bringing more robust activation for quantization without extra computation burden. As shown in Fig. 5.10, γ will be excluded from the LayerNorm and moved to the shortcut branch and weight of the next layer. As a result, the LayerNorm becomes the Non-scaling LayerNorm. The shortcut branch and weight of the next layer absorb a new parameter γ. From Fig. 5.10, the "Quant" process quantizes X'. Then the quantized output engages two branches respectively. The first is the matrix multiplication on the bottom branch. The second is multiplying parameter γ and experiencing the "DeQuant" process. In fact, the γ calculation is delayed from LayerNorm to the shortcut branch. Thus, this new design will not increase the computation overhead.

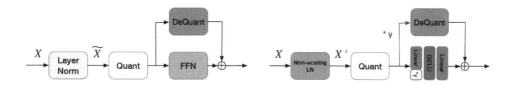

FIGURE 5.10

Left: quantization flow before. Right: gamma migration.

5.6.3　Token-Wise Clipping

The token-wise clipping further efficiently finds a suitable clipping range to achieve minimal final quantization loss in a coarse-to-fine procedure. At the coarse-grained stage, by leveraging the fact that those less important outliers only belong to a few tokens, the authors propose to obtain a preliminary clipping range quickly in a token-wise manner. In particular, this stage aims to quickly skip over the area where clipping causes little accuracy influence. According to the second finding, the long tail area only matches with a few tokens. Therefore, the max value of the embedding at a token can be its representative. Also, the min value can be representative of negative outliers. Then, a new tensor with T elements can be constructed by taking out the maximum signal for each token:

$$
\begin{aligned}
O^u &= \{max(token_1), max(token_2), ..., max(token_T)\}, \\
O^l &= \{min(token_1), min(token_2), ..., min(token_T)\},
\end{aligned}
\tag{5.15}
$$

where O^u is marked as the collection of upper bounds, O^l is the collection of lower bounds. The clipping value is determined by:

$$
\begin{aligned}
c^u &= quantile(O^u, \alpha), \\
c^l &= quantile(O^l, \alpha),
\end{aligned}
\tag{5.16}
$$

where the *quantile* is the quantile function that computes the α-th quantiles of its input. A α that minimizes the final loss is searched in a grid search manner. The author chooses to use a uniform quantizer. Thus, according to c^u and c^l, a step size s_0 of the uniform quantizer can be computed given the bit-width b by $s = \frac{c^u - c^l}{2^b - 1}$.

At the fine-grained stage, the preliminary clipping range is optimized to obtain a better results. The aim is to make some fine-grained adjustments in the critical area to further provide a guarantee for the final effect. In detail, with the resulting step size s_0 from the coarse-grained stage is adopted for initialization. Then, a learning based on gradient descent is used to update parameter step size s toward the final loss with learning rate η:

$$
s = s - \eta \frac{\partial L}{\partial s}.
\tag{5.17}
$$

Due to the wide range of outliers only corresponding to a few tokens, passing through the unimportant area from the token perspective (the coarse-grained stage) needs much fewer iterations than from the value perspective (the fine-grained stage). The special design of the two stages adequately exploits this feature and thus leads a high efficiency.

5.7　BinaryBERT: Pushing the Limit of BERT Quantization

Bai *et al.* [6] established the pioneer work for Binary BERT Pre-Trained Models. They first studied the potential rationales behind the sharp drop from ternarization to binarization of BERT. They begin with comparing the loss landscapes of full-precision, ternary, and binary BERT models. In detail, the parameters $\mathbf{W}_1, \mathbf{W}_2$ from the value layers of multi-head attention in the first two transformer layers are assigned with the following perturbations on parameters:

$$
\tilde{\mathbf{W}}_1 = \mathbf{W}_1 + x \cdot \mathbf{1}_x, \quad \tilde{\mathbf{W}}_2 = \mathbf{W}_2 + y \cdot \mathbf{1}_y,
\tag{5.18}
$$

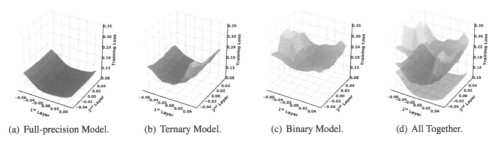

(a) Full-precision Model.   (b) Ternary Model.   (c) Binary Model.   (d) All Together.

FIGURE 5.11
Loss landscapes visualization of the full-precision, ternary, and binary models on MRPC [230].

where $x \in \{\pm 0.2\bar{\mathbf{W}}_1, \pm 0.4\bar{\mathbf{W}}_1, ..., \pm 1.0\bar{\mathbf{W}}_1\}$ are perturbation magnitudes based the absolute mean value $\bar{\mathbf{W}}_1$ of $\mathbf{W}_1$, and similar rules hold for y. $\mathbf{1}_x$ and $\mathbf{1}_y$ are vectors with all elements being 1. For each pair of (x, y), the corresponding training loss is shown in Fig. 5.11. As can be seen, the full-precision model has the lowest overall training loss, and its loss landscape is flat and robust to the perturbation. For the ternary model, despite the surface tilts up with larger perturbations, it looks locally convex and is thus easy to optimize. This may also explain why the BERT models can be ternarized without severe accuracy drop [285]. However, the loss landscape of the binary model turns out to be higher and more complex. By stacking the three landscapes together, the loss surface of the binary BERT stands on the top with a clear margin with the other two. The steep curvature of loss surface reflects a higher sensitivity to binarization, which attributes to the training difficulty.

The authors further quantitatively measured the steepness of loss landscape, starting from a local minima $\mathbf{W}$ and apply the second order approximation to the curvature. According to the Taylor's expansion, the loss increase induced by quantizing $\mathbf{W}$ can be approximately upper bounded by

$$\ell(\hat{\mathbf{W}}) - \ell(\mathbf{W}) \approx \boldsymbol{\epsilon}^\top \mathbf{H}\boldsymbol{\epsilon} \leq \lambda_{\max}\|\boldsymbol{\epsilon}\|^2, \qquad (5.19)$$

where $\boldsymbol{\epsilon} = \mathbf{W} - \hat{\mathbf{W}}$ is the quantization noise, and $\lambda_{\max}$ is the largest eigenvalue of the Hessian $\mathbf{H}$ at $\mathbf{w}$. Note that the first-order term is skipped due to $\nabla\ell(\mathbf{W}) = 0$. By taking $\lambda_{\max}$ [208] as a quantitative measurement for the steepness of the loss surface, the authors separately calculated $\lambda_{\max}$ for each part of BERT as (1) the query/key layers (MHA-QK), (2) the value layer (MHA-V), (3) the output projection layer (MHA-O) in the multi-head attention, (4) the intermediate layer (FFN-Mid), and (5) the output layer (FFN-Out) in the feed-forward network. From Fig. 5.12, the top-1 eigenvalues of the binary model are higher

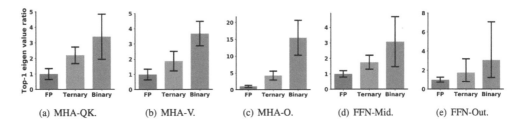

(a) MHA-QK.   (b) MHA-V.   (c) MHA-O.   (d) FFN-Mid.   (e) FFN-Out.

FIGURE 5.12
The top-1 eigenvalues of parameters at different Transformer parts of the full-precision (FP), ternary, and binary BERT.

both on expectation and standard deviation compared to the full-precision baseline and the ternary model. For instance, the top-1 eigenvalues of MHA-O in the binary model are $\sim 15\times$ larger than the full-precision counterpart. Therefore, the quantization loss increases of full-precision and ternary model are tighter bounded than the binary model in Eq. (5.19). The highly complex and irregular landscape by binarization thus poses more challenges to the optimization.

5.7.1 Ternary Weight Splitting

Given the challenging loss landscape of binary BERT, the authors proposed ternary weight splitting (TWS) that exploits the flatness of ternary loss landscape as the optimization proxy of the binary model. As is shown in Fig. 2.4, they first train the half-sized ternary BERT to convergence, and then split both the latent full-precision weight $\mathbf{W}^t$ and quantized $\hat{\mathbf{W}}^t$ to their binary counterparts $\mathbf{W}_1^b, \mathbf{W}_2^b$ and $\hat{\mathbf{W}}_1^b, \hat{\mathbf{W}}_2^b$ via the TWS operator. To inherit the performance of the ternary model after splitting, the TWS operator requires the splitting equivalency (*i.e.*, the same output given the same input):

$$\mathbf{W}^t = \mathbf{W}_1^b + \mathbf{W}_2^b, \quad \hat{\mathbf{W}}^t = \hat{\mathbf{W}}_1^b + \hat{\mathbf{W}}_2^b \ . \tag{5.20}$$

While solution to Eq. (5.20) is not unique, the latent full-precision weights $\mathbf{W}_1^b, \mathbf{W}_2^b$ are constrained after splitting to satisfy $\mathbf{W}^t = \mathbf{W}_1^b + \mathbf{W}_2^b$ as

$$\mathbf{W}_{1,i}^b = \begin{cases} a \cdot \mathbf{W}_i^t & \text{if } \hat{\mathbf{W}}_i^t \neq 0 \\ b + \mathbf{W}_i^t & \text{if } \hat{\mathbf{W}}_i^t = 0, \mathbf{W}_i^t > 0 \ , \\ b & \text{otherwise} \end{cases} \tag{5.21}$$

$$\mathbf{W}_{2,i}^b = \begin{cases} (1-a)\mathbf{W}_i^t & \text{if } \hat{\mathbf{W}}_i^t \neq 0 \\ -b & \text{if } \hat{\mathbf{W}}_i^t = 0, \mathbf{W}_i^t > 0 \ , \\ -b + \mathbf{W}_i^t & \text{otherwise} \end{cases} \tag{5.22}$$

where a and b are the variables to solve. By Eq. (5.21) and Eq. (5.22) with $\hat{\mathbf{W}}^t = \hat{\mathbf{W}}_1^b + \hat{\mathbf{W}}_2^b$, we get

$$a = \frac{\sum_{i \in \mathcal{I}} |\mathbf{W}_i^t| + \sum_{j \in \mathcal{J}} |\mathbf{W}_j^t| - \sum_{k \in \mathcal{K}} |\mathbf{W}_k^t|}{2 \sum_{i \in \mathcal{I}} |\mathbf{W}_i^t|},$$

$$b = \frac{\frac{n}{|\mathcal{I}|} \sum_{i \in \mathcal{I}} |\mathbf{W}_i^t| - \sum_{i=1}^n |\mathbf{W}_i^t|}{2(|\mathcal{J}| + |\mathcal{K}|)}, \tag{5.23}$$

where we denote $\mathcal{I} = \{i \mid \hat{\mathbf{W}}_i^t \neq 0\}$, $\mathcal{J} = \{j \mid \hat{\mathbf{W}}_j^t = 0 \text{ and } \mathbf{W}_j^t > 0\}$ and $\mathcal{K} = \{k \mid \hat{\mathbf{W}}_k^t = 0 \text{ and } \mathbf{W}_k^t < 0\}$. $|\cdot|$ denotes the cardinality of the set.

5.7.2 Knowledge Distillation

Further, the authors proposed to boost the performance of binarized BERT by Knowledge Distillation (KD), which is shown to benefit BERT quantization [285]. Following [106, 285], they first performed *intermediate-layer distillation* from the full-precision teacher network's embedding $\mathbf{E}$, layer-wise MHA output $\mathbf{M}_l$ and FFN output $\mathbf{F}_l$ to the quantized student counterpart $\hat{\mathbf{E}}, \hat{\mathbf{M}}_l, \hat{\mathbf{F}}_l$ ($l = 1, 2, ...L$). To minimize their mean squared errors, *i.e.*, $\ell_{emb} = \text{MSE}(\hat{\mathbf{E}}, \mathbf{E})$, $\ell_{mha} = \sum_l \text{MSE}(\hat{\mathbf{M}}_l, \mathbf{M}_l)$, and $\ell_{ffn} = \sum_l \text{MSE}(\hat{\mathbf{F}}_l, \mathbf{F}_l)$, the objective function falls in

$$\ell_{int} = \ell_{emb} + \ell_{mha} + \ell_{ffn}. \tag{5.24}$$

TABLE 5.5
Quantization results of BinaryBERT on SQuAD and MNLI-m.

Method	#Bits	Size	SQuAD-v1.1	MNLI-m
BERT-base	*full-prec.*	418	80.8/88.5	84.6
DistilBERT	*full-prec.*	250	79.1/86.9	81.6
LayerDrop-6L	*full-prec.*	328	-	82.9
LayerDrop-3L	*full-prec.*	224	-	78.6
TinyBERT-6L	*full-prec.*	55	79.7/87.5	82.8
ALBERT-E128	*full-prec.*	45	82.3/89.3	81.6
ALBERT-E768	*full-prec.*	120	81.5/88.6	82.0
Quant-Noise	PQ	38	-	83.6
Q-BERT	2/4-8-8	53	79.9/87.5	83.5
Q-BERT	2/3-8-8	46	79.3/87.0	81.8
Q-BERT	2-8-8	28	69.7/79.6	76.6
GOBO	3-4-32	43	-	83.7
GOBO	2-2-32	28	-	71.0
TernaryBERT	2-2-8	28	79.9/87.4	83.5
BinaryBERT	**1-1-8**	**17**	**80.8/88.3**	**84.2**
BinaryBERT	**1-1-4**	**17**	**79.3/87.2**	**83.9**

Then, the *prediction-layer distillation* minimizes the soft cross-entropy (SCE) between quantized student logits $\hat{\mathbf{y}}$ and teacher logits $\mathbf{y}$, *i.e.*,

$$\ell_{pred} = \text{SCE}(\hat{\mathbf{y}}, \mathbf{y}). \tag{5.25}$$

After splitting from the half-sized ternary model, the binary model inherits its performance on a new architecture with full width. However, the original minimum of the ternary model may not hold in this new loss landscape after splitting. Thus, the authors further proposed to fine-tune the binary model with prediction-layer distillation to look for a better solution.

For implementation, the authors took DynaBERT [89] sub-networks as backbones, offering both half-sized and full-sized models for easy comparison. Firstly, a ternary model of width $0.5\times$ with the two-stage knowledge distillation is trained until convergence. Then, the authors splited it into a binary model with width $1.0\times$, and perform further fine-tuning with prediction-layer distillation. Table 5.5 compares their proposed BinaryBERT with a variety of state-of-the-art counterparts, including Q-BERT [208], GOBO [279], Quant-Noise [65] and TernaryBERT [285] for quantizing BERT on MNLI of GLUE [230] and SQuAD [198]. Aside from quantization, other general compression approaches are also compared such as DistillBERT [206], LayerDrop [64], TinyBERT [106], and ALBERT [126]. BinaryBERT has the smallest model size with the best performance among all quantization approaches. Compared with the full-precision model, BinaryBERT retains competitive performance with significantly reduced model size and computation. For example, it achieves more than **24×** compression ratio compared with BERT-base, with only 0.4% ↓ and 0.0%/0.2% ↓ drop on MNLI-m and SQuAD v1.1, respectively.

In summary, this paper's contributions can be concluded as: (1) The first work to explore BERT binarization with an analysis for the performance drop of binarized BERT models. (2) A ternary weight-splitting method splits a trained ternary BERT to initialize BinaryBERT, followed by fine-tuning for further refinement.

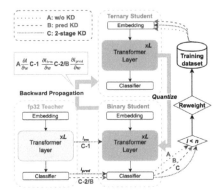

FIGURE 5.13
Structure of BinaryBERT-based BEBERT. The dashed lines denoted with A, B, and C represent combining ensemble with different KD strategies.

5.8   BEBERT: Efficient and Robust Binary Ensemble BERT

On the basis of BinaryBERT, Tian *et al.*[222] proposed to employ ensemble learning on binary BERT models, yielding Binary Ensemble BERT (BEBERT). Figure 5.13 shows the architecture of BEBERT based on BinaryBERT [6]. During the training process, BEBERT updates the sample weights of the training dataset in each iteration, focusing on the wrongly predicted elements. When using knowledge distillation (KD), the forward propagation is performed with the full-precision teacher and the binary student. Then the gradient of distillation loss is computed to update the weights of the ternary student during backward propagation (BP). After that, the parameters are binarized. The training process of BEBERT based on BiBERT is similar to that based on BinaryBERT, except that BiBERT is quantized from a full-precision student and distilled by the DMD method[195]. Note that the original two-stage KD [106] contains distillation for Transformer layers and the prediction layer, introducing extra forward and backward propagation steps in training. Therefore, the authors proposed distilling the prediction layer or removing the KD procedures to reduce the training costs.

In detail, the authors used AdaBoost [67] to integrate multiple binary BERTs to build BEBERT. AdaBoost is a popular ensemble learning method mainly collects the results from multiple weak learners to decrease the prediction bias. The AdaBoost-based BEBERT takes as input a training set S of m examples $(x_1, y_1), ..., (x_m, y_m)$, where $y_j \in Y$ represents the label of j-th sample. Afterward, the boosting algorithm calls the binary BERT to train for N rounds, generating a binary model in each round. In the i-th round, AdaBoost provides the training set with a distribution D_i as the sample weight; The initial distribution D_1 is uniform over S, so D1(i) = 1/m for all i. And then, the BERT training algorithm computes a classifier h_i (or h_i^S when KD is employed), focusing on minimizing the error $e_i = P_{j \sim D_i}(h_i(x_j) \neq y_j)$. At last, the booster combines the weak hypotheses into a single final hypothesis $H \leftarrow \Sigma_{i=1}^N \alpha_i h_i(x_i)$.

TABLE 5.6

Quantization results of BEBERT on GLUE benchmark. The average results of all tasks are reported.

Method	#Bits	Size	GLUE
BERT-base	*full-prec.*	418	82.84
DynaBERT	*full-prec.*	33	77.36
DistilBERT6L	*full-prec.*	264	78.56
BinaryBERT	1-1-4	16.5	78.76
BEBERT	1-1-4	33	**80.96**
TinyBERT6L	*full-prec.*	264	81.91
TernaryBERT	2-2-8	28	81.91
BinaryBERT	1-1-4	16.5	81.57
BEBERT	1-1-4	33	**82.53**

Inspired by the empirical opinion in [3] that convolutional neural networks can improve little accuracy if using ensemble learning after the KD procedures, the authors removed the KD during ensemble for accelerating the training of BEBERT. Although the two-stage KD performs better in [106], it is time-consuming to conduct forward and backward propagation twice. Ensemble with prediction KD can avoid double propagation and ensemble can even remove the evaluation process of the teacher model. The authors further conducted experiments to show whether applying KD in ensemble BinaryBERT has a minor effect on its accuracy in the GLUE datasets, showing that BEBERT without KD can save training time while preserving accuracy. They further compared BEBERT to various SOTA compressed BERTs. The results listed in Table 5.6 suggest BEBERT outperforms BinaryBERT in accuracy by up to 6.7%. Compared to the full-precision BERT, it also saves 15× and 13× on FLOPs and model size, respectively, with a negligible accuracy loss of 0.3%, showing the potential for practical deployment.

In summary, this paper's contributions can be concluded as: (1) The first work that introduces ensemble learning to binary BERT models to improve accuracy and robustness. (2) Removing the KD procedures during ensemble accelerates the training process.

5.9 BiBERT: Accurate Fully Binarized BERT

Though BinaryBERT [6] and BEBERT [222] pushed down the weight and word embedding to be binarized, they have not achieved to binarize BERT with 1-bit activation accurately. To mitigate this, Qin *et al.* [195] proposed BiBERT toward fully binarized BERT models. BiBERT includes an efficient Bi-Attention structure for maximizing representation information statistically and a Direction-Matching Distillation (DMD) scheme to optimize the full binarized BERT accurately.

5.9.1 Bi-Attention

To address the information degradation of binarized representations in the forward propagation, the authors proposed an efficient Bi-Attention structure based on information theory, which statistically maximizes the entropy of representation and revives the attention mechanism in the fully binarized BERT. Since the representations (weight, activation, and embedding) with extremely compressed bit-width in fully binarized BERT have lim-

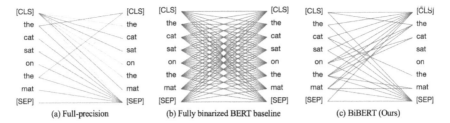

      (a) Full-precision   (b) Fully binarized BERT baseline   (c) BiBERT (Ours)

FIGURE 5.14
Attention-head view for (a) full-precision BERT, (b) fully binarized BERT baseline, and (c) BiBERT for same input. BiBERT with Bi-Attention shows similar behavior with the full-precision model, while baseline suffers indistinguishable attention for information degradation.

ited capabilities, the ideal binarized representation should preserve the given full-precision counterparts as much as possible means the mutual information between binarized and full-precision representations should be maximized. When the deterministic sign function is applied to binarize BERT, the goal is equivalent to maximizing the information entropy $\mathcal{H}(\mathbf{B})$ of binarized representation $\mathbf{B}$ [171], which is defined as

$$\mathcal{H}(\mathbf{B}) = - \sum_B p(B) \log p(B), \tag{5.26}$$

where $B \in \{-1, 1\}$ is the random variable sampled from $\mathbf{B}$ with probability mass function p. Therefore, the information entropy of binarized representation should be maximized to better preserve the full-precision counterparts and let the attention mechanism function well.

    As for the attention structure in full-precision BERT, the normalized attention weight obtained by softmax is essential. But direct application of binarization function causes a complete information loss to binarized attention weight. Specifically, since the softmax($\mathbf{A}$) is regarded as following a probability distribution, the elements of $\mathbf{B}_A^s$ are all quantized to 1 (Fig. 5.14(b)) and the information entropy $\mathcal{H}(\mathbf{B}_A^s)$ degenerates to 0. A common measure to alleviate this information degradation is to shift the distribution of input tensors before applying the sign function, which is formulated as

$$\hat{\mathbf{B}}_{\mathbf{A}}^s = \mathrm{sign}\left(\mathrm{softmax}(\mathbf{A}) - \tau\right), \tag{5.27}$$

where the shift parameter τ, also regarded as the threshold of binarization, is expected to maximize the entropy of the binarized $\hat{\mathbf{B}}_{\mathbf{A}}^s$ and is fixed during the inference. Moreover, the attention weight obtained by the sign function is binarized to $\{-1, 1\}$, while the original attention weight has a normalized value range $[0, 1]$. The negative value of attention weight in the binarized architecture is contrary to the intuition of the existing attention mechanism and is also empirically proved to be harmful to the attention structure.

    To mitigate the information degradation caused by binarization in the attention mechanism, the authors introduced an efficient Bi-Attention structure for fully binarized BERT, which maximizes information entropy of binarized representations statistically and applies bitwise operations for fast inference. In detail, they proposed to binarize the attention weight into the Boolean value, while the design is driven by information entropy maximization. In Bi-Attention, bool function is leveraged to binarize the attention score $\mathbf{A}$, which is defined as

$$\mathrm{bool}(x) = \begin{cases} 1, & \text{if } x \geq 0 \\ 0, & \text{otherwise} \end{cases}, \tag{5.28}$$

$$\frac{\partial \operatorname{bool}(x)}{\partial x} = \begin{cases} 1, & \text{if } |x| \leq 1 \\ 0, & \text{otherwise.} \end{cases} \tag{5.29}$$

By applying $\operatorname{bool}(\cdot)$ function, the elements in attention weight with lower value are binarized to 0. Thus the obtained entropy-maximized attention weight can filter the crucial part of elements. And the proposed Bi-Attention structure is finally expressed as

$$\mathbf{B_A} = \operatorname{bool}(\mathbf{A}) = \operatorname{bool}\left(\frac{1}{\sqrt{D}}\left(\mathbf{B_Q} \otimes \mathbf{B_K}^\top\right)\right), \tag{5.30}$$

$$\operatorname{Bi-Attention}(\mathbf{B_Q}, \mathbf{B_K}, \mathbf{B_V}) = \mathbf{B_A} \boxtimes \mathbf{B_V}, \tag{5.31}$$

where $\mathbf{B_V}$ is the binarized value obtained by $\operatorname{sign}(\mathbf{V})$, $\mathbf{B_A}$ is the binarized attention weight, and $\boxtimes$ is a well-designed Bitwise-Affine Matrix Multiplication (BAMM) operator composed by $\otimes$ and bitshift to align training and inference representations and perform efficient bitwise calculation.

In a nutshell, in Bi-Attention structure, the information entropy of binarized attention weight is maximized (as Fig. 5.14(c) shows) to alleviate its immense information degradation and revive the attention mechanism. Bi-Attention also achieves greater efficiency since the softmax is excluded.

5.9.2 Direction-Matching Distillation

As an optimization technique based on element-level comparison of activation, distillation allows the binarized BERT to mimic the full-precision teacher model about intermediate activation. However, distillation causes direction mismatch for optimization in the fully binarized BERT baseline, leading to insufficient optimization and even harmful effects. To address the direction mismatch occurred in fully binarized BERT baseline in the backward propagation, the authors further proposed a DMD scheme with apposite distilled activations and the well-constructed similarity matrices to effectively utilize knowledge from the teacher, which optimizes the fully binarized BERT more accurately.

Their efforts first fall into reselecting the distilled activations for DMD by distilling the upstream query $\mathbf{Q}$ and key $\mathbf{K}$ instead of attention score in DMD for distillation to utilize its knowledge while alleviating direction mismatch. Besides, the authors also distilled the value $\mathbf{V}$ to further cover all the inputs of MHA. Then, similarity pattern matrices are constructed for distilling activation, which can be expressed as

$$\mathbf{P_Q} = \frac{\mathbf{Q} \times \mathbf{Q}^\top}{\|\mathbf{Q} \times \mathbf{Q}^\top\|}, \mathbf{P_K} = \frac{\mathbf{K} \times \mathbf{K}^\top}{\|\mathbf{K} \times \mathbf{K}^\top\|}, \mathbf{P_V} = \frac{\mathbf{V} \times \mathbf{V}^\top}{\|\mathbf{V} \times \mathbf{V}^\top\|}, \tag{5.32}$$

where $\|\cdot\|$ denotes $\ell 2$ normalization. The corresponding $\mathbf{P_{Q}}_T, \mathbf{P_{K}}_T, \mathbf{P_{V}}_T$ are constructed in the same way by the teacher's activation. The distillation loss is expressed as:

$$\ell_{\text{distill}} = \ell_{\text{DMD}} + \ell_{\text{hid}} + \ell_{\text{pred}}, \tag{5.33}$$

$$\ell_{\text{DMD}} = \sum_{l \in [1,L]} \sum_{\mathbf{F} \in \mathcal{F}_{\text{DMD}}} \|\mathbf{P_F}l - \mathbf{P_F}_{Tl}\|, \tag{5.34}$$

where L denotes the number of transformer layers, $\mathcal{F}_{\text{DMD}} = \{\mathbf{Q}, \mathbf{K}, \mathbf{V}\}$. The loss term ℓ_{hid} is constructed as the $\ell 2$ normalization form.

The overall pipeline for BiBERT is shown in Fig. 5.15. The authors conducted experiments on the GLUE benchmark for binarizing various BERT-based pre-trained models. The results listed in Table 5.7 shows that BiBERT surpasses BinaryBERT by a wide margin in the average accuracy.

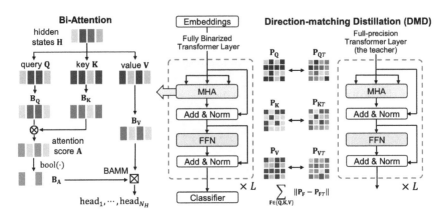

FIGURE 5.15

Overview of BiBERT, applying Bi-Attention structure for maximizing representation information and Direction-Matching Distillation (DMD) scheme for accurate optimization.

TABLE 5.7

Quantization results of BiBERT on GLUE benchmark. The average results of all tasks are reported.

Method	#Bits	Size	GLUE
BERT-base	*full-prec.*	418	82.84
BinaryBERT	1-1-4	16.5	79.9
TernaryBERT	2-2-2	28.0	45.5
BinaryBERT	1-1-2	16.5	53.7
TernaryBERT	2-2-1	28.0	42.3
BinaryBERT	1-1-1	16.5	41.0
BiBERT	1-1-1	**13.4**	**63.2**
BERT-base$_{6L}$	*full-prec.*	257	79.4
BiBERT$_{6L}$	1-1-1	**6.8**	**62.1**
BERT-base$_{4L}$	*full-prec.*	55.6	77.0
BiBERT$_{4L}$	1-1-1	**4.4**	**57.7**

In summary, this paper's contributions can be concluded as: (1) The first work to explore fully binary pre-trained BERT-models. (2) An efficient Bi-Attention structure for maximizing representation information statistically. (3) A Direction-Matching Distillation (DMD) scheme to optimize the full binarized BERT accurately.

5.10   BiT: Robustly Binarized Multi-Distilled Transformer

Liu *et al.*[156] further presented BiT to boost the performance of fully-binarized BERT pre-trained models. In their work, a series of improvements that enable binary BERT was identified, which includes a two-set binarization scheme, an elastic binary activation function with learned parameters, a method to quantize a network to its limit by successively

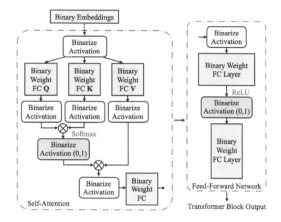

FIGURE 5.16
Overview of BiT. A transformer block contains the multi-head self-attention and feed-forward network. All the weights are binarized to $\{-1, 1\}$ in the Embedding/Fully-Connected layers and binarize activations to $\{0, 1\}$ for ReLU/Softmax outputs and to $\{-1, 1\}$ for other layers.

distilling higher precision models into lower precision students. They are introduced in detail as follows.

5.10.1 Two-Set Binarization Scheme

In contrast to CNNs on images where activations exhibit comparable distributions, different activations in transformer blocks are performing different functionalities, and thus vary in their output distributions. In particular, these activations can be divided into two categories: the activations after Softmax/ReLU layer that contains positive values only and the remaining activations with both positive and negative values (e.g., after matrix multiplication). If we denote by $\mathbf{X_R}$ the vector of activation values, then the two cases are $\mathbf{X}_\mathbf{R}^i \in \mathbb{R}_+$ and $\mathbf{X}_\mathbf{R}^i \in \mathbb{R}$ respectively.

For the former set, mapping to the binary levels $\{-1, 1\}$ would result in a severe distribution mismatch. Therefore, the authors instead mapped non-negative activation layers to $\hat{\mathbf{X}}_\mathbf{B} \in \{0, 1\}^n$ and binarize activation layers with $\mathbf{X_R} \in \mathbb{R}^n$ to $\hat{\mathbf{X}}_\mathbf{B} \in \{-1, 1\}^n$, shown in Fig. 5.16. BiBERT [195] also suggests binarizing attention to $\{0, 1\}$, but with bool function replacing SoftMax, while the authors empirically found that simply binarizing attentions after SoftMax to $\{0, 1\}$ works better and binarizing ReLU output to $\{0, 1\}$ instead of $\{-1, 1\}$ brings further improvements.

Additionally, they applied a layer-wise scaling factor to binarized activations to reduce the binarization error, *i.e.*, $\mathbf{X_B} = \alpha\hat{\mathbf{X}}_\mathbf{B}$. The optimal values of α are different for the $\hat{\mathbf{X}}_\mathbf{B} \in \{0, 1\}^n$ and $\hat{\mathbf{X}}_\mathbf{B} \in \{-1, 1\}^n$ cases and can be calculated by minimizing the $l2$ error:

$$\mathcal{J}(\alpha) = ||\mathbf{X_R} - \alpha\hat{\mathbf{X}}_\mathbf{B}||^2$$
$$\alpha^* = \underset{\alpha \in \mathbb{R}_+}{\arg\min}\, \mathcal{J}(\alpha) \tag{5.35}$$

Following XNOR-Net [199], by expanding Eq. 5.35, we have

$$\mathcal{J}(\alpha) = \alpha^2 \hat{\mathbf{X}}_B^T \hat{\mathbf{X}}_\mathbf{B} - 2\alpha \mathbf{X_R}^T \hat{\mathbf{X}}_\mathbf{B} + \mathbf{X_R}^T \mathbf{X_R} \tag{5.36}$$

The activations are binarized following previous works as:

$$\hat{\mathbf{X}}_{\mathbf{B}}^i = \text{Sign}(\mathbf{X}_{\mathbf{R}}^i) = \begin{cases} -1, & \text{if } \mathbf{X}_{\mathbf{R}}^i < 0 \\ +1, & \text{if } \mathbf{X}_{\mathbf{R}}^i \geqslant 0 \end{cases} \tag{5.37}$$

In that case, $\hat{\mathbf{X}}_B^T \hat{\mathbf{X}}_{\mathbf{B}} = n_{\mathbf{X_R}}$, where $n_{\mathbf{X_R}}$ is number of elements in $\mathbf{X_R}$, and α^* can be solved as:

$$\alpha^* = \frac{\mathbf{X_R}^T \hat{\mathbf{X}}_{\mathbf{B}}}{n_{\mathbf{X_R}}} = \frac{||\mathbf{X_R}||_{l1}}{n_{\mathbf{X_R}}} \tag{5.38}$$

For the activations in attention layers or after the ReLU non-linearity layers with $\mathbf{X_R} \in \mathbb{R}_+^n$, the authors binarized the activations to $\hat{\mathbf{X}}_{\mathbf{B}} \in \{0,1\}^n$ by rounding the real-valued activations:

$$\hat{\mathbf{X}}_{\mathbf{B}}^i = \lfloor \text{Clip}(\mathbf{X}_{\mathbf{R}}^i, 0, 1) \rceil = \begin{cases} 0, & \text{if } \mathbf{X}_{\mathbf{R}}^i < 0.5 \\ 1, & \text{if } \mathbf{X}_{\mathbf{R}}^i \geqslant 0.5 \end{cases} \tag{5.39}$$

In that case, $\hat{\mathbf{X}}_B^T \hat{\mathbf{X}}_{\mathbf{B}} = n_{\{\mathbf{X_R} \geqslant 0.5\}}$ where $n_{\{\mathbf{X_R} \geqslant 0.5\}}$ denotes the number of elements in $\mathbf{X_R}$ that are greater than or equal to 0.5. Then α^* can be solved as:

$$\alpha^* = \frac{||\mathbf{X_R} \cdot \mathbf{1}_{\{\mathbf{X_R} \geqslant 0.5\}}||_{l1}}{n_{\{\mathbf{X_R} \geqslant 0.5\}}} \tag{5.40}$$

5.10.2 Elastic Binarization Function

The fixed scaling and threshold derived previously works reasonably well, but might not be optimal since it ignores the distribution of the variable which is being binarized. Ideally, these parameters can be learned during training to minimize the target loss.

When using classical binarization methods, *i.e.*, $\hat{\mathbf{X}}_{\mathbf{B}}^i = \text{Sign}(\mathbf{X}_{\mathbf{R}}^i)$, the binary output is independent of the scale of the real-valued input. However, in our case where $\hat{\mathbf{X}}_{\mathbf{B}}^i = \lfloor \text{Clip}(\mathbf{X}_{\mathbf{R}}^i, 0, 1) \rceil$, this independence no longer holds. Learning the scaling and threshold parameters, and how to approximate the gradients precisely in the process becomes crucial for the final accuracy.

To handle this, the authors proposed the elastic binarization function to learn both the scale $\alpha \in \mathbb{R}_+$ and the threshold $\beta \in \mathbb{R}$:

$$\mathbf{X}_{\mathbf{B}}^i = \alpha \hat{\mathbf{X}}_{\mathbf{B}}^i = \alpha \lfloor \text{Clip}(\frac{\mathbf{X}_{\mathbf{R}}^i - \beta}{\alpha}, 0, 1) \rceil \tag{5.41}$$

In the function, α is initialized with α^* in Eq. (5.38) and β to be 0, and it is trained with gradients from the final loss. To back-propagate the gradients to α through the discretized binarization function, the straight-through estimator (STE) [9] is leveraged to bypass the incoming gradients to the round function to be the outgoing gradients:

$$\begin{aligned} \frac{\partial \mathbf{X}_{\mathbf{B}}^i}{\partial \alpha} &= \hat{\mathbf{X}}_{\mathbf{B}}^i + \alpha \frac{\partial \hat{\mathbf{X}}_{\mathbf{B}}^i}{\partial \alpha} \\ &\stackrel{STE}{\approx} \hat{\mathbf{X}}_{\mathbf{B}}^i + \alpha \frac{\partial \text{Clip}(\frac{\mathbf{X}_{\mathbf{R}}^i - \beta}{\alpha}, 0, 1)}{\partial \alpha} \\ &= \begin{cases} 0, & \text{if } \mathbf{X}_{\mathbf{R}}^i < \beta \\ \frac{\beta - \mathbf{X_R}^i}{\alpha}, & \text{if } \beta \leqslant \mathbf{X}_{\mathbf{R}}^i < \alpha/2 + \beta \\ 1 - \frac{\mathbf{X_R}^i - \beta}{\alpha}, & \text{if } \alpha/2 + \beta \leqslant \mathbf{X}_{\mathbf{R}}^i < \alpha + \beta \\ 1, & \text{if } \mathbf{X}_{\mathbf{R}}^i \geqslant \alpha + \beta \end{cases} \end{aligned} \tag{5.42}$$

Then the gradients *w.r.t.* β can be similarly calculates as:

$$\frac{\partial \mathbf{X}_{\mathbf{B}}^i}{\partial \beta} \overset{STE}{\approx} \alpha \frac{\partial \mathrm{Clip}(\frac{\mathbf{X}_{\mathbf{R}}^i - \beta}{\alpha}, 0, 1)}{\partial \beta}$$
$$= \begin{cases} -1, & \text{if } \beta \leqslant \mathbf{X}_{\mathbf{R}}^i < \alpha + \beta \\ 0, & \text{otherwise} \end{cases} \tag{5.43}$$

For the layers that contain both positive and negative real-valued activations *i.e.*, $\mathbf{X}_{\mathbf{R}} \in \mathbb{R}^n$, the binarized values $\hat{\mathbf{X}}_{\mathbf{B}} \in \{-1, 1\}^n$ are indifferent to the scale inside the Sign function: $\mathbf{X}_{\mathbf{B}}^i = \alpha \cdot \mathrm{Sign}(\frac{\mathbf{X}_{\mathbf{R}}^i - \beta}{\alpha}) = \alpha \cdot \mathrm{Sign}(\mathbf{X}_{\mathbf{R}}^i - \beta)$. In that case, since the effect of scaling factor α inside the Sign function can be ignored, the gradient *w.r.t.* α can be simply calculated as $\frac{\partial \mathbf{X}_{\mathbf{B}}^i}{\partial \alpha} = \mathrm{Sign}(\mathbf{X}_{\mathbf{R}}^i - \beta)$.

5.10.3   Multi-Distilled Binary BERT

Classical knowledge distillation (KD) [87] trains the outputs (*i.e.*, logits) of a student network to be close to those of a teacher, which is typically larger and more complex. This approach is quite general, and can work with any student-teacher pair which conforms to the same output space. However, knowledge transfer happens faster and more effectively in practice if the intermediate representations are also distilled [1]. This approach has been useful when distilling to student models with similar architecture [206], particularly for quantization [6, 116].

Note that having a similar student-teacher pair is a requirement for distilling representations. While how similar they need to be is an open question, intuitively, a teacher who is architecturally closer to the student should make transfer of internal representations easier. In the context of quantization, it is easy to see that lower precision students are progressively less similar to the full-precision teacher, which is one reason why binarization is difficult.

This suggests a multi-step approach, where instead of directly distilling from a full-precision teacher to the desired quantization level, the authors first distilled into a model with sufficient precision to preserve quality. This model can then be used as a teacher to distill into a further quantized student. This process can be repeated multiple times, while at each step ensuring that the teacher and student models are sufficiently similar, and the performance loss is limited.

The multi-step distillation follows a *quantization schedule*, $\mathbf{Q} = \{(b_w^1, b_a^1), (b_w^2, b_a^2), \dots, (b_w^k, b_a^k)\}$ with $(b_w^1, b_a^1) > (b_w^2, b_a^2) > \dots > (b_w^k, b_a^k)^1$. (b_w^k, b_a^k) is the target quantization level. In practice, the authors found that down to a quantization level of W1A2, and one can distill models of reasonable accuracy in single shot. As a result, they followed a fixed quantization schedule, W32A32 $\to$ W1A2 $\to$ W1A1.

BiT, which is shown in Fig. 5.16, combines the elastic binary activations with multi-distillation obtain, BiT simultaneously ensures good initialization for the eventual student model. Since the binary loss landscape is highly irregular, good initialization is critical to aid optimization.

In summary, this paper's contributions can be concluded as: (1) The first demonstration of fully binary pre-trained BERT models with less performance degradation. (2) A two-set binarization scheme, an elastic binary activation function with learned parameters, a multi-distillation method to boost the performance of binarzed BERT models.

---

[1] $(a, b) > (c, d)$ if $a > c$ and $b \geq d$ or $a \geq c$ and $b > d$.

5.11   Post-Training Embedding Binarization for Fast Online Top-K Passage Matching

To lower the complexity of BERT, the recent state-of-the-art model ColBERT[113] employs Contextualized Late Interaction paradigm to independently learn fine-grained query-passage representations. It comprises: (1) a query encoder f_Q, (b) a passage encoder f_D, and (3) a query-passage score predictor. Specifically, given a query q and a passage d, f_Q and f_D encode them into a bag of fixed-size embeddings $\mathbf{E}_q$ and $\mathbf{E}_d$ as follows:

$$
\begin{aligned}
\mathbf{E}_q &= \text{Normalize}(\text{CNN}(\text{BERT}(``[Q]q_0q_1 \cdot q_l"))), \\
\mathbf{E}_d &= \text{Filter}(\text{Normalize}(\text{CNN}(\text{BERT}(``[D]d_0d_1 \cdot d_n")))),
\end{aligned}
\tag{5.44}
$$

where q and d are tokenized into tokens $q_0q_q \cdot q_l$ and $d_0d_1 \cdot d_n$ by BERT-based WordPiece, respectively. $[Q]$ and $[D]$ indicate the sequence types.

Despite the advances of ColBERT over the vanilla BERT model, its massive computation and parameter burden still hinder the deployment on edge devices. Recently, Chen *et al.*[40] proposed Bi-ColBERT to binarize the embedding to relieve the computation burden. Bi-ColBERT involves (1) semantic diffusion to hedge the information loss against embedding binarization, and (2) approximation of Unit Impulse Function [18] for more accurate gradient estimation.

5.11.1   Semantic Diffusion

Binarization with $\text{sign}(\cdot)$ inevitably smoothes the embedding informativeness into the binarized space, *e.g.*, $-1, 1^d$ regardless of its original values. Thus, intuitively, one wants to avoid condensing and gathering informative latent semantics in (relatively-small) sub-structures of embedding bags. In other words, the aim falls into diffusing the embedded semantics in all embedding dimensions as one effective strategy to hedge the inevitable information loss caused by the numerical binarization and retain the semantic uniqueness after binarization as much as possible.

Recall in singular value decomposition (SVD), singular values and vectors reconstruct the original matrix; normally, large singular values can be interpreted to associate with major semantic structures of the matrix [242]. To achieve semantic diffusion via normalizing singular values for equalizing their respective contributions in constituting latent semantics, the authors introduced a lightweight semantic diffusion technique as follows. Concretely, let $\mathbf{I}$ denote the identity matrix and a standard normal random vector $\mathbf{p}^{(h)} \in \mathbb{R}^d$. During training, the diffusion vector $\mathbf{p}^{(h)}$ is iteratively updated as $\mathbf{p}^{(h)} = \mathbf{E}_q^T\mathbf{E}_q\mathbf{p}^{(h-1)}$. Then, the projection matrix $\mathbf{P}_q$ is obtained via:

$$
\mathbf{P}_q = \frac{\mathbf{p}^{(h)}\mathbf{p}^{(h)^T}}{||\mathbf{p}^{(h)}||_2^2}.
\tag{5.45}
$$

Then, the semantic-diffused embedding with the hyper-parameter $\epsilon \in (0, 1)$ as:

$$
\hat{\mathbf{E}}_q = \mathbf{E}_q(\mathbf{I} - \epsilon\mathbf{P}_q).
\tag{5.46}
$$

Compare to the unprocessed embedding bag, *i.e.*, $\mathbf{E}_q$, embedding presents a diffused semantic structure with a more balanced spectrum (distribution of singular values) in expectation.

5.11.2 Gradient Estimation

After obtaining the semantic-diffused embedding bag, a rescaled embedding binarization for each one embedding of the contextualized bag is constructed as:

$$\mathbf{B}_{q_i} = \frac{||\hat{\mathbf{E}}_{q_i}||_1}{c} \cdot \text{sign}(\hat{\mathbf{E}}_{q_i}), \tag{5.47}$$

where $i \in ||\hat{\mathbf{E}}_q||$ and c denotes the embedding dimension. The binarized embedding bag $\mathbf{B}_q$ sketches the original embeddings via (1) binarized codes and (2) embedding scaler, both of which collaboratively reveal the value range of original embedding entries. Moreover, such rescaled binarization supports the bit-wise operations for computation acceleration in match-scoring prediction. To mitigate this, the authors further utilized the approximation of Unit Impulse Function [58] to furnish the accordant gradient estimation as:

$$\frac{\partial \mu(t)}{\partial t} = \begin{cases} 1, & t = 1, \\ 0, & \text{otherwise}. \end{cases} \tag{5.48}$$

It is obvious to take a translation by $\text{sign}(t) = 2\mu(t) - 1$, and theoretically $\frac{\partial \text{sign}(t)}{\partial t} = 2\frac{\partial \mu(t)}{\partial t}$. Furthermore, $\frac{\partial \mu(t)}{\partial t}$ can be introduced with zero-centered Gaussian probability density function as:

$$\frac{\partial \mu(t)}{\partial t} = \lim_{\beta \to \infty} \frac{|\beta|}{\sqrt{\pi}} exp(-(\beta t)^2), \tag{5.49}$$

which implies that:

$$\frac{\partial \text{sign}(t)}{\partial t} \approx \frac{2\gamma}{\sqrt{\pi}} exp(-(\gamma t)^2). \tag{5.50}$$

Intuitively, the estimator in Eq. (5.50) follows the main direction of factual gradients of $\text{sign}(\cdot)$, which produces a coordinated embedding optimization for inputs with diverse value ranges.

Similarly to ColBERT [113], Bi-ColBERT employed its proposed Late Interaction Mechanism for matching score computation, which is implemented by a sum of maximum similarity computation with embedding dot-products:

$$S_{q,d} = \sum_{i \in [|\mathbf{B}_p|]} \max_{j \in [|\mathbf{B}_p|]} \mathbf{B}_{q_i} \cdot \mathbf{B}_{\mathbf{d_j}}^{\mathbf{T}}, \tag{5.51}$$

which can be equivalently implemented with bit-wise operations as follows:

$$S_{q,d} = \sum_{i \in [|\mathbf{B}_q|]} \max_{j \in [|\mathbf{B}_p|]} \mathbf{B}_{q_i} \text{count}(\text{signxnor}(\text{sign}(\mathbf{B}_{q_i} \cdot \text{sign}(\mathbf{B}_{d_i}^T)))). \tag{5.52}$$

The above equation replaces most of floating-point arithmetics with bit-wise operations, providing the potentiality of online computation acceleration. Lastly, Bi-ColBERT adopts the training paradigm of ColBERT that is optimized via the pairwise softmax cross-entropy loss over the computed scores of positive and negative passage samples.

The proposed Bi-ColBERT is evaluated on the MS-MARCO Ranking dataset [182]. It is a collection of 8.8M passages from 1M real-world queries to Bing. Each query is associated with sparse relevance judgments of one (or a small number of) documents marked as relevant and no documents explicitly marked as irrelevant. The results listed in Table 5.8 suggests a trade-off between passage searching quality and retrieval cost, where ColBERT aims to simplify the neural architecture and Bi-ColBERT focuses on effective embedding binarization.

TABLE 5.8

Quantization results of Bi-ColBERT.

Model	MRR@10
$BERT_{base}$	16.7
$BERT_{large}$	19.8
ColBERT	32.8
Bi-ColBERT	31.7

In summary, this paper's contributions can be concluded as: (1) The first work to binarize ColBERT. (2) A semantic diffusion method to hedge the information loss against embedding binarization. (3) An approximation of Unit Impulse Function [18] for more accurate gradient estimation.

6

Applications in Computer Vision

6.1 Introduction

In this section, we introduce the applications of binary neural networks in the field of computer vision. Specifically, we introduce the vision tasks including person re-identification, 3D point cloud processing, object detection, and speech recognition. First, we briefly overview these areas.

6.1.1 Person Re-Identification

A large family of person re-id research focuses on metric learning loss. Some of them introduce verification loss [248] into identification loss, others apply triplet loss with hard sample mining [41, 203]. Recent efforts employ pedestrian attributes to improve supervision and work for multi-task learning [213, 232]. One of the mainstream methods is horizontally splitting input images or feature maps to take advantage of local spatial cues [132, 219, 271]. Similarly, pose estimation is incorporated into the learning of local features [212, 214]. Furthermore, human parsing is used in [111] to enhance spatial matching. In comparison, our DG-Net relies only on simple identification loss for Re-ID learning and does not require extra auxiliary information such as pose or human parsing for image generation.

Another active research line is to use GANs [76] to augment training data. [294] is first introduced to use unconditional GAN to generate images from random vectors. Huang et al. proceed in this direction with WGAN [4] and assign pseudo-labels to generated images [95]. Li et al. propose to share weights between re-id model and discriminator of GAN [76]. In addition, some recent methods use pose estimation to generate pose-conditioned images. In [103] a two-stage generation pipeline is developed based on pose to refine the generated images. Similarly, pose is also used in [71] to generate images of a pedestrian in different poses to make the learned features more robust to pose variances.

Meanwhile, some recent studies also exploit synthetic data for the style transfer of pedestrian images to compensate for the disparity between the source and target domains. Cycle-GAN [300] is applied in [296] to transfer the style of pedestrian image from one data set to another. StarGAN [44] is used in [295] to generate pedestrian images with different camera styles. Bak et al. [7] employ a game engine to render pedestrians using various illumination conditions. Wei et al. [241] take semantic segmentation to extract the foreground mask to assist with style transfer.

6.1.2 3D Point Cloud Processing

PointNet [192] is the first deep learning model that processes the point cloud. The basic building blocks proposed by PointNet, such as multi-layer perceptrons for point-wise feature extraction and max/average pooling for global aggregation, have become a popular design choice for various categories of newer backbones. PointNet++ [193] exploits the met-

DOI: 10.1201/9781003376132-6

ric space distances to learn local features with increasing contextual scales, with novel set learning layers to adaptively combine features from multi-scale based on uniform densities. PointCNN [134] is introduced to learn an X transformation from input points to simultaneously weigh the input features associated with the points and then permute them into latent potentially canonical order. Grid-GCN [256] takes advantage of the Coverage-Aware Grid Query (CAGQ) strategy for point-cloud processing, which leverages the efficiency of grid space. In this way, Grid-GCN improves spatial coverage while reducing theoretical time complexity.

6.1.3   Object Detection

Deep Learning based object detection can generally be classified into two categories: two-stage and single-stage object detection. Two-stage detectors, for example, Faster R-CNN [201], FPN [143], and Cascade R-CNN [30], generate region proposals in the first stage and refine them in the second. In localization, R-CNN [73] utilizes the L2 norm between predicted and target offsets as the object function, which can cause gradient explosions when errors are significant. Fast R-CNN [72] and Faster R-CNN [201] proposed a smooth loss of L1 that keeps the gradient of large prediction errors consistent. One-stage detectors, e.g., RetinaNet [144] and YOLO [200], classify and regress objects concurrently, which are highly efficient but suffer from lower accuracy. Recent methods [276, 202] have been used to improve localization accuracy using IoU (Insertion over Union)-related values as regression targets. IoU Loss [276] utilized the negative log of IoU as object functions directly, which incorporates the dependency between box coordinates and adapts to multi-scale training. GIoU [202] extends the IoU loss to non-overlapping cases by considering the shape properties of the compared objects. CIoU Loss [293] incorporates more geometric measurements, that is, overlap area, central point distance, and aspect ratio, and achieves better convergence.

6.1.4   Speech Recognition

Speech recognition is an automatic technology that converts human voice content into the corresponding text by computers. Because of its widespread prospects, speech recognition has become one of the most popular topics in academic research and industrial applications. In recent years, speech recognition has improved rapidly with th'e development of deep convolutional neural networks (DCNNs). WaveNet [183] is one of the most advanced frameworks for speech recognition. When assigned languages and audio spectrograms are given, they can be recognized vividly and converse text to speech in high quality. The data-driven vocoders avoid the error of the process of estimating the speech spectrum and phase information, then combine them to return the speech waveform. The data-driven vocoders is the key to which WaveNets naturally produce voice. The key to naturally produce voice about WaveNets is that new data-driven vocoders [178] avoid the error problem of the process when estimating the speech spectrum and phase information separately and then combine them to return the speech waveform. Instead of traditional speech recognition applications on remote servers, speech recognition is gradually becoming popular on mobile devices. However, the requirements of abundant memory and computational resources restrict full precision neural networks. Before solving the hardware deployment problem on mobile devices, we were unable to run or store these DCNNs with huge amounts of parameters.

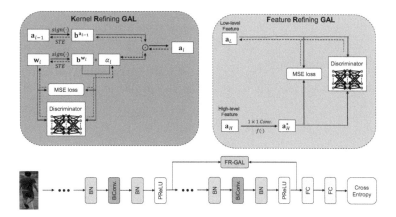

FIGURE 6.1
An illustration of BiRe-ID based on KR-GAL and FR-GAL, applying **K**ernel **R**efining **G**enerative **A**dversarial **L**earning (KR-GAL) and **F**eature **R**efining **G**enerative **A**dversarial **L**earning (FR-GAL). KR-GAL consists of the unbinarized kernel $\mathbf{w}_i$, corresponding binarized kernel $\mathbf{b}^{\mathbf{w}_i}$, and the attention-aware scale factor α_i. α_i is employed to channel-wise reconstruct the binarized kernel $\mathbf{b}^{\mathbf{w}_i}$. We employ conventional MSE loss and a GAN to fully refine $\mathbf{w}_i$ and α_i. FR-GAL is a self-supervision tool to refine the features of the low-level layers with the semantic information contained by the high-level features. To compare the features of the low- and high-level parts, we employ a 1×1 convolution and nearest neighbor interpolation $f(\cdot)$ to keep the channel dimension identical. Then the high-level features can be utilized to refine the low-level feature through a GAN.

6.2 BiRe-ID: Binary Neural Network for Efficient Person Re-ID

This section proposes a new BNN-based framework for efficient person Re-ID (BiRe-ID) [262]. We introduce the kernel and feature refinement based on generative adversarial learning (GAL) [76] to improve the representation capacity of BNNs. Specifically, we exploit GAL to efficiently refine the kernel and feature of BNNs. We introduce an attention-aware factor to refine the 1-bit convolution kernel under the GAL framework (KR-GAL). We reconstruct real-valued kernels by their corresponding binarized counterparts and the attention-aware factor. This reconstruction process is well supervised by GAL and MSE loss as shown in the upper left corner of Fig. 6.1.

Furthermore, we employ a self-supervision framework to refine the low-level features under the supervision of the high-level features with semantic information. As shown in the upper right corner of Fig. 6.1, we use a feature-refining generative adversarial network (FR-GAL) to supervise the low-level feature maps. In this way, the low-level features will be refined by the semantic information contained in the high-level features to improve the training process and lead to a sufficiently trained BNN.

6.2.1 Problem Formulation

We first consider a general quantization problem for deeply accelerating convolution operations to calculate the quantized or discrete weights. We design a quantization process by projecting the real-valued (32-bit) variable x onto a set as

$$\mathbb{Q} = \{a_1, a_2, \cdots, a_n\}, \tag{6.1}$$

where $\mathbb{Q}$ is a discrete set and n is the bit size of the set $\mathbb{Q}$. For example, n is set as 2^{16} when performing 16-bit quantization. Then, we define the projection of $x \in \mathbb{R}$ onto the set $\mathbb{Q}$ as

$$P_{\mathbb{R}\to\mathbb{Q}}(x) = \begin{cases} a_1, & x < \frac{a_1+a_2}{2} \\ \cdots \\ a_i, & \frac{a_{i-1}+a_i}{2} \leq x < \frac{a_i+a_{i+1}}{2} \\ \cdots \\ a_n, & \frac{a_{n-1}+a_n}{2} \leq x \end{cases} . \tag{6.2}$$

By projecting 32-bit wights and activations into low bit cases, the computation source will be reduced to a great deal. For extreme cases, binarizing weights and activations of neural networks decreases the storage and computation cost by $32\times$ and $64\times$, respectively. Considering the binarization process of BNNs, Eqs. 6.34 and 6.79 are relaxed into

$$P_{\mathbb{R}\to\mathbb{B}}(x) = \begin{cases} -1, & x < 0 \\ +1, & 0 \leq x \end{cases} , \ s.t. \ \mathbb{B} = \{-1, +1\}, \tag{6.3}$$

where we set $a_1 = -1$ and $a_2 = +1$. Then $P_{\mathbb{R}\to\mathbb{B}}(\cdot)$ is equivalent to the sign function *i.e.*, $sign(\cdot)$.

The learning objective of conventional BNNs (XNOR-Net) is defined to minimize the geometry distance between x and $P_{\mathbb{R}\to\mathbb{B}}(x)$ as

$$\arg\min_{x,\alpha} \|x - \alpha P_{\mathbb{R}\to\mathbb{B}}(x)\|_2^2, \tag{6.4}$$

where α is an auxiliary scale factor. In recent works of binarized neural networks (BNNs) [199, 159], they explicitly solve the objective as

$$\alpha = \frac{\|x\|_1}{\text{size}(x)}, \tag{6.5}$$

where $\text{size}(x)$ denotes the number of elements in x. However, this objective is insufficient to maintain the information of the real-valued counterpart x. To overcome this shortcoming, we introduce the kernel refining convolution.

Furthermore, XNOR-Net, which aligns with most BNNs, leads to intrachannel feature homogenization, thus causing degradation of feature representation capacity. Hence, a new feature refinement method should be introduced.

6.2.2   Kernel Refining Generative Adversarial Learning (KR-GAL)

Given a conventional CNN model, we denote $\mathbf{w}_i \in \mathbb{R}_{n_i}$ and $\mathbf{a}_i \in \mathbb{R}_{m_i}$ as its weights and feature maps in the i-th layer, where $n_i = C_i \cdot C_{i-1} \cdot K_i \cdot K_i$ and $m_i = C_i \cdot W_i \cdot H_i$. C_i represents the number of output channels of the i-th layer. (W_i, H_i) are the width and height of the feature maps and K_i is the kernel size. Then we have the following.

$$\mathbf{a}_i = \mathbf{a}_{i-1} \otimes \mathbf{w}_i, \tag{6.6}$$

where $\otimes$ is the convolutional operation. As mentioned above, the BNN model aims to binarize $\mathbf{w}_i$ and $\mathbf{a}_i$ into $P_{\mathbb{R}\to\mathbb{B}}(\mathbf{w}_i)$ and $P_{\mathbb{R}\to\mathbb{B}}(\mathbf{a}_i)$. For simplification, in this chapter, we denote $P_{\mathbb{R}\to\mathbb{B}}(\mathbf{w}_i)$ and $P_{\mathbb{R}\to\mathbb{B}}(\mathbf{a}_i)$ as $\mathbf{b}^{\mathbf{w}_i} \in \mathbb{B}_{m_i}$ and $\mathbf{b}^{\mathbf{a}_i} \in \mathbb{B}_{n_i}$ in this chapter, respectively.

Then, we use efficient XNOR and Bit-count operations to replace real-valued operations. Following [199], the forward process of the BNN is

$$\mathbf{a}_i = \mathbf{b^{a_{i-1}}} \odot \mathbf{b^{w_i}}, \tag{6.7}$$

where $\odot$ represents efficient XNOR and Bit-count operations. Based on XNOR-Net, we introduce a learnable channel-wise scale factor to modulate the amplitude of real-valued convolution. Aligned with the Batch Normalization (BN) and activation layers, the 1-bit convolution is formulated as

$$\mathbf{b^{a_i}} = sign(\Phi(\boldsymbol{\alpha}_i \circ \mathbf{b^{a_{i-1}}} \odot \mathbf{b^{w_i}})). \tag{6.8}$$

In KR-GAL, the original output feature $\mathbf{a}_i$ is first scaled by a channel-wise scale factor (vector) $\boldsymbol{\alpha}_i \in \mathbb{R}_{C_i}$ to modulate the amplitude of the real-valued counterparts. It then enters $\Phi(\cdot)$, which represents a composite function built by stacking several layers, *e.g.*, BN layer, non-linear activation layer, and max pool layer. The output is then binarized to obtain the binary activations $\mathbf{b^{a_i}} \in \mathbb{B}_{n_i}$, using the sign function. sign$(\cdot)$ denotes the sign function that returns $+1$ if the input is greater than zeros and -1 otherwise. Then, the 1-bit activation $\mathbf{b^{a_i}}$ can be used for the efficient XNOR and Bit-count of $(i+1)$-th layer.

However, the gap in representational capability between $\mathbf{w}_i$ and $\mathbf{b^{w_i}}$ could lead to a large quantization error. We aim to minimize this performance gap to reduce the quantization error while increasing the binarized kernels' ability to provide information gains. Therefore, $\boldsymbol{\alpha}_i$ is also used to reconstruct $\mathbf{b^{w_i}}$ into $\mathbf{w}_i$. This learnable scale factor can lead to a novel learning process with more precise estimation of convolutional filters by minimizing a novel adversarial loss. Discriminators $D(\cdot)$ with weights W_D are introduced to distinguish unbinarized kernels $\mathbf{w}_i$ from reconstructed ones $\boldsymbol{\alpha}_i \circ \mathbf{b^{w_i}}$. Therefore, $\boldsymbol{\alpha}_i$ and W_D are learned by solving the following optimization problem.

$$\arg \min_{\mathbf{w}_i, \mathbf{b^{w_i}}, \boldsymbol{\alpha}_i} \max_{W_D} \mathscr{L}_{Adv}^K(\mathbf{w}_i, \mathbf{b^{w_i}}, \alpha_i, W_D) + \mathscr{L}_{MSE}^K(\mathbf{w}_i, \mathbf{b^{w_i}}, \alpha_i) \ \forall \ i \in N, \tag{6.9}$$

where $\mathscr{L}_{Adv}^K(\mathbf{w}_i, \mathbf{b^{w_i}}, \alpha_i, W_D)$ is the adversarial loss as

$$\mathscr{L}_{Adv}^K(\mathbf{w}_i, \mathbf{b^{w_i}}, \alpha_i, W_D) = log(D(\mathbf{w}_i; W_D)) + log(1 - D(\mathbf{b^{w_i}} \circ \alpha_i; W_D)), \tag{6.10}$$

where $D(\cdot)$ consists of several basic blocks, each with a fully connected layer and a LeakyReLU layer. In addition, we employ discriminators to refine every binarized convolution layer during the binarization training process.

Furthermore, $\mathscr{L}_{MSE}(\mathbf{w}_i, \mathbf{b^{w_i}}, \alpha_i)$ is the kernel loss between the learned real-valued filters $\mathbf{w}_i$ and the binarized filters $\mathbf{b^{w_i}}$, which is expressed by MSE as

$$\mathscr{L}_{MSE}^K(\mathbf{w}_i, \mathbf{b^{w_i}}, \alpha_i) = \frac{\lambda}{2}||\mathbf{w}_i - \alpha_i \circ \mathbf{b^{w_i}}||_2^2, \tag{6.11}$$

where MSE is used to balance the gap between real value $\mathbf{w}_i$ and binarized $\mathbf{b^{w_i}}$. λ is a balance hyperparameter.

6.2.3 Feature Refining Generative Adversarial Learning (FR-GAL)

We introduce generative adversarial learning (GAL) to refine the low-level characteristic through self-supervision. We employ the high-level feature with abundant semantic information $\mathbf{a}_H \in R_{m_H}$ to supervise the low-level feature $\mathbf{a}_L \in R_{m_L}$, where $m_H = C_H \cdot W_H \cdot H_H$ and $m_L = C_L \cdot W_L \cdot H_L$. To keep the channel dimension identical, we first employ a 1×1 convolution to reduce C_H to C_L as

$$\mathbf{a}_H^* = f(W_{1 \times 1} \otimes \mathbf{a}_H), \tag{6.12}$$

where $f(\cdot)$ is the nearest-neighbor interpolation. Therefore, we formulate the learning objective for feature refinement as

$$\arg \min_{\mathbf{a}_L, \mathbf{a}_H^*} \max_{W_D} \mathscr{L}_{Adv}^F(\mathbf{a}_L, \mathbf{a}_H^*, W_D) + \mathscr{L}_{MSE}^F(\mathbf{a}_L, \mathbf{a}_H^*) \ \forall \ i \in N, \tag{6.13}$$

where $\mathscr{L}_{Adv}^K(\mathbf{w}_i, \mathbf{b}^{\mathbf{w}_i}, \alpha_i, W_D)$ is the adversarial loss as

$$\mathscr{L}_{Adv}^F(\mathbf{a}_L, \mathbf{a}_H^*, W_D) = log(D(\mathbf{a}_H^*; W_D)) + log(1 - D(\mathbf{a}_L; W_D)), \tag{6.14}$$

where $D(\cdot)$ consists of several basic blocks, each with a fully connected layer and a LeakyReLU layer. In addition, we adopt several discriminators to refine the features during the binarization training process.

Moreover, $\mathscr{L}_{MSE}^F(\mathbf{w}_i, \mathbf{b}^{\mathbf{w}_i}, \alpha_i)$ is the feature loss between the low-level and high-level features, which is expressed by MSE as

$$\mathscr{L}_{MSE}^F(\mathbf{a}_L, \mathbf{a}_H^*) = \frac{\mu}{2}||\mathbf{a}_L - \mathbf{a}_H^*||_2^2, \tag{6.15}$$

where μ is a balancing hyperparameter.

6.2.4   Optimization

For a specific task, the conventional problem-dependent loss $\mathscr{L}_S$ *e.g.*, the cross entropy, is considered, thus the learning objective is defined as

$$\arg \min_{\mathbf{w}_i, \alpha_i, \mathbf{p}_i} = \mathscr{L}_S(\mathbf{w}_i, \alpha_i, \mathbf{p}_i) \ \forall \ i \in N, \tag{6.16}$$

where $\mathbf{p}_i$ denotes the other parameters of BNN, *e.g*, parameters of BN and PReLU. Therefore, the general learning objective of BiRe-ID is Eqs. 6.79, 6.13, and 6.16. For each convolutional layer, we sequentially update $\mathbf{w}_i$, α_i and $\mathbf{p}_i$.

Updating $\mathbf{w}_i$: Consider $\delta_{\mathbf{w}_i}$ as the gradient of the real-valued kernels $\mathbf{w}_i$. Thus,

$$\delta_{\mathbf{w}_i} = \frac{\partial \mathscr{L}}{\partial \mathbf{w}_i} = \frac{\partial \mathscr{L}_S}{\partial \mathbf{w}_i} + \frac{\partial \mathscr{L}_{Adv}^K}{\partial \mathbf{w}_i} + \frac{\partial \mathscr{L}_{Adv}^F}{\partial \mathbf{w}_i} + \frac{\partial \mathscr{L}_{MSE}^K}{\partial \mathbf{w}_i} + \frac{\partial \mathscr{L}_{MSE}^F}{\partial \mathbf{w}_i}. \tag{6.17}$$

During the backpropagation of softmax loss $\mathscr{L}_S(\mathbf{w}_i, \alpha_i, \mathbf{p}_i)$, the gradients go to $\mathbf{b}^{\mathbf{w}_i}$ first and then to $\mathbf{w}_i$. Thus, we formulate is as

$$\frac{\partial \mathscr{L}_S}{\partial \mathbf{w}_i} = \frac{\partial \mathscr{L}_S}{\partial \mathbf{b}^{\mathbf{w}_i}} \frac{\partial \mathbf{b}^{\mathbf{w}_i}}{\partial \mathbf{w}_i}, \tag{6.18}$$

where

$$\frac{\partial \mathbf{b}^{\mathbf{w}_i}}{\partial \mathbf{w}_i} = \begin{cases} 2 + 2\mathbf{w}_i, & -1 \le \mathbf{w}_i < 0, \\ 2 - 2\mathbf{w}_i, & 0 \le \mathbf{w}_i < 1, \\ 0, & \text{otherwise}, \end{cases} \tag{6.19}$$

which is an approximation of the 2×dirac-delta function [159]. Furthermore,

$$\frac{\partial \mathscr{L}_{Adv}^K}{\partial \mathbf{w}_i} = \frac{1}{D(\mathbf{w}_i; W_D)} \frac{\partial D}{\partial \mathbf{w}_i}. \tag{6.20}$$

$$\frac{\partial \mathscr{L}_{MSE}^K}{\partial \mathbf{w}_i} = \lambda(\mathbf{w}_i - \alpha_i \circ \mathbf{b}^{\mathbf{w}_i}) \circ \alpha_i, \tag{6.21}$$

$$\frac{\partial \mathscr{L}_{Adv}^F}{\partial \mathbf{w}_i} = -\frac{1}{1 - D(\mathbf{a}_i; W_D)} \frac{\partial D}{\partial \mathbf{a}_i} \frac{\partial \mathbf{a}_i}{\partial \mathbf{w}_i} \mathbb{I}(i \in L), \tag{6.22}$$

$$\frac{\partial \mathscr{L}_{MSE}^{F}}{\partial \mathbf{w}_i} = \mu(\mathbf{a}_i - \mathbf{a}_H^*)\frac{\partial \mathbf{a}_i}{\partial \mathbf{w}_i}\mathbb{I}(i \in L), \tag{6.23}$$

where $\mathbb{I}$ is an indicator function defined as

$$\mathbb{I}(i \in L) = \begin{cases} 1, & i-\text{th layer is supervised with FR} - \text{GAL} \\ 0, & else \end{cases}. \tag{6.24}$$

As mentioned above, we employ several FR-GALs in the training process. Therefore, $\mathbb{I}(i \in L)$ denotes whether i-th layer is supervised with FR-GAL. Note that FR-GAL is only used to supervise the low-level feature. Thus, no gradient is aroused to the high-level feature.

In this way, we calculate every specific gradient of $\mathbf{w}_i$ as

$$\mathbf{w}_i \leftarrow \mathbf{w}_i - \eta_1 \delta_{\mathbf{w}_i}, \tag{6.25}$$

where η_1 is a learning rate.

Update α_i: We further update the learnable matrix α_i with $\mathbf{w}_i$ fixed. Let δ_{α_i} be the gradient of α_i, we then have

$$\delta_{\alpha_i} = \frac{\partial \mathscr{L}}{\partial \alpha_i} = \frac{\partial \mathscr{L}_S}{\partial \alpha_i} + \frac{\partial \mathscr{L}_{Adv}^{K}}{\partial \alpha_i} + \frac{\partial \mathscr{L}_{MSE}^{K}}{\partial \alpha_i} + \frac{\partial \mathscr{L}_{Adv}^{F}}{\partial \alpha_i} + \frac{\partial \mathscr{L}_{MSE}^{F}}{\partial \alpha_i}, \tag{6.26}$$

and

$$\alpha_i \leftarrow \alpha_i - \eta_2 \delta_{\alpha_i}, \tag{6.27}$$

where η_2 is the learning rate for α_i. Furthermore,

$$\frac{\partial \mathscr{L}_{Adv}^{K}}{\partial \alpha_i} = -\frac{1}{(1 - D(\alpha_i \circ \mathbf{b}^{\mathbf{w}_i}; W_D))}\frac{\partial D}{\partial(\alpha_i \circ \mathbf{b}^{\mathbf{w}_i})}\mathbf{b}^{\mathbf{w}_i}. \tag{6.28}$$

$$\frac{\partial \mathscr{L}_{MSE}^{K}}{\partial \alpha_i} = -\lambda(\mathbf{w}_i - \alpha_i \circ \mathbf{b}^{\mathbf{w}_i})\mathbf{b}^{\mathbf{w}_i}, \tag{6.29}$$

$$\frac{\partial \mathscr{L}_{Adv}^{F}}{\partial \alpha_i} = -\frac{1}{1 - D(\mathbf{a}_i; W_D)}\frac{\partial D}{\partial \mathbf{a}_i}\frac{\partial \mathbf{a}_i}{\partial \alpha_i}\mathbb{I}(i \in L), \tag{6.30}$$

$$\frac{\partial \mathscr{L}_{MSE}^{F}}{\partial \alpha_i} = \mu(\mathbf{a}_i - \mathbf{a}_H^*)\frac{\partial \mathbf{a}_i}{\partial \alpha_i}\mathbb{I}(i \in L), \tag{6.31}$$

Update $\mathbf{p}_i$: Finally, we update the other parameters $\mathbf{p}_i$ with $\mathbf{w}_i$ and $\boldsymbol{\alpha}_i$ fixed. $\delta_{\mathbf{p}_i}$ is defined as the gradient of $\mathbf{p}_i$ as

$$\delta_{\mathbf{p}_i} = \frac{\partial L_S}{\partial \mathbf{p}_i} \tag{6.32}$$

$$\mathbf{p}_i \leftarrow \mathbf{p}_i - \eta_3 \delta_{\mathbf{p}_i}, \tag{6.33}$$

where η_3 is the learning rate for other parameters. These derivations demonstrate that the refining process can be trained from the beginning to the end. The training process of our BiRe-ID is summarized in Algorithm 13. We independently update the parameters while fixing other parameters of convolutional layers to enhance the variation of the feature maps in every layer. In this way, we can accelerate the convergence of training and fully explore the potential of our 1-bit networks.

Algorithm 11 BiRe-ID Training

Input: The training dataset, and the hyper-parameters such as initial learning rate, weight decay, convolution stride and padding size.

Output: BiRe-ID model with weights $\mathbf{b^w}$, learnable scale factors α, and other parameters $\mathbf{p}$.

1: Initialize $\mathbf{w}$, α, $\mathbf{p}$, and W_D randomly;
2: **repeat**
3:    Randomly sample a mini-batch from dataset;
4:    // Forward propagation
5:    **for all** $i = 1$ to N convolution layer **do**
6:       $\mathbf{b^{a_i}} = sign(\Phi(\boldsymbol{\alpha}_i \circ \mathbf{b^{a_{i-1}}} \odot \mathbf{b^{w_i}}))$;
7:    **end for**
8:    // Backward propagation
9:    **for all** $l = L$ to 1 **do**
10:       Update the kernel refining discriminators $D(\cdot)$ of GAN by ascending their stochastic gradients:
11:          $\nabla_D(log(D(\mathbf{w}_i; W_D)) + log(1 - D(\mathbf{b^{w_i}} \circ \alpha_i; W_D)))$;
12:       Update the feature refining discriminators $D(\cdot)$ of GAN by ascending their stochastic gradients:
13:          $\nabla_D(log(D(\mathbf{a}_H^*; W_D)) + log(1 - D(\mathbf{a}_L; W_D)))$;
14:       Calculate the gradients $\delta_{\mathbf{w}_i}$; // Using Eq. 7-12
15:       $\mathbf{w}_i \leftarrow \mathbf{w}_i - \eta_1 \delta_{\mathbf{w}_i}$; // Update the weights
16:       Calculate the gradient δ_{α_i}; // Using Eq. 13-16
17:       $\alpha_i \leftarrow \alpha_i - \eta_2 \delta_{\alpha_i}$; // Update the scale factor
18:       Calculate the gradient $\delta_{\mathbf{p}_i}$; // Using Eq. 13-16
19:       $\mathbf{p}_i \leftarrow \mathbf{p}_i - \eta_3 \delta_{\mathbf{p}_i}$; // Update other parameters
20:    **end for**
21: **until** the maximum epoch
22: $\mathbf{b^w} = sign(\mathbf{w})$.

6.2.5 Ablation Study

In this section, we conduct a performance study for the components of BiRe-ID, including kernel MSE loss (hyperparameter λ), KR-GAL, feature MSE loss (hyperparameter μ) and FR-GAL. Market-1501 [289] and ResNet-18 are used in this experiment. We separate this subsection into two parts: selecting hyperparameters and evaluating the components of BiRe-ID.

Selecting Hyper-Parameters We first set the kernel refining GAL (KR-GAL) and the feature refining GAL (FR-GAL) as the invariant variable to compare the impact of the hyperparameter λ and μ on the ResNet-18 backbone. As plotted in Fig. 6.2, we set the ablation study at λ and μ. We vary λ from 0 to $1e-4$ and μ from 0 to $1e-2$ to evaluate BiRe-ID's mAP with different hyperparameter settings. From bottom to top, BiRe-ID obtains the obviously better mAPs with μ set as $5e-3$ (green mAP curve). From left to right, BiRe-ID obtains the best mAP with λ set as $5e-5$. Therefore, we set μ and λ as $5e-3$ and $5e-5$ experiments on the Re-ID task.

Evaluating the Components of BiRe-ID As shown in Table 6.5, the use of GANs dramatically increases the performance of the proposed baseline network. More specifically, we first introduce our baseline network by adding a single BN layer ahead of the 1-bit convolutions of XNOR-Net, which brings a 14.1% improvement in mAP. The introduction of KR-GAL and FR-GAL improves mAP by 7.1% and 4.1%, respectively, on the proposed

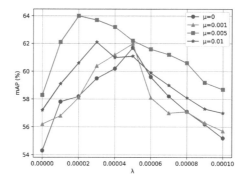

FIGURE 6.2
The variety of BiRe-ID's final mAPs on Market-1501. An ablation study on λ and μ. ResNet-18 backbone is employed.

baseline network, as shown in the second section of Table 6.5. By adding all KR-GAL and FR-GAL, our BiRe-ID achieves 10.0% higher mAP and 9.8% higher Rank@1 accuracy than the baseline, even approximating the corresponding real-valued network accuracy.

6.3 POEM: 1-Bit Point-Wise Operations Based on E-M for Point Cloud Processing

In this section, we first implement a baseline XNOR-Net-based [199] 1-bit point cloud network, which shows that the performance drop is mainly caused by two drawbacks. First, the layer-wise weights of XNOR-Net roughly follow a Gaussian distribution with a mean value around 0. However, such a distribution is subject to disturbance caused by the noise contained in the raw point cloud data [86]. As a result, such a Gaussian distributed weight (around 0) will accordingly change its sign, *i.e.*, the binarization result will change dramatically. This explains why the baseline network is ineffective in processing the point cloud data and achieves a worse convergence, as shown in Fig. 6.3 (a). In contrast, the bimodal distribution will gain its robustness against this noise. Second, XNOR-Net fails to adapt itself to the characteristics of cloud data, when computing the scale factor using a nonlearning method.

To address these issues, we introduce 1-bit point-wise operations based on Expectation-Maximization (POEM) [261] to efficiently process the point cloud data. We exploit the

TABLE 6.1
The effects of different components in BiRe-ID on the Rank@1 and mAP on the Market-1501 dataset.

ResNet-18	Rank@1 (%)	mAP (%)
XNOR-Net	63.8	40.1
Proposed baseline network	74.9	54.0
Proposed baseline network + KR-GAL	80.0	61.1
Proposed baseline network + FR-GAL	78.5	58.1
Proposed baseline network + KR-GAL + FR-GAL (BiRe-ID)	**84.1**	**64.0**
Real-valued Counterpart	**85.1**	**64.3**

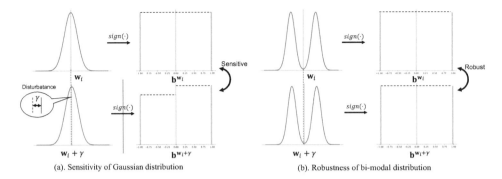

(a). Sensitivity of Gaussian distribution   (b). Robustness of bi-modal distribution

FIGURE 6.3
Subfigure (a) and (b) illustrate the robustness of the Gaussian distribution and the bimodal distribution. From left to right in each subfigure, we plot the distribution of the unbinarized weights $\mathbf{w}_i$ and the binarized weights $\mathbf{b}^{\mathbf{w}_i}$. The XNOR-Net's drawback lies in subfigure (a). If a disturbance γ is on the unbinarized weights by the discrete activation, there will be a significant disturbance on the binarized weight. The subfigure (b) shows the robustness of the bimodal distribution when influenced by the same disturbance.

Expectation-Maximization (EM) [175] method to constrain the distribution of weights. As shown in Fig. 6.3 (b), the model is robust to disturbances. Furthermore, we introduce a learnable and adaptive scale factor for every 1-bit layer to enhance the feature representation capacity of our binarized networks. Finally, we lead a powerful 1-bit network for point cloud processing, which can reconstruct real-valued counterparts' amplitude via a new learning-based method.

6.3.1   Problem Formulation

We first consider a general quantization problem for deep-accelerating pointwise operations to calculate quantized or discrete weights. We design a quantization process by projecting the full-precision (32-bit) variable x onto a set as

$$\mathbb{Q} = \{a_1, a_2, \cdots, a_n\}, \tag{6.34}$$

where $\mathbb{Q}$ is a discrete set and n is the bit size of the set $\mathbb{Q}$. For example, n is set as 2^{16} when performing 16-bit quantization.

Then, we define the projection of $x \in \mathbb{R}$ onto the set $\mathbb{Q}$ as

$$P_{\mathbb{R}\to\mathbb{Q}}(x) = \begin{cases} a_1, & x < \frac{a_1+a_2}{2} \\ \cdots \\ a_i, & \frac{a_{i-1}+a_i}{2} \le x < \frac{a_i+a_{i+1}}{2} \\ \cdots \\ a_n, & \frac{a_{n-1}+a_n}{2} \le x \end{cases} . \tag{6.35}$$

By projecting 32-bit wights and activations into low bit cases, the computation source will be reduced to a great deal. For extreme cases, binarizing weights and activations of neural networks decreases the storage and computation cost by $32\times$ and $64\times$, respectively. Considering the binarization process of BNNs, Eqs. 6.34 and 6.79 are relaxed into

$$P_{\mathbb{R}\to\mathbb{B}}(x) = \begin{cases} -1, & x < 0 \\ +1, & 0 \le x \end{cases} , \ s.t. \ \mathbb{B} = \{-1, +1\}, \tag{6.36}$$

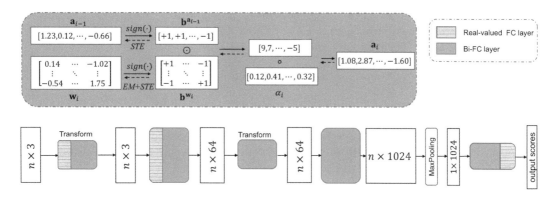

FIGURE 6.4

Outline of the 1-bit PointNet obtained by our POEM on the classification task. We save the first and last fully connected layer as real valued, which is with horizontal stripes. We give the detailed forward and back propagation process of POEM, where EM denotes the Expectation-Maximization algorithm, and STE denotes Straight-Through-Estimator.

where we set $a_1 = -1$ and $a_2 = +1$. Then $P_{\mathbb{R} \to \mathbb{B}}(\cdot)$ is equivalent to the sign function, *i.e.*, $sign(\cdot)$.

However, The binarization procedure achieved by $P_{\mathbb{R} \to \mathbb{B}}(x)$ is sensitive to disturbance when x follows a Gaussian distribution, *e.g.*, XNOR-Net. That is, the binarization results are subjected to the noise of the raw point cloud data, as shown in Fig. 6.3. To address this issue, we first define an objective as

$$\arg \min_{x} P_{\mathbb{R} \to \mathbb{B}}(x) - P_{\mathbb{R} \to \mathbb{B}}(x + \gamma), \tag{6.37}$$

where γ denotes a disturbance.

Another objective is defined to minimize the geometry distance between x and $P_{\mathbb{R} \to \mathbb{B}}(x)$ as

$$\arg \min_{x, \alpha} \|x - \alpha P_{\mathbb{R} \to \mathbb{B}}(x)\|_2^2, \tag{6.38}$$

where α is an auxiliary scale factor. In recent works of binarized neural networks (BNNs) [199, 159], they explicitly solve the objective as

$$\alpha = \frac{\|x\|_1}{\text{size}(x)}, \tag{6.39}$$

where $\text{size}(x)$ denotes the number of elements in x. However, this objective neglects that α also influences the output of the 1-bit layer. In contrast, we also consider this shortcoming and modify this learning object for our POEM.

6.3.2 Binarization Framework of POEM

We briefly introduce the framework based on our POEM, as shown in Fig. 6.4. We extend the binarization process from 2D convolution (XNOR-Net) to fully connected layers (FCs) for feature extraction, termed 1-bit fully connected (Bi-FC) layers, based on extremely efficient bit-wise operations (XNOR and Bit-count) via the lightweight binary weight and activation.

Given a conventional FC layer, we denote $\mathbf{w}_i \in \mathbb{R}_{m_i}$ and $\mathbf{a}_i \in \mathbb{R}_{C_i}$ as its weights and features in the i-th layer, where $m_i = C_i \times C_{i-1}$. C_i represents the number of output channels of i-th layer. Then we have the following.

$$\mathbf{a}_i = \mathbf{a}_{i-1} \otimes \mathbf{w}_i, \tag{6.40}$$

where $\otimes$ denotes full-precision multiplication. As mentioned above, the BNN model aims to binarize $\mathbf{w}_i$ and $\mathbf{a}_i$ into $P_{\mathbb{R}\to\mathbb{B}}(\mathbf{w}_i)$ and $P_{\mathbb{R}\to\mathbb{B}}(\mathbf{a}_i)$. For simplification, in this chapter we denote $P_{\mathbb{R}\to\mathbb{B}}(\mathbf{w}_i)$ and $P_{\mathbb{R}\to\mathbb{B}}(\mathbf{a}_i)$ as $\mathbf{b}^{\mathbf{w}_i} \in \mathbb{B}_{m_i}$ and $\mathbf{b}^{\mathbf{a}_i} \in \mathbb{B}_{C_i}$ in this paper, respectively. Then, we use the efficient XNOR and Bit-count operations to replace full-precision operations. Following [199], the forward process of the BNN is

$$\mathbf{a}_i = \mathbf{b}^{\mathbf{a}_{i-1}} \odot \mathbf{b}^{\mathbf{w}_i}, \tag{6.41}$$

where $\odot$ represents efficient XNOR and Bit-count operations. Based on XNOR-Net [199], we introduce a learnable channel-wise scale factor to modulate the amplitude of real-valued convolution. Aligned with the Batch Normalization (BN) and activation layers, the process is formulated as

$$\mathbf{b}^{\mathbf{a}_i} = sign(\Phi(\boldsymbol{\alpha}_i \circ \mathbf{b}^{\mathbf{a}_{i-1}} \odot \mathbf{b}^{\mathbf{w}_i})), \tag{6.42}$$

where we divide the data flow in POEM into units for detailed discussions. In POEM, the original output feature $\mathbf{a}_i$ is first scaled by a channel-wise scale factor (vector) $\boldsymbol{\alpha}_i \in \mathbb{R}_{C_i}$ to modulate the amplitude of its full-precision counterparts. It then enters $\Phi(\cdot)$, which represents a composite function built by stacking several layers, *e.g.*, the BN layer, the non-linear activation layer, and the max-pooling layer. Then the output is binarized to obtain the binary activations $\mathbf{b}^{\mathbf{a}_i} \in \mathbb{B}_{C_i}$, through the sign function. $sign(\cdot)$ denotes the sign function that returns $+1$ if the input is greater than zeros and -1 otherwise. Then, 1-bit activation $\mathbf{b}^{\mathbf{a}_i}$ can be used for efficient XNOR and Bit-count of the $(i+1)$-th layer.

6.3.3   Supervision for POEM

To constrain Bi-FC to have binarized weights with amplitudes similar to their real-valued counterparts, we introduce a new loss function in our supervision for POEM. We consider that unbinarized weights should be reconstructed based on binarized weights, as revealed in Eq. 6.38. We define the reconstruction loss according to Eq. 6.38 as

$$L_R = \frac{1}{2}\|\mathbf{w}_i - \boldsymbol{\alpha}_i \circ \mathbf{b}^{\mathbf{w}_i}\|_2^2, \tag{6.43}$$

where L_R is the reconstruction loss. Taking into account the impact of $\boldsymbol{\alpha}_i$ on the layer output, we define the learning objective of our POEM as

$$\underset{\{\mathbf{w}_i, \boldsymbol{\alpha}_i, \mathbf{p}_i\}, \forall i \in N}{\arg\min} \; L_S(\mathbf{w}_i, \boldsymbol{\alpha}_i, \mathbf{p}_i) + \lambda L_R(\mathbf{w}_i, \boldsymbol{\alpha}_i), \tag{6.44}$$

where $\mathbf{p}_i$ denotes the other parameters of real-valued layers in the network, *e.g.*, BN layer, activation layer, and unbinarized fully-connected layer. N denotes the number of layers in the network. L_S is the cross entropy.

And λ is a hyperparameter. Unlike binarization methods (such as XNOR-Net [199] and Bi-Real Net [159]) where only the reconstruction loss is considered in the weight calculation. By fine-tuning the value of λ, our proposed POEM can achieve much better performance than XNOR-Net, which shows the effectiveness of combined loss against only softmax loss. Our discrete optimization method comprehensively calculates the Bi-FC layers considering the reconstruction loss and the softmax loss in a unified framework.

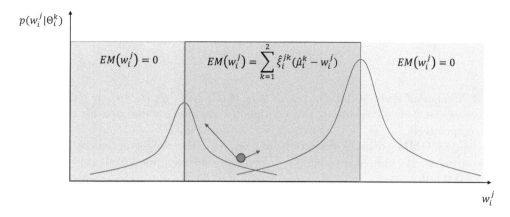

$p(w_i^j | \Theta_i^k)$

$EM(w_i^j) = 0$

$$EM(w_i^j) = \sum_{k=1}^{2} \hat{\xi}_i^{jk}(\hat{\mu}_i^k - w_i^j)$$

$EM(w_i^j) = 0$

w_i^j

FIGURE 6.5
Illustration of training w_i^j via Expectation-Maximization. We set a free constraint for the weights obeying one specific distribution, *i.e.*, which is lower than the minimum mean value or higher than the maximum mean value. For the ones in the middle area (distribution not transparent), we apply $EM(\cdot)$ to constrain it to converge to a specific distribution.

6.3.4 Optimization for POEM

In our POEM, what needs to be learned and updated are unbinarized weights $\mathbf{w}_i$, scale factor $\boldsymbol{\alpha}_i$ and other parameters $\mathbf{p}_i$. These three kinds of filters are jointly learned. In each Bi-FC layer, POEM sequentially updates unbinarized weights $\mathbf{w}_i$ and scale factor $\boldsymbol{\alpha}_i$. For other layers, we directly update the parameters $\mathbf{p}_i$ through backpropagation.

Updating $\mathbf{w}_i$ via Expectation-Maximization: Given a conventional binarization framework, it learns weights $\mathbf{w}_i$ based on Eq. 6.44. $\delta_{\mathbf{w}_i}$ corresponding to $\mathbf{w}_i$ is defined as

$$\delta_{\mathbf{w}_i} = \frac{\partial L_S}{\partial \mathbf{w}_i} + \lambda \frac{\partial L_R}{\partial \mathbf{w}_i} \tag{6.45}$$

$$\mathbf{w}_i \leftarrow \mathbf{w}_i - \eta \delta_{\mathbf{w}_i}, \tag{6.46}$$

where L_S and L_R are loss functions, and η is the learning rate. $\frac{\partial L_S}{\partial \mathbf{w}_i}$ can be computed by backpropagation, and, furthermore, we have

$$\frac{\partial L_R}{\partial \mathbf{w}_i} = (\mathbf{w}_i - \boldsymbol{\alpha}_i \circ \mathbf{b}^{\mathbf{w}_i}) \circ \boldsymbol{\alpha}_i. \tag{6.47}$$

However, this backpropagation process without the necessary constraint will result in a Gaussian distribution of $\mathbf{w}_i$, which degrades the robustness of Bi-FCs as revealed in Eq. 6.80. Our POEM takes another learning objective as

$$\arg \min_{\mathbf{w}_i} \mathbf{b}^{\mathbf{w}_i} - \mathbf{b}^{\mathbf{w}_i + \gamma}. \tag{6.48}$$

To learn Bi-FCs capable of overcoming this obstacle, we introduce the EM algorithm in the update of $\mathbf{w}_i$. First, we assume that the ideal distribution of $\mathbf{w}_i$ should be bimodal.

Assumption 6.3.1. *For every unbinarized weight of the i-th 1-bit layer, i.e., $\forall w_i^j \in \mathbf{w}_i$, it can be constrained to follow a Gaussian Mixture Model (GMM).*

Based on our assumption, for $\mathbf{w}_i$ we formulate the ideal bimodal distribution as

$$\mathcal{P}(\mathbf{w}_i|\mathbf{\Theta}_i) = \beta_i^k \sum_{k=1}^{2} p(\mathbf{w}_i|\Theta_i^k), \tag{6.49}$$

where the number of distributions is set as 2 in this paper. $\Theta_k^l = \{\mu_i^k, \sigma_i^k\}$ denotes the parameters of the k-th distribution, *i.e.*, μ_i^k denotes the mean value and σ_i^k denotes the variance, respectively.

To solve the GMM with the observed data $\mathbf{w}_i$, *i.e.*, the weight ensemble in the i-th layer. We introduce the hidden variable ξ_i^{jk} to formulate the maximum likelihood estimation (MLE) of GMM as

$$\xi_i^{jk} = \begin{cases} 1, & w_i^j \in p_i^k \\ 0, & \text{else} \end{cases}, \tag{6.50}$$

where ξ_i^{jk} is the hidden variable that describes the affiliation of w_i^j and p_i^k (simplified denotation of $p(\mathbf{w}_i|\Theta_i^k)$). We then define the likelihood function $\mathcal{P}(w_i^j, \xi_i^{jk}|\Theta_i^k)$ as

$$\mathcal{P}(w_i^j, \xi_i^{jk}|\Theta_i^k) = \prod_{k=1}^{2} (\beta_i^k)^{|p_i^k|} \prod_{j=1}^{m_i} \left\{ \frac{1}{\Omega} f(w_i^j, \mu_i^k, \sigma_i^k) \right\}^{\xi_i^{jk}}, \tag{6.51}$$

where $\Omega = \sqrt{2\pi|\sigma_i^k|}$, $|p_i^k| = \sum_{j=1}^{m_i} \xi_i^{jk}$, and $m_i = \sum_{k=1}^{2} |p_i^k|$. And $f(w_i^j, \mu_i^k, \sigma_i^k)$ is defined as

$$f(w_i^j, \mu_i^k, \sigma_i^k) = \exp(-\frac{1}{2\sigma_i^k}(w_i^j - \mu_i^k)^2). \tag{6.52}$$

Hence, for every single weight w_i^j, ξ_i^{jk} can be computed by maximizing the likelihood as

$$\max_{\xi_i^{jk}, \forall j, k} E\left[\log \mathcal{P}(w_i^j, \xi_i^{jk}|\Theta_i^k)|w_i^j, \Theta_i^k \right] \tag{6.53}$$

where $E(\cdot)$ represents the estimate. Therefore, the maximum likelihood estimate $\hat{\xi}_i^{jk}$ is calculated as

$$\begin{aligned} \hat{\xi}_i^{jk} &= E(\xi_i^{jk}|w_i^j, \Theta_i^k) \\ &= \mathcal{P}(\xi_i^{jk} = 1|w_i^j, \Theta_i^k) \\ &= \frac{\beta_i^k p(w_i^j|\Theta_i^k)}{\sum_{k=1}^{2} \beta_i^k p(w_i^j|\Theta_i^k)}. \end{aligned} \tag{6.54}$$

After the expectation step, we perform the maximization step to compute Θ_i^k as

$$\hat{\mu}_i^k = \frac{\sum_{j=1}^{m_i} \hat{\xi}_i^{jk} w_i^j}{\sum_{j=1}^{m_i} \hat{\xi}_i^{jk}}, \tag{6.55}$$

$$\hat{\sigma}_i^k = \frac{\sum_{j=1}^{m_i} \hat{\xi}_i^{jk} (w_i^j - \hat{\mu}_i^k)^2}{\sum_{j=1}^{m_i} \hat{\xi}_i^{jk}}, \tag{6.56}$$

$$\hat{\alpha}_i^k = \frac{\sum_{j=1}^{m_i} \hat{\xi}_i^{jk}}{m_i}. \tag{6.57}$$

Algorithm 12 POEM training. L is the loss function (summation of L_S and L_R) and N is the number of layers. Binarize() binarizes the filters obtained using the binarization Eq. 6.36, and Update() updates the parameters according to our update scheme.

Input: a minibatch of inputs and their labels, unbinarized weights $\mathbf{w}$, scale factor $\boldsymbol{\alpha}$, learning rates η.
Output: updated unbinarized weights $\mathbf{w}^{t+1}$, updated scale factor $\boldsymbol{\alpha}^{t+1}$.

1: {1. Computing gradients with aspect to the parameters:}
2: {1.1. Forward propagation:}
3: **for** $i = 1$ to N **do**
4:     $\mathbf{b}^{\mathbf{w}_i} \leftarrow$ Binarize($\mathbf{w}_i$) (using Eq. 6.36)
5:     Bi-FC features calculation using Eq. 6.87 – 6.72
6:     Loss calculation using Eq. 6.88 – 6.44
7: **end for**
8: {1.2. Backward propagation:}
9: **for** $i = N$ to 1 **do**
10:     {Note that the gradients are not binary.}
11:     Computing $\delta_{\mathbf{w}}$ using Eq. 6.89 – 6.59
12:     Computing $\delta_{\boldsymbol{\alpha}}$ using Eq. 6.60 – 6.62
13:     Computing $\delta_{\mathbf{p}}$ using Eq. 6.63 – 6.64
14: **end for**
15: {Accumulating the parameters gradients:}
16: **for** $i = 1$ to N **do**
17:     $\mathbf{w}^{t+1} \leftarrow$ Update($\delta_{\mathbf{w}}, \eta$) (using Eq. 6.89)
18:     $\boldsymbol{\alpha}^{t+1} \leftarrow$ Update($\delta_{\boldsymbol{\alpha}}, \eta$) (using Eq. 6.61)
19:     $\mathbf{p}^{t+1} \leftarrow$ Update($\delta_{\mathbf{w}}, \eta$) (using Eq. 6.64)
20:     $\eta^{t+1} \leftarrow$ Update(η) according to learning rate schedule
21: **end for**

Then, we optimize w_i^j as

$$\delta_{w_i^j} = \frac{\partial L_S}{\partial w_i^j} + \lambda \frac{\partial L_R}{\partial w_i^j} + \tau EM(w_i^j), \tag{6.58}$$

where τ is the hyperparameter to control the proportion of the Expectation-Maximization operator $EM(w_i^j)$. $EM(w_i^j)$ is defined as

$$EM(w_i^j) = \left\{ \begin{array}{cc} \sum_{k=1}^{2} \hat{\xi}_i^{jk}(\hat{\mu}_i^k - w_i^j), & \hat{\mu}_i^1 < w_i^j < \hat{\mu}_i^2 \\ 0, & \text{else} \end{array} \right. . \tag{6.59}$$

Updating $\boldsymbol{\alpha}_i$: We further update the scale factor $\boldsymbol{\alpha}_i$ with $\mathbf{w}_i$ fixed. $\delta_{\boldsymbol{\alpha}_i}$ is defined as the gradient of $\boldsymbol{\alpha}_i$, and we have

$$\delta_{\boldsymbol{\alpha}_i} = \frac{\partial L_S}{\partial \boldsymbol{\alpha}_i} + \lambda \frac{\partial L_R}{\partial \boldsymbol{\alpha}_i} \tag{6.60}$$

$$\boldsymbol{\alpha}_i \leftarrow |\boldsymbol{\alpha}_i - \eta \delta_{\boldsymbol{\alpha}_i}|, \tag{6.61}$$

where η is the learning rate. The gradient derived from softmax loss can be easily calculated on the basis of backpropagation. Based on Eq. 6.44, we have

$$\frac{\partial L_R}{\partial \boldsymbol{\alpha}_i} = (\mathbf{w}_i - \boldsymbol{\alpha}_i \circ \mathbf{b}^{\mathbf{w}_i}) \cdot \mathbf{b}^{\mathbf{w}_i}. \tag{6.62}$$

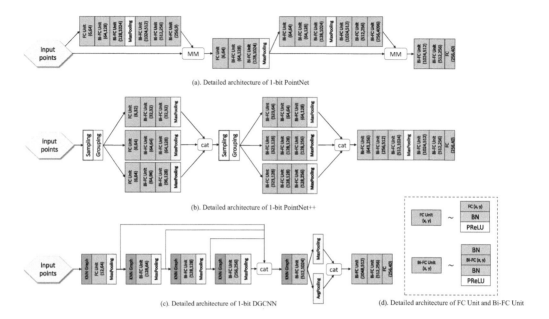

(a). Detailed architecture of 1-bit PointNet

(b). Detailed architecture of 1-bit PointNet++

(c). Detailed architecture of 1-bit DGCNN

(d). Detailed architecture of FC Unit and Bi-FC Unit

FIGURE 6.6
Detailed architecture of 1-bit networks implemented by us. (a) detailed architecture of 1-bit PointNet. MM denotes matrix multiplication in short; (b) detailed architecture of 1-bit PointNet++. Cat denotes the concatenation operation; (c) detailed architecture of 1-bit DGCNN; (d) detailed architecture of the FC unit and the Bi-FC unit used from (a) to (c). We use 2 BNs in the Bi-FC Unit.

Updating $\mathbf{p}_i$: We finally update other parameters $\mathbf{p}_i$ with $\mathbf{w}_i$ and $\boldsymbol{\alpha}_i$ fixed. $\delta_{\mathbf{p}_i}$ is defined as the gradient of $\mathbf{p}_i$. We formulate it as

$$\delta_{\mathbf{p}_i} = \frac{\partial L_S}{\partial \mathbf{p}_i} \tag{6.63}$$

$$\mathbf{p}_i \leftarrow \mathbf{p}_i - \eta \delta_{\mathbf{p}_i}. \tag{6.64}$$

The above derivations show that POEM is learnable with the BP algorithm. Our POEM is supervised on the basis of a simple and effective reconstruction loss function. Moreover, we introduce an efficient Expectation-Maximization algorithm to optimize unbinarized weights, thus constraining them to formulate a bimodal distribution.

6.3.5   Ablation Study

Hyper-parameter selection: There are hyperparameters λ and τ in Eqs. 6.44 and 6.58 that are related to the reconstruction loss and the EM algorithm. The effect of parameters λ and τ is evaluated in ModelNet40 for 1-bit PointNet, the architectural details of which can be found in Fig. 6.6 (a). The Adam optimization algorithm is used during the training process, with a batch size of 592. Using different values of λ and τ, the performance of POEM is shown in Table 6.2. In Table 6.2, from left to right lie the overall accuracies (OAs) with different λ from 1×10^{-3} to 0.

And the OAs with different τ from 1×10^{-2} to 0 lie from top to bottom. With a decrease of λ, the OA increases first and then drops dramatically. The same trend is shown when we

TABLE 6.2

Ablation study on hyperparameters λ and τ. We vary λ from 1×10^{-3} to 0 and τ from 1×10^{-2} to 0, respectively. We show the overall accuracy (OA) in this table.

1-bit PointNet		λ			
		1×10^{-3}	1×10^{-4}	1×10^{-5}	0
τ	1×10^{-2}	89.3	89.0	86.3	81.9
	1×10^{-3}	88.3	**90.2**	87.9	82.5
	1×10^{-4}	86.5	87.1	85.5	81.4
	0	82.7	85.3	83.7	80.1

decrease τ. We get the optimal 1-bit PointNet with POEM with $\{\lambda, \tau\}$ set as $\{1 \times 10^{-4}, 1 \times 10^{-3}\}$. Hence, we extend this hyperparameter set to the other experiments involved in this paper.

We also set τ as 1×10^{-3} and plot the growth curve of POEM training accuracies with different λ and XNOR-Net. Figure 6.7 shows that the 1-bit PointNet obtained by POEM achieves optimal training accuracy when λ is set as 1×10^{-4}. Also, with EM-optimized back propagation, the weight convergence becomes better than XNOR-Net (in purple), as shown in Fig. 6.7.

Evaluating the components of POEM: In this part, we evaluate every critical part of POEM to show how we compose the novel and effective POEM. We first introduce our baseline network by adding a single BN layer ahead of the 1-bit convolutions of XNOR-Net, which brings about an improvement 2.8% in OA. As shown in Table 6.5, the introduction of PReLU, EM, and the learnable scale factor improves accuracy by 1.9%, 3.1%, and 3.4%, respectively, over the baseline network, as shown in the second section of Table 6.5. By adding all the PReLU, EM and the learnable scale factor, our POEM achieves 7.1% higher accuracy than the baseline, even surpassing the accuracy of the corresponding real-valued network.

Compared to merely using the PReLU, the use of our main contributions, EM and the learnable scale factor, increases the accuracy by 5.2%, which is very significant for the point cloud classification task. The 1-bit PointNet achieves the performance, which even approaches the real-valued PointNet++ baseline within 2.0% (90.2% vs. 91.9%).

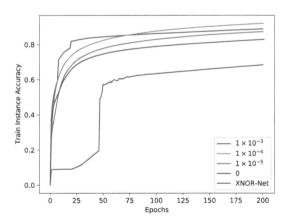

FIGURE 6.7

Training accuracies of POEM ($\tau = 1 \times 10^{-3}$) with different λ and XNOR-Net.

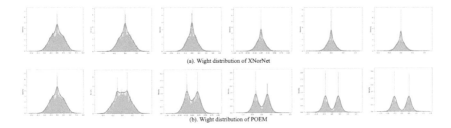

FIGURE 6.8
(a) and (b) illustrate the distribution of the unbinarized weights $\mathbf{w}_i$ of the 6-th 1-bit layer in 1-bit PointNet backbone when trained under XNOR-Net and our POEM, respectively. From left to right, we report the weight distribution of initialization, 40-th, 80-th, 120-th, 160-th, and 200-th epoch. Our POEM obtains an apparent bimodal distribution, which is much more robust.

Weight distribution: The POEM-based model is based on an Expectation-Maximization process implemented in PyTorch [186] platform. We compare the weight distribution of training XNOR-Net and POEM, which can subtly confirm our motivation. For a 1-bit PointNet model, we analyze the 6-th 1-bit layer sized $(64, 64)$ and having 4096 elements. We plot its weight distribution at the $\{0, 40, 60, 120, 160, 200\}$-th epochs. Figure 6.8 shows that the initialization (0-th epoch) is the same for XNOR-Net and POEM. However, our POEM efficiently employs the Expectation-Maximization algorithm to supervise the backpropagation process, leading to an effective and robust bimodal distribution. This analysis also complies with the performance comparison in Table 6.5.

6.4   LWS-Det: Layer-Wise Search for 1-bit Detectors

The performance of 1-bit detectors typically degrades to the point where they are not widely deployed on real-world embedded devices. For example, BiDet [240] only achieves 13.2% mAP@[.5, .95] on the COCO `minival` dataset [145], resulting in an accuracy gap of 10.0% below its real value counterpart (on the SSD300 framework). The reason, we believe, lies in the fact that the layer-wise binarization error significantly affects 1-bit detector learning.

TABLE 6.3
The effects of different components of POEM on OA.

1-bit PointNet	OA (%)
XNOR-Net	81.9
Proposed baseline network	83.1
Proposed baseline network + PReLU	85.0
Proposed baseline network + EM	86.2
Proposed baseline network + LSF	86.5
Proposed baseline network + PReLU + EM + LSF (POEM)	90.2
Real-valued Counterpart	89.2

Note: PReLU, EM, and LSF denote components that are introduced into our proposed baseline network. The proposed baseline network + PReLU + EM + LSF denotes the POEM we propose. LSF denotes the learnable scale factor, in short.

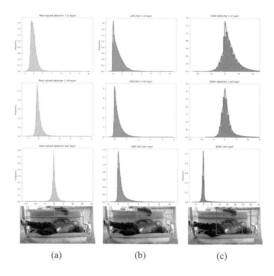

(a) (b) (c)

FIGURE 6.9

Example layer-wise feature map distribution and detection results of (a) a real-valued detector, (b) LWS-Det, and (c) BiDet. We extract the feature maps of the first, second, and final binarized layers and illustrate their distributions based on the frequency-value histogram in rows 1–3. The last row shows the detection result.

Figure 6.9 shows the layer-wise feature map distribution and detection results of a real-valued detector, our LWS-Det, and BiDet [240] from left to right. The first three rows show the distributions of feature maps. The distribution of BiDet's feature map has a variance less similar to the one of the real-value detector, leading to a result with false positives and missed detection in the 4-th row. In comparison, our LWS-Det can reduce the binarization error and provide better detection results.

In this section, we present the layer-wise search method to produce an optimized 1-bit detector (LWS-Det) [264] using the student-teacher framework to narrow the performance gap. As shown in Fig. 6.10, we minimize the binarization error by decoupling it into angular and amplitude errors. We search for binarized weight supervised by well-designed losses between real-valued convolution and 1-bit convolution under differentiable binarization search (DBS) framework, following the DARTS method [151, 305]. We formulate the binarization problem as the combination of -1 and 1, while a differentiable search can explore the binary space to significantly improve the capacity of 1-bit detectors. To improve the representation ability of LWS-Det, we design two losses to supervise the 1-bit convolution layer from angular and amplitude perspective. In this way, we obtain a powerful 1-bit detector (LWS-Det) that can minimize angular and amplitude errors in the same framework.

6.4.1 Preliminaries

Given a conventional CNN model, we denote $\mathbf{w}_i \in \mathbb{R}_{n_i}$ and $\mathbf{a}_i \in \mathbb{R}_{m_i}$ as its weights and feature maps in the i-th layer, where $n_i = C_i \cdot C_{i-1} \cdot K_i \cdot K_i$ and $m_i = C_i \cdot W_i \cdot H_i$. C_i represents the number of output channels of the i-th layer. (W_i, H_i) are the width and height of the feature maps and K_i is the kernel size. Then we have the following.

$$\mathbf{a}_i = \mathbf{a}_{i-1} \otimes \mathbf{w}_i, \tag{6.65}$$

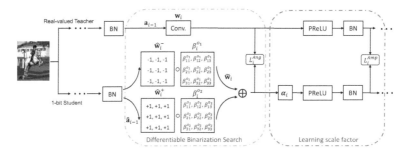

FIGURE 6.10
Our LWS-Det. From left to right are the input, search, and learning processes. For a given 1-bit convolution layer, LWS-Det first searches for the binary weight ($+1$ or -1) by minimizing the angular loss supervised by a real-valued teacher detector. LWS-Det learns the real-valued scale factor $\boldsymbol{\alpha}$ to enhance the feature representation ability.

where $\otimes$ is the convolution operation. We omit the batch normalization (BN) and activation layers for simplicity. The 1-bit model aims to quantize $\mathbf{w}_i$ and $\mathbf{a}_i$ into $\widehat{\mathbf{w}}_i \in \{-1, +1\}$ and $\widehat{\mathbf{a}}_i \in \{-1, +1\}$ using efficient xnor and bit-count operations to replace full-precision operations. Following [99], the forward process of the 1-bit CNN is:

$$\widehat{\mathbf{a}}_i = \text{sign}(\widehat{\mathbf{a}}_{i-1} \odot \widehat{\mathbf{w}}_i), \tag{6.66}$$

where $\odot$ represents the xnor and bit-count operations and $\text{sign}(\cdot)$ denotes the sign function, which returns 1 if the input is greater than zero and -1 otherwise. This binarization process will bring about the binarization error, which can be seen in Figs. 6.11 (a) and (b). The product of the 1-bit convolution (b) cannot simulate the one of real value (a) both in angularity and in amplitude.

Substantial efforts have been made to optimize this error. [199, 228] formulate the object as

$$L_i^{\mathbf{w}} = \|\mathbf{w}_i - \boldsymbol{\alpha}_i \circ \widehat{\mathbf{w}}_i\|_2^2, \tag{6.67}$$

where $\circ$ denotes the channel-wise multiplication and $\boldsymbol{\alpha}_i$ is the vector consisting of channel-wise scale factors. Figure 6.11 (c) [199, 228] learns α_i by directing optimizing $L_i^{\mathbf{w}}$ to 0, and thus the explicit solution is

$$\alpha_i^j = \frac{\|\mathbf{w}_i^j\|_1}{C_{i-1} \cdot K_i^j \cdot K_i^j}, \tag{6.68}$$

where j denotes the j-th channel of i-th layer. Other works [77] dynamically evaluate Eq. 6.80 rather than explicitly solving or modifying $\boldsymbol{\alpha}_i$ to other shapes [26].

Previous work mainly focuses on kernel reconstruction but neglects angular information, as shown in Fig. 6.11 (d). One drawback of existing methods lies in its ineffectiveness when binarizing a very small float value as shown in Fig. 6.11. On the contrary, we leverage the strong capacity of a differentiable search to fully explore a binary space for an ideal combination of -1 and $+1$ without a ambiguous binarization process involved.

6.4.2   Formulation of LWS-Det

We regard the 1-bit object detector as a student network, which can be searched and learned based on a teacher network (real-valued detector) layer by layer. Our overall framework is

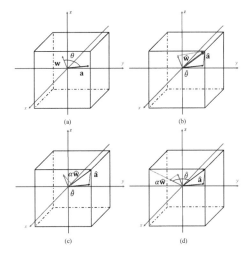

FIGURE 6.11
An illustration of binarization error in the 3-dimension space. (a) The intersection angle θ of real-valued weight $\mathbf{w}$ and activation $\mathbf{a}$ is significant. (b) After binarization $(\hat{\mathbf{w}}, \hat{\mathbf{a}})$ based on sign function, the intersection angle $\hat{\theta} = 0$. (c) $\hat{\theta} = 0$ based on XNOR-Net binarization. (d) Ideal binarization via angular and amplitude error minimization.

illustrated in Fig. 6.10. As depicted above, the main learning objective (layer-wise binarization error) is defined as

$$E = \sum_{i=1}^{N} \|\mathbf{a}_{i-1} \otimes \mathbf{w}_i - \widehat{\mathbf{a}}_{i-1} \odot \widehat{\mathbf{w}}_i \circ \boldsymbol{\alpha}_i\|_2^2, \tag{6.69}$$

where N is the number of binarized layers. We then optimize E layer-wise as

$$\underset{\widehat{\mathbf{w}}_i, \boldsymbol{\alpha}_i}{\operatorname{argmin}} E_i(\widehat{\mathbf{w}}_i, \boldsymbol{\alpha}_i; \mathbf{w}_i, \mathbf{a}_{i-1}, \widehat{\mathbf{a}}_{i-1}), \quad \forall i \in [1, \ N]. \tag{6.70}$$

In LWS-Det, we learn Equ. 6.70 by decoupling it into angular loss and amplitude loss, where we optimize the angular loss by differentiable binarization search (DBS) and the amplitude loss by learning the scale factor.

6.4.3 Differentiable Binarization Search for the 1-Bit Weight

We formulate the binarization task as a differentiable search problem. Considering that the 1-bit weight is closely related to the angular, as shown in Fig. 6.11, we define an angular loss to supervise our search process as

$$\begin{aligned} L_i^{Ang} &= \|\cos\theta_i - \cos\widehat{\theta}_i\|_2^2 \\ &= \|\frac{\mathbf{a}_{i-1} \otimes \mathbf{w}_i}{\|\mathbf{a}_{i-1}\|_2 \|\mathbf{w}_i\|_2} - \frac{\widehat{\mathbf{a}}_{i-1} \odot \widehat{\mathbf{w}}_i}{\|\widehat{\mathbf{a}}_{i-1}\|_2 \|\widehat{\mathbf{w}}_i\|_2}\|_2^2. \end{aligned} \tag{6.71}$$

For the learning process of the i-th layer, the objective is formulated as

$$\underset{\widehat{\mathbf{w}}_i}{\operatorname{argmin}} L_i^{Ang}(\widehat{\mathbf{w}}_i; \widehat{\mathbf{a}}_i, \mathbf{w}_i, \mathbf{a}_i). \tag{6.72}$$

Algorithm 13 Training 1-bit detectors via LWS-Det.

Input: The training dataset, pre-trained teacher model. **Output:** 1-bit detector.

1: Initialize $\boldsymbol{\alpha}_i$ and $\boldsymbol{\beta}_i^{o_i} \sim \mathcal{N}(0, 1)$ and other real-valued parameters layer-wise;
2: **for** $i = 1$ to N **do**
3:     **while** Differentiable search **do**
4:         Compute L_i^{Ang}, L_i^{Amp}, L_i^W
5:     **end while**
6: **end for**
7: Compute L^{GT}, L^{Lim}
8: **for** $i = N$ to 1 **do**
9:     Update parameters via back propagation
10: **end for**

We introduce the DARTS framework to solve Eq. 6.72, named differential binarization search (DBS). We follow [151] to efficiently find $\widehat{\mathbf{w}}_i$. Specifically, we approximate $\widehat{\mathbf{w}}_i$ by the weighted probability of two matrices whose weights are all set as -1 and $+1$, respectively. We relax the choice of a particular weight by the probability function defined as

$$p_i^{o_k} = \sum_{o_k \in \mathcal{O}} \frac{\exp(\boldsymbol{\beta}_i^{o_k})}{\sum_{o_k' \in \mathcal{O}} \exp(\boldsymbol{\beta}_i^{o_k'})}, \quad \text{s.t.} \quad \mathcal{O} = \{\widehat{\mathbf{w}}_i^-, \widehat{\mathbf{w}}_i^+\}, \tag{6.73}$$

where $p_i^{o_k}$ is the probability matrix belonging to the operation $o_k \in \mathcal{O}$. The search space $\mathcal{O}$ is defined as the two possible weights: $\{\widehat{\mathbf{w}}_i^-, \widehat{\mathbf{w}}_i^+\}$. For the inference stage, we select the weight owning the max probability as

$$\widetilde{\mathbf{w}}_{i,l} = \arg\max_{o_k} p_{i,l}^{o_k}, \tag{6.74}$$

where $p_{i,l}^{o_k}$ denotes the probability that the l-th weight of the i-th layer belongs to operation o_k. Therefore, the l-th weight of $\widetilde{\mathbf{w}}$, *that is*, $\widetilde{\mathbf{w}}_{i,l}$, is defined by the operation having the highest probability. In this way, we modify Eq. 6.87 by substituting $\widehat{\mathbf{w}}_i$ to $\widetilde{\mathbf{w}}_i$ as

$$L_i^{Ang} = \|\frac{\mathbf{a}_{i-1} \otimes \mathbf{w}_i}{\|\mathbf{a}_{i-1}\|_2 \|\mathbf{w}_i\|_2} - \frac{\widehat{\mathbf{a}}_{i-1} \odot \widetilde{\mathbf{w}}_i}{\|\widehat{\mathbf{a}}_{i-1}\|_2 \|\widetilde{\mathbf{w}}_i\|_2}\|_2^2. \tag{6.75}$$

By this, we retain the top-1 strongest operations (from distinct weights) for each weight of $\widehat{\mathbf{w}}_i$ in the discrete set $\{+1, -1\}$.

6.4.4   Learning the Scale Factor

After searching for $\widehat{\mathbf{w}}_i$, we learn the real-valued layers between the i-th and $(i+1)$-th 1-bit convolution. We omit the batch normalization (BN) and activation layers for simplicity. We can directly simplify Eq. 6.69 as

$$L_i^{Amp} = E_i(\boldsymbol{\alpha}_i; \mathbf{w}_i, \widetilde{\mathbf{w}}_i, \mathbf{a}_{i-1}, \widehat{\mathbf{a}}_{i-1}). \tag{6.76}$$

Following conventional BNNs [77, 287], we employ Eq. 6.80 to further supervise the scale factor $\boldsymbol{\alpha}_i$. According to [235], we employ a fine-grained limitation of the features to aid in the prior detection. Hence, the supervision of LWS-Det is formulated as

$$L = L^{GT} + \lambda L^{Lim} + \mu \sum_{i=1}^{N}(L_i^{Ang} + L_i^{Amp}) + \gamma \sum_{i=1}^{N} L_i^{\mathbf{w}}, \tag{6.77}$$

where L^{GT} is the detection loss derived from the ground truth label and L^{Lim} is the fine-grained feature limitation defined in [235]. The LWS-Det process is outlined in Algorithm 13.

6.4.5 Ablation Study

Effectiveness of DBS. We first compare our DBS method with three other methods to produce binarized weights–Random Search [277], Sign [99], and RSign [158]. As shown in Table 6.4, we evaluate the effectiveness of DBS on two detectors: one-stage SSD and two-stage Faster-RCNN. On the Faster-RCNN detector, the usage of DBS improves the mAP by 8.1%, 4.3%, and 9.1% compared to Sign, RSign, and Random Search, respectively, under the same student-teacher framework. On the SSD detector, DBS also enhances mAP by 5.5%, 3.3% and 11.3% compared to other binarization methods, respectively, which is very significant for the object detection task.

Convergence analysis. We evaluate the convergence of detection loss during the training process compared to other situations on two detectors: Faster-RCNN with ResNet-18 backbone and SSD with VGG-16 backbone. As plotted in Fig. 6.12, the LWS-Det training curve based on random search oscillates vigorously, which is suspected to be triggered by a less optimized angular error resulting from the randomly searched binary weights. Additionally, our DBS achieves a minimum loss during training compared to Sign and RSign. This also confirms that our DBS method can binarize the weights with minimum angular error, which explains the best performance in Table 6.4.

6.5 IDa-Det: An Information Discrepancy-Aware Distillation for 1-bit Detectors

The recent art [264] employs fine-grained feature imitation (FGFI) [235] to enhance the performance of 1-bit detectors. However, it neglects the intrinsic information discrepancy between 1-bit detectors and real-valued detectors. As shown in Fig. 6.13, we demonstrate that saliency maps of real-valued Faster-RCNN of the ResNet-101 backbone (often used as the teacher network) and the ResNet-18 backbone, compared to 1-bit Faster-RCNN of the ResNet-18 backbone (often used as the student network) from top to bottom. They show

TABLE 6.4
Ablation study: comparison of the performance of different binarization methods with DBS.

Framework	Backbone	Binarization Method	mAP
Faster-RCNN	ResNet-18	Sign	65.1
		RSign	68.9
		Random Search	64.1
		DBS	73.2
		Real-valued	76.4
SSD	VGG-16	Sign	65.9
		RSign	68.1
		Random Search	60.1
		DBS	71.4
		Real-valued	74.3

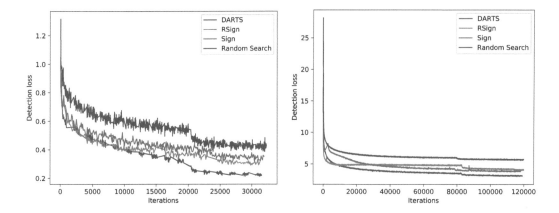

FIGURE 6.12

Convergence Faster-RCNN with ResNet-18 backbone (left) and SSD with VGG-16 backbone (right) based on different binarizations training on VOC `trainval2007` and `trainval2012`.

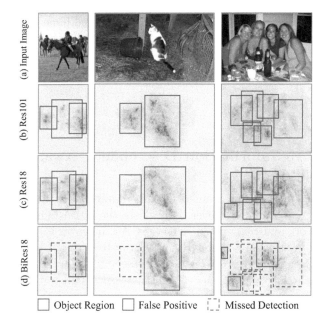

FIGURE 6.13

The input images and the saliency maps follow [79]. The images are randomly selected from VOC `test2007`. Each row includes: (a) input images, saliency maps of (b) Faster-RCNN with ResNet-101 backbone (Res101), (c) Faster-RCNN with ResNet-18 backbone (Res18), (d) 1-bit Faster-RCNN with ResNet-18 backbone (BiRes18), respectively.

that knowledge distillation (KD) methods such as [235] are effective for distilling real-valued Faster-RCNNs, only when their teacher model and their student counterpart share small information discrepancy on proposals, as shown in Fig. 6.13 (b) and (c). This phenomenon does not happen for 1-bit Faster-RCNN, as shown in Fig. 6.13 (b) and (d). This might explain why existing KD methods are less effective in 1-bit detectors. A statistic on the COCO and PASCAL VOC datasets in Fig. 6.14 shows that the discrepancy between the

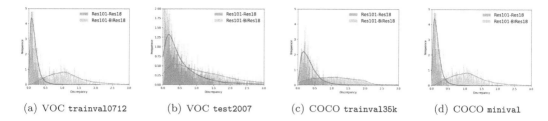

(a) VOC `trainval0712`   (b) VOC `test2007`   (c) COCO `trainval35k`   (d) COCO `minival`

FIGURE 6.14

The Mahalanobis distance of the gradient in the intermediate neck feature between Res101-Res18 (gathering on the left) and Res101-BiRes18 (uniformly dispersed) in various datasets.

proposal saliency maps of Res101 and Res18 (blue) is much smaller than that of Res101 and BiRes18 (orange). That is to say, the smaller the distance, the smaller the discrepancy. Briefly, conventional KD methods show their effectiveness in distilling real-valued detectors, but seem to be less effective on distilling 1-bit detectors.

We are motivated by the observation above and present an information discrepancy-aware distillation for 1-bit detectors (IDa-Det) [260]. This can effectively address the information discrepancy problem, leading to an efficient distillation process. As shown in Fig. 6.15, we introduce a discrepancy-aware method to select proposal pairs and facilitate distilling 1-bit detectors, rather than only using object anchor locations of student models or ground truth as in existing methods [235, 264, 79]. We further introduce a novel entropy distillation loss to leverage more comprehensive information than conventional loss functions. By doing so, we achieve a powerful information discrepancy-aware distillation method for 1-bit detectors (IDa-Det).

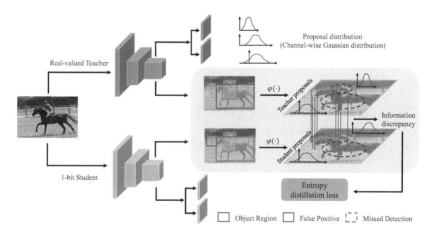

FIGURE 6.15

Overview of the proposed information discrepancy-aware distillation (IDa-Det) framework. We first select representative proposal pairs based on the information discrepancy. Then we propose the entropy distillation loss to eliminate the information discrepancy.

6.5.1   Preliminaries

In a specific convolution layer, $\mathbf{w} \in \mathbb{R}^{C_{out} \times C_{in} \times K \times K}$, $\mathbf{a}_{in} \in \mathbb{R}^{C_{in} \times W_{in} \times H_{in}}$, and $\mathbf{a}_{out} \in \mathbb{R}^{C_{out} \times W_{out} \times H_{out}}$ represent its weights and feature maps, where C_{in} and C_{out} represents the number of channels. (H, W) are the height and width of the feature maps, and K denotes the size of the kernel. Then we have the following.

$$\mathbf{a}_{out} = \mathbf{a}_{in} \otimes \mathbf{w}, \tag{6.78}$$

where $\otimes$ is the convolution operation. We omit the batch normalization (BN) and activation layers for simplicity. The 1-bit model aims to quantize $\mathbf{w}$ and $\mathbf{a}_{in}$ into $\mathbf{b^w} \in \{-1, +1\}^{C_{out} \times C_{in} \times K \times K}$ and $\mathbf{b^{a_{in}}} \in \{-1, +1\}^{C_{in} \times H \times W}$ using efficient XNOR and Bit-count operations to replace full-precision operations. Following [48], the forward process of the 1-bit CNN is

$$\mathbf{a}_{out} = \boldsymbol{\alpha} \circ \mathbf{b^{a_{in}}} \odot \mathbf{b^w}, \tag{6.79}$$

where $\odot$ is the XNOR, and bit-count operations, and $\circ$ denotes channel-wise multiplication. $\boldsymbol{\alpha} = [\alpha_1, \cdots, \alpha_{C_{out}}] \in \mathbb{R}_+$ is the vector consisting of channel-wise scale factors. $\mathbf{b} = \text{sign}(\cdot)$ denotes the binarized variable using the sign function, which returns 1 if the input is greater than zero and -1 otherwise. It then enters several non-linear layers, *e.g.*, BN layer, non-linear activation layer, and the max-pooling layer. We omit these for simplification. Then, the output $\mathbf{a}_{out}$ is binarized to $\mathbf{b^{a_{out}}}$ via the sign function. The fundamental objective of BNNs is to calculate $\mathbf{w}$. We want it to be as close as possible before and after binarization to minimize the binarization effect. Then, we define the reconstruction error as

$$L_R(\mathbf{w}, \boldsymbol{\alpha}) = \mathbf{w} - \boldsymbol{\alpha} \circ \mathbf{b^w}. \tag{6.80}$$

6.5.2   Select Proposals with Information Discrepancy

To eliminate the large magnitude scale difference between the real valued teacher and the 1-bit student, we introduce a channelwise transformation for the proposals[1] of the intermediate neck. We first apply a transformation $\varphi(\cdot)$ on a proposal $\tilde{R}_n \in \mathbb{R}^{C \times W \times H}$ and have

$$R_{n;c}(x,y) = \varphi(\tilde{R}_{n;c}(x,y)) = \frac{\exp(\frac{\tilde{R}_{n;c}(x,y)}{\mathcal{T}})}{\sum_{(x',y') \in (W,H)} \exp(\frac{\tilde{R}_{n;c}(x'y')}{\mathcal{T}})}, \tag{6.81}$$

where $(x, y) \in (W, H)$ denotes a specific spatial location (x, y) in the spatial range (W, H), and $c \in \{1, \cdots, C\}$ is the channel index. $n \in \{1, \cdots, N\}$ is the proposal index. N denotes the number of proposals. $\mathcal{T}$ denotes a hyper-parameter controlling the statistical attributions of the channel-wise alignment operation[2]. After the transformation, the features in each channel of a proposal are projected into the same feature space [231] and follow a Gaussian distribution as

$$p(R_{n;c}) \sim \mathcal{N}(\mu_{n;c}, \sigma^2_{n;c}). \tag{6.82}$$

We further evaluate the information discrepancy between the teacher and the student proposals. As shown in Fig. 6.16, the teacher and the student have N_T and N_S proposals, respectively. Every proposal in one model generates a counterpart feature map patch in the same location as in the other model. Thus, total $N_T + N_S$ proposal pairs are considered. To evaluate the information discrepancy, we introduce the Mahalanobis distance of each

---

[1] In this paper, the proposal denotes the neck/backbone feature map patched by the region proposal of detectors.

[2] In this section, we set $\mathcal{T} = 4$.

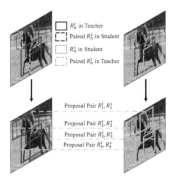

FIGURE 6.16
Illustration for the generation of the proposal pairs. Every single proposal in one model generates a counterpart feature map patch in the same location as the other model.

channel-wise proposal feature and measure the discrepancy as

$$\varepsilon_n = \sum_{c=1}^{C} ||(R_{n;c}^t - R_{n;c}^s)^T \Sigma_{n;c}^{-1} (R_{n;c}^t - R_{n;c}^s)||_2, \qquad (6.83)$$

where $\Sigma_{n;c}$ denotes the covariance matrix of the teacher and the student in the c-th channel of the n-th proposal pair. The Mahalanobis distance takes into account both the pixel-level distance between proposals and the differences in statistical characteristics in pair of proposals.

To select representative proposals with maximum information discrepancy, we first define a binary distillation mask m_n as

$$m_n = \begin{cases} 1, & \text{if pair } (R_n^t, R_n^s) \text{ is selected} \\ 0, & \text{otherwise} \end{cases} \qquad (6.84)$$

where $m_n = 1$ denotes that the distillation will be applied on this proposal pair; otherwise, it remains unchanged. For each pair of proposals, only when their distribution is quite different can the student model learn from the teacher counterpart where a distillation process is needed.

On the basis of the derivation above, discrepant proposal pairs will be optimized through distillation. To distill the selected pairs, we resort to maximizing the conditional probability $p(R_n^s | R_n^t)$. That is, after distillation or optimization, the feature distributions of the teacher proposals and the student counterparts become similar. To this end, we define $p(R_n^s | R_n^t)$ with $m_n, n \in \{1, \cdots, N_T + N_S\}$ in consideration as

$$p(R_n^s | R_n^t; m_n) \sim m_n \mathcal{N}(\mu_n^t, \sigma_n^{t\,2}) + (1 - m_n)\mathcal{N}(\mu_n^s, \sigma_n^{s\,2}). \qquad (6.85)$$

Subsequently, we introduce a bilevel optimization formulation to solve the distillation problem as

$$\max_{R_n^s} p(R_n^s | R_n^t; \mathbf{m}^*), \ \ \forall\, n \in \{0, \cdots, N_T + N_S\},$$
$$\text{s.t. } \mathbf{m}^* = \arg\max_{\mathbf{m}} \sum_{n=1}^{N_T + N_S} m_n \varepsilon_n, \qquad (6.86)$$

where $\mathbf{m} = [m_1, \cdots, m_{N_T + N_S}]$ and $||\mathbf{m}||_0 = \gamma \cdot (N_T + N_S)$. γ is a hyperparameter. In this way, we select $\gamma \cdot (N_T + N_S)$ pairs of proposals that contain the most representative information discrepancy for distillation. γ controls the proportion of discrepant proposal pairs, further validated in Section 6.5.4.

For each iteration, we first solve the inner-level optimization, *that is,* the selection of the proposal, by exhaustive sorting [249]; and then solve the upper-level optimization, distilling the selected pair, based on the entropy distillation loss discussed in Section 6.5.3. Considering that there are not too many proposals involved, the process is relatively efficient for inner-level optimization.

6.5.3   Entropy Distillation Loss

After selecting a specific number of proposals, we crop the feature based on the proposals we obtained. Most SOTA detection models are based on Feature Pyramid Networks (FPN) [143], which can significantly improve the robustness of multiscale detection. For the Faster-RCNN framework in this paper, we resize the proposals and crop the features from each stage of the neck feature maps. We generate the proposals from the regression layer of the SSD framework and crop the features from the feature map of maximum spatial size. Then we formulate the entropy distillation process as follows.

$$\max_{R_n^s} \; p(R_n^s | R_n^t). \tag{6.87}$$

Here is **the upper level** of the bi-level optimization, where m is solved and therefore omitted. We rewrite Eq. 6.87 and further achieve our entropy distillation loss as

$$L_P(\mathbf{w}, \boldsymbol{\alpha}; \gamma) = (R_n^s - R_n^t) + \mathrm{Cov}(R_n^s, R_n^t)^{-1}(R_n^s - R_n^t)^2 + \log(\mathrm{Cov}(R_n^s, R_n^t)), \tag{6.88}$$

where $\mathrm{Cov}(R_n^s, R_n^t) = \mathbb{E}(R_n^s R_n^t) - \mathbb{E}(R_n^s)\mathbb{E}(R_n^t)$ denotes the covariance matrix.

Hence, we train the 1-bit student model end-to-end, the total loss for distilling the student model is defined as

$$L = L_{GT}(\mathbf{w}, \boldsymbol{\alpha}) + \lambda L_P(\mathbf{w}, \boldsymbol{\alpha}; \gamma) + \mu L_R(\mathbf{w}, \boldsymbol{\alpha}), \tag{6.89}$$

where L_{GT} is the detection loss derived from the ground truth label, and L_R is defined in Equ. 6.80.

6.5.4   Ablation Study

Selecting the hyper-parameter. As mentioned above, we select hyperparameters λ, γ, and μ in this part. First, we select μ, which controls the binarization process. As plotted in Fig. 6.17 (a), we first fine-tune the hyperparameter μ controlling the binarization process in four situations: raw BiRes18 and BiRes18 distilled by Hint [33], FGFI [235], and our IDa-Det, respectively. In general, performance increases first and then decreases when the value of μ increases. On raw BiRes18 and IDa-Det BiRes18, the 1-bit student performs best when μ is set as 1e-4. And μ valued 1e-3 is better for the Hint and the FGFI distilled 1-bit student. Therefore, we set μ as 1e-4 for an extended ablation study. Figure 6.17 (b) shows that the performances increase first and then decrease with increasing λ from left to right. In general, IDa-Det performs better with λ set as 0.4 and 0.6. With a variable value of γ, we find $\{\lambda, \gamma\} = \{0.4, 0.6\}$ boost the performance of IDa-Det most, achieving 76.9% mAP on VOC test2007. Based on the ablative study above, we set the hyperparameters λ, γ, and μ as 0.4, 0.6, and 1e-4 for the experiments in this chapter.

Effectiveness of components. We first compare our information discrepancy-aware (IDa) proposal selecting method with other methods to select proposals: Hint [33] (using the neck feature without region mask) and FGFI [235]. We show the effectiveness of IDa on two-stage Faster-RCNN in Table 6.5. In Faster-RCNN, the introduction of IDa improves mAP

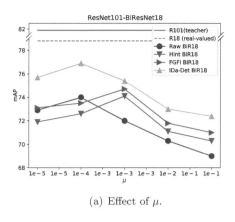

(a) Effect of μ.

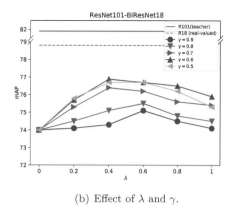

(b) Effect of λ and γ.

FIGURE 6.17

On VOC, we (a) select μ on the raw detector and different KD methods including Hint [33], FGFI [235], and IDa-Det; (b) select λ and γ on IDa-Det with μ set as 1e–4.

by 2.5%, 2.4%, and 1.8% compared to non-distillation, Hint and FGFI, under the same student-teacher framework. Then we evaluate the proposed entropy distillation loss against the conventional ℓ_2 loss, the loss of the inner product and the loss of cosine similarity. As depicted in Table 6.5, our entropy distillation loss improves the distillation performance by 0.4%, 0.3%, and 0.4% with the Hint, FGFI, and IDa method compared with ℓ_2 loss. Compared to the loss of the inner product and cosine similarity, the loss of entropy outperforms them by 2.1% and 0.5% in mAP in our framework, which further reflects the effectiveness of our method.

TABLE 6.5

The effects of different components in IDa-Det with Faster-RCNN model on PASCAL VOC dataset.

Model	Proposal selection	Distillation method	mAP
Res18	✗	✗	78.6
BiRes18	✗	✗	74.0
Res101-BiRes18	Hint	ℓ_2	74.1
Res101-BiRes18	Hint	Entropy loss	74.5
Res101-BiRes18	FGFI	ℓ_2	74.7
Res101-BiRes18	FGFI	Entropy loss	75.0
Res101-BiRes18	IDa	Inner-product	74.8
Res101-BiRes18	IDa	Cosine similarity	76.4
Res101-BiRes18	IDa	ℓ_2	76.5
Res101-BiRes18	**IDa**	**Entropy loss**	**76.9**

Note: Hint [33] and FGFI[235] are used to compare with our information discrepancy-aware proposal selection (IDa). IDa and Entropy loss denote main components of the proposed IDa-Det.

Bibliography

[1] Gustavo Aguilar, Yuan Ling, Yu Zhang, Benjamin Yao, Xing Fan, and Chenlei Guo. Knowledge distillation from internal representations. In *Proceedings of the AAAI Conference on Artificial Intelligence*, pages 7350–7357, 2020.

[2] Milad Alizadeh, Javier Fernández-Marqués, Nicholas D Lane, and Yarin Gal. An empirical study of binary neural networks' optimisation. In *Proceedings of the International Conference on Learning Representations*, 2018.

[3] Zeyuan Allen-Zhu and Yuanzhi Li. Towards understanding ensemble, knowledge distillation and self-distillation in deep learning. *arXiv preprint arXiv:2012.09816*, 2020.

[4] Martin Arjovsky, Soumith Chintala, and Léon Bottou. Wasserstein generative adversarial networks. In *Proceedings of the International Conference on Machine Learning*, pages 214–223, 2017.

[5] Haoli Bai, Lu Hou, Lifeng Shang, Xin Jiang, Irwin King, and Michael R Lyu. Towards efficient post-training quantization of pre-trained language models. *arXiv preprint arXiv:2109.15082*, 2021.

[6] Haoli Bai, Wei Zhang, Lu Hou, Lifeng Shang, Jing Jin, Xin Jiang, Qun Liu, Michael Lyu, and Irwin King. Binarybert: Pushing the limit of bert quantization. *arXiv preprint arXiv:2012.15701*, 2020.

[7] Slawomir Bak, Peter Carr, and Jean-Francois Lalonde. Domain adaptation through synthesis for unsupervised person re-identification. In *Proceedings of the European Conference on Computer Vision*, pages 189–205, 2018.

[8] Ron Banner, Itay Hubara, Elad Hoffer, and Daniel Soudry. Scalable methods for 8-bit training of neural networks. *Advances in neural information processing systems*, 31, 2018.

[9] Yoshua Bengio, Nicholas Léonard, and Aaron Courville. Estimating or propagating gradients through stochastic neurons for conditional computation. *arXiv preprint arXiv:1308.3432*, 2013.

[10] Joseph Bethge, Christian Bartz, Haojin Yang, Ying Chen, and Christoph Meinel. Meliusnet: Can binary neural networks achieve mobilenet-level accuracy? *arXiv preprint arXiv:2001.05936*, 2020.

[11] Joseph Bethge, Marvin Bornstein, Adrian Loy, Haojin Yang, and Christoph Meinel. Training competitive binary neural networks from scratch. *arXiv preprint arXiv:1812.01965*, 2018.

[12] Joseph Bethge, Haojin Yang, Marvin Bornstein, and Christoph Meinel. Binarydensenet: developing an architecture for binary neural networks. In *Proceedings of the IEEE/CVF International Conference on Computer Vision Workshops*, pages 0–0, 2019.

[13] Yash Bhalgat, Jinwon Lee, Markus Nagel, Tijmen Blankevoort, and Nojun Kwak. Lsq+: Improving low-bit quantization through learnable offsets and better initialization. In *Proceedings of the IEEE/CVF Conference on Computer Vision and Pattern Recognition Workshops*, pages 696–697, 2020.

[14] Christopher M Bishop. Bayesian neural networks. *Journal of the Brazilian Computer Society*, 4(1):61–68, 1997.

[15] David M Blei, John D Lafferty, et al. A correlated topic model of science. *The annals of applied statistics*, 1(1):17–35, 2007.

[16] Charles Blundell, Julien Cornebise, Koray Kavukcuoglu, and Daan Wierstra. Weight uncertainty in neural network. In *Proceedings of the International Conference on Machine Learning*, pages 1613–1622, 2015.

[17] Yelysei Bondarenko, Markus Nagel, and Tijmen Blankevoort. Understanding and overcoming the challenges of efficient transformer quantization. *arXiv preprint arXiv:2109.12948*, 2021.

[18] Ronald Newbold Bracewell and Ronald N Bracewell. *The Fourier transform and its applications*, volume 31999. McGraw-Hill New York, 1986.

[19] Leo Breiman. Bias, variance, and arcing classifiers. Technical report, Tech. Rep. 460, Statistics Department, University of California, Berkeley . . . , 1996.

[20] Andrew Brock, Theodore Lim, James M Ritchie, and Nick Weston. Smash: one-shot model architecture search through hypernetworks. *arXiv preprint arXiv:1708.05344*, 2017.

[21] Tom Brown, Benjamin Mann, Nick Ryder, Melanie Subbiah, Jared D Kaplan, Prafulla Dhariwal, Arvind Neelakantan, Pranav Shyam, Girish Sastry, Amanda Askell, et al. Language models are few-shot learners. *Advances in neural information processing systems*, 33:1877–1901, 2020.

[22] A. Buades, B. Coll, and J. Morel. A non-local algorithm for image denoising. In *CVPR*, 2005.

[23] Adrian Bulat, Jean Kossaifi, Georgios Tzimiropoulos, and Maja Pantic. Matrix and tensor decompositions for training binary neural networks. *arXiv preprint arXiv:1904.07852*, 2019.

[24] Adrian Bulat, Brais Martinez, and Georgios Tzimiropoulos. Bats: Binary architecture search. In *Proc. of ECCV*, pages 309–325, 2020.

[25] Adrian Bulat and Georgios Tzimiropoulos. Binarized convolutional landmark localizers for human pose estimation and face alignment with limited resources. In *Proceedings of the IEEE International Conference on Computer Vision*, pages 3706–3714, 2017.

[26] Adrian Bulat and Georgios Tzimiropoulos. Xnor-net++: Improved binary neural networks. *arXiv preprint arXiv:1909.13863*, 2019.

[27] Han Cai, Tianyao Chen, Weinan Zhang, Yong Yu, and Jun Wang. Efficient architecture search by network transformation. In *Proceedings of the AAAI Conference on Artificial Intelligence*, volume 32, 2018.

[28] Han Cai, Jiacheng Yang, Weinan Zhang, Song Han, and Yong Yu. Path-level network transformation for efficient architecture search. In *International Conference on Machine Learning*, pages 678–687. PMLR, 2018.

[29] Han Cai, Ligeng Zhu, and Song Han. Proxylessnas: Direct neural architecture search on target task and hardware. *arXiv preprint arXiv:1812.00332*, 2018.

[30] Zhaowei Cai and Nuno Vasconcelos. Cascade r-cnn: Delving into high quality object detection. In *Proceedings of the IEEE conference on computer vision and pattern recognition*, pages 6154–6162, 2018.

[31] Nicolas Carion, Francisco Massa, Gabriel Synnaeve, Nicolas Usunier, Alexander Kirillov, and Sergey Zagoruyko. End-to-end object detection with transformers. In *Computer Vision–ECCV 2020: 16th European Conference, Glasgow, UK, August 23–28, 2020, Proceedings, Part I 16*, pages 213–229. Springer, 2020.

[32] John G Carney, Pádraig Cunningham, and Umesh Bhagwan. Confidence and prediction intervals for neural network ensembles. In *IJCNN'99. International Joint Conference on Neural Networks. Proceedings (Cat. No. 99CH36339)*, volume 2, pages 1215–1218. IEEE, 1999.

[33] Guobin Chen, Wongun Choi, Xiang Yu, Tony Han, and Manmohan Chandraker. Learning efficient object detection models with knowledge distillation. In *Proc. of NeurIPS*, 2017.

[34] Hanlin Chen, Baochang Zhang, Song Xue, Xuan Gong, Hong Liu, Rongrong Ji, and David Doermann. Anti-bandit neural architecture search for model defense. In *Computer Vision–ECCV 2020: 16th European Conference, Glasgow, UK, August 23–28, 2020, Proceedings, Part XIII 16*, pages 70–85, 2020.

[35] Hanlin Chen, Li'an Zhuo, Baochang Zhang, Xiawu Zheng, Jianzhuang Liu, Rongrong Ji, David Doermann, and Guodong Guo. Binarized neural architecture search for efficient object recognition. *International Journal of Computer Vision*, 129:501–516, 2021.

[36] Hanlin Chen, Li'an Zhuo, Baochang Zhang, Xiawu Zheng, Jianzhuang Liu, Rongrong Ji, David Doermann, and Guodong Guo. Binarized neural architecture search for efficient object recognition. *International Journal of Computer Vision*, 129(2):501–516, 2021.

[37] Mingzhe Chen, Ursula Challita, Walid Saad, Changchuan Yin, and Mérouane Debbah. Artificial neural networks-based machine learning for wireless networks: A tutorial. *IEEE Communications Surveys & Tutorials*, 21(4):3039–3071, 2019.

[38] Shangyu Chen, Wenya Wang, and Sinno Jialin Pan. Metaquant: Learning to quantize by learning to penetrate non-differentiable quantization. *Proc. of NeurIPS*, 32:3916–3926, 2019.

[39] Xin Chen, Lingxi Xie, Jun Wu, and Qi Tian. Progressive differentiable architecture search: Bridging the depth gap between search and evaluation. In *Proceedings of the IEEE/CVF international conference on computer vision*, pages 1294–1303, 2019.

[40] Yankai Chen, Yifei Zhang, Huifeng Guo, Ruiming Tang, and Irwin King. An effective post-training embedding binarization approach for fast online top-k passage matching. In *Proceedings of the 2nd Conference of the Asia-Pacific Chapter of the Association*

for Computational Linguistics and the 12th International Joint Conference on Natural Language Processing, pages 102–108, 2022.

[41] De Cheng, Yihong Gong, Sanping Zhou, Jinjun Wang, and Nanning Zheng. Person re-identification by multi-channel parts-based cnn with improved triplet loss function. In *Proceedings of the IEEE Conference on Computer Vision and Pattern Recognition*, pages 1335–1344, 2016.

[42] Brian Chmiel, Liad Ben-Uri, Moran Shkolnik, Elad Hoffer, Ron Banner, and Daniel Soudry. Neural gradients are near-lognormal: improved quantized and sparse training. *arXiv preprint arXiv:2006.08173*, 2020.

[43] Jungwook Choi, Zhuo Wang, Swagath Venkataramani, Pierce I-Jen Chuang, Vijayalakshmi Srinivasan, and Kailash Gopalakrishnan. Pact: Parameterized clipping activation for quantized neural networks. *arXiv preprint arXiv:1805.06085*, 2018.

[44] Yunjey Choi, Minje Choi, Munyoung Kim, Jung-Woo Ha, Sunghun Kim, and Jaegul Choo. Stargan: Unified generative adversarial networks for multi-domain image-to-image translation. In *Proceedings of the IEEE Conference on Computer Vision and Pattern Recognition*, pages 8789–8797, 2018.

[45] Kevin Clark, Urvashi Khandelwal, Omer Levy, and Christopher D Manning. What does bert look at? An analysis of bert's attention. *arXiv preprint arXiv:1906.04341*, 2019.

[46] Benoît Colson, Patrice Marcotte, and Gilles Savard. An overview of bilevel optimization. *Annals of operations research*, 153(1):235–256, 2007.

[47] Matthieu Courbariaux, Yoshua Bengio, and Jean-Pierre David. Training deep neural networks with low precision multiplications. *arXiv preprint arXiv:1412.7024*, 2014.

[48] Matthieu Courbariaux, Yoshua Bengio, and Jean-Pierre David. Binaryconnect: Training deep neural networks with binary weights during propagations. *Advances in neural information processing systems*, 28, 2015.

[49] Richard Crandall and Carl Pomerance. *Prime numbers*. Springer, 2001.

[50] M. Dehghani, S. Gouws, O. Vinyals, J. Uszkoreit, and L. Kaiser. Universal transformers. In *International Conference on Learning Representations*, 2019.

[51] Mostafa Dehghani, Stephan Gouws, Oriol Vinyals, Jakob Uszkoreit, and Łukasz Kaiser. Universal transformers. *arXiv preprint arXiv:1807.03819*, 2018.

[52] Alessio Del Bue, Joao Xavier, Lourdes Agapito, and Marco Paladini. Bilinear modeling via augmented lagrange multipliers (balm). *IEEE transactions on pattern analysis and machine intelligence*, 34(8):1496–1508, 2011.

[53] Jia Deng, Wei Dong, Richard Socher, Li-Jia Li, Kai Li, and Li Fei-Fei. Imagenet: A large-scale hierarchical image database. In *Proceedings of the IEEE/CVF Conference on Computer Vision and Pattern Recognition*, pages 248–255, 2009.

[54] Jacob Devlin, Ming-Wei Chang, Kenton Lee, and Kristina Toutanova. Bert: Pre-training of deep bidirectional transformers for language understanding. *arXiv preprint arXiv:1810.04805*, 2018.

[55] Jacob Devlin, Ming-Wei Chang, Kenton Lee, and Kristina Toutanova. Bert: Pre-training of deep bidirectional transformers for language understanding. In *NAACL-HLT*, 2019.

[56] Ruizhou Ding, Ting-Wu Chin, Zeye Liu, and Diana Marculescu. Regularizing activation distribution for training binarized deep networks. In *Proceedings of the IEEE/CVF Conference on Computer Vision and Pattern Recognition*, pages 11408–11417, 2019.

[57] Ruizhou Ding, Zeye Liu, Rongye Shi, Diana Marculescu, and RD Blanton. Lightnn: Filling the gap between conventional deep neural networks and binarized networks. In *Proceedings of the on Great Lakes Symposium on VLSI 2017*, pages 35–40, 2017.

[58] Paul Adrien Maurice Dirac. The physical interpretation of the quantum dynamics. *Proceedings of the Royal Society of London. Series A, Containing Papers of a Mathematical and Physical Character*, 113(765):621–641, 1927.

[59] Zhen Dong, Zhewei Yao, Daiyaan Arfeen, Amir Gholami, Michael W Mahoney, and Kurt Keutzer. Hawq-v2: Hessian aware trace-weighted quantization of neural networks. In *Neural Information Processing Systems(NeurIPS)*, pages 18518–18529, 2020.

[60] Alexey Dosovitskiy, Lucas Beyer, Alexander Kolesnikov, Dirk Weissenborn, Xiaohua Zhai, Thomas Unterthiner, Mostafa Dehghani, Matthias Minderer, Georg Heigold, Sylvain Gelly, et al. An image is worth 16x16 words: Transformers for image recognition at scale. *arXiv preprint arXiv:2010.11929*, 2020.

[61] Steven K Esser, Jeffrey L McKinstry, Deepika Bablani, Rathinakumar Appuswamy, and Dharmendra S Modha. Learned step size quantization. *arXiv preprint arXiv:1902.08153*, 2019.

[62] Mark Everingham, Luc Van Gool, Christopher KI Williams, John Winn, and Andrew Zisserman. The pascal visual object classes (voc) challenge. *International journal of computer vision*, 88(2):303–338, 2010.

[63] Fartash Faghri, Iman Tabrizian, Ilia Markov, Dan Alistarh, Daniel M Roy, and Ali Ramezani-Kebrya. Adaptive gradient quantization for data-parallel sgd. *Advances in neural information processing systems*, 33:3174–3185, 2020.

[64] Angela Fan, Edouard Grave, and Armand Joulin. Reducing transformer depth on demand with structured dropout. *arXiv preprint arXiv:1909.11556*, 2019.

[65] Angela Fan, Pierre Stock, Benjamin Graham, Edouard Grave, Rémi Gribonval, Herve Jegou, and Armand Joulin. Training with quantization noise for extreme model compression. *arXiv preprint arXiv:2004.07320*, 2020.

[66] Pedro Felzenszwalb and Ramin Zabih. Discrete optimization algorithms in computer vision. *Tutorial at IEEE International Conference on Computer Vision*, 2007.

[67] Yoav Freund, Robert E Schapire, et al. Experiments with a new boosting algorithm. In *icml*, volume 96, pages 148–156. Citeseer, 1996.

[68] D. Gabor. Electrical engineers part iii: Radio and communication engineering, j. *Journal of the Institution of Electrical Engineers - Part III: Radio and Communication Engineering 1945-1948*, 1946.

[69] D. Gabor. Theory of communication. part 1: The analysis of information. *Journal of the Institution of Electrical Engineers-Part III: Radio and Communication Engineering*, 1946.

[70] Peng Gao, Minghang Zheng, Xiaogang Wang, Jifeng Dai, and Hongsheng Li. Fast convergence of detr with spatially modulated co-attention. In *Proceedings of the IEEE/CVF International Conference on Computer Vision*, pages 3621–3630, 2021.

[71] Yixiao Ge, Zhuowan Li, Haiyu Zhao, Guojun Yin, Shuai Yi, Xiaogang Wang, et al. Fd-gan: Pose-guided feature distilling gan for robust person re-identification. In *Proceedings of the European Conference on Computer Vision*, pages 1222–1233, 2018.

[72] Ross Girshick. Fast r-cnn. In *Proceedings of the IEEE international conference on computer vision*, pages 1440–1448, 2015.

[73] Ross Girshick, Jeff Donahue, Trevor Darrell, and Jitendra Malik. Rich feature hierarchies for accurate object detection and semantic segmentation. In *Proceedings of the IEEE conference on computer vision and pattern recognition*, pages 580–587, 2014.

[74] Ruihao Gong, Xianglong Liu, Shenghu Jiang, Tianxiang Li, Peng Hu, Jiazhen Lin, Fengwei Yu, and Junjie Yan. Differentiable soft quantization: Bridging full-precision and low-bit neural networks. In *Proceedings of the IEEE/CVF International Conference on Computer Vision*, pages 4852–4861, 2019.

[75] I. J. Goodfellow, J. Shlens, and C. Szegedy. Explaining and harnessing adversarial examples. *arXiv*, 2014.

[76] Ian Goodfellow, Jean Pouget-Abadie, Mehdi Mirza, Bing Xu, David Warde-Farley, Sherjil Ozair, Aaron Courville, and Yoshua Bengio. Generative adversarial nets. In *Proceedings of the European Conference on Computer Vision*, pages 2672–2680, 2014.

[77] Jiaxin Gu, Ce Li, Baochang Zhang, Jungong Han, Xianbin Cao, Jianzhuang Liu, and David Doermann. Projection convolutional neural networks for 1-bit cnns via discrete back propagation. In *Proceedings of the AAAI Conference on Artificial Intelligence*, 2019.

[78] Jiaxin Gu, Junhe Zhao, Xiaolong Jiang, Baochang Zhang, Jianzhuang Liu, Guodong Guo, and Rongrong Ji. Bayesian optimized 1-bit cnns. In *Proceedings of the IEEE/CVF International Conference on Computer Vision*, pages 4909–4917, 2019.

[79] Jianyuan Guo, Kai Han, Yunhe Wang, Han Wu, Xinghao Chen, Chunjing Xu, and Chang Xu. Distilling object detectors via decoupled features. In *Proc. of CVPR*, 2021.

[80] Suyog Gupta, Ankur Agrawal, Kailash Gopalakrishnan, and Pritish Narayanan. Deep learning with limited numerical precision. In *International conference on machine learning*, pages 1737–1746. PMLR, 2015.

[81] David Ha, Andrew Dai, and Quoc V Le. Hypernetworks. *arXiv preprint arXiv:1609.09106*, 2016.

[82] Trevor Hastie, Robert Tibshirani, Jerome Friedman, and James Franklin. The elements of statistical learning: data mining, inference and prediction. *The Mathematical Intelligencer*, 27(2):83–85, 2005.

[83] Kaiming He, Xinlei Chen, Saining Xie, Yanghao Li, Piotr Dollár, and Ross Girshick. Masked autoencoders are scalable vision learners. *arXiv preprint arXiv:2111.06377*, 2021.

[84] Kaiming He, Xiangyu Zhang, Shaoqing Ren, and Jian Sun. Deep residual learning for image recognition. In *Proceedings of the IEEE/CVF Conference on Computer Vision and Pattern Recognition*, pages 770–778, 2016.

[85] Koen Helwegen, James Widdicombe, Lukas Geiger, Zechun Liu, Kwang-Ting Cheng, and Roeland Nusselder. Latent weights do not exist: Rethinking binarized neural network optimization. *Advances in neural information processing systems*, 32, 2019.

[86] Pedro Hermosilla, Tobias Ritschel, and Timo Ropinski. Total denoising: Unsupervised learning of 3d point cloud cleaning. In *Proceedings of the IEEE/CVF international conference on computer vision*, pages 52–60, 2019.

[87] Geoffrey Hinton, Oriol Vinyals, and Jeff Dean. Distilling the knowledge in a neural network. *Computer Science*, 14(7):38–39, 2015.

[88] Lu Hou, Zhiqi Huang, Lifeng Shang, Xin Jiang, Xiao Chen, and Qun Liu. Dynabert: Dynamic bert with adaptive width and depth. *Advances in Neural Information Processing Systems*, 33:9782–9793, 2020.

[89] Lu Hou, Zhiqi Huang, Lifeng Shang, Xin Jiang, Xiao Chen, and Qun Liu. Dynabert: Dynamic bert with adaptive width and depth. In *NeurIPs*, 2020.

[90] Andrew G Howard, Menglong Zhu, Bo Chen, Dmitry Kalenichenko, Weijun Wang, Tobias Weyand, Marco Andreetto, and Hartwig Adam. Mobilenets: Efficient convolutional neural networks for mobile vision applications. *arXiv preprint arXiv:1704.04861*, 2017.

[91] Qinghao Hu, Peisong Wang, and Jian Cheng. From hashing to cnns: Training binary weight networks via hashing. In *Proceedings of the AAAI Conference on Artificial Intelligence*, volume 32, 2018.

[92] Gao Huang, Zhuang Liu, Laurens Van Der Maaten, and Kilian Q Weinberger. Densely connected convolutional networks. In *Proceedings of the IEEE/CVF Conference on Computer Vision and Pattern Recognition*, pages 4700–4708, 2017.

[93] Kun Huang, Bingbing Ni, and Xiaokang Yang. Efficient quantization for neural networks with binary weights and low bitwidth activations. In *Proceedings of the AAAI Conference on Artificial Intelligence*, volume 33, pages 3854–3861, 2019.

[94] Lianghua Huang, Xin Zhao, and Kaiqi Huang. Got-10k: A large high-diversity benchmark for generic object tracking in the wild. *IEEE transactions on pattern analysis and machine intelligence*, 43(5):1562–1577, 2019.

[95] Yan Huang, Jingsong Xu, Qiang Wu, Zhedong Zheng, Zhaoxiang Zhang, and Jian Zhang. Multi-pseudo regularized label for generated data in person re-identification. *IEEE Transactions on Image Processing*, 28(3):1391–1403, 2018.

[96] Yanping Huang, Youlong Cheng, Ankur Bapna, Orhan Firat, Dehao Chen, Mia Chen, HyoukJoong Lee, Jiquan Ngiam, Quoc V Le, Yonghui Wu, et al. Gpipe: Efficient training of giant neural networks using pipeline parallelism. *Advances in neural information processing systems*, 32, 2019.

[97] Zehao Huang and Naiyan Wang. Data-driven sparse structure selection for deep neural networks. In *Proc. of ECCV*, pages 304–320, 2018.

[98] Zhiqi Huang, Lu Hou, Lifeng Shang, Xin Jiang, Xiao Chen, and Qun Liu. Ghostbert: Generate more features with cheap operations for bert. In *Proceedings of the 59th Annual Meeting of the Association for Computational Linguistics and the 11th International Joint Conference on Natural Language Processing (Volume 1: Long Papers)*, pages 6512–6523, 2021.

[99] Itay Hubara, Matthieu Courbariaux, Daniel Soudry, Ran El-Yaniv, and Yoshua Bengio. Binarized neural networks. *Advances in neural information processing systems*, 29, 2016.

[100] Itay Hubara, Matthieu Courbariaux, Daniel Soudry, Ran El-Yaniv, and Yoshua Bengio. Quantized neural networks: Training neural networks with low precision weights and activations. *The Journal of Machine Learning Research*, 18(1):6869–6898, 2017.

[101] Itay Hubara, Yury Nahshan, Yair Hanani, Ron Banner, and Daniel Soudry. Improving post training neural quantization: Layer-wise calibration and integer programming. *arXiv preprint arXiv:2006.10518*, 2020.

[102] Sergey Ioffe and Christian Szegedy. Batch normalization: Accelerating deep network training by reducing internal covariate shift. In *Proceedings of International conference on machine learning*, pages 448–456, 2015.

[103] Phillip Isola, Jun-Yan Zhu, Tinghui Zhou, and Alexei A Efros. Image-to-image translation with conditional adversarial networks. In *Proceedings of the IEEE Conference on Computer Vision and Pattern Recognition*, pages 1125–1134, 2017.

[104] Benoit Jacob, Skirmantas Kligys, Bo Chen, Menglong Zhu, Matthew Tang, Andrew Howard, Hartwig Adam, and Dmitry Kalenichenko. Quantization and training of neural networks for efficient integer-arithmetic-only inference. In *Proceedings of the IEEE conference on computer vision and pattern recognition*, pages 2704–2713, 2018.

[105] Tianchu Ji, Shraddhan Jain, Michael Ferdman, Peter Milder, H Andrew Schwartz, and Niranjan Balasubramanian. On the distribution, sparsity, and inference-time quantization of attention values in transformers. *arXiv preprint arXiv:2106.01335*, 2021.

[106] X. Jiao, Y. Yin, L. Shang, X. Jiang, X. Chen, L. Li, F. Wang, and Q. Liu. Tinybert: Distilling bert for natural language understanding. In *Findings of Empirical Methods in Natural Language Processing*, 2020.

[107] Xiaoqi Jiao, Yichun Yin, Lifeng Shang, Xin Jiang, Xiao Chen, Linlin Li, Fang Wang, and Qun Liu. Tinybert: Distilling bert for natural language understanding. *arXiv preprint arXiv:1909.10351*, 2019.

[108] Amin Jourabloo and Xiaoming Liu. Pose-invariant 3d face alignment. In *Proceedings of the IEEE international conference on computer vision*, pages 3694–3702, 2015.

[109] Felix Juefei-Xu, Vishnu Naresh Boddeti, and Marios Savvides. Local binary convolutional neural networks. In *Proceedings of the IEEE conference on computer vision and pattern recognition*, pages 19–28, 2017.

[110] Sangil Jung, Changyong Son, Seohyung Lee, Jinwoo Son, Youngjun Kwak, Jae-Joon Han, and Changkyu Choi. Joint training of low-precision neural network with quantization interval parameters. *arXiv preprint arXiv:1808.05779*, 2, 2018.

[111] Mahdi M Kalayeh, Emrah Basaran, Muhittin Gökmen, Mustafa E Kamasak, and Mubarak Shah. Human semantic parsing for person re-identification. In *Proceedings of the IEEE Conference on Computer Vision and Pattern Recognition*, pages 1062–1071, 2018.

[112] Mohammad Emtiyaz Khan and Haavard Rue. Learningalgorithms from bayesian principles. *arXiv preprint arXiv:2002.10778*, 2(4), 2020.

[113] Omar Khattab and Matei Zaharia. Colbert: Efficient and effective passage search via contextualized late interaction over bert. In *Proceedings of the 43rd International ACM SIGIR conference on research and development in Information Retrieval*, pages 39–48, 2020.

[114] Dahyun Kim, Kunal Pratap Singh, and Jonghyun Choi. Learning architectures for binary networks. In *Proc. of ECCV*, pages 575–591, 2020.

[115] Hyungjun Kim, Kyungsu Kim, Jinseok Kim, and Jae-Joon Kim. Binaryduo: Reducing gradient mismatch in binary activation network by coupling binary activations. In *International Conference on Learning Representations*.

[116] Jangho Kim, Yash Bhalgat, Jinwon Lee, Chirag Patel, and Nojun Kwak. Qkd: Quantization-aware knowledge distillation. *arXiv preprint arXiv:1911.12491*, 2019.

[117] Minje Kim and Paris Smaragdis. Bitwise neural networks. *arXiv preprint arXiv:1601.06071*, 2016.

[118] Sehoon Kim, Amir Gholami, Zhewei Yao, Michael W Mahoney, and Kurt Keutzer. I-bert: Integer-only bert quantization. In *International conference on machine learning*, pages 5506–5518. PMLR, 2021.

[119] Seungryong Kim, Dongbo Min, Stephen Lin, and Kwanghoon Sohn. Dctm: Discrete-continuous transformation matching for semantic flow. In *Proceedings of the IEEE International Conference on Computer Vision*, volume 6, 2017.

[120] Durk P Kingma, Tim Salimans, and Max Welling. Variational dropout and the local reparameterization trick. *Proceedings of the Advances in neural information processing systems*, pages 2575–2583, 2015.

[121] Martin Koestinger, Paul Wohlhart, Peter M Roth, and Horst Bischof. Annotated facial landmarks in the wild: A large-scale, real-world database for facial landmark localization. In *2011 IEEE international conference on computer vision workshops (ICCV workshops)*, pages 2144–2151. IEEE, 2011.

[122] Alex Krizhevsky, Geoffrey Hinton, et al. Learning multiple layers of features from tiny images. 2009.

[123] Alex Krizhevsky, Ilya Sutskever, and Geoffrey E Hinton. Imagenet classification with deep convolutional neural networks. In *Proceedings of the Advances in Neural Information Processing Systems*, pages 1097–1105, 2012.

[124] Jouko Lampinen and Aki Vehtari. Bayesian approach for neural networks—review and case studies. *Neural networks*, 14(3):257–274, 2001.

[125] Zhenzhong Lan, Mingda Chen, Sebastian Goodman, Kevin Gimpel, Piyush Sharma, and Radu Soricut. Albert: A lite bert for self-supervised learning of language representations. *arXiv preprint arXiv:1909.11942*, 2019.

[126] Zhenzhong Lan, Mingda Chen, Sebastian Goodman, Kevin Gimpel, Piyush Sharma, and Radu Soricut. Albert: A lite bert for self-supervised learning of language representations. In *ICLR*, 2020.

[127] Emanuel Laude, Jan-Hendrik Lange, Jonas Schüpfer, Csaba Domokos, Leal-Taix? Laura, Frank R. Schmidt, Bjoern Andres, and Daniel Cremers. Discrete-continuous admm for transductive inference in higher-order mrfs. In *Proceedings of the IEEE/CVF Conference on Computer Vision and Pattern Recognition*, pages 4539–4548, 2018.

[128] Cong Leng, Zesheng Dou, Hao Li, Shenghuo Zhu, and Rong Jin. Extremely low bit neural network: Squeeze the last bit out with admm. In *Proceedings of the AAAI Conference on Artificial Intelligence*, pages 3466–3473, 2018.

[129] Feng Li, Hao Zhang, Shilong Liu, Jian Guo, Lionel M Ni, and Lei Zhang. Dn-detr: Accelerate detr training by introducing query denoising. In *Proceedings of the IEEE/CVF conference on computer vision and pattern recognition*, pages 13619–13627, 2022.

[130] Fengfu Li, Bo Zhang, and Bin Liu. Ternary weight networks. *arXiv preprint arXiv:1605.04711*, 2016.

[131] Mu Li, David G Andersen, Alexander J Smola, and Kai Yu. Communication efficient distributed machine learning with the parameter server. *Advances in Neural Information Processing Systems*, 27, 2014.

[132] Wei Li, Xiatian Zhu, and Shaogang Gong. Person re-identification by deep joint learning of multi-loss classification. In *Proceedings of the International Joint Conference on Artificial Intelligence*, pages 2194–2200, 2017.

[133] Yanghao Li, Naiyan Wang, Jiaying Liu, and Xiaodi Hou. Factorized bilinear models for image recognition. In *Proc. of ICCV*, pages 2079–2087, 2017.

[134] Yangyan Li, Rui Bu, Mingchao Sun, Wei Wu, Xinhan Di, and Baoquan Chen. Pointcnn: Convolution on x-transformed points. In *Proceedings of Advances in Neural Information Processing Systems*, pages 820–830, 2018.

[135] Yanjing Li, Sheng Xu, Xianbin Cao, Li'an Zhuo, Baochang Zhang, Tian Wang, and Guodong Guo. Dcp–nas: Discrepant child–parent neural architecture search for 1-bit cnns. *International Journal of Computer Vision*, pages 1–23, 2023.

[136] Yanjing Li, Sheng Xu, Baochang Zhang, Xianbin Cao, Peng Gao, and Guodong Guo. Q-vit: Accurate and fully quantized low-bit vision transformer. In *Advances in neural information processing systems*, 2022.

[137] Yuhang Li, Ruihao Gong, Xu Tan, Yang Yang, Peng Hu, Qi Zhang, Fengwei Yu, Wei Wang, and Shi Gu. Brecq: Pushing the limit of post-training quantization by block reconstruction. *arXiv preprint arXiv:2102.05426*, 2021.

[138] Zefan Li, Bingbing Ni, Wenjun Zhang, Xiaokang Yang, and Wen Gao. Performance guaranteed network acceleration via high-order residual quantization. In *Proceedings of the IEEE International Conference on Computer Vision*, pages 2584–2592, 2017.

[139] Faming Liang, Qizhai Li, and Lei Zhou. Bayesian neural networks for selection of drug sensitive genes. *Journal of the American Statistical Association*, 113(523):955–972, 2018.

[140] Mingbao Lin, Rongrong Ji, Zihan Xu, Baochang Zhang, Yan Wang, Yongjian Wu, Feiyue Huang, and Chia-Wen Lin. Rotated binary neural network. In *Proc. of NeurIPS*, pages 1–9, 2020.

[141] Shaohui Lin, Rongrong Ji, Yuchao Li, Yongjian Wu, Feiyue Huang, and Baochang Zhang. Accelerating convolutional networks via global & dynamic filter pruning. In *Proceedings of the International Joint Conference on Artificial Intelligence*, pages 2425–2432, 2018.

[142] Shaohui Lin, Rongrong Ji, Chenqian Yan, Baochang Zhang, Liujuan Cao, Qixiang Ye, Feiyue Huang, and David Doermann. Towards optimal structured cnn pruning via generative adversarial learning. In *Proceedings of the IEEE/CVF Conference on Computer Vision and Pattern Recognition*, pages 2790–2799, 2019.

[143] Tsung-Yi Lin, Piotr Dollár, Ross Girshick, Kaiming He, Bharath Hariharan, and Serge Belongie. Feature pyramid networks for object detection. In *Proceedings of IEEE Conference on Computer Vision and Pattern Recognition*, 2017.

[144] Tsung-Yi Lin, Priya Goyal, Ross Girshick, Kaiming He, and Piotr Dollár. Focal loss for dense object detection. In *Proceedings of the IEEE international conference on computer vision*, pages 2980–2988, 2017.

[145] Tsung-Yi Lin, Michael Maire, Serge Belongie, James Hays, Pietro Perona, Deva Ramanan, Piotr Dollár, and C Lawrence Zitnick. Microsoft coco: Common objects in context. In *Proceedings of the European Conference on Computer Vision*, pages 740–755, 2014.

[146] Tsung-Yu Lin, Aruni RoyChowdhury, and Subhransu Maji. Bilinear cnn models for fine-grained visual recognition. In *Proc. of ICCV*, pages 1449–1457, 2015.

[147] Xiaofan Lin, Cong Zhao, and Wei Pan. Towards accurate binary convolutional neural network. In *Proceedings of the Advances in Neural Information Processing Systems*, pages 345–353, 2017.

[148] Chunlei Liu, Wenrui Ding, Yuan Hu, Baochang Zhang, Jianzhuang Liu, Guodong Guo, and David Doermann. Rectified binary convolutional networks with generative adversarial learning. *International Journal of Computer Vision*, 129:998–1012, 2021.

[149] Chunlei Liu, Wenrui Ding, Xin Xia, Baochang Zhang, Jiaxin Gu, Jianzhuang Liu, Rongrong Ji, and David Doermann. Circulant binary convolutional networks: Enhancing the performance of 1-bit dcnns with circulant back propagation. In *Proceedings of the IEEE/CVF Conference on Computer Vision and Pattern Recognition*, pages 2691–2699, 2019.

[150] Chunlei Liu, Wenrui Ding, Xin Xia, Baochang Zhang, Jiaxin Gu, Jianzhuang Liu, Rongrong Ji, and David Doermann. Circulant binary convolutional networks: Enhancing the performance of 1-bit dcnns with circulant back propagation. In *Proceedings of the IEEE/CVF Conference on Computer Vision and Pattern Recognition*, pages 2691–2699, 2019.

[151] Hanxiao Liu, Karen Simonyan, and Yiming Yang. Darts: Differentiable architecture search. In *Proceedings of the International Conference on Learning Representations*, pages 1–13, 2019.

[152] Risheng Liu, Jiaxin Gao, Jin Zhang, Deyu Meng, and Zhouchen Lin. Investigating bi-level optimization for learning and vision from a unified perspective: A survey and beyond. *IEEE Transactions on Pattern Analysis and Machine Intelligence*, 2021.

[153] Wei Liu, Dragomir Anguelov, Dumitru Erhan, Christian Szegedy, Scott Reed, Cheng-Yang Fu, and Alexander C Berg. Ssd: Single shot multibox detector. In *Proceedings of the European Conference on Computer Vision*, pages 21–37, 2016.

[154] Ze Liu, Yutong Lin, Yue Cao, Han Hu, Yixuan Wei, Zheng Zhang, Stephen Lin, and Baining Guo. Swin transformer: Hierarchical vision transformer using shifted windows. In *Proc. of ICCV*, pages 10012–10022, 2021.

[155] Zechun Liu, Kwang-Ting Cheng, Dong Huang, Eric P Xing, and Zhiqiang Shen. Nonuniform-to-uniform quantization: Towards accurate quantization via generalized straight-through estimation. In *Proceedings of the IEEE/CVF Conference on Computer Vision and Pattern Recognition*, pages 4942–4952, 2022.

[156] Zechun Liu, Barlas Oguz, Aasish Pappu, Lin Xiao, Scott Yih, Meng Li, Raghuraman Krishnamoorthi, and Yashar Mehdad. Bit: Robustly binarized multi-distilled transformer. In *Advances In Neural Information Processing Systems*, 2022.

[157] Zechun Liu, Zhiqiang Shen, Shichao Li, Koen Helwegen, Dong Huang, and Kwang-Ting Cheng. How do adam and training strategies help bnns optimization. In *Proc. of ICML*, pages 6936–6946, 2021.

[158] Zechun Liu, Zhiqiang Shen, Marios Savvides, and Kwang-Ting Cheng. Reactnet: Towards precise binary neural network with generalized activation functions. In *Proceedings of the European Conference on Computer Vision*, pages 143–159, 2020.

[159] Zechun Liu, Baoyuan Wu, Wenhan Luo, Xin Yang, Wei Liu, and Kwang-Ting Cheng. Bi-real net: Enhancing the performance of 1-bit cnns with improved representational capability and advanced training algorithm. In *Proceedings of the European Conference on Computer Vision*, pages 747–763, 2018.

[160] Zhen-Tao Liu, Si-Han Li, Min Wu, Wei-Hua Cao, Man Hao, and Lin-Bo Xian. Eye localization based on weight binarization cascade convolution neural network. *Neurocomputing*, 378:45–53, 2020.

[161] Zhenhua Liu, Yunhe Wang, Kai Han, Wei Zhang, Siwei Ma, and Wen Gao. Post-training quantization for vision transformer. *Advances in Neural Information Processing Systems*, 34:28092–28103, 2021.

[162] Zhuang Liu, Jianguo Li, Zhiqiang Shen, Gao Huang, Shoumeng Yan, and Changshui Zhang. Learning efficient convolutional networks through network slimming. In *Proceedings of the IEEE International Conference on Computer Vision*, pages 2736–2744, 2017.

[163] Jonathan Long, Evan Shelhamer, and Trevor Darrell. Fully convolutional networks for semantic segmentation. In *Proceedings of the IEEE conference on computer vision and pattern recognition*, pages 3431–3440, 2015.

[164] Ilya Loshchilov and Frank Hutter. Decoupled weight decay regularization. In *Proceedings of the International Conference on Learning Representations*, pages 1–18, 2017.

[165] Ziyang Luo, Artur Kulmizev, and Xiaoxi Mao. Positional artefacts propagate through masked language model embeddings. *arXiv preprint arXiv:2011.04393*, 2020.

[166] X. Ma, P. Zhang, S. Zhang, N. Duan, Y. Hou, D. Song, and M. Zhou. A tensorized transformer for language modeling. In *Advances in Neural Information Processing Systems*, 2019.

[167] A. Madry, A. Makelov, L. Schmidt, D. Tsipras, and A. Vladu. Towards deep learning models resistant to adversarial attacks. In *ICLR*, 2017.

[168] Brais Martinez, Jing Yang, Adrian Bulat, and Georgios Tzimiropoulos. Training binary neural networks with real-to-binary convolutions. *arXiv preprint arXiv:2003.11535*, 2020.

[169] Depu Meng, Xiaokang Chen, Zejia Fan, Gang Zeng, Houqiang Li, Yuhui Yuan, Lei Sun, and Jingdong Wang. Conditional detr for fast training convergence. In *Proceedings of the IEEE/CVF International Conference on Computer Vision*, pages 3651–3660, 2021.

[170] Xiangming Meng, Roman Bachmann, and Mohammad Emtiyaz Khan. Training binary neural networks using the bayesian learning rule. In *International conference on machine learning*, pages 6852–6861. PMLR, 2020.

[171] D Messerschmitt. Quantizing for maximum output entropy (corresp.). *IEEE Transactions on Information Theory*, 17(5):612–612, 1971.

[172] Paul Michel, Omer Levy, and Graham Neubig. Are sixteen heads really better than one? *Advances in neural information processing systems*, 32, 2019.

[173] Luca Mocerino and Andrea Calimera. Tentaclenet: A pseudo-ensemble template for accurate binary convolutional neural networks. In *2020 2nd IEEE International Conference on Artificial Intelligence Circuits and Systems (AICAS)*, pages 261–265. IEEE, 2020.

[174] Jonas Mockus, Vytautas Tiesis, and Antanas Zilinskas. The application of bayesian methods for seeking the extremum. *Towards global optimization*, 2(117-129):2, 1978.

[175] Todd K Moon. The expectation-maximization algorithm. *IEEE Signal processing magazine*, 13(6):47–60, 1996.

[176] Jean-Jacques Moreau. Proximité et dualité dans un espace hilbertien. *Bulletin de la Société mathématique de France*, 93:273–299, 1965.

[177] Matthias Mueller, Neil Smith, and Bernard Ghanem. A benchmark and simulator for uav tracking. In *Computer Vision–ECCV 2016: 14th European Conference, Amsterdam, The Netherlands, October 11–14, 2016, Proceedings, Part I 14*, pages 445–461. Springer, 2016.

[178] Prasanna Kumar Muthukumar and Alan W Black. A deep learning approach to data-driven parameterizations for statistical parametric speech synthesis. *arXiv preprint arXiv:1409.8558*, 2014.

[179] Markus Nagel, Rana Ali Amjad, Mart Van Baalen, Christos Louizos, and Tijmen Blankevoort. Up or down? adaptive rounding for post-training quantization. In *International Conference on Machine Learning*, pages 7197–7206. PMLR, 2020.

[180] Markus Nagel, Mart van Baalen, Tijmen Blankevoort, and Max Welling. Data-free quantization through weight equalization and bias correction. In *Proceedings of the IEEE/CVF International Conference on Computer Vision*, pages 1325–1334, 2019.

[181] Yuval Netzer, Tao Wang, Adam Coates, Alessandro Bissacco, Bo Wu, and Andrew Y Ng. Reading digits in natural images with unsupervised feature learning. 2011.

[182] Tri Nguyen, Mir Rosenberg, Xia Song, Jianfeng Gao, Saurabh Tiwary, Rangan Majumder, and Li Deng. Ms marco: A human generated machine reading comprehension dataset. In *CoCo@ NIPs*, 2016.

[183] Aaron van den Oord, Sander Dieleman, Heiga Zen, Karen Simonyan, Oriol Vinyals, Alex Graves, Nal Kalchbrenner, Andrew Senior, and Koray Kavukcuoglu. Wavenet: A generative model for raw audio. *arXiv preprint arXiv:1609.03499*, 2016.

[184] Nikunj C Oza and Stuart J Russell. Online bagging and boosting. In *International Workshop on Artificial Intelligence and Statistics*, pages 229–236. PMLR, 2001.

[185] Adam Paszke, Sam Gross, Soumith Chintala, Gregory Chanan, Edward Yang, Zachary DeVito, Zeming Lin, Alban Desmaison, Luca Antiga, and Adam Lerer. Automatic differentiation in pytorch. In *Proceedings of the Advances in Neural Information Processing Systems Workshops*, pages 1–4, 2017.

[186] Adam Paszke, Sam Gross, Francisco Massa, Adam Lerer, James Bradbury, Gregory Chanan, Trevor Killeen, Zeming Lin, Natalia Gimelshein, Luca Antiga, et al. Pytorch: An imperative style, high-performance deep learning library. In *Advances in Neural Information Processing Systems*, pages 8026–8037, 2019.

[187] KB Petersen, MS Pedersen, et al. The matrix cookbook. *Technical University of Denmark*, 15, 2008.

[188] Hieu Pham, Melody Guan, Barret Zoph, Quoc Le, and Jeff Dean. Efficient neural architecture search via parameters sharing. In *International conference on machine learning*, pages 4095–4104. PMLR, 2018.

[189] Hai Phan, Zechun Liu, Dang Huynh, Marios Savvides, Kwang-Ting Cheng, and Zhiqiang Shen. Binarizing mobilenet via evolution-based searching. In *Proceedings of the IEEE/CVF Conference on Computer Vision and Pattern Recognition*, pages 13420–13429, 2020.

[190] Gabriele Prato, Ella Charlaix, and Mehdi Rezagholizadeh. Fully quantized transformer for machine translation. *arXiv preprint arXiv:1910.10485*, 2019.

[191] Juan C. Pérez, Motasem Alfarra, Guillaume Jeanneret, Adel Bibi, Ali Kassem Thabet, Bernard Ghanem, and Pablo Arbeláez. Robust gabor networks. *arXiv*, 2019.

[192] Charles R Qi, Hao Su, Kaichun Mo, and Leonidas J Guibas. Pointnet: Deep learning on point sets for 3d classification and segmentation. In *Proceedings of the IEEE Conference on Computer Vision and Pattern Recognition*, pages 652–660, 2017.

[193] Charles Ruizhongtai Qi, Li Yi, Hao Su, and Leonidas J Guibas. Pointnet++: Deep hierarchical feature learning on point sets in a metric space. In *Proceedings of Advances in Neural Information Processing Systems*, pages 5099–5108, 2017.

[194] Haotong Qin, Zhongang Cai, Mingyuan Zhang, Yifu Ding, Haiyu Zhao, Shuai Yi, Xianglong Liu, and Hao Su. Bipointnet: Binary neural network for point clouds. In *Proceedings of the International Conference on Learning Representations*, 2021.

[195] Haotong Qin, Yifu Ding, Mingyuan Zhang, Qinghua Yan, Aishan Liu, Qingqing Dang, Ziwei Liu, and Xianglong Liu. Bibert: Accurate fully binarized bert. *arXiv preprint arXiv:2203.06390*, 2022.

[196] Haotong Qin, Ruihao Gong, Xianglong Liu, Mingzhu Shen, Ziran Wei, Fengwei Yu, and Jingkuan Song. Forward and backward information retention for accurate binary neural networks. In *Proceedings of the IEEE/CVF Conference on Computer Vision and Pattern Recognition*, pages 2250–2259, 2020.

[197] Maithra Raghu, Thomas Unterthiner, Simon Kornblith, Chiyuan Zhang, and Alexey Dosovitskiy. Do vision transformers see like convolutional neural networks? *Advances in Neural Information Processing Systems*, 34:12116–12128, 2021.

[198] Pranav Rajpurkar, Jian Zhang, Konstantin Lopyrev, and Percy Liang. Squad: 100,000+ questions for machine comprehension of text. *arXiv preprint arXiv:1606.05250*, 2016.

[199] Mohammad Rastegari, Vicente Ordonez, Joseph Redmon, and Ali Farhadi. Xnor-net: Imagenet classification using binary convolutional neural networks. In *Proceedings of the European Conference on Computer Vision*, pages 525–542, 2016.

[200] Joseph Redmon and Ali Farhadi. Yolov3: An incremental improvement. *arXiv preprint arXiv:1804.02767*, 2018.

[201] Shaoqing Ren, Kaiming He, Ross Girshick, and Jian Sun. Faster r-cnn: Towards real-time object detection with region proposal networks. In *Proceedings of the Advances in Neural Information Processing Systems*, pages 91–99, 2015.

[202] Hamid Rezatofighi, Nathan Tsoi, JunYoung Gwak, Amir Sadeghian, Ian Reid, and Silvio Savarese. Generalized intersection over union: A metric and a loss for bounding box regression. In *Proceedings of the IEEE/CVF conference on computer vision and pattern recognition*, pages 658–666, 2019.

[203] Ergys Ristani and Carlo Tomasi. Features for multi-target multi-camera tracking and re-identification. In *Proceedings of the IEEE Conference on Computer Vision and Pattern Recognition*, pages 6036–6046, 2018.

[204] Olga Russakovsky, Jia Deng, Hao Su, Jonathan Krause, Sanjeev Satheesh, Sean Ma, Zhiheng Huang, Andrej Karpathy, Aditya Khosla, Michael Bernstein, et al. Imagenet large scale visual recognition challenge. *International journal of computer vision*, 115:211–252, 2015.

[205] Mark Sandler, Andrew Howard, Menglong Zhu, Andrey Zhmoginov, and Liang-Chieh Chen. Mobilenetv2: Inverted residuals and linear bottlenecks. In *Proceedings of the IEEE conference on computer vision and pattern recognition*, pages 4510–4520, 2018.

[206] Victor Sanh, Lysandre Debut, Julien Chaumond, and Thomas Wolf. Distilbert, a distilled version of bert: smaller, faster, cheaper and lighter. *arXiv preprint arXiv:1910.01108*, 2019.

[207] Shibani Santurkar, Dimitris Tsipras, Andrew Ilyas, and Aleksander Madry. How does batch normalization help optimization? In *Proceedings of Advances in neural information processing systems*, pages 1–11, 2018.

[208] S. Shen, Z. Dong, J. Ye, L. Ma, Z. Yao, A. Gholami, M. W. Mahoney, and K. Keutzer. Q-bert: Hessian based ultra low precision quantization of bert. In *Proceedings of the AAAI Conference on Artificial Intelligence*, 2020.

[209] Sheng Shen, Zhen Dong, Jiayu Ye, Linjian Ma, Zhewei Yao, Amir Gholami, Michael W Mahoney, and Kurt Keutzer. Q-bert: Hessian based ultra low precision quantization of bert. In *Proceedings of the AAAI Conference on Artificial Intelligence*, volume 34, pages 8815–8821, 2020.

[210] Ravid Shwartz-Ziv and Naftali Tishby. Opening the black box of deep neural networks via information. *arXiv:1703.00810*, 2017.

[211] Karen Simonyan and Andrew Zisserman. Very deep convolutional networks for large-scale image recognition. In *Proceedings of the International Conference on Learning Representations*, pages 1–15, 2015.

[212] Chi Su, Jianing Li, Shiliang Zhang, Junliang Xing, Wen Gao, and Qi Tian. Pose-driven deep convolutional model for person re-identification. In *Proceedings of the IEEE International Conference on Computer Vision*, pages 3960–3969, 2017.

[213] Chi Su, Shiliang Zhang, Junliang Xing, Wen Gao, and Qi Tian. Deep attributes driven multi-camera person re-identification. In *Proceedings of the European Conference on Computer Vision*, pages 475–491, 2016.

[214] Yumin Suh, Jingdong Wang, Siyu Tang, Tao Mei, and Kyoung Mu Lee. Part-aligned bilinear representations for person re-identification. In *Proceedings of the European Conference on Computer Vision*, pages 402–419, 2018.

[215] Shengyang Sun, Changyou Chen, and Lawrence Carin. Learning structured weight uncertainty in bayesian neural networks. In *Proceedings of the Artificial Intelligence and Statistics*, pages 1283–1292, 2017.

[216] Shengyang Sun, Guodong Zhang, Jiaxin Shi, and Roger Grosse. Functional variational bayesian neural networks. In *Proceedings of the International Conference on Learning Representations*, pages 1–22, 2019.

[217] Siqi Sun, Yu Cheng, Zhe Gan, and Jingjing Liu. Patient knowledge distillation for bert model compression. *arXiv preprint arXiv:1908.09355*, 2019.

[218] Siyang Sun, Yingjie Yin, Xingang Wang, De Xu, Wenqi Wu, and Qingyi Gu. Fast object detection based on binary deep convolution neural networks. *CAAI transactions on intelligence technology*, 3(4):191–197, 2018.

[219] Yifan Sun, Liang Zheng, Yi Yang, Qi Tian, and Shengjin Wang. Beyond part models: Person retrieval with refined part pooling (and a strong convolutional baseline). In *Proceedings of the European Conference on Computer Vision*, pages 480–496, 2018.

[220] Christian Szegedy, Wei Liu, Yangqing Jia, Pierre Sermanet, Scott Reed, Dragomir Anguelov, Dumitru Erhan, Vincent Vanhoucke, and Andrew Rabinovich. Going deeper with convolutions. In *Proceedings of the IEEE conference on computer vision and pattern recognition*, pages 1–9, 2015.

[221] Chaofan Tao, Lu Hou, Wei Zhang, Lifeng Shang, Xin Jiang, Qun Liu, Ping Luo, and Ngai Wong. Compression of generative pre-trained language models via quantization. *arXiv preprint arXiv:2203.10705*, 2022.

[222] Jiayi Tian, Chao Fang, Haonan Wang, and Zhongfeng Wang. Bebert: Efficient and robust binary ensemble bert. *arXiv preprint arXiv:2210.15976*, 2022.

[223] Naftali Tishby, Fernando C Pereira, and William Bialek. The information bottleneck method. *arXiv preprint physics/0004057*, 2000.

[224] Hugo Touvron, Matthieu Cord, Matthijs Douze, Francisco Massa, Alexandre Sablay-rolles, and Hervé Jégou. Training data-efficient image transformers & distillation through attention. In *International conference on machine learning*, pages 10347–10357. PMLR, 2021.

[225] VW-S Tseng, Sourav Bhattachara, Javier Fernández-Marqués, Milad Alizadeh, Catherine Tong, and Nicholas D Lane. Deterministic binary filters for convolutional neural networks. International Joint Conferences on Artificial Intelligence Organization, 2018.

[226] Frederick Tung and Greg Mori. Similarity-preserving knowledge distillation. In *Proc. of ICCV*, pages 1365–1374, 2019.

[227] Ashish Vaswani, Noam Shazeer, Niki Parmar, Jakob Uszkoreit, Llion Jones, Aidan N Gomez, Łukasz Kaiser, and Illia Polosukhin. Attention is all you need. *Advances in neural information processing systems*, 30, 2017.

[228] Diwen Wan, Fumin Shen, Li Liu, Fan Zhu, Jie Qin, Ling Shao, and Heng Tao Shen. Tbn: Convolutional neural network with ternary inputs and binary weights. In *Proceedings of the European Conference on Computer Vision (ECCV)*, pages 315–332, 2018.

[229] Diwen Wan, Fumin Shen, Li Liu, Fan Zhu, Jie Qin, Ling Shao, and Heng Tao Shen. Tbn: Convolutional neural network with ternary inputs and binary weights. In *Proceedings of the European Conference on Computer Vision*, pages 315–332, 2018.

[230] Alex Wang, Amanpreet Singh, Julian Michael, Felix Hill, Omer Levy, and Samuel R Bowman. Glue: A multi-task benchmark and analysis platform for natural language understanding. *arXiv preprint arXiv:1804.07461*, 2018.

[231] Guo-Hua Wang, Yifan Ge, and Jianxin Wu. Distilling knowledge by mimicking features. *IEEE Transactions on Pattern Analysis and Machine Intelligence*, 2021.

[232] Jingya Wang, Xiatian Zhu, Shaogang Gong, and Wei Li. Transferable joint attribute-identity deep learning for unsupervised person re-identification. In *Proceedings of the IEEE Conference on Computer Vision and Pattern Recognition*, pages 2275–2284, 2018.

[233] Peisong Wang, Qinghao Hu, Yifan Zhang, Chunjie Zhang, Yang Liu, and Jian Cheng. Two-step quantization for low-bit neural networks. In *Proceedings of the IEEE Conference on computer vision and pattern recognition*, pages 4376–4384, 2018.

[234] Song Wang, Dongchun Ren, Li Chen, Wei Fan, Jun Sun, and Satoshi Naoi. On study of the binarized deep neural network for image classification. *arXiv preprint arXiv:1602.07373*, 2016.

[235] Tao Wang, Li Yuan, Xiaopeng Zhang, and Jiashi Feng. Distilling object detectors with fine-grained feature imitation. In *Proc. of CVPR*, 2019.

[236] Xiaodi Wang, Baochang Zhang, Ce Li, Rongrong Ji, Jungong Han, Xianbin Cao, and Jianzhuang Liu. Modulated convolutional networks. In *Proceedings of the IEEE Conference on Computer Vision and Pattern Recognition*, pages 840–848, 2018.

[237] Xiaodi Wang, Baochang Zhang, Ce Li, Rongrong Ji, Jungong Han, Xianbin Cao, and Jianzhuang Liu. Modulated convolutional networks. In *Proceedings of the IEEE/CVF Conference on Computer Vision and Pattern Recognition*, pages 840–848, 2018.

[238] Yulin Wang, Zanlin Ni, Shiji Song, Le Yang, and Gao Huang. Revisiting locally supervised learning: an alternative to end-to-end training. In *Proceedings of the International Conference on Learning Representations*, pages 1–21, 2021.

[239] Ziwei Wang, Jiwen Lu, Chenxin Tao, Jie Zhou, and Qi Tian. Learning channel-wise interactions for binary convolutional neural networks. In *Proceedings of the IEEE/CVF conference on computer vision and pattern recognition*, pages 568–577, 2019.

[240] Ziwei Wang, Ziyi Wu, Jiwen Lu, and Jie Zhou. Bidet: An efficient binarized object detector. In *Proceedings of the IEEE/CVF Conference on Computer Vision and Pattern Recognition*, pages 2049–2058, 2020.

[241] Longhui Wei, Shiliang Zhang, Wen Gao, and Qi Tian. Person transfer gan to bridge domain gap for person re-identification. In *Proceedings of the IEEE Conference on Computer Vision and Pattern Recognition*, pages 79–88, 2018.

[242] Xing Wei, Yue Zhang, Yihong Gong, Jiawei Zhang, and Nanning Zheng. Grassmann pooling as compact homogeneous bilinear pooling for fine-grained visual classification. In *Proceedings of the European Conference on Computer Vision (ECCV)*, pages 355–370, 2018.

[243] Xiuying Wei, Yunchen Zhang, Xiangguo Zhang, Ruihao Gong, Shanghang Zhang, Qi Zhang, Fengwei Yu, and Xianglong Liu. Outlier suppression: Pushing the limit of low-bit transformer language models. *arXiv preprint arXiv:2209.13325*, 2022.

[244] Liangjian Wen, Xuanyang Zhang, Haoli Bai, and Zenglin Xu. Structured pruning of recurrent neural networks through neuron selection. *Neural Networks*, 123:134–141, 2020.

[245] Yandong Wen, Kaipeng Zhang, Zhifeng Li, and Yu Qiao. A discriminative feature learning approach for deep face recognition. In *Proceedings of the European Conference on Computer Vision*, pages 499–515, 2016.

[246] Ronald J Williams and David Zipser. A learning algorithm for continually running fully recurrent neural networks. *Neural computation*, 1(2):270–280, 1989.

[247] Eric Wong, Leslie Rice, and J. Zico Kolter. Fast is better than free: Revisiting adversarial training. In *ICLR*, 2020.

[248] Lin Wu, Yang Wang, Junbin Gao, and Xue Li. Where-and-when to look: Deep siamese attention networks for video-based person re-identification. *IEEE Transactions on Multimedia*, 21(6):1412–1424, 2018.

[249] Nailong Wu. *The maximum entropy method*, volume 32. Springer Science & Business Media, 2012.

[250] Yi Wu, Jongwoo Lim, and Ming-Hsuan Yang. Online object tracking: A benchmark. In *Proceedings of the IEEE conference on computer vision and pattern recognition*, pages 2411–2418, 2013.

[251] Yi Wu, Jongwoo Lim, and Ming-Hsuan Yang. Object tracking benchmark. *IEEE Transactions on Pattern Analysis & Machine Intelligence*, 37(09):1834–1848, 2015.

[252] Xu Xiang, Yanmin Qian, and Kai Yu. Binary deep neural networks for speech recognition. In *INTERSPEECH*, pages 533–537, 2017.

[253] C. Xie, Y. Wu, L. V. D. Maaten, A. L. Yuille, and K. He. Feature denoising for improving adversarial robustness. In *CVPR*, 2019.

[254] Sirui Xie, Hehui Zheng, Chunxiao Liu, and Liang Lin. Snas: stochastic neural architecture search. *arXiv preprint arXiv:1812.09926*, 2018.

[255] Ji Xin, Raphael Tang, Jaejun Lee, Yaoliang Yu, and Jimmy Lin. Deebert: Dynamic early exiting for accelerating bert inference. *arXiv preprint arXiv:2004.12993*, 2020.

[256] Qiangeng Xu, Xudong Sun, Cho-Ying Wu, Panqu Wang, and Ulrich Neumann. Grid-gcn for fast and scalable point cloud learning. In *Proceedings of the IEEE Conference on Computer Vision and Pattern Recognition*, pages 5661–5670, 2020.

[257] Sheng Xu, Yanjing Li, Mingbao Lin, Peng Gao, Guodong Guo, Jinhu Lü, and Baochang Zhang. Q-detr: An efficient low-bit quantized detection transformer. In *Proceedings of the IEEE/CVF Conference on Computer Vision and Pattern Recognition*, pages 3842–3851, 2023.

[258] Sheng Xu, Yanjing Li, Teli Ma, Mingbao Lin, Hao Dong, Baochang Zhang, Peng Gao, and Jinhu Lu. Resilient binary neural network. In *Proceedings of the AAAI Conference on Artificial Intelligence*, pages 10620–10628, 2023.

[259] Sheng Xu, Yanjing Li, Tiancheng Wang, Teli Ma, Baochang Zhang, Peng Gao, Yu Qiao, Jinhu Lü, and Guodong Guo. Recurrent bilinear optimization for binary neural networks. In *European Conference on Computer Vision*, pages 19–35. Springer, 2022.

[260] Sheng Xu, Yanjing Li, Bohan Zeng, Teli Ma, Baochang Zhang, Xianbin Cao, Peng Gao, and Jinhu Lü. Ida-det: An information discrepancy-aware distillation for 1-bit detectors. In *European Conference on Computer Vision*, pages 346–361. Springer, 2022.

[261] Sheng Xu, Yanjing Li, Junhe Zhao, Baochang Zhang, and Guodong Guo. Poem: 1-bit point-wise operations based on expectation-maximization for efficient point cloud processing. In *Proceedings of the British Machine Vision Conference*, 2021.

[262] Sheng Xu, Chang Liu, Baochang Zhang, Jinhu Lü, Guodong Guo, and David Doermann. Bire-id: Binary neural network for efficient person re-id. *ACM Transactions on Multimedia Computing, Communications, and Applications (TOMM)*, 18(1s):1–22, 2022.

[263] Sheng Xu, Zhendong Liu, Xuan Gong, Chunlei Liu, Mingyuan Mao, and Baochang Zhang. Amplitude suppression and direction activation in networks for 1-bit faster r-cnn. In *Proceedings of the 4th International Workshop on Embedded and Mobile Deep Learning*, pages 19–24, 2020.

[264] Sheng Xu, Junhe Zhao, Jinhu Lu, Baochang Zhang, Shumin Han, and David Doermann. Layer-wise searching for 1-bit detectors. In *Proceedings of the IEEE/CVF Conference on Computer Vision and Pattern Recognition*, pages 5682–5691, 2021.

[265] Yuhui Xu, Lingxi Xie, Xiaopeng Zhang, Xin Chen, Guo-Jun Qi, Qi Tian, and Hongkai Xiong. Pc-darts: Partial channel connections for memory-efficient architecture search. *arXiv preprint arXiv:1907.05737*, 2019.

[266] Zhe Xu and Ray CC Cheung. Accurate and compact convolutional neural networks with trained binarization. *arXiv preprint arXiv:1909.11366*, 2019.

[267] Zihan Xu, Mingbao Lin, Jianzhuang Liu, Jie Chen, Ling Shao, Yue Gao, Yonghong Tian, and Rongrong Ji. Recu: Reviving the dead weights in binary neural networks. *arXiv preprint arXiv:2103.12369*, 2021.

[268] Haojin Yang, Martin Fritzsche, Christian Bartz, and Christoph Meinel. Bmxnet: An open-source binary neural network implementation based on mxnet. In *Proceedings of the 25th ACM international conference on Multimedia*, pages 1209–1212, 2017.

[269] Li Yang, Zhezhi He, and Deliang Fan. Binarized depthwise separable neural network for object tracking in fpga. In *Proceedings of the 2019 on Great Lakes Symposium on VLSI*, pages 347–350, 2019.

[270] Zhewei Yao, Amir Gholami, Qi Lei, Kurt Keutzer, and Michael W Mahoney. Hessian-based analysis of large batch training and robustness to adversaries. *Advances in Neural Information Processing Systems*, 31, 2018.

[271] Dong Yi, Zhen Lei, Shengcai Liao, and Stan Z Li. Deep metric learning for person re-identification. In *Proceedings of the International Conference on Pattern Recognition*, pages 34–39, 2014.

[272] Penghang Yin, Shuai Zhang, Jiancheng Lyu, Stanley Osher, Yingyong Qi, and Jack Xin. Binaryrelax: A relaxation approach for training deep neural networks with quantized weights. *SIAM Journal on Imaging Sciences*, 11(4):2205–2223, 2018.

[273] Shouyi Yin, Peng Ouyang, Shixuan Zheng, Dandan Song, Xiudong Li, Leibo Liu, and Shaojun Wei. A 141 uw, 2.46 pj/neuron binarized convolutional neural network based self-learning speech recognition processor in 28nm cmos. In *2018 IEEE Symposium on VLSI Circuits*, pages 139–140. IEEE, 2018.

[274] C. Ying, A. Klein, E. Real, E. Christiansen, K. Murphy, and F. Hutter. Nas-bench-101: Towards reproducible neural architecture search. In *ICML*, 2019.

[275] Yang You, Jing Li, Sashank Reddi, Jonathan Hseu, Sanjiv Kumar, Srinadh Bhojanapalli, Xiaodan Song, James Demmel, Kurt Keutzer, and Cho-Jui Hsieh. Large batch optimization for deep learning: Training bert in 76 minutes. *Proc. of ICLR*, pages 1–37, 2020.

[276] Jiahui Yu, Yuning Jiang, Zhangyang Wang, Zhimin Cao, and Thomas Huang. Unitbox: An advanced object detection network. In *Proceedings of the 24th ACM international conference on Multimedia*, pages 516–520, 2016.

[277] Kaicheng Yu, Christian Sciuto, Martin Jaggi, Claudiu Musat, and Mathieu Salzmann. Evaluating the search phase of neural architecture search. *arXiv preprint arXiv:1902.08142*, 2019.

[278] Zhou Yu, Jun Yu, Jianping Fan, and Dacheng Tao. Multi-modal factorized bilinear pooling with co-attention learning for visual question answering. In *Proc. of ICCV*, pages 1821–1830, 2017.

[279] Ali Hadi Zadeh, Isak Edo, Omar Mohamed Awad, and Andreas Moshovos. Gobo: Quantizing attention-based nlp models for low latency and energy efficient inference. In *2020 53rd Annual IEEE/ACM International Symposium on Microarchitecture (MICRO)*, pages 811–824. IEEE, 2020.

[280] Ofir Zafrir, Guy Boudoukh, Peter Izsak, and Moshe Wasserblat. Q8bert: Quantized 8bit bert. In *2019 Fifth Workshop on Energy Efficient Machine Learning and Cognitive Computing-NeurIPS Edition (EMC2-NIPS)*, pages 36–39. IEEE, 2019.

[281] Sergey Zagoruyko and Nikos Komodakis. Wide residual networks. In *Proceedings of the British Machine Vision Conference*, pages 1–15, 2016.

[282] Matthew D Zeiler. Adadelta: an adaptive learning rate method. *arXiv preprint arXiv:1212.5701*, 2012.

[283] Baochang Zhang, Alessandro Perina, Zhigang Li, Vittorio Murino, Jianzhuang Liu, and Rongrong Ji. Bounding multiple gaussians uncertainty with application to object tracking. *International journal of computer vision*, 118:364–379, 2016.

[284] Dongqing Zhang, Jiaolong Yang, Dongqiangzi Ye, and Gang Hua. Lq-nets: Learned quantization for highly accurate and compact deep neural networks. In *Proceedings of the European conference on computer vision (ECCV)*, pages 365–382, 2018.

[285] Wei Zhang, Lu Hou, Yichun Yin, Lifeng Shang, Xiao Chen, Xin Jiang, and Qun Liu. Ternarybert: Distillation-aware ultra-low bit bert. *arXiv preprint arXiv:2009.12812*, 2020.

[286] Xiangyu Zhang, Xinyu Zhou, Mengxiao Lin, and Jian Sun. Shufflenet: An extremely efficient convolutional neural network for mobile devices. *arXiv preprint arXiv:1707.01083*, 2017.

[287] Junhe Zhao, Sheng Xu, Baochang Zhang, Jiaxin Gu, David Doermann, and Guodong Guo. Towards compact 1-bit cnns via bayesian learning. *International Journal of Computer Vision*, pages 1–25, 2022.

[288] Feng Zheng, Cheng Deng, and Heng Huang. Binarized neural networks for resource-efficient hashing with minimizing quantization loss. In *IJCAI*, pages 1032–1040, 2019.

[289] Liang Zheng, Liyue Shen, Lu Tian, Shengjin Wang, Jingdong Wang, and Qi Tian. Scalable person re-identification: A benchmark. *Proceedings of the IEEE International Conference on Computer Vision*, pages 1116–1124, 2015.

[290] Shixuan Zheng, Peng Ouyang, Dandan Song, Xiudong Li, Leibo Liu, Shaojun Wei, and Shouyi Yin. An ultra-low power binarized convolutional neural network-based speech recognition processor with on-chip self-learning. *IEEE Transactions on Circuits and Systems I: Regular Papers*, 66(12):4648–4661, 2019.

[291] Xiawu Zheng, Rongrong Ji, Lang Tang, Yan Wan, Baochang Zhang, Yongjian Wu, Yunsheng Wu, and Ling Shao. Dynamic distribution pruning for efficient network architecture search. *arXiv preprint arXiv:1905.13543*, 2019.

[292] Xiawu Zheng, Rongrong Ji, Lang Tang, Baochang Zhang, Jianzhuang Liu, and Qi Tian. Multinomial distribution learning for effective neural architecture search. In *Proc. of ICCV*, 2019.

[293] Zhaohui Zheng, Ping Wang, Wei Liu, Jinze Li, Rongguang Ye, and Dongwei Ren. Distance-iou loss: Faster and better learning for bounding box regression. In *Proceedings of the AAAI conference on artificial intelligence*, volume 34, pages 12993–13000, 2020.

[294] Zhedong Zheng, Liang Zheng, and Yi Yang. generated by gan improve the person re-identification baseline in vitro. In *Proceedings of the IEEE International Conference on Computer Vision*, pages 3754–3762, 2017.

[295] Zhun Zhong, Liang Zheng, Shaozi Li, and Yi Yang. Generalizing a person retrieval model hetero-and homogeneously. In *Proceedings of the European conference on computer vision (ECCV)*, pages 172–188, 2018.

[296] Zhun Zhong, Liang Zheng, Zhiming Luo, Shaozi Li, and Yi Yang. Invariance matters: Exemplar memory for domain adaptive person re-identification. In *Proceedings of the IEEE Conference on Computer Vision and Pattern Recognition*, pages 598–607, 2019.

[297] Denny Zhou, Mao Ye, Chen Chen, Tianjian Meng, Mingxing Tan, Xiaodan Song, Quoc Le, Qiang Liu, and Dale Schuurmans. Go wide, then narrow: Efficient training of deep thin networks. In *International Conference on Machine Learning*, pages 11546–11555. PMLR, 2020.

[298] Wangchunshu Zhou, Canwen Xu, Tao Ge, Julian McAuley, Ke Xu, and Furu Wei. Bert loses patience: Fast and robust inference with early exit. *Advances in Neural Information Processing Systems*, 33:18330–18341, 2020.

[299] Chenzhuo Zhu, Song Han, Huizi Mao, and William J Dally. Trained ternary quantization. In *Proceedings of the International Conference on Learning Representations*, pages 1–10, 2017.

[300] Jun-Yan Zhu, Taesung Park, Phillip Isola, and Alexei A Efros. Unpaired image-to-image translation using cycle-consistent adversarial networks. In *Proceedings of the IEEE International Conference on Computer Vision*, pages 2223–2232, 2017.

[301] Shilin Zhu, Xin Dong, and Hao Su. Binary ensemble neural network: More bits per network or more networks per bit? In *Proceedings of the IEEE/CVF Conference on Computer Vision and Pattern Recognition*, pages 4923–4932, 2019.

[302] Xiangyu Zhu, Zhen Lei, Xiaoming Liu, Hailin Shi, and Stan Z Li. Face alignment across large poses: A 3d solution. In *Proceedings of the IEEE conference on computer vision and pattern recognition*, pages 146–155, 2016.

[303] Bohan Zhuang, Chunhua Shen, Mingkui Tan, Lingqiao Liu, and Ian Reid. Structured binary neural networks for accurate image classification and semantic segmentation. In *Proceedings of the IEEE/CVF Conference on Computer Vision and Pattern Recognition*, pages 413–422, 2019.

[304] Li'an Zhuo, Baochang Zhang, Hanlin Chen, Linlin Yang, Chen Chen, Yanjun Zhu, and David Doermann. Cp-nas: Child-parent neural architecture search for 1-bit cnns. In *Proceedings of the Twenty-Ninth International Conference on International Joint Conferences on Artificial Intelligence*, pages 1033–1039, 2020.

[305] Barret Zoph and Quoc V Le. Neural architecture search with reinforcement learning. In *arXiv*, 2016.

[306] Barret Zoph, Vijay Vasudevan, Jonathon Shlens, and Quoc V. Le. Learning transferable architectures for scalable image recognition. In *Proceedings of the IEEE/CVF Conference on Computer Vision and Pattern Recognition*, pages 8697–8710, 2018.

[307] Barret Zoph, Vijay Vasudevan, Jonathon Shlens, and Quoc V Le. Learning transferable architectures for scalable image recognition. In *Proc. of CVPR*, pages 8697–8710, 2018.

Index

ABC-Net, 4, 13
Accelerated Proximal Gradient (APG), 79
Accuracy occupy (AO), 14
AdaBoost, 138
AFLW, 14
AFLW2000-3D, 14
AFLW-PIFA, 14
ALBERT, 137
Alternating Direction Method of Multipliers (ADMM), 11
Anti-Bandit for Neural Architecture Search (ABanditNAS), 92
Average precision (AP), 32

Batch Normalization, 2
BayesBiNN, 12
Bayesian neural network (BayesNN), 68
BEBERT, 138
BENN, 12
BERT, 119
BiBERT, 138
Bi-ColBERT, 147
BiDet, 166
Bi-FC, 159
BinaryBERT, 134
BinaryConnect, 2
BinaryDenseNet, 7
BinaryDuo, 12
BinaryNet, 2
Binarized Neural Architecture Search (BNAS), 10
Binary Neural Networks (BNN), 1, 2
BinaryRelax, 11
Binary-Weight-Networks (BWN), 4
Bi-Real Net, 3
BiRe-ID, 151
BLEU, 124
BMES, 91
BMXNet, 12
BONN, 14
BWNH, 11

Cascade R-CNN, 150
CBCNs, 11

Child-Parent (CP) Model, 10
CIFAR-10, 13
CIFAR-100, 13
CI-BCNN, 11
CIoU, 150
Circulant Binary Convolution, 11
Circulant Filters (CiFs), 11
CNN, 13
COCO, 34
ColBERT, 146
Computer vision (CV), 21
CoNNL-03, 126
Coverage-Aware, 150
CP-NAS, 14
CycleGAN, 149

DA, 35
DARTS, 167
Deep Neural Networks (DNN), 13
DeiT, 24
Density-ReLU (DReLU), 82
Detection transformer (DETR), 28
Deterministic Binary Filters (DBFs), 11
Differentiable Binarization Search (DBS), 167
Differentiable Soft Quantization, 3
Directed Acyclic Graph (DAG), 95
Direction-Matching Distillation (DMD), 141
Discrepant Child-Parent Neural Architecture Search (DCP-NAS), 105
Discrete Backpropagation via Projection (DBPP), 50
DistillBERT, 137
Distribution Guided Distillation (DGD), 22
Distribution Rectification Distillation (DRD), 30
DynaBERT, 137

Error Decay Estimator (EDE), 84

Fast Iterative Shrinkage-Thresholding Algorithm (FISTA), 79

Fast Gradient Sign Method (FGSM), 97
Faster-RCNN, 150
Feed-Forward Network (FFN), 120
FGFI, 177
FPN, 150
FQM, 35
FR-GAL, 151
FullyQT, 121
Fully quantized ViT (Q-ViT), 22

GAL, 151
GELU, 127
Generalized Gauss-Newton matrix (GGN),
        105
GIoU, 34
GMM, 78
GOBO, 131
GOT-10K, 14
Gradient Approximation, 3
Grid-GCN, 149
Grid Query (CAGQ), 149

Hessian AWare Quantization (HAWQ), 125
High-Order Residual Quantization
        (HORQ), 4

Image Classification, 12
ImageNet, 13
Information Bottleneck (IB), 32
Information Discrepancy-Aware Distillation
        for 1-bit Detectors (IDa-Det), 172
Information Rectification Module (IRM), 22
Integer-Only BERT Quantization
        (I-BERT), 127
IoU, 150
IR-Net, 84

KL divergence, 110
KR-GAL, 151

LAMB, 27
LayerDrop, 137
Layer-Wise Search for 1-bit Detectors
        (LWS-Det), 166
Learned Step Size Quantization (LSQ), 18
LightNN, 8
Local Binary Convolutional Network
        (LBCNN), 5, 13
Loss Design, 9
Low-Bit Quantized Detection Transformer
        (Q-DETR), 28
Lower Confidence Bound (LCB), 92

LSQ+, 30

M-Filters, 40
Markov Chain Monte Carlo (MCMC), 68
Maximum A posteriori (MAP), 70
Maximum Likelihood Estimation (MLE),
        162
Maximum Output Entropy (MOE), 25
MCN Convolution (MCconv), 42
Mean Square Error (MSE), 104
MeliusNet, 7
MetaQuant, 84
Minimum Average Error (MAE), 25
MNIST, 13
MNLI, 126
Modulated Convolutional Networks (MCN),
        5
Module-wise Reconstruction Error
        Minimization (MREM), 129
MRPC, 135
Multi-Head Attention (MHA), 32
Multi-Head Self-Attention (MHSA), 23
Multi-Layer Perceptron (MLP), 23

Natural Language Processing (NLP), 21
Neural Architecture Search (NAS), 10
Neural networks (NN), 15
Non-Maximum Suppression (NMS), 28

Object Detection and Tracking, 13
Optimization, 10
OTB50, 14
OTB100, 14
Outlier Suppression, 132

PACT, 20
PC-DARTs, 10
PCNNs, 9, 13
POEM, 157
PointNet, 149
PointNet++, 149
Post-training quantization (PTQ), 118
Probability Density Function (PDF), 24

Q-BERT, 125
Q-FC, 32
Q-Linear, 23
QIL, 20
QQP, 128
Quantization, 3
Quantization-aware training (QAT), 21
Quantized neural network (QNN), 16

ReActNet, 6
Rectified Binary Convolutional Networks
    (RBCNs), 11
Rectified Binary Convolutional SiamFC
    Network (RB-SF), 14
Recurrent Bilinear Optimization for binary
    Neural Network (RBONN), 14
Resilient Binary Neural Networks (ReBNN)
RBConv, 66
RBNN, 84
ReCU, 90
ResNet, 54
RetinaNet, 150
RoBERTa, 128
Robustly Binarized Multi-Distilled
    Transformer (BiT), 142

SiamFC, 14
SMCA-DETR, 34
Speech Recognition, 13
SQuAD, 126
SSD, 166
SST-2, 126
StarGAN, 149
Stochastic gradient descent (SGD), 73
STS-B, 128

Straight-through estimator (STE), 23
Success rate (SR), 14
SVHN, 13

TernaryBERT, 137
Ternary-Binary Network (TBN), 5
Ternary weight splitting (TWS), 136
TentacleNet, 12

UAV123, 14
U-MCN, 48
Upper Confidence Bound (UCB), 92

Variational inference (VI), 68
VGG, 54
Vision Transformer (ViT), 21
Visual question answering (VQA), 79
VOC, 29

WaveNet, 150
WGAN, 149
WMT14, 124
WRN, 48

XNOR-Net, 13

YOLO, 14, 150